Modern American Queer History

In the series *Critical Perspectives on the Past*,
edited by Susan Porter Benson, Stephen Brier, and Roy Rosenzweig

Modern American Queer History

ALLIDA M. BLACK, EDITOR

Temple University Press PHILADELPHIA

Temple University Press, Philadelphia 19122

Published 2001
Printed in the United States of America

Library of Congress Cataloging-in-Publication Data

Modern American queer history / edited by Allida M. Black.
p. cm. — (Critical perspectives on the past)
Includes bibliographical references.
ISBN 1-56639-871-1 (cloth : alk. paper) — ISBN 1-56639-872-X (pbk. : alk. paper)
1. Gays—United States—History—20th century. 2. Homosexuality—United States—History—20th century. 3. Gay liberation movement—United States. 4. Gay rights—United States. I. Black, Allida M. (Allida Mae), 1952– II. Series.

HQ76.3.U5 M63 2001
305.9'0664'09730904—dc21 00-054515

ISBN 13: 978-1-56639-872-5 (pbk. : alk. paper)

021012P

For John Howard,
without whom this would
not have been possible

Contents

Acknowledgments

This book would not have been possible without John Howard, who, in the spirit of friendship and extraordinary collegiality, helped shepherd it to publication. His support for me parallels his staunch commitment to lesbian, gay, and transgender history.

In addition to the scholars who stuck with us through the trials and tribulations of assembling an edited anthology, we owe specific gratitude to Novid Parsi for a meticulous and perceptive reading of the entire manuscript, to Judy Beck for a thoughtful critique of its style and substance, and to Yvonne Ramsey for copyediting a myriad of writing styles. Janet Francendese, who certainly is the most patient editor on the planet, stayed with us when we wavered, delayed, and procrastinated. She is just marvelous, and I thank her for her vision, her dedication, and her friendship.

Introduction

1

Where Are We to Begin?

JOHN HOWARD

"THE problem is still at root the same," Alan Bray surmised in 1982: "Where are we to begin?" This question has pestered historians of sexuality, whether writing about twentieth-century America or, as Bray was, Renaissance England. Do we write a history of homosexuality, lesbian and gay history, or queer history? From the very start, we shape the past as we set the parameters of inquiry. We create boundaries that not only exclude some historical figures and events but also alienate many of today's readers. We privilege certain prior thoughts and acts over others, thereby giving primacy to seemingly related iterations in contemporary culture. Where, for example, does the category of gender or the transgendered person fit into these histories? As we assess what might still be called a minority history (or histories, plural), we participate in the making of majorities and minorities. Therefore, we must be careful when we ask, Who or what are we interested in studying?

Lesbians, gays, bisexuals, transgender persons, straights. Today, much disagreement can be found over the very definitions of these (limited and limiting) categories, if assessed in any depth. If the identities or self-conceptions that these labels denote prove varied and elastic from one person to the next, then the widely acknowledged desires and behaviors that, in part, tend to constitute them likewise carry divergent meanings. In these regards, *we are different* one from another; in these matters, *we differ* with one another. If today we differ, what about differences across time, in the past? Can we understand them? Even if we try, we must ask, again, where are we to begin?

First, I propose as a historian that we consider where we have been. Specifically, I'd like to offer the briefest account of academe's engagements over the last several years with sexuality. Thereby, implicitly, I hope to characterize the ground covered by this current collection and its impressive assembly of authors. I don't propose a definitive assessment of the field or historical subfield, so far as such a field can be said to exist; given the infinite perspectives that animate this subject area, I'll stop short of attempting to answer the provocative question posed so thoughtfully by Vicki Eaklor in this volume's conclusion: Where are we now? I trust, further, that the thorough, practical, and ultimately workable guidelines that this volume's editor, Allida Black, set out will require little elaboration. From the thicket of complex American queer historical endeavor, she has pulled together a user-friendly, conceptually fundamental set of essays for use by university faculty, college students, and everyday readers. The essays speak—and speak well—for themselves. Finally, I'll sidestep the yet more difficult question: Where are we going? I'll forego millennial prognostications, but instead suggest a set of concerns that I hope will inform historians, writers, and readers alike as they, and as we, seek understanding and, most importantly, justice in our future encounters with the past—that is, in our futures.

The Queer Studies Pioneer Narrative

I find myself complicit in an emergent genre of scholarly writing: the queer studies pioneer narrative. My colleagues and I, ostensibly atomized on hostile campuses across the globe, have been telling our stories of individual struggle, triumph over adversity, as we detail our successes in offering the first course in queer studies at our respective universities, in uncovering the first cache of queer archival materials on a particular topic, or in writing the first scholarly volume on this or that queer subject. There are problems in these self-congratulatory epistles.

Relying on poststructuralist and feminist rationales, the queer studies pioneer narrative is a positioned work of personal writing, a first-person account of firsts, that recirculates dominant notions of individualism and effaces the collective nature of political struggle. Exacerbated by entrenched reward systems within academe, it celebrates the path-breaking, the carving out of a niche, and thereby hinders coalition. Ahistorical in nature, it expunges queer studies predecessors and reinscribes progressivist ideas about change; in essence, it reinstates the "repressive hypothesis" that theorist Michel Foucault debunked. We are getting better and better, it implies. Historically squelched, the speaking about and studying of sexuality are now becoming freer and freer.

In reflecting on my own narratives and those of other queer historians and theorists, I see the need for a group dialectic that goes beyond the disciplines and even beyond interdisciplinary understandings and institutional structures, since this language has also been heard under race and ethnic studies and women's studies rubrics. I suggest that we teachers and students, as well as nonacademicians, decenter traditional pedagogical strategies in an effort to acknowledge and foster cocurricular and extracurricular linkages. Further, I urge us to reconsider the ways in which we privilege the institution of higher learning as a locus of social change. As we envision insurgent tactics within pervasive systems of oppression, we must historicize and contextualize today's queer academic endeavor as but a *part* of multiple resistances to be found in unpredictable places and times.

The queer studies pioneer narrative reached its zenith—or, depending on how you look at it, its nadir—at the 1997 annual meeting of the Modern Languages Association. Four scholars shared their stories on a Gay and Lesbian Caucus panel entitled "Voices in the Wilderness: Teaching Queer Studies in Strange Places." Strange places, it seems, are those located outside New York, San Francisco, or Los Angeles. They include Catholic liberal arts colleges and state universities situated in the exoticized American South, where I taught for almost a decade.

At the conference, an associate professor of English from Texas described her "long and arduous process of establishing a gay and lesbian literature course at . . . a formerly all-male military college that did not admit women . . . until 1967." Her paper's title: "Reconstructing Homophobia in the Bible Belt, or How I Stopped Worrying and Learned to Love Rednecks." Lengthy, cutesy titles by scholars lamenting their lot in the South—and thereby positioning themselves above or beyond perceived local ideologies—would seem by now clichéd, indeed formulaic. (A more recent example by a scholar in north Florida: "What the South Needs: Suggestions and Observations of One Queer Southerner, or How a Hypocritical Military Haircut and a Letter to the Editor of the *New Yorker* Make Life in Pensacola Possible.") Similar to the Texan's narrative, an assistant professor in his first-person account of teaching queer literature at the University of South Carolina (USC) reported that he was "subjected to repeated attacks in the campus right-wing press"—attacks that were "characterized by unnerving personal animosity . . . [and] *regional* inflections of homophobia" (emphasis added). "The student writer," he continued, "published my home address and urged students to confront me there."

While I don't want to diminish any scholar's very real and very serious experiences of homophobic vitriol and harassment, I do want to point up the utilitarian value of such attacks as the USC professor invokes them, the ways in which they sustain and even legitimize queer scholars. As the old saying goes, "There's honor in having certain individuals as enemies." Indeed, if reactionary student newspapers such as the *Dartmouth Review* or *Duke Review* attack a faculty member, many will rally to that scholar's cause. But the isolationism that many queer studies scholars seem to take on has often been unnecessary, if not disingenuous and counterproductive. At the very same university in South Carolina, a colleague on the education faculty used his actual and reinvented persecution to great effect. His personal web site declared, "Welcome to the home page of a gay educator, author, activist, and [as if to dispel questions of authenticity occasioned by his Indiana upbringing] Southerner. Yes I am the person who Pat Robertson lambasted on the 700 Club as 'Satan of the University,' the professor *Out Magazine* championed as 'Dr. Sodomite.'"

Such statements, of course, must be understood in light of a broader academic context that fosters self-promotion and encourages the individuation of discrete scholars and their projects. But while the Texan, at a mammoth state school of some forty-three thousand students, insisted that her only allies were straight, liberal faculty who were "themselves . . . interpersonally homophobic," didn't the two faculty members at the University of South Carolina at least know one another? Can we legitimately assume, as these scholars suggested, that they were going it alone in crafting queer curricula? And if so, need they have been? Most incredibly, why were they not in league with queer students and student organizations? Indeed, who was taking these classes, anyway? Didn't the students' numbers, their voices, figure into administration decision-making?

As much as we queer scholars like to or are encouraged to present ourselves as pioneers, such assertions obfuscate the queer collective action that historically has enabled our very existence, our presence on campus, our publications, and our preening at academic conferences. Let me assure you, I'm not immune to this. Up until very recently, my bio bragged of several firsts. For one, I billed myself as the first scholar—along with my colleague Rose Gladney—to (co)teach a course in lesbian and gay studies at the University of Alabama. This statement was not based on any research into prior university catalogues or curriculum committee minutes. It was based solely on conjecture. Surely, I assumed, patting myself on the back, no one had dared teach such a course in Tuscaloosa, Alabama, prior to my time there.

But even then, in 1992, I harbored some nagging suspicions. Rose, not given to bravado, gently pointed me to the lesbian content in many women's studies courses at the University of Alabama. Too, I had a vague knowledge of the irrepressible Louie Crew. Crew certainly had taught queer material at the university. Under his editorship there, *College English*—the official journal of the National Council of Teachers of English—published in 1974 an entire quarterly issue on the topic of "The Homosexual Imagination." Crew soon afterward took a position at Fort Valley State College in no stranger a place than Fort Valley, Georgia—where, his bio proclaimed, he was married to his male partner.

I even recently took to crediting myself with publishing the first history of lesbian and gay Southerners, partly as a way to distinguish myself from one of the aforementioned USC scholars. Technically, the statement was true. But of what use was such information? Perhaps tenure review committees might one day be impressed, but I surely didn't endear myself to queer activists throughout the South who had long written their own memoirs, biographies, and histories—without the support of institutions like Duke University, but with mimeographed copy and grassroots distribution systems.

But then again, I'm at least in esteemed company. I noticed recently a big boast by Eve Sedgwick, the "soft-spoken queen of gay studies," as referred to by *Rolling Stone* and as cited, in turn, on the back cover of a recent tome. In a *New York Times Book Review* advertisement placed by the Association of American University Presses, Sedgwick said:

> When I showed a queer studies manuscript to a university press [editor] in 1983, he said, "You know you're crazy, don't you?" But he published it anyway. It's only university presses that can nourish the minds of five or ten thousand readers at a time, and keep challenging books in print long enough to become a useable part of the way people think.

Actually, by 1983, a number of queer titles had been published by university presses, notably John Boswell's powerful *Christianity, Social Tolerance, and Homosexuality* and John D'Emilio's indispensable *Sexual Politics, Sexual Communities*. Indeed, Boswell's and D'Emilio's editor at the University of Chicago Press, Doug Mitchell—long credited with fostering queer scholarship—was recently acknowledged with a lifetime service award from the Lambda Literary Foundation.

And contrary to Sedgwick's thesis, before university presses jumped on the bandwagon, small independent presses were putting out the best scholarly history, notably Jonathan Ned Katz's *Gay American History*, published by Thomas Crowell in 1976; the best sociology, including Laud Humphreys' *Tearoom Trade: Impersonal Sex in Public Places*, published by Aldine in 1970; and certainly the best if not the only works on queers of color, most notably Cherríe Moraga and Gloria Anzaldúa's *This Bridge Called My Back*, published first in 1981 by Persephone and thereafter by Kitchen Table, Women of Color Press.

As Saralyn Chesnut and Amanda Gable have demonstrated in their compelling analysis of 1970s lesbian-feminist writing, independent publishing houses and the bookstores that sold their works were collective endeavors, antithetical to academic individualism. Lesbian-feminist bookstores, where lesbian scholarship flourished, were more than intellectual enclaves or even community centers. They were multifaceted loci of families and friends, texts and images, thoughts and ideas, reflecting local neighborhoods and communities in flux but also in solidarity.

Similarly, campus environments supportive of queer studies are never the product of a lone wolf. Queer studies courses emerged on the heels of queer student groups, which beginning in the 1960s waged battles in the courts for their right to exist. And they continue to battle for their fair share of student fees and access to university meeting space, as we know from a recent federal case out of Alabama. These students, you readers, fill and sustain queer studies classes, and yet these campus courses do not and cannot exist apart from broader struggles for queer equal rights. The American homophile movement of the 1950s predated and enabled the movement for queer curricula in academe. One popular history lists the first departmentally approved "homophile studies" course as being offered in 1970 at—would you have guessed it?—the University of Nebraska. Another public history project points to a course from 1970 at the University of Kentucky.

Among a long, pernicious tradition of American pioneer mythology, this particular evocation of the pioneer metaphor is perhaps useful only to the extent that it reveals the insidious assumptions of these queer tales. The queer studies pioneer narrative reflects a slash-and-burn policy that callously disregards predecessors, that trounces over territory marked by prior claims, that asserts bald individualism made possible by foregoing collective action. Underneath these heroics, the reality is a sober one. Failure to build coalition—with students and student groups, new lesbian-gay-bisexual-transgender (LGBT) resource centers housed within student affairs divisions, neighboring community activists, and large-scale movements for social change—will only endanger the scholar-activist's ability to effect change. It will threaten the very safety and solace of the life of the mind seemingly predicated on solitude, whether in Alabama and Nebraska, or strange places like New York and Los Angeles.

Future Histories

The position of queer studies is far from secure. Despite increasing numbers of course offerings, collective endeavor proves difficult. Would that we were as organized as the National Association of Scholars (NAS) thinks. In my first semester at Duke University—a reputed bastion of subversive queer pedagogy—during the winter of 1996–97, it was a full month before I realized that on our little campus of six thousand undergraduates, at least three of us adjunct faculty members were teaching queer courses, however defined. We had not coordinated class meeting times, compared syllabi for overlap, or even met one another.

One of those instructors marveled at the large enrollment his class generated; that is, until he discovered that six of his students had assumed that "GLB Cultural Studies" referred to "Global Cultural Studies." Would that our courses enticed unsuspecting, wayward students in droves as the NAS fears. And yet, perhaps a lesson in recruitment is to be learned here. Of those six students, four remained in the class.

Meanwhile, zealously committed to full disclosure, I offered a special topics course with the out title, appearing on each student's transcript, of "American Lesbian and Gay History." Made fully aware of that on the first day of class, one of my six registrants failed to return, leaving me with five. Fortunately for my standing in the department, my course the following semester—a broader regional history that included within its well-advertised, revisionist critique a significant queer component—was overenrolled.

This brings us to a central dilemma posed by queer pedagogy: to teach queer history or to queer the teaching of history. Answers lie not solely or even primarily in the ability to draw large, engaged audiences. Rather, I would suggest that they lie in the ability to engage audiences in the theoretical exercise of destabilizing present categories, such that we all see our individual and varied collective investments in multiple histories of gender, sexuality, and difference. Such a post-identity politics positioning in relation to historical subjects and phenomena moves us well beyond the early queer historiographical preoccupation with prominent "lesbian" and "gay" predecessors—the often race- and class-biased paeans to this or that famous person, king or, uhm, queen, or figure from classical Greece. It further animates the very useful discourse theory critiques of normalcy; its ever-changing production, maintenance, and reproduction over time; and its perpetual, dialectical relationship to deviancy. Melding social history with histories of consciousness, it illuminates and complicates the most fundamental practices of everyday life across time, with the potential to elicit diverse student bodies' differing and ever-shifting senses of connectedness to the past.

The revolutionary potential of queering instruction became apparent to me when I was asked for the first (and last) time to serve at Duke on a university-wide committee, in this case on diversity and the curriculum. When some members claimed that great diversity already existed in campus course offerings—that is, in the number of courses that, using today's identity categories, mentioned non-white races, non-elite classes, non-Anglo-Saxon ethnicities, non-male genders, non-hetero sexualities—when they suggested a pick-and-choose system that would still allow the average student to slip through four years without any explicit brush with difference, Paula Giddings boldly (in light of Stanford's well-publicized debacle) suggested a single course to be required of all undergraduates: "The Historical Production of Human Difference." I've rarely seen a group of academic administrators more troubled.

Barring for the foreseeable future such systemic change in the curriculum, how might historians best utilize what pedagogical freedom is afforded when we shut the classroom door? What teaching strategies belie or rightly betray the more public course title, course syllabus, and departmental and college political posturing? How might sexualities become a principal concern of myriad historical projects? How might the conceptual dominance of identity, community, and politics—the presumably safer topics—be eclipsed or opened up by focuses on desire, pleasure, and behavior across time? How might complex histories of desire subvert the primacy of sexual object choice or sexual orientation as a primary category of analysis?

Further, don't these questions themselves demonstrate that any historical project inevitably reflects the historical context of its creation? For example, identity politics of the 1970s through the 1990s stressed the import of gay identity and community. Unsurprisingly, histories generated during that time privileged and, in part, produced identity and community in prior eras. My call today for a *queer* history, to be focused upon the ever-changing relationship of normalcy to deviancy, happens alongside a contemporary focus on queer desire over gay identity. A deeply historicist project thus situates in time not only the object of study but also the conductor of the study. Both the history and the historian must be historicized. We should ask not only what do we *study,* but who are *we* who study? Who are we in relationship to what we study?

The ongoing study of things queer, variously defined, would be a part of—and might even become tantamount to—Giddings's provocative proposed course on the production of human difference. Queer studies is part of the ongoing human story of drawing distinctions between what is normal and what is not. What we study is inclusive of but not limited to the terms we now use to mark our perceived cultural predecessors and their practices: "homosexual," "lesbian," "gay," "bisexual," "transgender," "intersexual"—but also, "heterosexual," "straight," and so on. What we might best choose to study, perhaps, is the phenomenon of distinction-making itself, sexual and otherwise. Indeed, what becomes understood as sexual or not changes over time.

How, then, do we study? What constitutes evidence? As many essays in this volume show, queer history was not always documented. Letters were burned, lives went unremarked. Similarly, as I've suggested, queer teaching hasn't always been recognized. Generations of teachers and professors have taught queer material without queer titles or syllabi. They taught normative texts and topics queerly. By privileging documents over other yet-to-be-imagined implements of history, traditional historical methodology ill-serves queer history. The method as well as the object of study should be queered. If, as these essays show, the nature of queerness changes over time, then queer studies—recently claimed as "pioneering"—itself has changed over time. It has changed and been reinvented, but it is not new. It has a long history of its own, a history distinct from, yet connected to, a broad range of intellectual endeavor. This collection suggests that histories of sexuality inevitably engage pedagogical concerns relevant to all historical practice.

Part One

Categories of Sexuality

2

Romantic Friendship

LEILA J. RUPP

IN 1975, while married to a man, I fell in love with a woman. In the early stages, my new relationship was purely romantic. I thought about her all the time, we talked endlessly on the telephone, I gave her presents, I longed to be with her. The way all of us understood what was going on was that she was "really" heterosexual and had just happened to fall in love with me, while I was "really" a lesbian and in the process of coming out. And then the very first issue of a new journal, *Signs: Journal of Women in Culture and Society,* fell into my hands, featuring as its lead article an entrancing study entitled "The Female World of Love and Ritual: Relations between Women in Nineteenth-Century America."[1]

In these pages I read the story of Molly and Helena, who met in school in New York in 1868. Molly, in an early letter to Helena, wrote, "I have not said to you in so many or so few words that I was happy with you during those few so incredibly short weeks but surely you do not need words to tell you what you must know. Those two or three days so dark without, so bright with firelight and contentment within I shall always remember as proof that, for a time, at least—I fancy for quite a long time—we might be sufficient for each other. . . . Imagine yourself kissed many times by one who loved you so dearly." As their friendship deepened, they made plans to live together, but that never happened. In crisis about their commitment, Molly pledged her love: "I wanted so to put my arms round my girl of all the girls in the world and tell her . . . I love her as wives do love their husbands, as *friends* who have taken each other for life. . . ." But shortly thereafter Helena decided to marry, and Molly followed suit two years later. In the interval between their marriages, Molly confided, "You know dear Helena, I really was in love with you. It was a passion such as I had never known until I saw you." And to Helena's fiancé, in a letter of congratulations, Molly wrote bluntly, "Do you know sir, that until you came along I believe that she loved me almost as girls love their lovers. *I know I loved her so.* Don't you wonder that I can stand the sight of you."

And this was only one of dozens of examples of passionate, intense, loving, physically affectionate relationships—what have come to be called "romantic friendships"—that Carroll Smith-Rosenberg had uncovered in the correspondence of a wide range of American middle-class families between the 1760s and the 1880s. Perhaps most amazing, as Molly's forthrightness in addressing Helena's fiancé suggests, such friendships were widely accepted, even admired, and often lasted from adolescence through marriage and into old age. Smith-Rosenberg concluded that the supposedly repressive Victorian sexual system in fact allowed far more latitude in moving along a spectrum ranging from heterosexuality to homosexuality than did late-twentieth-century American society.

Now let me try to reconstruct for a moment what this article meant to me. It was not that it was all right to be a lesbian because there had been lesbians in the past. Nor was it that what I was feeling was not about "homosexuality." Rather, it was that our modern categories of heterosexuality and homosexuality (and even bisexuality) are not complex enough to capture the slippery reality of love and desire. I seized upon this article because Smith-Rosenberg's vision of a world in which love and sexuality had no easy relationship to sexual identity made sense to me, unsure as I was if I yet merited the label "lesbian."

I begin my consideration of romantic friendship with this personal story because it illustrates many of the issues involved in the historical interpretation and reinterpretation of this important and puzzling phenomenon in the history of same-sex love and sexuality. In this essay, I explore romantic friendship as first articulated by historians and then consider some more recent historical discoveries, including the persistence of romantic friendship well into the twentieth century, that have cast doubt on that original understanding. Finally, I suggest a way to incorporate these newer developments without throwing out the baby with the bathwater.

First let us look a bit further at the early scholarship on romantic friendship. The book that really fleshed out the concept and gave it a name—actually in use in the eighteenth and nineteenth centuries—was Lillian Faderman's provocative *Surpassing the Love of Men,* a study of romantic friendship and love between women in the Euroamerican world from the seventeenth century to the present.[2] Faderman gave a great deal of attention to women's romantic friendships, emphasizing (as Smith-Rosenberg had already pointed out) that assumptions of women's asexuality explain the societal acceptance of what might look to modern eyes like lesbian relationships. If women and men (or at least white middle-class women and men) were conceptualized as polar opposites, men represented by the head and hand and women by the heart, men inherently lustful and women naturally pure and without desire, then what could be more natural than that women would find their soul mates among each other, and that society would condone this? Although Faderman never denied the *possibility* that romantic friends might be sexual together, she clearly could imagine that they might really love one another and yet, conditioned as they were by their society, not act on any sexual feelings. "It is probable that many romantic friends, while totally open in expressing and demonstrating emotional and spiritual love, repressed any sexual inclinations . . . that they might have felt for each other, since during most eras of modern history women were well taught from childhood that only men or bad women were sexually aggressive" (80). This led Faderman to see romantic friends as foremothers of contemporary lesbians.

Certainly asexuality would help to explain why society accepted and even glorified romantic friendships. Take, for example, the case of the "Ladies of Llangollen," Eleanor Butler and Sarah Ponsonby, two upper-class Welsh women who eloped in 1778. When Sarah's family discovered that she had run off with a woman instead of a man, they were enormously relieved. A relative explained: "Sarah's conduct, though it has an appearance of imprudence, is I am sure void of serious impropriety. There were no gentlemen concerned, nor does it appear to be anything more than a scheme of Romantic Friendship."[3] They lived together for over fifty years, attracting visits from famous women and men and serving as a kind of model of the idyllic life for other romantic friends.

Or take the case of "Miss Woods and Miss Pirie against Dame Helen Cumming Gordon," an early-nineteenth-century Scottish case on which Lillian Hellman based her famous lesbian play, *The Children's Hour.* Marianne Woods and Jane Pirie were schoolteachers who fell from grace when one of their students told her aristocratic grandmother that they had engaged in sexual acts together. To be accurate, we do not really know what the schoolgirl, Jane Cumming, told her grandmother, but it was enough for Lady Cumming Gordon to contact the parents of all the other girls, resulting in the emptying out of the school. The Misses Woods and Pirie promptly sued Lady Cumming Gordon for libel, leading to their further ruin but leaving us with a rich, if tantalizing, record of the trial. Lillian Faderman, in a creative retelling of the story, presents a number of possible explanations of what really happened.[4]

One of the things that is most telling about the trial is the evidence of the acceptability of romantic friendship. One of the judges, for example, exclaims, "Are we to say that every woman who has formed an intimate friendship and has slept in the same bed with another is guilty? Where is the innocent woman in Scotland?" (281). Lady Cumming Gordon's counsel, in an attempt to prove the schoolteachers guilty and thus his client innocent of libel, asks the girls if they ever saw their teachers "kissing, caressing, and fondling more than ordinary female friends," showing that quite a lot of physical affection might seem perfectly natural (82).

Yet the case presented a nearly impossible dilemma for the judges, for they had to choose between believing, on the one hand, that respectable schoolteachers had engaged in sexual acts (in the bed one of them shared with a student, no less) or that respectable schoolgirls could have made up a story about something—sex between women—that some of the judges resolutely refused to believe could exist. Thus the case yielded a "scotch verdict," or inconclusive decision. In the end the racist and imperialist division of "respectable" middle-class white Scottish women from women of other classes and races provided a way out. For Jane Cumming, the accuser, had been born from a liaison between Lady Cumming Gordon's beloved son, who died in service to the British Empire, and an Indian woman. That Jane Cumming had spent her early years in India could explain how she might know of something the judges themselves worked hard to deny could even exist. As one judge explained, "The language of the Hindoo female domestics turns chiefly on the commerce of the sexes. . . . It is impossible to live in Indostan without learning through observation and instruction, by the age of eight or nine, something about venereal intercourse" (153).

So, from the rich evidence provided in Faderman's two books, the standard story emerged. Romantic friendship flourished in the eighteenth and nineteenth centuries because middle-class white women were perceived as asexual. With the "sexual revolution" of the turn of the nineteenth century, which accompanied the movement of these women into the public sphere of work and politics, a new public recognition of women's sexuality threw suspicion on romantic friendships. Furthermore, romantic friends increasingly had the option of foregoing marriage altogether and choosing to live together, forming what came to be known (because of their frequency in the northeastern United States) as "Boston marriages." So with the breakdown of the sex-segregated social worlds of the nineteenth century came a new public awareness—what was perceived as a "discovery"—of lesbianism. For Faderman, in particular, the new science of sexology, which detailed the phenomenon of "inversion" (a woman trapped in a man's body, or vice versa) or homosexuality, played a critical role in making romantic friendships deviant.

Thus African American poet Angelina Weld Grimké, the grandniece of abolitionists Sarah and Angelina Grimké, in the last decade of the nineteenth century formed a romantic friendship but later obscured her love for women, as demonstrated in Chapter 4 of this volume. As a member of the middle class, Grimké's friendship with her school friend Mamie Burrill followed the patterns Smith-Rosenberg described for white women. In 1896, Burrill wrote to Grimké: "Could I just come to meet thee once more, in the old sweet way, just coming at your calling, and like an angel bending o'er you breathe into your ear, 'I love you.'" Angelina, later that year, expressed her own longing: "Oh Mamie if you only knew how my heart beats when I think of you and it yearns and pants to gaze, if only for one second upon your lovely face." But Grimké, perhaps because of the increasing suspicion towards women's relationships that accompanied the creation of the deviant category of the lesbian, came to veil her desires in her published poetry. Yet in her unpublished lyrics and published verses addressed to a gender-unspecified lover, Grimké poured out the pain of an unidentified lost love.[5]

But the fundamental assumptions—of asexuality and societal acceptance—underlying the trajectory of romantic friendship have increasingly come under attack. First of all, Anthony Rotundo found that white, middle-class young men also formed romantic friendships, even though no one accused them of asexuality.[6] If men could be romantic friends, how could we argue that women's intense relationships merited acceptance because society assumed women to be without sexual passion? Listen to the story of Albert Dodd and Anthony Halsey, college students in the 1830s, who loved each other and slept together in the same bed. Albert, in his journal, referred to his "adored Anthony," "My most beloved of all," and described his friend as "so handsome." "Often too," he wrote, Anthony "shared my pillow—or I his, and then how sweet to sleep with him, to hold his beloved form in my embrace, to have his arms about my neck, to imprint upon his face sweet kisses" (7).

This sounds, of course, a great deal like the romantic friendship that flourished among women. But there was one big difference: however much these young men might long to live together, their friendships ended with adulthood and marriage, because success in the middle-class male professional and business worlds called for a competitive spirit quite at odds with such youthful devotion. No "Montana Marriages" (that is, no unions between men on the heavily male frontier of white settlement) for American men! Even so, we have to wonder how supposedly lust-filled men could be presumed to be innocently sharing beds. The answer, I think, can be found in the complex division of sexuality in the nineteenth century along the lines of race, class, and ethnicity. Gender was not the only cleavage in societal views of sexuality. White, native-born, middle-class men, while perhaps inherently sexual, were presumed to have the self-control necessary to behave as "Christian Gentlemen." In contrast, working-class, immigrant, and African-American men embodied unleashed sexuality.[7]

From quite a different angle, evidence that romantic friendship persisted into the twentieth century, long after the public recognition of women's sexual desires and passions, also raises questions about the traditional story.[8] In the international women's movement, for example, women discussed "fairies," used the terms "queer" and "perverse from a sexual point of view," referred to "manly-looking" women and women who "went about together . . . , hair cropped short and rather mannish in dress," and described a school-girl crush as "hero-worship . . . but there was nothing sordid or exaggerated about it," indicating familiarity with the work of the sexologists, who had supposedly forever banished innocence about women's relationships.[9] Yet these women matter-of-factly accepted coupled women as partners in Boston marriages.

Consider, for instance, the relationship of Hull House founder and international peace activist Jane Addams with Mary Rozet Smith. Addams and Smith, both members of the Women's International League for Peace and Freedom (WILPF), sent and received messages for one another, made arrangements for double-bedded rooms when they traveled, and took care of each other. Smith, whom Addams described to Heymann as "My most intimate friend," inspired a great deal of enthusiasm among Addams's colleagues.[10] "Will you kiss your dear friend, Miss Smith, for me and tell her that in sleepless nights and even in nice dreams I see her before me as a good angel," wrote Dutch feminist Aletta Jacobs in 1915. "I have a remembrance of her as one of the sweetest women I ever met in the world," Jacobs added four years later. And, even more extravagantly, Jacobs concluded in 1923 that "I always have admired her and if I would have been a man I should have fallen in love with her."[11]

Or what about Anna Howard Shaw, American minister, charismatic orator, and international leader, who had a reputation within suffrage circles for her "strong and passionate attachments to other women," some of which "have broken up in . . . tempestuous fashion."[12] Shaw described her "abiding love for home and home life" at her country house, Moylan, which she shared with Lucy Anthony, a niece of Shaw's idol Susan B. Anthony. Anthony called Shaw, after her death, "my Precious Love," "the joy of my life."[13] Clearly the story is more complicated than historians at first assumed.

In response to these kinds of puzzles, scholars have suggested that we have exaggerated the societal acceptability of romantic friendship and overlooked the possibility of the recognition of a sexual nature of these bonds.[14] Discussions of literature, in particular, reveal an awareness and horror of sex between women before the alleged "discovery of lesbianism" in the late nineteenth century. A conventional character in a Louisa May Alcott story, for example, describes romantic friends who plan to live together after one marries as a "different race of creatures."[15] Other literary works contrasted suitable and deviant romantic friendships, as in the case of Maria Edgeworth's 1801 novel *Belinda,* which contrasts the heroine Belinda's romantic friendship with the ladylike Lady Delacour and the freakish "man-woman" Harriet Freke.[16]

And even the case of Marianne Woods and Jane Pirie, which reveals judges marveling in disbelief about the possibility of anything amiss about women sharing a bed, raises questions about women's asexuality. After all, the judges recognized, in asking whether the women crossed the lines of "ordinary female friendship," that there were such lines and that they could be crossed. How much kissing, caressing, and fondling was too much? The discovery of mid-nineteenth-century letters between Addie Brown, a free-born African-American domestic worker, and Rebecca Primus, an African-American schoolteacher, reveals the practice of what has been called "bosom sex," the fondling of breasts while sharing a bed.[17] Surely that was too much?

Had her contemporaries known about Anne Lister's sexual activities, they would surely have considered them too much. An independent, mannish, early-nineteenth-century English gentlewoman, Anne described in her elaborately coded diary her numerous sexual affairs with women, some of them married.[18] Fleeing England and the love of her life, who married a man and passed on to Anne a venereal disease contracted from her husband through his own extramarital exploits, Anne landed in Paris in 1824 and almost immediately began to court a widow, Mrs. Barlow, staying at the same pension. One night, Mrs. Barlow came to her room and climbed in bed with her: "I was contented that my naked left thigh should rest upon her naked left thigh and thus she let me grubble her over her petticoats. All the while I was pressing her between my thighs. . . . Now and then I held my hand still and felt her pulsation, let her rise towards my hand two or three times and gradually open her thighs, and felt . . . that she was excited."[19] Lister was a woman who, before the invention of the term "homosexuality" in 1869 and before the emergence of the first lesbian cultures around the turn of the century, not only loved and desired women but saw this as her defining characteristic. She knew the term "Saffic," considered her attraction to women natural, and proclaimed proudly that "I love, & only love, the fairer sex & thus beloved by them in turn, my heart revolts from any other love than theirs."[20]

Lister's amazing diary has seemed to undermine our understanding of romantic friendship by developing the sexual possibilities between women in a supposedly asexual era, but I do not think we should be so quick to dismiss entirely the idea of societal acceptance. Lister, after all, openly courted the women she loved, and although she encountered some ridicule and harassment, it came mostly, I think, because of her mannish dress and her utter disinterest in men. Rather than evidence that romantic friendship was unacceptable, her story suggests that some women pursued openly sexual relationships under the guise of acceptable romantic friendships. And some women got away with it.

I think we have to recognize that sexuality was never an impossibility between romantic friends, that romantic friendship was quite complex, and that the key to acceptance was respectability, which was not a permanent status but rather one that could be easily shattered. Any hint of gender deviance or overt sexuality or, perhaps, dismissal of men was enough to push romantic friends across the line, even before the late nineteenth century. In the case of the Scottish schoolteachers, the testimony of Jane Cumming that they came to each other's beds, lay one on top of the other, kissed, whispered "Oh, do it, darling," and made a noise similar to "putting one's finger into the neck of a wet bottle," if true, clearly put them beyond the bounds of respectability. Harriet Freke, the character in the Edgeworth novel, crossed the line in part because of her fondness for wearing men's clothes, and the romantic friends in the Louise May Alcott story stay safely on the side of respectability because they turn out not to be "mannish and rough." Rebecca Primus's aunt warned Addie Brown not to tell her male beau that she loved Rebecca more than him, suggesting that the women's relationship was acceptable only as long as it did not preclude marriage. And perhaps if Molly and Helena had not married men, if Molly had written to Helena's fiancé to tell him to go away, she might have crossed the line of respectability as surely as did Alice Mitchell, who slit the throat of her lover on the streets of Memphis in 1892 out of fear of losing her.[21]

Recent biographies of three well-respected women—M. Carey Thomas, president of Bryn Mawr College; First Lady Eleanor Roosevelt; and Miriam Van Waters, prison reformer—show us that well past the "discovery of lesbianism" women formed couples, made lives together, and expressed their love and erotic longing at the same time that they and the world around them could distinguish what they were from "female homosexuals." These life stories help us to understand the persistence of romantic friendship, as in the cases of Jane Addams and Mary Rozet Smith, and Anna Howard Shaw and Lucy Anthony, in a more complex way.

M. Carey Thomas, a redoubtable lady if ever there was one, chose as her life's loves two women, with some overlap. As a student in Switzerland in the early 1880s, she formed with her Baltimore friend Mamie Gwinn what they both considered a marriage. As Helen Lefkowitz Horowitz tells it in her sensitive biography, they lived together, loved each other passionately, and left a record of kisses exchanged and heads nestled in laps.[22] By the time Thomas became president of Bryn Mawr in 1894, she was also in love with another Baltimore friend, Mary Garrett, who in addition played the role of her financial patron. Unable to give up Gwinn's "little love" for the intense and fully requited passion of Garrett, Thomas carefully arranged the two women's comings and goings so that they did not have to meet, although they of course knew of each other. But what is particularly striking about Thomas's story is the way she bridges the worlds of romantic friendship and homosexuality. For she read about lesbianism, including sexual acts between women, she admired and followed the trial of Oscar Wilde, she kept lists of books labeled "Lesbianism" and "Books on Sapphism." While she shared a bed with Mary Garrett, as had countless romantic friends, she had also read texts that linked love between women and sexuality. As Horowitz wisely concludes, however, the fact that Thomas never seemingly took in any negative portrayals of lesbianism, never expressed any guilt or unease, is significant. "Both before and after she learned about female sexuality and lesbianism, Carey Thomas believed her attachments to Mamie and Mary were right and fitting, that love of a woman for a woman was better than any love for a man" (291).

What Eleanor Roosevelt knew or thought about lesbianism is a mystery, but the fact that she was a married woman and moved in a world of respectable but indubitably lesbian women certainly confused those looking in from the outside, both then and now. In what has become a famous passage, the journalist Lorena Hickok wrote to Roosevelt remembering "the feeling of that soft spot just north-east of the corner of your mouth against my lips," and Roosevelt confided her wish to "lie down beside you tonight and take you in my arms."[23] Although Franklin Roosevelt called some of Eleanor's necktie-wearing friends "she-men," Roosevelt herself did not transgress the boundaries of respectability enough to merit consideration as a lesbian or bisexual woman. How she viewed herself we shall never know, in part because Lorena Hickok burned most of Eleanor's letters after her death. Only Blanche Wiesen Cook's perceptive biography has allowed us to see Eleanor in context, in her world of coupled women who exchanged pinky rings and brought each other violets.[24] They reveled, she tells us, in the romance of the closet. And it was their respectability, their class privilege, their ladylike pearls, that protected them.

The importance of respectability is nowhere clearer than in the story of Miriam Van Waters, told so beautifully, in part in this volume's Chapter 5, by Estelle Freedman.[25] Van Waters formed a deeply romantic relationship with her benefactor, Geraldine Thompson, herself a married woman. In the 1920s, when the two women first met, the concept of homosexuality was no mystery, and Van Waters had read the work of the sexologists. But "lesbianism" suggested gender inversion, the "mannish" lesbian, or a Freudian notion of pathology, and Van Waters and Thompson considered themselves "normal." Yet they were also careful to conceal their relationship in certain ways, and Van Waters expressed self-doubt about her sexuality. And, as in the case of Eleanor Roosevelt, they systematically burned their letters when Van Waters came under attack for tolerating homosexuality at the women's prison she supervised. On the one hand, Van Waters did not see her relationship with Thompson as in the same category as lesbianism among prison inmates. On the other, she was scared that others would.[26]

These women's stories make clear that much had changed by the mid-twentieth century. The formulation of lesbianism as a syndrome may have made some romantic friends wary, but others, such as M. Carey Thomas, found potential self-definition and understanding even in the negative portrayals of the sexologists.[27] But I also believe that romantic friendship was throughout its history a complex phenomenon that took many forms. From the "bosom sex" of Addie Brown and Rebecca Primus to the "grubbling" of Anne Lister, some women acted on their erotic desires. Perhaps others did not, or found satisfaction in the kissing, caressing, and fondling of "ordinary" romantic friendship. But it was respectability, closely tied to class and ethnicity and gender (in the sense of not transgressing the boundary of gender by cross-dressing or otherwise appearing "mannish") that was key to determining the acceptability of romantic friendship. The rules of respectability, of course, changed over time, and certainly by the second "sexual revolution" of the 1960s and 1970s, romantic friendship was no more. It was too bad, for, as Carroll Smith-Rosenberg pointed out at the very beginning of our contemporary consideration of the phenomenon, the sexual system that permitted it offered a flexibility that we can only envy. Although in fact I do identify as a lesbian and my former lover is now married to a man, from a historical perspective those were not the only possible outcomes of the scenario that unfolded in 1975.

Notes

1. Carroll Smith-Rosenberg, "The Female World of Love and Ritual: Relations between Women in Nineteenth-Century America," *Signs: Journal of Women in Culture and Society* 1 (1975): 1–29.

2. Lillian Faderman, *Surpassing the Love of Men: Romantic Friendship and Love between Women from the Renaissance to the Present* (New York: William Morrow, 1981).

3. Quoted in Faderman, *Surpassing,* 75. See Elizabeth Mavor, *The Ladies of Llangollen: A Study in Romantic Friendship* (New York: Penguin, 1971).

4. Lillian Faderman, *Scotch Verdict: Miss Pirie and Miss Woods v. Dame Cumming Gordon* (1983; repr. New York: Columbia University Press, 1993).

5. Gloria T. Hull, *Color, Sex, and Poetry: Three Women Writers of the Harlem Renaissance* (Bloomington: Indiana University Press, 1987), quotation on 139. Another study shows that romantic friendships were not confined to white women; see Karen V. Hanse, "'No Kises Is Like Youres': An Erotic Friendship between Two African-American Women during the Mid-Nineteenth Century," *Gender & History* 7 (1995): 153–82.

6. E. Anthony Rotundo, "Romantic Friendship: Male Intimacy and Middle-Class Youth in the Northern United States, 1800–1900," *Journal of Social History* 23 (1989): 1–25.

7. See John D'Emilio and Estelle B. Freedman, *Intimate Matters: A History of Sexuality in America* (New York: Harper and Row, 1988).

8. See Leila J. Rupp, "'Imagine My Surprise': Women's Relationships in Mid-Twentieth Century America," in *Hidden from History: Reclaiming the Gay and Lesbian Past,* ed. Martin Bauml Duberman, Martha Vicinus, and George Chauncey, Jr. (New York: New American Library, 1989), 395–410.

9. RG [Rosika Schwimmer] to Wilhelmina [van Wulfften Palthe], July 29, 1917, Schwimmer-Lloyd collection, box A-90, New York Public Library (NYPL), for "fairies" and "queer;" MG [Marguerite Gobat] to Vilma Glocklich [French], October 27, 1924, Women's International League for Peace and Freedom (WILPF) papers, reel 1, for "perverse au point de vue sexuel;" Aletta Jacobs to Rosika Schwimmer, May 3, 1909, Schwimmer-Lloyd collection, box A-20, NYPL, for "manly-looking"; Helen Archdale to Anna Nilsson, May 17, 1933, Equal Rights International (ERI) papers, box 331, Fawcett Library (FL), London Guildhall University, for cropped hair and mannish dress; Mia Boissevain, tribute to Rosa Manus, n.d., Rosa Manus papers, Internationaal Informatiecentrum en Archief voor de Vrouwenbeweging (IIAV), Amsterdam.

10. Anne Zueblin to M. Illova, June 10, 1929, WILPF papers, reel 19; [Mary Sheepshanks] to Mary Rozet Smith, July 5, 1929, Addams papers, reel 20; [Jane Addams] to Lida Gustava Heymann, February 23, 1924, Addams papers, reel 16.

11. Aletta Jacobs to Jane Addams, December 23, 1915, Addams papers, reel 9; Aletta Jacobs to Jane Addams and Alice Hamilton, September 26, 1919, Addams papers, reel 12; Aletta Jacobs to Jane Addams, June 12, 1923, Addams papers, reel 15.

12. Rachel Foster Avery to Aletta Jacobs, July 14, 1910, Jacobs papers, IIAV.

13. Biography of Anna Howard Shaw, Dillon collection, box 18, Schlesinger Library (SL), Radcliffe College, Cambridge, Mass.; Anna Howard Shaw to Aletta Jacobs, March 19, 1914, Jacobs papers, IIAV; Aletta H. Jacobs, *Uit het leven van merkwaardige vrouwen* (Amsterdam: F. van Rossen, 1905), 37, quoted in Mineke Bosch with Annemarie Kloosterman, *Politics and Friendship: Letters from the International Woman Suffrage Alliance, 1902–1942* (Columbus: Ohio State University Press, 1990), 25; Barbara R. Finn, "Anna Howard Shaw and Women's Work," *Frontiers: A Journal of Women Studies* 4(3) (1979): 21–25, quoted in Bosch, *Politics and Friendship,* 26.

14. Liz Stanley, "Romantic Friendship? Some Issues in Researching Lesbian History and Biography," *Women's History Review* 1 (1992): 193–216; Martha Vicinus, "'They Wonder

to Which Sex I Belong': The Historical Roots of the Modern Lesbian Identity," *Feminist Studies* 18 (1992): 467–97; Sylvia Martin, "'These Walls of Flesh': The Problem of the Body in the Romantic Friendship/Lesbianism Debate," *Historical Reflections/Réflexions Historiques* 20 (1994): 243–66; and Lisa Moore, "'Something More Tender Still than Friendship': Romantic Friendship in Early-Nineteenth-Century England," *Feminist Studies* 18 (1992): 499–520.

15. Marylynne Diggs, "Romantic Friends or a 'Different Race of Creatures?' The Representation of Lesbian Pathology in Nineteenth-Century America," *Feminist Studies* 21 (1995): 317–40, quotation on 321.

16. Moore, "Something More Tender."

17. Karen V. Hansen, "'No Kisses Is Like Yours': An Erotic Friendship between Two African-American Women during the Mid-Nineteenth Century." *Gender & History* 7(2) (1995): 153–82.

18. Helena Whitebread, ed., *I Know My Own Heart: The Diaries of Anne Lister (1791–1840)*, (London: Virago, 1988); Helena Whitebread, ed., *No Priest But Love: The Journals of Anne Lister from 1824–1826* (New York: New York University Press, 1992).

19. Whitebread, *No Priest*, 65.

20. Whitebread, *I Know My Own Heart*, xxv.

21. Lisa Duggan, "The Trials of Alice Mitchell: Sensationalism, Sexology, and the Lesbian Subject in Turn-of-the-Century America," *Signs* 18 (1993): 791–814.

22. Helen Lefkowitz Horowitz, *The Power and Passion of M. Carey Thomas* (New York: Alfred Knopf, 1994).

23. Quoted in Doris Faber, *The Life of Lorena Hickok: E. R.'s Friend* (New York: William Morrow, 1980), 152, 176.

24. Blanche Wiesen Cook, *Eleanor Roosevelt, Volume One. 1884–1933* (New York: Viking, 1992).

25. Estelle B. Freedman, *Maternal Justice: Miriam Van Waters and the Female Reform Tradition* (Chicago: University of Chicago Press, 1996).

26. See also Estelle B. Freedman, "The Prison Lesbian: Race, Class, and the Construction of the Aggressive Female Homosexual," *Feminist Studies* 222 (Summer 1996): 397–423.

27. This is a point made also by Esther Newton, "The Mythic Mannish Lesbian: Radclyffe Hall and the New Woman," *Signs: Journal of Women in Culture and Society* 9 (1984): 557–75.

3

"Someone to Talk Our Language"

Jane Heap, Margaret Anderson, and the *Little Review* in Chicago

HOLLY A. BAGGETT

THE lives of Margaret Anderson and Jane Heap, lesbian partners and coeditors of the avant-garde literary journal the *Little Review,* founded in Chicago in 1914, were examples of open lesbianism in early twentieth-century America. Their journeys as two young women from Indiana and Kansas to Chicago at the turn of the century give some insight into the process of the creation of modern lesbian identity. Many questions are debated by historians in this foggy landscape between Victorian and modern: What was the relationship between the literature of sexologists and the creation of the "homosexual"? How should we interpret the mannish lesbian? At what point can we begin to speak of gay urban subcultures? While the lives of Anderson and Heap could not completely answer these questions, they do aid our understanding of the definitive and unambiguous steps taken by women who would come to publicly represent themselves as lesbians. The sources for this examination lie in the published pages of the *Little Review* as edited by Margaret Anderson and in the private correspondence of Jane Heap.

The *Little Review* was published from 1914 to 1929 and became famous as a journal of literary modernism, radical politics, and avant-garde art. Anderson and Heap are perhaps best remembered in American literary history for their 1920 obscenity trial over their serialization of James Joyce's *Ulysses.* The two moved the journal from Chicago to New York to Paris, where by the 1920s they became members of the American expatriate community. For the purposes of this essay, I will examine the early Chicago years of Anderson, Heap, and the *Little Review* to explore the commencement of two lesbian lives that became progressively radical and public.

The correspondence of Jane Heap gives us a view into the private hopes and concerns of a woman who would go from proper Midwestern girl to urban butch

Permission to include material from The Florence Reynolds Collection Related to Jane Heap and the *Little Review* granted by University of Delaware Library, Newark, Delaware, and Karen L. Clark.

Figure 1. Jane Heap, Chicago, 1909. Courtesy of Special Collections, Morris Library, University of Delaware, and Karen L. Clark.

Figure 2. Jane Heap, Paris, ca. 1926. Courtesy of Berenice Abbott / Commerce Graphics Ltd., Inc.

(Figures 1 and 2). The letters demonstrate her love for another woman, her hopes for their lives together, and the confusion that characterized the transition from Kansas daughter to Chicago cross-dresser.

In 1901 after graduating from Topeka High School, Jane Heap traveled to Chicago to study at the Art Institute with aspirations of becoming a professional artist.[1] Also consumed with a love of poetry and theater, Heap had made her way to the city just a few years before the onset of "the Chicago Renaissance." In the first two decades of the twentieth century Chicagoans witnessed a variety of events, trends, and movements in art, theater, and literature. In sum, these developments pushed the city beyond the vestiges of a genteel culture dictated by image-conscious late Victorian philanthropists toward the radical innovations of young iconoclasts passionately carrying the banner of the "New." The arrival of the Post-Impressionists Armory Art show at the Art Institute, the creation of the Chicago Little Theater by Maurice Browne, the editorship by Floyd Dell of the *Friday Literary Review,* the founding of the journal *Poetry* by Harriet Monroe, and the *Little Review* all dramatically transformed Chicago's literary and artistic landscape. After graduating from the Art Institute in 1905, Heap would find a position teaching at the Lewis Institute, now the Illinois Institute of Technology. At some point she met Florence Reynolds, the daughter of a Chicago insurance executive. In the summers of 1908 and 1909, Heap returned to visit with her family in Topeka and wrote frequent letters to Reynolds in Chicago.

Although fond of her family, Heap was not happy to leave Chicago. "Coming home always upsets me," she wrote Reynolds in August of 1908. "Here it is the Real—In Chicago it is Love and Art and Play."[2] What is quite clear is that Heap missed Reynolds more than she missed Chicago: that same month Heap wrote, "I wish I could be near you tonight—close—close—or near enough that a look or touch would let either into the other's heart—or to feel the heart stagger under the added load of a kiss—since it cannot be—we can wait—and waiting love the more."[3] On July 20, 1909, Heap declared, "I have always felt that I was a good lover, but since I have loved you I feel how utterly impossible it is to convey my love to you. Good night—loved so well. I wish you were here tonight and every night to go to sleep on my arm."[4] The following day she added, "Sometimes I lie quite still at night and imagine you close, touching me all along—until it becomes so real I nearly cry of emptiness."[5]

How can we determine if such letters are not another example of romantic friendship, but rather evidence that Heap and Reynolds saw themselves as self-consciously modern lesbian women who erotically desired one another? In response to a letter from Reynolds, Heap wrote, "I wish I could tell you of the thrill I got when reading that you wished my hands on 'My Home.' I wonder if it will ever die away. I wonder if the old hereditary way pulls us all whether we want it or not. I wonder have you wanted me this week. You *must* have. I love you, and want, want, want, you."[6]

The last letter helps us to frame crucial questions. Was the reference to Reynolds's wanting Heap's hands on her "Home" a coded sexual message? Or was Reynolds's "Home" her "Heart"? For Heap began most of her letters to Reynolds "Dear Tiny Heart"? What was Heap referring to when she wondered if "the old hereditary way pulls us all whether we want it or not"? Was it a reference to the biologically based theories of sexual inversion? Heap made no known statements specifically concerning the sexologists during this period either in the *Little Review* or her correspondence. But other evidence can lead us to some tentative conclusions. Over the course of her correspondence Heap gradually changed her signature from Jane to Lancelot to Richard. And we know it was this same period (1908–1909) that she began to occasionally cross-dress. Heap was in effect on her way to becoming what was seen by everyone who encountered her and later recorded it—"the mannish lesbian."

Furthermore, we know that Heap was not appropriating male names and dress in isolation; she and Reynolds had a circle of women friends who referred to themselves as Tommy, Jesse, and James and occasionally cross-dressed. In July of 1909, Heap wrote Reynolds of their mutual friend Marie Blanke, also known as James: "I have just written to James. She has been visiting at some very swell houses. She said she had been doing some of my stunts dressing up in men's clothes and making love to girls."[7] The meaning of cross-dressing has in itself been a subject of dispute among historians. Was cross-dressing a sign that women had internalized the sexologists' description of themselves as congenital inverts who were inherently masculine, or did they use it as a device to distance themselves from the Victorian tenet of female asexuality and declare their desire for other women? The answer, I believe, is both.

As Esther Newton has described the New Women of the late nineteenth and early twentieth centuries, "Before they could find one another, they had to become visible, at least to each other. What they needed was a new vocabulary built on the radical idea that women apart from men could have autonomous sexual feeling. . . . To become avowedly sexual, the New Woman had to enter the male world, either as a heterosexual on male terms . . . or as—or with—a lesbian in male body drag (a butch)."[8] The relationship of Heap and Reynolds was not a romantic friendship.

Heap was not a woman trying to literally pass as a man. Rather, her regard for Reynolds was the self-conscious construction of a modern lesbian.

This is not to suggest that Heap fervently believed everything sexologists pronounced. As George Chauncey has argued, such an assumption "attributes inordinate power to ideology as an autonomous force" and would "oversimplify the complex dialectic between social conditions, ideology and consciousness which produced gay identities."[9] Or more to the point in the case of Heap and Reynolds, what we have is, in the words of Lisa Duggan, "a polyvocal cultural dialogue" as a result of the interrelations of sexological representations and lesbian *self*-representations. What we see is a back and forth, an experimentation in gender and sex roles, and the response this provoked. In Duggan's words there was "an extended battle over the meaning of women's erotic partnerships at the turn of the century. Out of this battle, the first publicly visible forms of modern lesbianism were born."[10]

An interesting aspect of Heap's cross-dressing was her involvement in stage productions in Chicago in which she appeared only to play male roles. We know Heap acted in student productions at the Art Institute and later joined Maurice Brownes's Chicago Little Theater, which was responsible for fostering a nationwide little theater movement. Most of the extant photographs of Heap in these productions are, I believe, from "Blanke and Heap's Nickel Theater," a group of teachers from the Lewis Institute. Blanke is Marie Blanke, a.k.a. James. At a time, 1910, when Heap was not yet cross-dressing full time, the theater could provide a safe environment in which to publicly appear in male dress. Heap's interest in the theater went beyond acting; she worked in the Little Theater as a set designer and even authored a play, which remains today among her papers. This work is a fascinating piece of evidence demonstrating that Heap was preoccupied with questions of gender and sex roles. The play is entitled "Pyg-male-one," a takeoff on Shaw's *Pygmalion*. In her version, however, Heap reversed both the storyline and the gender roles. The professor is not Henry Higgins but a woman named Vera Still Bible, "Professor of Neurotics." The flower girl is a male character named William Grabbed For. In the play Professor Still Bible, referring to Grabbed For, states, "I'll wager that I can make a nervous and financial wreck of him in six months."[11] The professor and William marry, only to have the professor run away with another character of indeterminate sex named "Bunny."

The wedding of Heap's sister Edna provides another example of how Heap both utilized the idea of her self as a man and yet interpreted her relationship with Reynolds as something other than mimicry of heterosexuality. To her prospective brother-in-law Herbert Clark, Heap wrote, "Herb, I really want to tell you as man to man that if Edna has chosen you to be married I am glad it is you. It is hard for a woman to be married—and if Edna is not happy always I think I could kill the man who made her unhappy."[12] But to Reynolds, Heap confided, "It would make one tired to see Edna and Herb. They don't know the first idea of love. They don't even look at one another. Tiny heart when all the records are in—I think we will find that we have all the great Ecstasy's of Love."[13]

In spite of such language it would be misleading to portray Heap as a woman full of confidence in her joyous quest for the construction of modern lesbianism. She was self-conscious and clearly plagued by doubts. In one letter Heap wrote, "You dear little thing—I sat 'feeling' just now and I could feel how small you were in my arms. It seems to me now as if I did not 'love you up' often enough when we were together. Why did I always feel conscious when there were people present—as if it were not fair to you or something to love you publicly or what was it? I think we feel a difference that others did not suspect. I feel that I can be a part of everything and that nothing can be a part of me[,] being so different. . . . They never feel the difference in any way. I am the only one who knows the differences—that is what makes the distance stretch out so far on all sides and leaves me all alone. Except that distance between you and me—everything seems to shorten it, if possible, making the need of you almost unbearable."[14]

The sense of difference, and of distance from others, of despair, hurt, anger, and sadness repeatedly comes through in many of Heap's letters. "Perhaps we all feel," she disclosed in another letter, "like foreigners and long for someone to talk our language—How I have longed for someone to understand."[15] Heap was a young woman struggling at this point in her life on a number of levels. She was not yet totally free of her family, not financially independent, and felt hemmed in by her circumstances. She was a woman trying to break out in any number of ways. It was the support and love of Reynolds and her circle of friends that sustained Heap. "Late yesterday your letter came—it was not just a letter it was so much to me that I cannot tell—what your love, your faith and your understanding are to me I can never tell you—I do not believe that I myself know. . . ."[16]

JANE Heap met Margaret Anderson in 1916. The Little Theater and *Little Review* were both housed in the Fine Arts Building, and one day Heap appeared in Anderson's studio. Anderson had founded the *Little Review* two years earlier. A native of Indiana, she came to Chicago to escape what she felt to be the "suffocating" atmosphere of the Midwest. After working as a bookstore clerk, a freelance reviewer, and an editor of a religious journal whose principles she did not share, Anderson established the *Little Review,* an arts journal to be based on the "New." Anderson began her magazine in the midst of the Chicago Renaissance, and she quickly fell in with other young Midwesterners who had migrated to the city to escape their provincial surroundings.

Participants in and enthusiastic supporters of a revolution in both arts and politics, these young Americans loudly proclaimed the virtues of socialism, anarchism, cubism, futurism, psychoanalysis, and sexual liberation. Most were self-styled bohemians whose ability to live out their philosophy was in part formed by a concomitant transformation of the city's economic and social landscape. The emergence of three rooming-house districts on the west, south, and north sides of the city, populated mostly by wage earners and transient lodgers, led to the creation of social networks and peer subcultures that tolerated a fairly liberal lifestyle among its inhabitants. Two of these working-class districts helped to forge nonconformist enclaves in Chicago: on the south side between 57th Street and Stony Island Avenue and on the north side in Towertown, an area surrounding a water tower. Both areas were known, in the words of one historian of the Renaissance, "for strong assertions of the individual—artiness, intellectuality, radical politics, anti-religion, free love and homosexuality."[17]

Through the inhabitants of the south-side bohemia, Margaret Anderson found herself falling into the literary vortex of the Chicago Renaissance. Many of her friends and future contributors to the *Little Review*—Floyd Dell, Margery Currey, Sherwood Anderson, Theodore Dreiser, Ben Hecht, Maxwell Bodenheim, Vachel Lindsay, Carl Sandburg, and Arthur Davison Ficke—lived in dwellings that were essentially storefronts left over from the 1893 Colombian Exposition. Single-room structures with one large window in front, often without plumbing, these buildings had the advantage of being across from Jackson Park and near a railroad stop on the Loop. It was in the storefront home of Floyd Dell and Margery Currey that Anderson announced her plans for the *Little Review*.

The circle of the 57th Street bohemia, in which Anderson traveled, was aware of and somewhat anxious about male and female homosexuality. They had read Havelock Ellis, Edward Carpenter, and Otto Weininger, among others; they talked endlessly about the subject and treated it in their fictional work. Part of their interest in homosexuality was their fascination with psychoanalysis. Sherwood Anderson recalled the constant efforts of the 57th Street group to "psyche" one another. In his autobiography he wrote of one evening at Dell's and "the unfortunate moment when I brought up the subject of homosexuality." Anderson had spoken of his confusion upon observing "unashamed" homosexual behavior when he worked in a Chicago warehouse. Elaborating upon the episode later that same evening in Jackson Park, Anderson picked up a twig and absentmindedly broke it in two, whereupon his companion excitedly "psyched" him. Anderson, the friend concluded, was trying to destroy the phallic in himself and hence secretly desired to be a woman.[18]

If Chicago bohemians were uneasy about male homosexuality, their feelings toward lesbians were somewhat harsher. Margaret Anderson was a beautiful woman who was very aware of the impact of her looks. As she wrote in her first autobiography *My Thirty Years' War*, "It would be unbecoming of me not to know that I was extravagantly pretty in those days."[19] Others concurred. Dell observed that she was "austerely idealistic, matching her starry-eyed, unearthly young loveliness which was too saintlike."[20] Ben Hecht described her as "blonde, shapely with lean ankles and a Scandinavian face."[21] Anderson's beauty was matched with a personal intensity, which rarely escaped her peers. The Chicago poet Eunice Tietjens held that "anyone who could resist Margaret Anderson was granite and cold steel."[22]

And yet, at the same time there existed diametrically opposed descriptions of Anderson as cold, aloof, and detached, often by the very same people. Dell wrote that Anderson was "beautiful in a cool and standoffish way,"[23] and Hecht stated that she was seen as "chaste" and "frigid."[24] Maxwell Bodenheim, whose first poems were published in the *Little Review,* based a character in his novel *Blackguard,* a thinly veiled autobiographical portrait of the Chicago Renaissance literary scene, on Anderson. The character was Martha Apperson, editor of a magazine called *Art and Life,* who resembled in Bodenheims's words a "distressed virginal doll." The hero, based of course on Bodenheim, expressed an attraction to Apperson/Anderson. He "wanted her body" but only because "it was the only mystery that she seemed to possess and because he wondered whether it might not be able to make her thoughts less obvious."[25] These descriptions of Anderson as cold, cool, chaste, and virginal came from the knowledge of and resentment over her lesbianism. She was at once painted as an impassioned editor and an icy, untouchable woman. The descriptions of her as chaste and virginal depreciated her relations with women. It was well known in the early years of the *Little Review* that Anderson was having a relationship with Helen Dean, an assistant with the journal. (Bodenheim based a stereotypical masculine lesbian character in *Blackguard* on Dean.) Hecht recorded in his autobiography that another *Little Review* contributor, Alexander Kaun, referred to Anderson as "your idiot friend Sappho."[26] Such characterizations revealed the sexual tensions among the so-called enlightened members of early-twentieth-century bohemia.

If some readers and contributors were unaware of Anderson's sexual inclinations, there existed strong evidence in the *Little Review.* Anderson's lesbianism and feminism directly affected her editorial decisions. The first two years of the journal focused on the relationship between literature, sexuality, and politics. In her debut editorial of March 1914, Anderson queried, "Feminism? A clear thinking magazine can only have one attitude and the degree of ours is ardent."[27] "Birth control," she wrote in an editorial defending Margaret Sanger, "was one of the milestones by which civilization marked its progress."[28] In one of her more outspoken essays about American women entitled "Incense and Splendor," Anderson declared that "the American woman is pathetically undersexed."[29] She defended controversial morality in literature, decried censorship, reviewed the works of Ellen Key and Charlotte Perkins Gilman, and published the poetry of Amy Lowell and H. D.

One of the most important influences on Anderson during the Chicago years was Emma Goldman. Catching the famous radical during a speaking engagement in the city, Anderson rushed back to the *Little Review* office exclaiming, "I had just enough time to turn anarchist before the presses closed."[30] Goldman was of course one of the first public figures to defend homosexuals. Her lover Ben Reitman was somewhat jealous of Goldman's friendship with Anderson, stating emphatically, "She is crazy about you."[31] Goldman had told Reitman that she "was not inclined that way" but also admitted that she felt "stirrings as a result of my friendship with Margaret—expressive of my theoretic interest in sex variation."[32]

The most potent example of Anderson's willingness to be public was an editorial she wrote in the March 1916 issue of the *Little Review,* in which she criticized a public lecture by Edith Lees Ellis, wife of Havelock Ellis. On a speaking tour of America, Edith Ellis was to deliver a talk entitled "Sex and Eugenics," sponsored by The Medical Women of Chicago. Among other topics, the talk had been advertised as including a defense of the "sexually abnormal." Anderson criticized Ellis for not speaking forthrightly about homosexuality, as she seemed to have promised. Anderson complained that Ellis said "she meant to talk of those people who, through perverted or inverted sexual tendencies, faced the problem of having to turn their abnormality—perhaps their gift of genius if we understood these things better—into creative channels." However, Anderson concluded, "She said nothing really at all. She said in brief that there should be no war between the body and the soul, and that Oscar Wilde should have been understood rather then sent to jail. These things are not ideas; they are common sense. She can be blamed for that attitude that promises more than it gives." As Anderson continued, "in her reference to intermediate types, she didn't mention homosexuality; she had nothing to say about the differences between perversion and inversion, nor did she even hint at Carpenter's social efforts on behalf of the homosexualist. What does Mrs. Ellis think about Weininger's statement that intermediate forms are 'normal, not pathological phenomena, in all classes of organisms, and their appearance is no proof of physical decadence?' Does she agree with him, in his reference to the idea that inversion is an acquired character and one that has superseded normal sexual impulses, when he says, 'It might equally be sought to prove that the sexual inclination of a normal man for a normal woman was an unnatural, acquired habit. In the abstract there is no difference between the normal and inverted type.'"

Anderson elaborated, "It is not enough to repeat that Shakespeare and Michel Angelo, and Alexander the Great, and Rosa Bonheur and Sappho were intermediate types: how is the science of the future to meet these issues?" Anderson then quoted from Edward Carpenter: "The rays of sunshine in the night of our existence are so rare that we are responsive and deeply grateful for the least movement, for every single voice that speaks in our favor in the forum of mankind."

Anderson made clear what she had gone through in an effort to read the sexologists: "it is worth your life to get Havelock Ellis's six volumes from a bookstore or a library. You can only do it with a doctor's certificate or something of the sort. Even if you ask about Weininger you are taken behind locked doors, forced to swear that you want it out of no morbid curiosity, that you will keep it only a week, and above all that you won't let anyone else read it."

In her concluding paragraph Anderson passionately stated, "With us love is just as punishable as murder or robbery. Mrs. Ellis knows the workings of our courts; she knows of boys and girls, men and women, tortured or crucified every day for their love—because it is not expressed according to conventional morality. All of this was part of her responsibility on Feb. 4th; and that is why I say she failed."[33]

Jonathan Katz has identified Anderson's critique of Ellis's talk as constituting "the earliest militant public defense of homosexuality known to have been published by a lesbian in the United States." Katz also cites Anderson's quote from Weininger's 1906 book *Sex and Character* in defense of homosexuality as an example of how "a blatantly misogynist work could be used selectively in the interests of inverts."[34] Indeed in the March 1918 issue of the *Little Review* Anderson published a withering review of *Sex and Character* by Ford Madox Ford entitled "Men and Women," which pinpointed and savaged the anti-woman statements of Weininger.[35] This is a clear example of how lesbians could pick and choose among the writings of the sexologists to express their own interpretations of who they really were.

When they met in 1916 the outspoken Anderson and the cross-dressing Heap quickly fell in love. Heap became coeditor of the *Little Review*. And what of Florence Reynolds? Her affair with Heap ended with great feelings of friendship and support that lasted until Reynolds's death in 1949. When Anderson and Heap moved the *Little Review* to New York in 1917, Heap continued to write Reynolds, only now with a new twist in the relationship. Heap's letters began with the salutation "Dear Mother," the contents consisting mostly of complaints about Anderson. As for Anderson, she too had formed a friendship with Reynolds, often writing to her in Chicago and complaining about the behavior of her "son" Heap.

The *Little Review* went on to become one of the most important radical literary journals in the early twentieth century. Along with the publication of Joyce's *Ulysses*, Anderson and Heap are noted in literary history for publishing the work of Ezra Pound, Hart Crane, William Carlos Williams, and T. S. Eliot. Less frequently noted is their publication of women writers who incorporated lesbian themes into their poetry and fiction, such as H. D., Amy Lowell, Djuna Barnes, May Sinclair, Dorothy Richardson, Mina Loy, and Gertrude Stein. After their relationship ended in the early twenties, Heap continued the *Little Review* until 1929 when the two women reunited for the farewell issue. Heap died in 1964, Anderson in 1973.

THE letters of Jane Heap and Florence Reynolds demonstrate one way women crossed the chasm from romantic friendship to modern lesbian identity. As two Midwestern girls who were grew up in the final decades of the nineteenth century, their private letters appropriated the language we have come to associate with asexual friendship as defined by historians. However, in between the lines we see a consciousness of self—and of togetherness—that tells us these women were moving beyond simply a passionate companionship. The erotic references to touching, kissing, and sleeping together, coupled with the appropriation of male names and costume, confirms steps toward a new identity. That identity was explored in private within a small coterie of friends, but it was encouraged by transformations in the big city and a new awareness of sexuality. By the time Heap met Anderson seven years after her 1909 letters to Reynolds, the Chicago Renaissance and the growth of bohemian subcultures could allow Anderson to publish openly what Heap's letters had privately begged for—the right to unashamed love. What we have in effect are two strategies by two very different women who came together in a love affair during a critical juncture in the history of sexuality. The cross-dressing butch who had confessed her anxieties in private correspondence and the feminine beauty who splashed her demands for tolerance in public print each knew exactly who she was. When these two women came together, the significance of the situation was not lost on their contemporaries. If the judgment of their fellow iconoclasts in urban bohemia was sometimes as harsh as the medical "experts," these women clearly were not deterred. The journey they navigated was not altogether comfortable or clear, but for Margaret Anderson, Jane Heap, and other couples who saw themselves as lesbians and not simply friends, there was no turning back.

Notes

1. Office of Registrar, Art Institute of Chicago, Letter to author, September 28, 1989.

2. Jane Heap to Florence Reynolds, August 18, 1908, Heap-Reynolds Collection, University of Delaware, Newark, DE.

3. Jane Heap to Florence Reynolds, August 21, 1908.

4. Jane Heap to Florence Reynolds, July 20, 1909.

5. Jane Heap to Florence Reynolds, July 21, 1909.

6. Jane Heap to Florence Reynolds, July 19, 1909.

7. Jane Heap to Florence Reynolds, July 25, 1908

8. Esther Newton, "The Mythic Mannish Lesbian: Radclyffe Hall and the New Woman," *Signs: Journal of Women in Culture and Society* 9 (1984): 565–73.

9. George Chauncey, "From Sexual Inversion to Homosexuality: Medicine and the Changing Concept of Female Deviance," *Salmagundi* (Fall 1982/Winter 1983): 140.

10. Lisa Duggan, "The Trials of Alice Mitchell: Sensationalism, Sexology, and the Lesbian Subject in Turn of the Century America," *Signs: Journal of Women in Culture and Society* 18 (1993): 791–814.

11. Jane Heap, "Pyg-male-one," Heap-Reynolds Collection, Box 5.

12. Jane Heap to Herbert Clark, May 29, 1909, Heap-Reynolds Collection.

13. Jane Heap to Florence Reynolds, July 9, 1909.

14. Jane Heap to Florence Reynolds, August 2, 1909.

15. Jane Heap to Florence Reynolds, August 29, 1908.

16. Ibid.

17. Bernard Duffey, *The Chicago Renaissance in American Letters* (East Lansing: Michigan State College Press, 1954), 130.

18. Sherwood Anderson, *Memoirs* (New York: Harcourt, Brace, and Co., 1942), 234–35.

19. Margaret Anderson, *My Thirty Years' War* (New York: Horizon Press, 1969), 15.

20. Floyd Dell, *Homecoming* (New York: Farrar and Rinehart, 1933), 228.

21. Ben Hecht, *Child of the Century* (New York: Simon and Schuster, 1964), 233.

22. Eunice Tietjens, *The World At My Shoulder* (New York: Macmillan, 1938), 64.

23. Floyd Dell, Letter to Jackson Bryer, April 8, 1964.

24. Hecht, *Child of the Century,* 233.

25. Maxwell Bodenheim, *Blackguard* (Chicago: Covici: McGee, 1923), 136–38.

26. Hecht, *Child of the Century,* 238.

27. Anderson, "Announcement," *Little Review* (March 1914): 2.

28. Anderson, "Mr. Comstock and the Resourceful Police," *Little Review* (April 1915): 3.

29. Anderson, "Incense and Splendor," *Little Review* (June 1914): 1.

30. Ibid.

31. Alice Wexler, *Emma Goldman, An Intimate Life* (New York: Pantheon Books, 1984), 309 n35.

32. Wexler, n. xv 199.

33. Anderson, "Mrs. Ellis's Failure," *Little Review* (March 1915): 16–19.

34. Jonathan Katz, *Gay/Lesbian Almanac: A New Documentary* (New York: Harper and Row, 1983), 363–64.

35. Ford Madox Ford, "Men and Women," *Little Review* (April 1918): 54–65.

4

The New Negro Renaissance, A Bisexual Renaissance

The Lives and Works of Angelina Weld Grimké and Richard Bruce Nugent

BRETT BEEMYN

THE decade of the 1920s is often dubbed the New Negro or Harlem Renaissance because it witnessed a boom in the number of literary and artistic works produced by African Americans, particularly by the new, younger generation of African Americans who had migrated to northern and mid-Atlantic cities. Many critics have noted that a renewed sense of race consciousness among these emerging Black writers and artists played a central role in the development of the Renaissance, but virtually ignored is the significance in some cases of a growing awareness of being attracted to both women and men. Not only were a number of the period's leading figures behaviorally bisexual—including Wallace Thurman, Richard Bruce Nugent, Angelina Weld Grimké, Countee Cullen, Claude McKay, Bessie Smith, Ma Rainey, and possibly Langston Hughes—but this frequently had as much of an impact on their lives as being African American. And while the New Negro Renaissance helped solidify a Black literary canon, it also established a body of work that was specifically rooted in being African American and attracted to both women and men.[1]

In this essay, I will consider the relationship between bisexuality and the New Negro Renaissance by examining the lives and works of Angelina Weld Grimké and Richard Bruce Nugent, two of the period's important but undervalued writers. On the surface, Grimké and Nugent could not seem more different. Grimké sought above all else to live up to her family's prestigious name and her father's bourgeois expectations, which forced her to sublimate her attraction to other women and placed severe limits on her relationships with men. While she subtly wrote about her attraction to women in her poetry and more openly about her desire for men, she was rarely able to act on her feelings and eventually gave up writing altogether. Nugent, in contrast, considered himself a bohemian and deliberately sought to violate the strictures of his Black middle-class upbringing, in part by openly pursuing relationships with men and writing "Smoke, Lilies and Jade," the first published work of African-American fiction to have same-sex sexuality as its central theme.[2] Nevertheless, like Grimké, he struggled to find sexual satisfaction, which at times led to bouts of depression that interfered with his ability to write. Thus bisexuality not only provided the context and content of Grimké's and Nugent's work, but also helps account at times for their lack of work.

Due in part to their limited literary output during the 1920s, Grimké and Nugent have received less recognition than other New Negro Renaissance writers until recently, when they have been rediscovered and reclaimed by feminist and queer studies scholars. Yet while both are now receiving some much-needed critical attention, they are almost exclusively treated as lesbian and gay, respectively. This not only does a disservice to their lives and work, but also obscures some of the larger historical factors involved here, including the difficulties that Black lesbians, gay men, *and* bisexuals have faced in writing about their experiences and the role of behaviorally bisexual people in the development of Black lesbigay literary traditions.

Middle-class African Americans who were attracted to others of the same sex often faced a particularly arduous struggle to create an affirming sexual identity during the Renaissance—perhaps best illustrated by the life of Angelina Weld Grimké. As critic Gloria Hull first documented, Grimké was attracted to women but was unable to overcome the sexual strictures embraced by her family and other members of the Black bourgeoisie in the 1920s. The extent to which she felt sexually thwarted is evident in her poetry, especially in the poems that she never tried to have published. Filled with images of longing, heartbreak, and death, these works offer a glimpse into Grimké's sense of despair and hopelessness, which so affected her that she gave up writing altogether and became a recluse for the last twenty-eight years of her life. Citing one of Grimké's unpublished poems, Hull states that she was "buried 'Under the Days.'"[3]

Grimké *was* clearly attracted to women, but I want to challenge the contention made by Hull and others that the muting of her voice proceeded solely from a repressed lesbianism. While Grimké wrote poems about her unfulfilled same-sex desire and composed love letters to a female classmate, she also addressed a substantial number of her poems to a male love interest and kept a diary when she was twenty-three that documents her feelings for a white man who does not return her affections. Since most scholars before me have relied on Hull's reading of Grimké and have not reexamined the original manuscripts for themselves, the material that would challenge a strict lesbian reading has gone unnoticed, resulting in the continued misinterpretation of Grimké's life and writing. To cite one example, Hull assumes that Grimké's love poem "If" is a tribute to a woman, but her diary reveals that she wrote it for a man whom she desired.[4]

Hull, though, does deserve credit for recognizing the frequent references to a woman lover in Grimké's unpublished poetry and for uncovering a romantic letter that she wrote to a female friend (although Hull and others misidentify the intended recipient as Mary Burrill).[5] Grimké wrote poetry on a range of subjects, from personal tributes and mild protests against racial injustice to nature and romantic poems, and her work appeared regularly in *The Crisis* and *Opportunity* and in Black literature anthologies during the 1920s. Yet she chose not to publish the largest body of her work—the vast majority of her love poetry—seemingly because most of these poems openly express desire for women.[6] For example, in "Rosabel" the speaker appeals to the wind to tell the object of her affection that she "find[s] her fair," because the narrator herself "do[es] not dare." It concludes with the speaker affirming, "my love is . . . for her,—for her." In another poem, Grimké even more desperately longs for this woman's affections:

> A kiss
> A little thing
> Perhaps. But I would give my [hand],
> And all my heart holds dear, my wealth,
> My power, my life, my very soul,
> If I might taste but once—just once
> The dew
> Upon her lips.[7]

Perhaps the woman Grimké yearned for here was Mamie Edith Karn, a white classmate at Carleton Academy in Northfield, Minnesota, in the mid-1890s.[8] On the back of notes that she took for a physics class, Grimké wrote two love letters to Karn, one of which reads in part:[9]

> My own darling Mamie;
>
> I hope you will not be offended my love if I, your purest devoted admirer, call you by such familiar names. Oh Mamie if you only knew how my heart beats when I think of you and it yearns and pants to gaze, if only for one second upon your lovely face. . . .
>
> I know you are too young now to become my wife but I hope beloved that in a few years you will come to me and be my love, my wife!
>
> How my brain whirls how my pulses leap with joy and madness when I think of those two words, "my wife." . . . Oh my love I pray do that [which] makes me happy forever more. . . .
>
> Your passionate lover—[10]

It is unknown whether Grimké recopied and sent the letter to Karn. A close reading of her most intimate poetry—in which she often assumes the voice of a woman rejected by a female lover—suggests that Grimké did act, but that Karn spurned her interest, perhaps after initially responding favorably.[11] Her poem "To Her of the Cruel Lip," for example, ends with the lines: "Ah cruel lady, far away / Whose laughing lips have said me nay / . . . You laugh because your heart is glad / . . . I laugh, yes,—my heart is sad." The speaker in a similar poem, "Caprichosa," reveals that she "oft ha[s] dreamed the bliss / Of the nectar in one kiss" from a "cruel, dainty, little lady" who frequently flirts with her, but will not respond to her advances.[12]

Like many of her poems about women, these laments to an unfulfilled female love exist solely as holographs, suggesting that Grimké had no intention of publishing them. Only "Caprichosa" seems to have reached the typescript stage, at which point Grimké adopted a pseudonym, "Wag," by changing the order of her initials. Ultimately, though, this poem was also left unpublished, perhaps because Grimké still found it too personal.

Instead of concealing her authorship, Grimké much more often obscured the intended recipient of her poetry, avoiding the use of feminine pronouns that would reveal the nature of her unrequited love.[13] But the fact that she addresses a woman remains evident in her use of traditionally feminine imagery and metaphors. For example, one of her most frequently reprinted poems, "A Mona Lisa," begins: "I should like to creep / Through the long brown grasses / That are your lashes," and another popular poem, "When the Green Lies Over the Earth," refers to "your curls so shining and sweet." Some of these works were not published, though, including poems that describe the object of her desire as having a throat "so fragrant, fair," "little fingers frail and thin," and "lips and hands which are soft, sweet, and fragrant."[14]

At the same time, Grimké wrote a number of poems that use imagery indicating a male love interest, such as "Your Hands":

> I love your hands.
> They are big hands, firm hands, gentle hands;
> Hair grows on the back near the wrist . . . .
> I have seen the nails broken and stained.
> From hard work.
> And yet, when you touch me,
> I grow small . . . . and quiet . . . .
> . . . And happy . . . .[15]

While Grimké's poems to women have been cited by scholars such as Hull and Carolivia Herron, works expressing a desire for men have been completely disregarded, even though some are very direct and repeatedly use masculine pronouns. For example, her poem "Little Red Heart of Mine" reads in part:

> Little red eager trusting heart of mine
> You must die
> Yesterday you lay asleep. Today he came
> And you awoke
> Unforgettable is the touch of his strong caressing hands
> Piercing sweet the power of his lips . . .

The yearning of his eyes.
Hush! Hush! Little heart. It may never be.[16]

An untitled holograph is even more pessimistic about the possibility of a love affair with this man and how she will cope in his absence:

Oh that he would love me
Oh that he would love me
But he will not but he will not
Though I pray eternally
Oh that I might see his face
Oh that I might see his face
But he comes not, never comes he
What is life without him
Let me sleep then, die and sleep then
For I cannot, cannot live
Without him.[17]

The sense of desperation and despair evident in these two poems is more fully expressed in the diary she kept from July 18 to September 10, 1903. Like her poems addressed to men, the diary is filled with longings for a male love interest—and has similarly been disregarded by scholars, who insist on treating her as a lesbian despite such evidence to the contrary.[18] The diary, which is often directly addressed to an unnamed white man whom Grimké had met and spent time with in Boston the previous year, chronicles the severe emotional suffering she endures when he fails to return her affections. In an early entry she writes:

> I said last night that I must forget you, sweet, but I can't God help me, I can't. Every thought, every word, every feeling of mine is wrapped up in you and lives in you. . . . I wonder how long I can keep up this smiling face and laughter and jokes. . . . I think and think and think until my brain grows wild and I long for mere physical suffering. . . . I shall probably break-down some time. The only thing that saved me last winter was my school teaching. I cannot simply express how much I love you. . . . I love you so much I could kiss your feet and I, God knows, am a proud woman. . . . I must stop for I am losing my self control.[19]

Eventually, she relinquishes hope for a relationship, but with it she also forsakes the possibility of future happiness, writing in her diary:

> I shall never know what it means to be a mother, for I shall never marry. I am through with love and the like forever, and oh I am so tired. . . . I am so very very tired of living. There is nothing to look forward to . . . but the great emptiness of many years . . .[20]

The diary ends here, so it is unclear whether Grimké ever overcame her sense of hopelessness and loved again. She never did marry, although she would have readily wed the man who spurned her,[21] and none of the letters among her surviving papers refer to a serious romantic relationship in subsequent years.

But even if Grimké recovered from her heartbreak and met a man or a woman who returned her affections, she would have been unable to enter a committed relationship because of a near total dependence on her father for emotional support and approval. In a sense, her life revolved around him, with Angelina continually trying—mostly unsuccessfully—to measure up in his eyes. After failing to heed her father's advice to forget the man mentioned in her diary, she vowed never again to disappoint him, even if that meant sacrificing her own happiness and abandoning the possibility for other significant relationships. In one of her last entries, she wrote:

> I am going to try and do some work every day. I must keep sane and cheerful for my father's sake. Dear father, I shall never do anything desperate while I have you. You have had trouble enough without my giving you any more. . . . I have two reasons only for living—my dear dear father and my writing. They must fill my life absolutely. I never expect to love again. . . .[22]

Seen from this perspective, there was no room in her life for a lover—whether male or female—and in any event, no one could possibly measure up to her father.

By failing to recognize that Grimké was attracted to men as well as women, scholars have underestimated the pervasiveness of her depression and the extent to which she had to struggle to live up to the demands of her father. Even after Archibald's death in 1930, she still felt bound to meet the standards he set for her and could not risk bringing dishonor to the family name. Moreover, without her father—the emotional center of her life— and unable to develop close relationships with either women or men, she had to suffer in isolation, with only her poetry as an outlet for her despair and loneliness. It was not enough, and over time she became even more withdrawn. Without the two things that had sustained her—her father and her writing—she appears to have simply given up on living.

Nugent's life was far less tragic, although he too often had a difficult time finding happiness in relationships, and his ability to write suffered as a result. But whereas Grimké seems to have been unable to pursue her same-sex desires and had no one to whom she could reveal her sadness, Nugent had no trouble meeting male sex partners. His problem, as he told his longtime confidant Alain Locke, was often "get[ting] a friend of the sort I want. Everyone else seems to have one close friend who thinks of all the small niceties and petty things, except me."[23]

Locke, a gay Howard University professor who had known Nugent since the writer and artist was a youth, was someone Nugent frequently turned to for help and support on matters relating to men.[24] In a letter from 1937, for example, Nugent updated Locke on his latest partner, telling Locke that the man, whom he referred to as Flash, was "completely faithful in a way that I find is becoming of greater and greater importance to me. . . . He is good for me in that paradoxically enough, he brings out in me all of the so-called normal instincts that have been lying dormant." Unlike many of his previous relationships, which seem to have been primarily about sex and involved no commitments, Nugent wrote that the "constancy and ready and willing companionship" of Flash had "relegated [sex] to a more fitting and comfortable place" and "[made] me more and more aware of some of the beauties of the possibility of more conventional marriage. And that despite the role I play in our immediate physical relationship," which apparently was that of the "active" partner or "top." But while sex had become "comparatively unimportant," he cautioned Locke "not [to] think for a moment that I mean that it becomes uninteresting. . . . The physical expression of it becomes unimportant in its *method* of expression." Because of Locke's homosexuality and his own difficulties with men, Nugent felt that his friend could empathize: "I very likely sound very muddled but I think that *you* can understand what I am trying to say."[25]

Such upbeat letters to Locke were rare, though; more often, Nugent expressed his frustration and despair over his inability to form lasting, emotionally satisfying relationships with men. In a 1928 letter that he admitted was a "pleading weak depressive note," Nugent complained that all of his sexual partners were either using him or depending on him too much, which was "sapping all of [him] away" and causing him to be "at a terrible crisis psychologically." In exasperation, he asked, "Don't they ever realize that a prop (of nothing more than honest affection) might help me too?"[26]

He hoped that he was only "passing thru" what he characterized as "one of those awful spells of depression during which I am irritable (and hide it), have an insane desire to weep (and hide it), and feel as tho there is no one on earth that gives a damn."[27] But his depressive state continued throughout 1929 and, except for the time he was involved with Flash in the late 1930s, apparently for much of the next decade. Nugent understood that it was "a perfectly stupid way to feel and so easily explained psychologically as to appear childish, either from the angle of a homo- or duosexual's juxtaposition to life or an artist's." However, for him, it was "doubly hard" because his bisexual and artistic sensibilities were "rolled into one."[28]

Even though Nugent recognized the causes and futility of his sorrow, he replied that he couldn't help himself. Feeling "the need of someone to lean on so bad," he continued "to unload [his] burdens" on Locke while trying not to let his depression block his creativity.[29] This proved impossible, though, and Nugent's writing seems to have suffered greatly as a result of his romantic hardships. In a 1929 letter, he told his friend: "Only one thing has saved me from doing something—anything really desperate . . . and that [is] that I have several exceptionally good and ambitious ideas for writing and also the firm conviction that I can work them out."[30] But despite remaining hopeful that he could successfully develop these projects—among them a novel, short stories based on the Bible, and several ballets—and despite Locke's emotional and occasional financial support, Nugent published very little in the last years of the Renaissance and during the 1930s.[31]

Although Nugent was sexually inclined toward men, he also had relationships with women and was happily married for seventeen years, until his wife died from cancer in the 1960s. But just as with Grimké, this aspect of his life is typically overlooked by critics such as David Levering Lewis and Thomas Wirth, who insist on treating him as "homosexual" and even ignore the bisexual content of his most famous work, "Smoke, Lilies and Jade."[32] Largely autobiographical, it is a stream-of-consciousness story about Alex, a bohemian artist living in New York, who encounters a strikingly handsome youth he refers to as Beauty and takes the man home with him. A scene of passionate lovemaking follows, after which Alex wonders whether to continue seeing Beauty or the woman he has been involved with. But recognizing that "he loved them both," he decides that he does not have to choose, for "one *can* love two at the same time . . . one *can*."[33]

Ironically, while Nugent is now typically thought of as gay—under the misguided assumption that any historic figure who was involved in same-sex relationships was homosexual—during the 1920s he was known for being attracted to both women and men. For example, in his satirical novel of the New Negro Renaissance, *Infants of the Spring,* Nugent's friend and fellow bohemian Wallace Thurman portrayed him as Paul Arbian, a Black bisexual artist who draws "highly colored phalli" and openly flirts with people regardless of gender. The Arbian/Nugent character causes a stir when he not only acknowledges his sexual involvement with both women and men, but joyously admits that he "enjoy[s] one experience as much as the other."[34]

Infants of the Spring concludes tragically with the simultaneous deaths of the Renaissance and Arbian, who commits suicide after completing his much-anticipated novel, which is dedicated in part to Oscar Wilde, "whose golden spores of decadent pollen I shall broadcast and fertilize."[35] Yet any possibility for posthumous notoriety is thwarted when he accidentally destroys all but the title page and dedication during his suicide. While Nugent's faith in his writing ability apparently prevented him from deciding to take his own life, his inability to form emotionally satisfying relationships during and after the Renaissance meant that many of his "exceptionally good and ambitious ideas" similarly died within him. Like Grimké, Nugent was sustained by his writing but his sense of despair often overpowered his creativity. Consequently, neither he nor Grimké ever achieved the fame of many other Renaissance writers, and to the extent that their names are known today, it is largely because of the premise that they were gay/lesbian.

The fact that Nugent is now often seen as exclusively homosexual, or that Grimké's poetic and personal desire for men has been entirely ignored, demonstrates the need for a more complicated understanding of sexuality that moves us away from a zero-sum paradigm. What, after all, is achieved by denying the complexity of people's personal lives and recognizing only those sexual relationships that affirm one's own needs and desires? Are Grimké and Nugent any less important in the queer studies canon because they were attracted to both women and men? Is the New Negro Renaissance thereby diminished as a time when same-sex sexual cultures began to flourish? I think any honest examination leads to the conclusion that there is little to lose and much to gain by acknowledging the place of bisexuality within society in general and within the Renaissance in particular. If we are to understand the factors that helped shape the era, we cannot leave critical aspects of people's lives "buried 'Under the Days.'"

Notes

1. For a general discussion of the New Negro Renaissance and the Black lesbian, gay, and bisexual cultures that developed in New York during that time, see Eric Garber, "A Spectacle in Color: The Lesbian and Gay Subculture of Jazz Age Harlem," in *Hidden from History: Reclaiming the Gay and Lesbian Past,* ed. Martin Bauml Duberman, Martha Vicinus, and George Chauncey, Jr. (New York: New American Library, 1989), 318–31.

2. However, to avoid parental disapproval, Nugent published "Smoke, Lilies and Jade" under the name "Richard Bruce." Eric Garber, "Richard Bruce Nugent," in *Dictionary of Literary Biography: Afro-American Writers from the Harlem Renaissance to 1940,* Vol. 51, ed. Trudier Harris (Detroit: Gale Research Co., 1987), 216.

3. Gloria T. Hull, *Color, Sex, and Poetry: Three Women Writers of the Harlem Renaissance* (Bloomington: Indiana University Press, 1987), 150–51.

4. Grimké diary, July 31, 1903, Angelina Weld Grimké Papers (hereafter Grimké Papers), Moorland-Spingarn Collection, Howard University, Washington, D.C.; Hull, *Color, Sex, and Poetry,* 139.

5. Hull, *Color, Sex, and Poetry,* 139. See also Carolivia Herron, ed., Introduction, *Selected Works of Angelina Weld Grimké* (New York: Oxford University Press, 1991), 6–7.

6. Grimké not only decided against sending most of her love poems to magazine and book editors, but when she was creating a table of contents for a proposed collection of her work, these poems were also notably absent, with the exception of "Rosabel." Instead, the volume, which she entitled *Dusk Dreams,* included a number of lesser quality poems—a fact that might explain why, if she carried through and sent it to a publisher, it never reached print. Grimké Papers.

7. "Rosabel" (initially entitled "Rosalie") and "Fragments," Grimké Papers.

8. Additional information about Karn's early life is limited. She was born in Canada in October 1879, one of three children of a doctor. When Mary was a few years old, the family moved to Ortonville, Minnesota, and became naturalized citizens. She attended Carleton Academy from 1895 to 1898, receiving a degree in music (piano, voice, and harmony theory). My thanks to the staffs at the Minnesota Historical Society and Carleton College for their assistance in locating information about Karn and her family.

9. Hull and the many critics who have relied on her findings mistakenly identify the love letters as being addressed to Mary (Mamie) Burrill, a one-time close friend who, like Grimké, was sexually attracted to women. Although the full name on the manuscript is

clearly Karn's, the confusion here is understandable. Not only did the two women have the same first name, but Burrill wrote a letter to Grimké on February 25, 1896, that seems to suggest they had earlier pursued a sexual relationship:

> Perhaps you will wonder why I am writing to you this is easy to explain. I write to apologize to you for having acted so mean towards you while you were visiting Washington City. . . . Dear Angie do forget how I have treated you. I could rest content if I thought you would cast all that I have ever done to you, into that deep chasm known as the "Forgotten" . . . Angelina do think of me again as your true Friend . . .
>
> Could I just come to meet thee once more, in the old sweet way, just coming at your calling, and like an angel bending o'er you breathe into your ear, "I love you."
>
> P.S. Angie do you love me as you used to?

It is possible that Grimké and Burrill were once sexually involved; they met in 1894 or 1895 when Grimké was living in Washington with her uncle before being sent to Carleton. At the time, though, Burrill was only thirteen or fourteen years old. (There has been some discrepancy about the date of Burrill's birth. According to her birth certificate, she was born on August 30, 1881.) While early adolescence is certainly not too young for the development of a mutually consenting same-sex sexual relationship—indeed, more contemporary coming-out stories commonly relate first experiences that occurred at even younger ages—critics must tread carefully in such cases so as not to impose modern concepts of lesbianism onto the past by confusing platonic friendships and school crushes with sexual intimacy. For an excellent discussion that mediates between a view that all women who had close relationships in the nineteenth and twentieth centuries were lesbians and a view that such relationships were loving but entirely asexual, see Leila J. Rupp, "'Imagine My Surprise': Women's Relationships in Mid-Twentieth-Century America," in *Hidden from History: Reclaiming the Gay and Lesbian Past,* ed. Martin Bauml Duberman, Martha Vicinus, and George Chauncey, Jr. (New York: New American Library, 1989), 395–410.

Whether or not they were sexually involved, Burrill was more interested in renewing their relationship than was Grimké, perhaps because Grimké did not forgive her as Burrill had hoped. For example, when Grimké was back in Washington during her holiday break from school in 1898, Burrill repeatedly came to visit. However, Archibald had to implore his daughter to show gratitude, telling her afterward that "you must not neglect Mamie Burrill, for she was devotion itself to you while home. Please write to her soon, for it would be very bad manners not to express to her your appreciation of all her attention." Archibald Grimké to Angelina Weld Grimké, January 11, 1899, Grimké Papers.

10. The physics notes are dated October 27, 1896. The language in these letters is reminiscent of the nineteenth-century romantic friendships considered by historians Carroll Smith-Rosenberg and Lillian Faderman, although they largely limit their discussions to the relationships between middle-class white women. Grimké's letters demonstrate that these intense emotional, and at times physical, relationships were also prevalent in elite Black social circles. See Smith-Rosenberg, "The Female World of Love and Ritual: Relations between Women in Nineteenth-Century America," in *Disorderly Conduct: Visions of Gender in Victorian America,* ed. Carroll Smith-Rosenberg (New York: Oxford University Press, 1985), 53–76, and

Faderman, *Surpassing the Love of Men: Romantic Friendship and Love between Women from the Renaissance to the Present* (New York: William Morrow, 1981), esp. Part II.

11. Even if Karn returned Grimké's affections, the relationship was short-lived. Grimké stayed at Carleton for less than two years—returning to live with her father and to attend school in Boston—and Karn married a Minnesota lawyer soon after graduating and moved to Sisseton, South Dakota, where they bought a house next door to his mother. In 1916, when she was thirty-seven, Karn had a daughter. It is unlikely that Grimké and Karn had any contact after Grimké moved back to Boston. There are no letters from Karn in Grimké's papers, and although she is listed in Grimké's address book from the 1890s, the entry only says "Ortonville, Minn."

12. "To Her of the Cruel Lip" and "Caprichosa," Grimké Papers. Other poems in which the speaker laments being rejected by a woman include "Your Eyes," "Ballade to My Lady's Eyes," and an untitled work that begins "We have touched hands."

13. Gloria Hull, citing Grimké's poem "My Shrine," suggests that Grimké also changed feminine pronouns to masculine ones at the typescript stage. However, I found no evidence in her manuscripts to support this contention; on the contrary, some of her poems use masculine pronouns from the start. Hull, *Color, Sex, and Poetry,* 141.

14. "A Mona Lisa" and "When the Green Lies Over the Earth" were both published, for example, in Countee Cullen's *Caroling Dusk: An Anthology of Verse by Negro Poets* (New York: Harper & Bros., 1927). The other works cited here are "You" and "Give Me Your Eyes," Grimké Papers. Many of her nature poems also use feminine imagery, often representing the woman she loves as a star, "softly leaning down," and herself as the one remaining bird or a tree, "lonely, apart, unyielding." See especially "A Winter Twilight," "At Autumn," "At the Autumn Dusk," "At Morn," "The Eyes of My Regret," and "My Star," Grimké Papers. All of these poems are also included in Herron, *Selected Works of Angelina Weld Grimké.*

15. "Your Hands," Grimké Papers. Another poem with masculine imagery is "Why?" It is an angry work, critical of a man who leads her on and makes her believe that he was "[her] dream-dove, longed-for, *king*" (my emphasis).

16. "Little Red Heart of Mine," Grimké Papers.

17. "Oh that he would love me," Grimké Papers. Interestingly, Herron includes neither of these poems in the *Selected Works of Angelina Weld Grimké.*

18. Any careful reading of the diary reveals that the object of her affection was male. Not only does Grimké consistently use masculine pronouns, but she frequently discusses the person in terms that clearly show he was a man. For example, in one entry she relates a dream that she has in which the man is married to the wife of Bruce Evans, her school principal. After describing the horror of the experience, she implores, "I hope you will never marry. I can stand it while I know there is no other girl. . . ." In a subsequent entry, Grimké states that an astrologer whom she had consulted had told her that she would marry in the next year. Addressing the person she loves, she writes, "What would I not give to believe that you are this man." Another entry reads: "Dear can I give you any more than this, a woman's first sweet love? Whether I ever see you again or not, you have done this for me, dear, you have made a woman of me. Is not that something to do? Not any man could have done that. I am proud that you were he my sweet." Grimké diary, July 19, July 24, and July 21, 1903, Grimké Papers. Despite the tremendous weight of this evidence, Hull

only reluctantly acknowledges that the person in the diary *may* not be a woman, due to the unlikelihood that Grimké would discuss a same-sex relationship with her father. Hull, *Color, Sex, and Poetry,* 139.

19. Grimké diary, July 22, July 24, and September 6, 1903, Grimké Papers. Although Grimké poured out her emotions in her diary, she could be quite cryptic at times. For example, in the July 24 entry, she wrote: "Friday night. X. I only know what this means, and it *shall* not appear again." Another aspect of her secretiveness was that she did not identify the man; the one time that Grimké mentioned his name, she later erased it. The man's race is also never directly stated. I am presuming that he was white because she refers to him as having blue eyes. Grimké's unfulfilled love for Karn and later this man may explain the association of whiteness with death and despair in much of her poetry.

20. Grimké diary, September 6 and September 10, 1903, Grimké Papers. The suicidal feelings evident in this quote seem to be confirmed by a subsequent passage that suggests she was contemplating taking her life, but decided against it because of her father:

> Before you do this thing remember that somewhere there lives a just God before whom sometime you will have to stand in judgement. Remember that you have a father who lives for you alone who would give his life blood for you. Think what it would mean to him—this knowledge remember that.

21. The extent to which she was willing to drop everything for this man—as well as her lack of self-esteem—is likewise evident in the last diary entry:

> If you but beckoned to me and said come, I would come and if you said, Nana [her nickname] will you marry tonight, this afternoon, now, I would. But dear, I am almost absolutely certain that this is not so. Why should you care for me? No reason. I know I am not attractive and fetching etc. like other girls. I ought not to expect to be loved.

22. Grimké diary, July 21, 1903, Grimké Papers.

23. Nugent to Locke, n.d. [late 1928], Alain Locke Papers (hereafter Locke Papers), Moorland-Spingarn Collection, Howard University, Washington, D.C.

24. James Hatch, "An Interview with Bruce Nugent," *Artists and Influences: 1982* (New York: Hatch-Billops Collection, 1982), 87.

25. Nugent to Locke, "Monday" [February 1937], Locke Papers. I provide a detailed discussion of Locke's homosexuality in my dissertation "A Queer Capital: Lesbian, Gay, and Bisexual Life in Washington, D.C., 1890–1955," University of Iowa, 1997.

26. Nugent to Locke, n.d. [late 1928], Locke Papers.

27. Nugent to Locke, n.d. [January 24, 1929], Locke Papers.

28. Ibid.

29. Nugent to Locke, n.d. [January 24, 1929] and n.d. [late 1928], Locke Papers.

30. Nugent to Locke, n.d. [October 16, 1929], Locke Papers.

31. As was the case for many Black writers, Nugent's ability to write and have his work published was also greatly affected by the Depression. Previously, he had relied on the goodwill of others to get by and was not very concerned about money. But unable to find work in the early 1930s and having to depend on small, irregular relief checks, he

became extremely worried about how he would survive. As Nugent told Locke: "[a job] is a terrifically important issue with me right now and I can think of very little else. . . . So until I have done something about working I am and have been in no frame of mind to do anything about the things I write." Eventually, Locke was able to secure a position for Nugent with the short-lived Federal Theatre Project. Nugent to Locke, n.d. [late 1936], February 5, 1937, and "Monday" [February 1937], Locke Papers.

32. Charles Michael Smith, "Bruce Nugent: Bohemian of the Harlem Renaissance," in *In the Life: A Black Gay Anthology,* ed. Joseph Beam (Boston: Alyson, 1986), 216–17; David Levering Lewis, *When Harlem Was in Vogue* (New York: Oxford University Press, 1989), 196–97; Thomas H. Wirth, "Fire!! in Retrospect," insert to the reprint of *Fire!!* (Metuchen, N.J.: The Fire!! Press, 1982).

33. Richard Bruce, "Smoke, Lilies and Jade," *Fire!!* 1 (November 1926). Reprinted in Wirth, "Fire!! in Retrospect," 33–39.

34. Wallace Thurman, *Infants of the Spring* (1932; repr. Boston: Northeastern University Press, 1992), 12, 47.

35. Ibid., 284.

PART TWO

Evidence, Narrative, and Biography

5

"The Burning of Letters Continues"

Elusive Identities and the Historical Construction of Sexuality

ESTELLE B. FREEDMAN

ON a clear June morning in 1948, the controversial prison reformer Miriam Van Waters made a painful and momentous decision. For months she had been embroiled in a political struggle with conservative state officials who wished to dismiss her as the liberal superintendent of the Massachusetts Reformatory for Women. Local newspapers headlined the claims that Van Waters coddled prisoners, hired ex-inmates, and condoned homosexual behavior in prison. Investigators from the Department of Corrections interrogated her staff and seized inmate files as evidence.

As she sat before a glowing fireplace in her home that June morning, Miriam Van Waters fueled the blaze with some of her most precious possessions. "The Burning of Letters continues," she wrote in her journal that day. "One can have no personal 'life' in this battle, so I have destroyed many letters of over 22 years." Van Waters had met her patron and romantic partner, Geraldine Thompson, twenty-two years earlier. Since the late 1920s they had corresponded almost daily, sharing their thoughts, their activities, and their love during the weeks between their regular visits with one another. All but a few of the daily letters Thompson had addressed to her "Old Sweet," her "Dearest Dearest Love," went up in flames that day. As she burned the letters, Van Waters recorded her sense of loss: "They might have been *inspiration,* history, joy, style—to me in 'old age.'" Instead, she resolved to keep their message within herself. "The letters are bone and sinew now in my carnage. Doubtless my character has been formed by them."[1]

As Van Waters's biographer, I felt deeply mixed emotions when I read this passage in her journal.[2] On the one hand, my empathic pain for her loss quickly turned to anger at the politicians, and the society, whose condemnation of love between women forced her to destroy this personally meaningful correspondence—and, in the process, prevented me from reading this significant historical evidence. On the other hand, uncovering the revelation that she had destroyed the bulk of her

Reprinted from Estelle B. Freedman, "The Burning of Letters Continues," *Journal of Women's History* 9(4) (1994): 181–200, by permission of the journal and Indiana University Press.

correspondence from Thompson provided in itself an important clue in my quest to understand Van Waters's elusive sexual identity. "The Burning of Letters" passage provided a smoking gun, of sorts, to explain the absence of evidence documenting the intimacy of the Van Waters-Thompson relationship. Furthermore, that threats of political scandal had prompted the burning helped to confirm my interpretation of Van Waters's ordeal as a precursor of the sexual surveillance of the McCarthy era.

Van Waters's decision to destroy the record of her intimate relationship with another woman was not unique for professional women of her generation. Born in the late nineteenth century, just as the modern concept of homosexuality emerged within European and American medical literature, educated women like Van Waters bridged two eras in the social construction of sexual identity. Although they came of age in a world that still valued female intimacy, over the course of their lifetimes romantic friendships lost the sexual innocence they had once enjoyed.[3] That so many women in public life destroyed their correspondence with close female friends or partners indicates their awareness of the process of stigmatization that took place in the early twentieth century. As a result, self-censorship—apart from familial or historical suppression of evidence—has created historical silences that speak worlds about the relationships between such women as Miriam Van Waters and Geraldine Thompson, Alice Paul and Elsie Hill, Molly Dewson and Polly Porter, M. Carey Thomas and Mamie Gwinn, and Frieda Miller and Pauline Newman, to name a few who burned all or part of their personal papers.[4]

Van Waters's conscious effort to conceal her relationship with Thompson represents only one of the many challenges I faced as a feminist biographer committed to interpreting private as well as public life. Two related problems complicated this task: first, evasion and contradiction within existing historical sources; and second, the weaknesses of my own preconceived historical categories.

These problems surfaced even before I became Van Waters's biographer. Years ago a historian who knew of my interest in women's prisons suggested that I write about Miriam Van Waters. When I seemed uninterested, he added the tantalizing comment: "She was a lesbian, you know." Although I was uninterested in biography at the time, I did become intrigued a few years later, when I looked up the heading "lesbian" in the Schlesinger Library card catalogue and found a lone reference to files in the Van Waters papers. Catalogue drawer in hand, I walked into the archivists' office, mentioned that someone had once told me that Miriam Van Waters was a lesbian, and asked, rather naively, "Was she?" An archivist responded—I paraphrase slightly—"We don't say that about anyone without proof." The implication, in tone and words, was that I was making an unpleasant accusation.

In retrospect, I realized that both my penchant for naming and the library's reluctance to do so were equally problematic. Each of us acted upon certain assumptions about lesbian identity. My modern "lesbian feminist" impulse sought to reject what Blanche Cook has called "the historical denial of lesbianism" in favor of restoring the lesbian element to women's history, without questioning the historical meaning of the term "lesbian." Or perhaps I was unconsciously adopting Adrienne Rich's concept of a lesbian continuum, which generously labeled a range of woman-centered behaviors as lesbian.[5] The archivist, it seemed to me, adopted a modern homophobic response, seeking to protect historical subjects from accusations of identities that might have offended them (or, I suspected, her). The library's policy, I later learned, was that only self-identified lesbians would be categorized as such.

Eventually, my simplistic question—"Was she a lesbian?"—would evolve into a more complex inquiry into Van Waters's sexual subjectivity. By the time I made the commitment to writing a biography of Van Waters, I recognized the need to historicize my own inherited categories, particularly those—such as homosexuality—that derive from modern, Western notions of the self, identity, and politics. The very category of sexual identity often rests upon concepts of a unified self and often describes the consciousness of a bourgeois (male) historical actor, for whom the taken-for-granted privileges of gender, class, and frequently race permit the foregrounding of sexual subjectivity. For many women, class, race, or ethnicity may be more salient than sexuality in the formation of modern identities. Moreover, as scholars such as Earl Lewis and Dana Takagi argue, for many women and people of color, multiplicities of identities are perpetually uncertain and in flux. Whether in the case of visible ethnicity or invisible sexuality, identity categories mask the complexity of incoherent identities. Recognizing this fact, however, does not preclude the need to understand the historical construction of identities, which in practice wields significant power on the levels of both individual and social relationships. Studies of sexuality thus face a dilemma similar to those that address ethnicity: should scholars and activists discard or claim social categories that we admit to be unstable?[6]

I believe that exploring the concept of sexual identity remains a critical task for historians, despite the difficulty of pinning down our subject. Let me briefly survey the historiographical landscape to contextualize my approach. While the historical denial of homosexuality has recently given way to extensive scholarly inquiry, competing theories continue to characterize the literature. At one extreme lie essentialist notions of a transcendent "gay" identity that disregard historical and cultural specificity. These theories range from the biological/hormonal/genetic to the historical argument that "gay" people have always existed, from the Greeks to the moderns, as a unique category. At the other extreme lies a postmodernist tendency to fragment identity into a category so fluid and unstable that it threatens to return, curiously enough, to the denial with which we began. In short, we cannot study lesbians in the past because the term is too modern and limiting, too falsely universalizing, and too much a figment of discursive imagination.[7]

A middle ground, where I am most comfortable, draws on the model of social construction first articulated by the British sociologist Mary McIntosh. This account of the historical transition from homosexual acts to homosexual identities emphasizes the impact of economic and social relations within Western industrial societies. John D'Emilio and I applied elements of this model to our survey of American sexual history, arguing implicitly against theories of the discursive creation of homosexual identity by modern medical and psychiatric authorities. Rather, we suggested, within an emerging capitalist society, the separation of reproduction and heterosexuality, along with the growth of wage labor, provided economic and social spaces for the emergence of self-conscious same-sex relationships, which are then labeled homosexual. The possibilities for these relationships, outside traditional family controls, in turn made possible, and likely, the formation of gay identity and, eventually, modern gay politics.[8]

As feminist scholarship reminds us, however, the timing and meaning of this transition differed by gender. Trying to fit women into the (traditional) acts of (capitalist) identity model raises problems, given women's continuing reproductive responsibilities and their economic dependence within both middle- and working-class families in the nineteenth century, when this transition was occurring. Nonetheless, distinct female constructions of same-sex relationships did emerge in response to new economic roles. These included, but were not limited to, women who passed as men and married other women, usually associated with the working class; romantic friendships, usually associated with middle-class women; and mutual households, known as "Boston marriages," largely associated with educated women but created by working women as well.[9]

Only in the twentieth century, however, as the U.S. consumer culture increasingly sexualized women of all classes, did an explicitly lesbian identity emerge, first within black and white working-class cultures and later among middle-class feminists. As I have suggested elsewhere, racial and class constructions of female sexuality deeply influenced this process. Given the sexual objectification of African-American and working-class women, and the denial of sexual agency to middle-class white women, the lesbian label was often applied to black and working-class women who were already associated with criminality and prostitution.[10] Despite their practices of same-sex love, white middle-class women rarely claimed lesbianism as an identity before the 1940s, with the notable exception of some artists, writers, and bohemians.[11]

This social constructionist account of the emergence of lesbian identity remains, I feel, too abstract. Its very insistence on the social, as opposed to individual, meaning of sexuality risks overlooking the fact that identity formation is in fact as much an individual as a social phenomenon. Indeed, the two are often in conflict, especially in periods of transition, when individuals raised with the sexual categories of an earlier culture partake in the social changes that redefine their behaviors. Historians too rarely acknowledge either the complications of contradictory and competing identities in their subjects, or the dilemmas we face in handling elusive identities.[12]

In the interest of becoming more explicit about how historians grapple with the elusive subject of sexual identity, I want to reflect on my own process of research and interpretation by recalling three kinds of evidence that combined to shape my understanding of Miriam Van Waters's sexuality: first, what her professional writings reveal about Van Waters's intellectual categories—in other words, the authoritative discourses she encountered and may have internalized or modified; second, how personal sources such as letters and diaries provide clues to her subjective experience of sexuality; and third, how rumors, accusations, and assumptions enter the historical record and influence the historian. Together these sources help explain why the burning of letters continued in Van Waters's lifetime and what it meant for her identity.

Discourses

In the early twentieth century, highly-educated women such as Miriam Van Waters might be exposed to published literature that clearly named both male and female homosexuality. Only a generation earlier, even romantic female friends and women who passed as men perceived their experiences within frameworks largely devoid of sexual references. The "female world of love and ritual" mapped by historian Carroll Smith-Rosenberg allowed same-sex attractions to "pass" as sexually innocent, whether they were or not. Beginning in the late nineteenth century, a modern conception of homosexuality emerged, articulated first as a form of gender inversion and later as an expression of erotic desire.[13] Gradually an explicitly sexual language characterized the literature on same-sex relationships. Helen Horowitz's insightful interpretation of M. Carey Thomas provides a good example of the transition. In the 1870s, Thomas's reading of romantic and pre-Raphaelite poets afforded her an initial and asexual framework for understanding passion between women; after the 1890s, however, the Oscar Wilde trial and the availability of works by sexologists such as Richard von Krafft-Ebing allowed Thomas to name sexual acts between women as well. Similarly, Lisa Duggan's analysis of the Alice Mitchell trial suggests that during the 1890s the popular press helped create a complex—and contested—erotic lesbian subject, associated in part with insanity and crime.[14]

As a graduate student at Clark University between 1910 and 1913, Van Waters easily discovered the scholarly literature on sexuality. She read Havelock Ellis, Krafft-Ebing, and some Sigmund Freud, as well as the work of her advisor, psychologist G. Stanley Hall. Her own writing recognized the power of sexuality and stressed the importance of sex education and the strategy of channeling youthful energies into recreation and social service. She also became curious about gender identity and same-sex relationships, as a questionnaire she designed reveals. The survey of adolescent girls asked, for example, "did you wish to be a boy?" and was your first "love for some one you knew closely, or for some distant person or for some older woman or girl friend?" A separate questionnaire for teachers asked if "crushes" between girls were "based on mutuality of interest and inclination; or are they more likely to exist between 'masculine,' and excessively 'feminine' types?"[15] The questions suggest Van Waters's interest in whether same-sex attractions correlated with gender identity, an inquiry prompted in part by Ellis's notion of sexual inversion, which associated "mannish" women with lesbianism.

Although Van Waters never conducted this survey, her intellectual curiosity about gender nonconformity and its relationship to homosexuality recurred in her doctoral dissertation, "The Adolescent Girl among Primitive People." At this time she consciously rejected Freudian interpretations of sexuality and adopted Ellis's language of inversion—albeit without the pathological notions of deviant sexuality. Her views also reflected the cultural relativism of Franz Boas. After describing institutionalized gender-crossing among North American Indians, for example, Van Waters concluded that "among primitive peoples, a useful and appropriate life-role is commonly furnished the inverted individual. . . . It is quite possible that modern policy could profitably go to school to the primitive in this regard."[16] Similarly, in an appendix on contemporary American approaches to adolescent delinquents, Van Waters analyzed the case of a cross-dressing young woman accused of being a "white slaver" because she brought girls to her room at night. Reluctant to label the girl a "true homosexual," she reported that "it is impossible for her to earn an honest and adequate living while dressed as a woman," and claimed that sympathy for women of the underworld rather than sexual proclivities accounted for her behavior.[17]

During her subsequent career working in juvenile and adult female reformatories, Van Waters retained a liberal tolerance for homosexuality, even as she increasingly incorporated Freudian views of sexual psychopathology. When she discussed the management of "'crushes' and sentimental attachment" among reformatory inmates in her 1925 book, *Youth in Conflict,* she advised that a trained social worker could draw out the girl and replace unhealthy attachments with healthy ones through a beneficial "transference." A harsher passage reflected conservative medical views of sex and gender when she labeled as the most perverse juvenile case she had encountered a narcissistic girl whose "emotional life will be self-centered or flow toward those of her own sex," and who would "never wish to live the biologically normal life."[18]

Despite these published critiques of unhealthy homosexual attachments, as superintendent of the Framingham, Massachusetts, reformatory for women from 1932 to 1957, Miriam Van Waters consistently resisted the labeling of prison relationships as homosexual. Her liberal administration emphasized education, social welfare services, psychiatric counseling, and work opportunities outside prison for the three to four hundred women inmates, the large majority of whom were young, white, Catholic, and working-class. Although the criminological literature then identified black women in prison as the aggressors in interracial sexual relationships, Van Waters and her staff did not draw a racial line around prison homosexuality.

Rather, they tried to distinguish between "true homosexuality" and temporary attractions. They believed the former could be detected by the Rorschach test; in the absence of such "positive evidence" they assumed that only the boredom of prison routine stimulated "unnatural" interest in same-sex relationships. Thus an active program of classes and clubs attempted to channel the energies of both black and white prisoners into what the staff considered healthier recreations. Even when staff discovered two women in bed together—of any racial combination—they hesitated to label them as homosexual.

Van Waters's tolerance of prison homosexual liaisons contributed to the conservative assault on her administration in the 1940s. In 1949, when the Commissioner of Corrections dismissed Van Waters from office, he charged

> that you have known of and failed to prevent the continuance of, or failed to know and recognize that an unwholesome relationship has existed between inmates of the Reformatory for Women which is called the "doll racket" by inmates and some officer personnel; the terms "stud" and "*queen*" are used with implied meanings, and such association has resulted in "crushes," "courtships", and homosexual practises [*sic*] among the inmates in the Reformatory.[19]

During several months of public hearings, Van Waters successfully defended her policies, in part by minimizing the existence of homosexuality at the reformatory, in part by deferring to psychiatric authorities when asked about homosexual tendencies among inmates. Typical of her strategic evasion was this response to hostile interrogation about whether certain acts or personal styles revealed homosexual tendencies:

> That, sir, is so distinctly a medical and technical question that I would not presume to answer it. One of the first things we are taught is that a homosexual tendency must be distinguished from a homosexual act. A homosexual tendency may be completely repressed and turned into a variety of other expressions, including a great aversion to emotion.[20]

By invoking the power of psychiatry, Van Waters acknowledged the shifting meaning of homosexuality—from an act to an identity. At the same time, she tried to avoid a labeling process that would mark close friends, mannish women, and those who had crushes on other inmates as confirmed homosexuals, a category she reserved for a treatable psychopathological condition that posed problems only when characterized by aggressive sexual behaviors.

Whether consciously or not, Van Waters's testimony represented a form of resistance to the use of accusations of homosexuality to discredit nonconforming women. Rather than sacrifice some "mannish" women or close female friends by calling them either "homosexuals," "latent homosexuals," or "women with homosexual tendencies," she firmly opposed labeling. At the same time, like psychologists of the period, she did so by accepting a definition of true homosexuality as pathology.

In the 1950s, partly in response to her reading of the Kinsey Reports, and partly in the wake of the accusations about prison lesbianism during her dismissal hearings, Van Waters's public lectures urged greater tolerance. Homosexuality, she explained, could be "found in all levels of society," in all types of people. Her emphasis, however, was on treatment. Once revealed through use of the Rorschach test, she believed, homosexual tendencies could be reversed with the aid of psychiatry.[21]

In short, for Miriam Van Waters, lesbianism was a curable social problem not unlike alcoholism. Although she initially encountered lesbianism among working-class, immigrant, and black reformatory inmates, she recognized that it occurred within other groups as well. Rather than emphasize a heterosexual solution, Van Waters placed great faith in "healthy" female bonding as an alternative to lesbianism. In this sense, whether or not she had internalized modern medical categories, she strategically invoked an earlier discourse of sexually innocent and nurturing female friendships as a corrective to the increasing stigmatization of women's love for women as a form of perversion.

Evidence of Subjectivity

When Superintendent Van Waters evaded the labeling of homosexuality during her dismissal hearings, she also sidestepped implicit questions about her own sexual identity. In her personal life, Van Waters had refused to label her love for a woman as a form of homosexuality, despite her long-term romantic partnership with Geraldine Thompson, a New Jersey philanthropist who was known publicly only as a wealthy benefactor and a supporter of Van Waters's reforms. So, too, she hesitated to assume that other women who appeared to fit the medical definition really were homosexuals, a term she reserved for women's pathological, though curable, sexual aggression toward other women.[22]

What of her internal consciousness of her own sexuality? The private story of Miriam Van Waters's own relationships with women both parallels and contradicts her public pronouncements. Beginning in adolescence, she fell deeply in love with other women and, for the most part, preferred their company to the attentions of male suitors. Never a sexual prude, Van Waters recognized the importance of the erotic, especially within the poetry and fiction she wrote in her late twenties. But she also placed great stock in the power of sublimation for harnessing erotic energy into expression as art, spirituality, or public service. Thus, upon reading Radclyffe Hall's *The Well of Loneliness* in 1929, Van Waters commented in her journal that had Stephen Gordon's parents been more loving, instead of becoming a lesbian Gordon might have "run a girls camp," become a high school counselor, or supervised a juvenile protective agency, all activities remarkably similar to those Van Waters chose.[23]

The detailed introspective journals Van Waters kept as an adult provide further clues about her subjective experience of sexuality, despite the frequently coded and intentionally obscure nature of her writing.[24] Tantalizing passages in Van Waters's journals made little sense to me until late into my research, when I gained access to a cache of personal papers that had not been deposited in the archives. Literally locked away within a rusting trunk and forgotten in an attic, that cache included passionate letters from two of Van Waters's ardent admirers: one set from Hans Weiss, a young Swiss social worker who wished to marry Van Waters; the other, a year's worth of daily letters from Geraldine Thompson, the older, wealthy, married philanthropist whose subsequent correspondence Van Waters burned in 1948. Working with both the journals and the "courtship letters," as I called them, I learned how Van Waters struggled to balance the erotic, the emotional, and the spiritual in each of these relationships.

Despite significant differences between the Weiss and Thompson correspondence—his letters were more erotic, hers more spiritual; he was more emotionally demanding, she longed to be of service to her beloved—I was struck by the consistency in Van Waters's response to her male and female suitors. In each case, she remained publicly silent, restrained in her responses to passion, and conflicted about making any lifelong commitment. The two relationships did present separate challenges to Van Waters's sexuality. The younger, less established Weiss frequently articulated his erotic longings; in response, Van Waters struggled to incorporate physical passion while subsuming it within her ideal of a spiritualized romantic friendship. The older, wealthier, and more powerful Thompson longed for "the Justice of the Peace and church bells" to signify their commitment; in response, Van Waters feared the dependency that could result from their union.[25]

In both cases, the management of passion was a recurrent theme for Miriam Van Waters. Although her journals were characteristically obscure about sexual experiences, one passage written after a visit with Weiss alluded to an unidentified young "Beloved" with whom she had experienced both a spiritual epiphany and a "yielding to love." In one entry, she recalled a candlelit scene in which her "hands were flung up by a strong clasp of young hands on my wrists—and with another soul—I plunged down a glittering waterfall immeasurably high, and sunk at last—into a pool—where two floated in weariness and content."[26] More typical, however, was her insistence on limiting their intimacy. "As a lover I yield to no one in sustained worship," she wrote in her journal. To Weiss she explained that their spiritual union transcended the need for physical proximity, suggesting that unrequited love could yield the "deepest spiritual gain."[27] By 1930, she had successfully encouraged Weiss to wed someone else; she had already informed him of another, unnamed attraction.

The Thompson courtship, begun during the late 1920s, overlapped with the waning of Van Waters's intimacy with Weiss. Both women valued romantic and spiritual intimacy, and neither wrote explicitly about their sexual experiences. Yet Van Waters left hints about her consciousness of lesbianism and her continuing management of erotic impulses. In 1930, she read an article about Katherine B.

Davis's 1929 study of female sexuality, which found that a quarter of unmarried women college graduates acknowledged a sexual component within their intense emotional relationships with other women. Van Waters starred the point that these were normal, not pathological, women, as if to differentiate her experience from the perversions she had earlier identified among juvenile delinquents.[28] As in her relationship with Weiss, however, Van Waters continued to place limits on erotic expression. Thus when Thompson expressed a desire "to 'catch your soul's breath' in kisses," Van Waters questioned the impulse in her journal: "What one calls appetite—satisfaction of warmth needs-hunger needs—is not just that. . . . In maturity some times in some circumstances—to feed hunger fully—is to lose hunger. There are other ways of quenching the fire—and all must be escaped." Professionally she had recommended channeling youthful sexual energies, whether heterosexual or homosexual. But her personal ideal suggested not simply sublimation but rather that desire could be maintained best by leaving it largely unfulfilled. While staying at Thompson's home, she again alluded to the value of control: "The secret of life is manifested in hunger—it can't safely be quenched—neither by denial, nor complete feeding, nor running away, nor escape—but by a new way."[29]

Whether or not she discovered this "new way" of managing desire, by the time she and Thompson pledged their love at the end of 1930, Van Waters recognized that she had crossed some line. "The object which arouses love—cannot be foreseen or controlled," she wrote in her journal. "All we know is—that same force which engulfs us, and makes us ready for service to husband and children—some times—to some persons—flows out to a man, woman, child, animal, 'cause,' idea." Van Waters did not, however, acknowledge her love publicly nor claim a lesbian identity. When Geraldine longed to "shout about" their love so that her family would "know what life through you is giving me," Miriam counseled discretion.[30] Similarly, when an acquaintance who lived openly with another woman later asked Van Waters in public about the ring she wore—a gift from Thompson—Van Waters seethed at the impudence of this inquiry into her private life. Perhaps her status as a civil service employee, and as the guardian and later adoptive mother of a child, made Van Waters more cautious than her independently wealthy partner, Thompson. Equally likely, Van Waters struggled to reconcile her passion with the psychological construction of lesbianism she had already formed.

Another cryptic journal entry suggests how powerfully that psychological construction influenced her. In a dream, she wrote, she had enjoyed a feeling of "Understanding" that derived in part from "the recent Rorshak [*sic*] and integration." Van Waters used the Rorschach test to detect "innate homosexuality" among inmates; in 1938, a trusted friend administered the test to her and the results made Van Waters feel confident and optimistic. One line in this passage was crossed out heavily in pencil, especially over someone's name, but the entry continued, "Geraldine and I shall learn together."[31] In my reading, the Rorschach test proved to Van Waters that she was not an innate homosexual, thus freeing her of the deviant label and, ironically, granting her permission to integrate her love for Thompson without adopting a lesbian identity.

Rumors

Why, then, the burning of letters? Even if Van Waters did not consider herself a lesbian, the world around her was not as thoroughly convinced. Although her close associates insisted to me that the relationship was much too spiritual to have been homosexual, Van Waters's partnership with Geraldine Thompson made her increasingly vulnerable to the insinuations of her political opponents.

In the conformist atmosphere after World War II, accusations of Communism, often conflated with homosexuality, fueled an attack on liberalism. Thus, in 1948, claims that Van Waters tolerated homosexuality at the Massachusetts women's reformatory facilitated her dismissal from office. Aside from the widely publicized claims about the "doll racket" among inmates, rumors about Van Waters's sexuality circulated underground, though never in print. For example, Eleanor Roosevelt—a friend of Thompson and supporter of Van Waters—learned of the whispering campaign when she received several "vile" letters so disturbing that she destroyed most of them. Similarly, a hostile postcard sent to supporters referred to Van Waters as "supt. (or Chief *Pervert*)" of the reformatory.[32] It was at this time that Van Waters burned most of Thompson's correspondence, carefully locking away only that one year of "courtship" letters.

Despite the private insinuations that led her to burn Thompson's letters, Van Waters survived the attempt to fire her. The publicity surrounding prison lesbianism during her hearings, however, contributed to a national preoccupation with homosexuality and to the naming of lesbianism as a social threat. No matter how confident Van Waters may have been that she was not a lesbian, outside observers often assumed that she was. Late in my research, after years of waiting to receive Van Waters's FBI file, I found a 1954 document that seemed to place an official government seal on her identity. While carrying out surveillance on Helen Bryan, a suspected Communist sympathizer with whom Van Waters had a romantic friendship later in life, a local FBI informant read the correspondence between the two women. Shocked by the "unusual" nature of the letters, which contained "numerous repeated terms of endearment and other statements," he came to "the definite opinion that Dr. VAN WATERS and BRYAN are Lesbians."[33] It was to prevent just such a conclusion from being drawn that Van Waters had earlier burned Thompson's letters.

That identity formation is often a social as much as an individual phenomenon is further revealed by a final anecdote from my research on Van Waters, a coda of sorts that brings the story into the 1990s. My book completed, I turned to the task of acquiring permission to quote from sources, including Geraldine Thompson's courtship letters. With trepidation I sent the permission form to Thompson's eldest surviving granddaughter, who soon called to discuss the request. Her initial words, "I will not grant permission," struck further terror in me, until I absorbed the completion of her sentence: "I will not grant permission to repeat any lies; I want the truth." Too much had been concealed in her family, she explained, too much smoothed over. By the end of our conversation, she had told me with confidence that her grandmother had been a lesbian and that she was sure that Thompson and Van Waters were lovers, for they had shared a bed during family vacations. "Do you know what we grandchildren called Miriam when she came to visit?" she asked. "Grammy Thompson's yum-yum." She gladly granted permission to quote when I seemed willing to reveal "the truth."[34]

I would like to close this retrospective account of my construction of Miriam Van Waters's sexuality with several reflections on the burning of letters. For one, my research affirms the insights of such historians as Blanche Cook and Leila Rupp—that we cannot depend on either labels or direct evidence of sexual behavior to locate the subjects of lesbian history. At the same time, however, we need to be historically specific about the meaning of sexual identity. For many middle-class women of Van Waters's generation, lesbianism connoted a psychopathology that did not resonate with their experience of loving women. Rejecting the label did not mean rejecting the practice, but it did mean distancing themselves from other women—notably the working-class and African-American women who were forging an explicitly erotic lesbian community in the postwar era. Class and race privilege thus took precedence over sexuality as a source of identity, especially for women in public office. Ultimately, however, even Van Waters's resistance to labeling could not prevent the public discourse on homosexuality from imposing an identity on her that seemed to be at odds with her self-understanding.

Social construction theory emphasizes how either medical, legal, and literary discourses or economic and familial relationships create the possibilities within which individuals can act out and interpret their sexuality. One weakness of social construction theory, however, is that as a collective argument it tends to flatten individual differences and does not account well for individual agency. Writing a biography of Miriam Van Waters allowed me to explore an individual case study of identity formed both in tandem and in conflict with the social construction of sexuality.

Van Waters came of age in a transitional moment, when the social possibilities for romantic and sexual love between women increased, but also while medical labeling pathologized these relationships. As an educated, professional woman, exposed to such sexologists as Ellis and Freud, she was both conscious of the erotic and aware of the psychopathic label then attached to same-sex relationships. At the same time, Van Waters was attracted to women; she was able to live outside of heterosexual institutions; and she could and did take advantage of the opportunity to establish a partnership with another woman, even as she fiercely resisted lesbian identification.

Perhaps the fear of losing her job, and her social standing, kept Van Waters from identifying as a lesbian. But her rejection of lesbianism as an identity was not merely self-serving, for she just as fiercely resisted the labeling of working-class prison inmates as lesbians, and during her dismissal hearings in 1949 she more or less placed her class and race privilege on the line to defend these women from such charges. In the end, it was Van Waters's privileges—combined with her distinguished career of service and her upper-class political connections—that protected her from public disgrace. The working-class women she tried to protect would forge their own public lesbian identity, one that equally rejected the pathological discourse of the early twentieth century.

I suspect that Miriam Van Waters would have liked to live in a world that no longer existed, one in which neither labels nor stigma surrounded women's passionate relationships. To contemporary feminists, who value our own historically constructed ideal of the openly lesbian sexual subject, Van Waters seems anything but progressive. Yet if we are serious about the feminist scholarly enterprise of recognizing women's historical agency, we have to be willing to accept it when beliefs, and possibly behaviors, go against the grain of a "progressive" narrative that embraces categories we have claimed for ourselves. And we must keep in mind that this narrative rests heavily upon a highly class- and race-specific lesbian identity constructed since the 1960s, one that depathologized white, middle-class women's love for women but simultaneously failed to recognize a range of other sources of identity.

For complex reasons, then, I think that historians must be careful not to impose upon the past identities constructed in our own times. Rather, we must read for past constructions and consider where they originated, how they changed, and how multiple layers of meaning—intellectual, emotional, and political—could influence individual identity. Miriam Van Waters's case suggests the ways that some women could simultaneously internalize, resist, manipulate, and ignore the cultural constructions of sexuality in their times. Above all, her story reminds us to look beyond our sources, to read both silences and speech, and, at times, to accept the historical integrity of elusive personal identities.

Notes

Acknowledgment: I would like to thank Blanche Wiesen Cook and Darlene Clark Hine for their helpful comments on the original version of this essay, presented at the 1996 Berkshire Conference on the History of Women; the members of the 1996 graduate seminar on Interdisciplinary Feminist Studies at Stanford and the graduate program in women's history at New York University for extremely stimulating discussions of the essay in progress; John D'Emilio, Lori Ginzberg, Susan Krieger, Joanne Meyerowitz, Leila Rupp, and Martha Vicinus for their insightful suggestions for revision; and Martha Mabie Gardiner for her exceptional research assistance.

1. Miriam Van Waters Journal (hereafter MVW Journal), 16 June 1948, 19 June 1948, and 22 June 1948, file 220v, Anne Gladding-Miriam Van Waters Papers, Schlesinger Library, Radcliffe College (hereafter Gladding-MVW Papers). A handful of surviving letters were scattered through Van Waters's correspondence in the papers she donated to the Schlesinger Library. Miriam Van Waters Papers, Schlesinger Library, Radcliffe College (hereafter MVW Papers).

2. For a full account of her life, see Estelle B. Freedman, *Maternal Justice: Miriam Van Waters and the Female Reform Tradition* (Chicago: University of Chicago Press, 1996).

3. On nineteenth-century women's middle-class romantic friendships and their transformation in the twentieth century, see Carroll Smith-Rosenberg, "The Female World of Love and Ritual: Relations between Women in Nineteenth-Century America," *Signs* 1(1) (1975): 1–29; Nancy Sahli, "Smashing: Women's Relationships before the Fall," *Chrysalis* 8 (Summer 1979): 17–27; Lillian Faderman, *Surpassing the Love of Men: Romantic Friendship between Women from the Renaissance to the Present* (New York: William Morrow, 1981); Blanche Cook, "Female Support Networks and Political Activism: Lillian Wald, Crystal Eastman, Emma Goldman," in *A Heritage of Her Own*, ed. Nancy F. Cott and Elizabeth H. Pleck (New York: Simon and Schuster, 1979), 412–44; Leila J. Rupp, "Imagine My Surprise: Women's Relationships in Historical Perspective," *Frontiers* 5(3) (1980): 61–70; and Lillian Faderman, *Odd Girls and Twilight Lovers: A History of Lesbian Life in Twentieth-Century America* (New York: Columbia University Press, 1991).

4. On the burning of other letters, see, for example, Susan Ware, "Unlocking the Porter-Dewson Partnership: A Challenge for the Feminist Biographer," in *The Challenge of Feminist Biography*, ed. Sara Alpern et al. (Urbana: University of Illinois Press, 1992); Annelise Orleck, *Common Sense and a Little Fire: Women and Working-Class Politics in the United States, 1900–1965* (Chapel Hill: University of North Carolina Press, 1995), 300; and Martha Freeman, ed., *Always, Rachel: The Letters of Rachel Carson and Dorothy Freeman, 1952–1964* (Boston: Beacon Press, 1995). The burning of parts of Alice Paul's letters was reported to me by Paul's grandniece, Eloise Lawrence. According to her grandchildren, Geraldine Thompson saved Miriam Van Waters's letters under her bed but destroyed them before her death. Geraldine Boone to author, 1989; Anne Bristow to author, 1989. According to Blanche Cook, every one of Eleanor Roosevelt's friends burned their letters. Blanche Cook, comment on an earlier version of this article at the Berkshire Conference on the History of Women, University of North Carolina, 7 June 1996. On reading historical silences about sexuality, see Darlene Clark Hine, "Rape and the Inner Lives of Black Women in the Middle West: Preliminary Thoughts on the Culture of Dissemblance: Conference Report," *Signs* 14(4) (1989): 912–20; and Elaine Sargent Apthorp, "Speaking of Silence: Willa Cather and the 'Problem' of Feminist Biography," *Women's Studies* 18(1) (1990): 1–11.

5. Blanche Cook, "The Historical Denial of Lesbianism," *Radical History Review* 20 (Spring/Summer 1979): 60–65; and Adrienne Rich, "Compulsory Heterosexuality and Lesbian Existence," *Signs* 5(4) (1980): 631–60.

6. On the dilemma of resolving versus holding the tension between categories of race, gender, ethnicity, or sexuality—categories that we know to be constructed—without

denying either the lived experience of identities or obliterating the political usefulness of these categories, see Stuart Hall, "Ethnicity: Identity and Difference," *Radical America* 23(4) (1989): 9–20; Dana Takagi, "Maiden Voyage: Excursion into Sexuality and Identity Politics in Asian America," *Amerasia Journal* 20(1) (1994): 1–17; and Earl Lewis, "To Turn as on a Pivot: Writing African Americans into a History of Overlapping Diasporas," *American Historical Review* 100(3) (1995): 765–88.

7. See, for example, Joan Scott, "The Evidence of Experience," in *The Lesbian and Gay Studies Reader,* ed. Henry Abelove, Michele Aina Barale, and David M. Halperin (New York: Routledge, 1993), 397–415. For a useful summary and critique of these theories, see Martha Vicinus, "Introduction," *Lesbian Subjects: A Feminist Studies Reader,* ed. Martha Vicinus (Bloomington: Indiana University Press, 1996), 1–12.

8. Mary McIntosh, "The Homosexual Role," *Social Problems* 16(2) (1968): 182–92; and John D'Emilio and Estelle B. Freedman, *Intimate Matters: A History of Sexuality in America,* rev. ed. (Chicago: University of Chicago Press, 1997). See also Jeffrey Weeks, *Coming Out: Homosexual Politics in Britain, from the Nineteenth Century to the Present* (London: Quartet, 1977); and John D'Emilio, "Capitalism and Gay Identity," in *Making Trouble: Essays on Gay History, Politics, and the University* (New York: Routledge, 1992), 3–16.

9. None of these forms of female relationships was strictly class-bound, for some middle-class women assumed male attire or male / female gender roles, while black and working-class women also formed romantic friendships and shared households with other women. See, for example, Lisa Duggan, "The Trials of Alice Mitchell: Sensationalism, Sexology, and the Lesbian Subject in Turn-of-the-Century America," *Signs* 18(4) (1993): 791–814; Karen V. Hansen, "'No Kisses Is Like Youres': An Erotic Friendship between Two African-American Women during the Mid-Nineteenth Century," *Gender and History* 7(2) (1995): 153–82; and Joanne Meyerowitz, *Women Adrift: Independent Wage Earners in Chicago, 1880–1930* (Chicago: University of Chicago Press, 1988), 113–14. On the varieties of working-class lesbian history, see Jonathan Katz, ed., *Gay American History: Lesbians and Gay Men in the U.S.A.* (New York: Thomas Crowell, 1976), esp. "Passing Women," 209–81; San Francisco Lesbian and Gay History Project, "She Even Chewed Tobacco: A Pictorial Narrative of Passing Women in America," in *Hidden from History: Reclaiming the Gay and Lesbian Past,* ed. Martin Bauml Duberman, Martha Vicinus, and George Chauncey, Jr. (New York: New American Library, 1989), 183–94; Eric Garber, "'T'Ain't Nobody's Bizness': Homosexuality in 1920s Harlem," in *Black Men / White Men,* ed. Michael J. Smith (San Francisco: Gay Sunshine Press, 1983); Allan Berube, *Coming Out Under Fire: The History of Gay Men and Women in World War Two* (New York: Free Press, 1990); Madeline Davis and Elizabeth Lapovsky Kennedy, "Oral History and the Study of Sexuality in the Lesbian Community: Buffalo, New York, 1940–1960," *Feminist Studies* 12(1) (1986): 7–26; Madeline Davis and Elizabeth Lapovsky Kennedy, *Boots of Leather, Slippers of Gold: The History of a Lesbian Community* (New York: Routledge, 1993); Katie Gilmartin, "'The Very House of Difference': Intersections of Identities in the Life Histories of Colorado Lesbians, 1940–1965" (Ph.D. diss., Yale University, 1995); and John D'Emilio, *Sexual Politics, Sexual Communities: The Making of a Homosexual Minority in the United States, 1940–1970* (Chicago: University of Chicago Press, 1983).

10. Estelle B. Freedman, "The Prison Lesbian: Race, Class, and the Construction of the Aggressive Female Homosexual, 1915–1965," *Feminist Studies* 22(2) (1996): 397–423.

On medical and psychiatric views of lesbianism, see George Chauncey, Jr., "From Sexual Inversion to Homosexuality: Medicine and the Changing Conceptualization of Female Deviance," *Salmagundi* 58–59 (Fall 1982–Winter 1983): 114–46; and Jennifer Terry, "Lesbians under the Medical Gaze: Scientists Search for Remarkable Differences," *Journal of Sex Research* 27(3) (1990): 317–39.

11. In this article I am concerned with women like Van Waters who rejected lesbian identity, rather than with women who understood themselves to be lesbians but discreetly avoided the term. On the latter, see, for example, Elizabeth Lapovsky Kennedy, "'But We Would Never Talk about It': The Structures of Lesbian Discretion in South Dakota, 1928–1933," in *Inventing Lesbian Cultures in America,* ed. Ellen Lewin (Boston: Beacon Press, 1996), 15–39.

12. A notable exception is Helen Lefkowitz Horowitz's masterful treatment of multiple subjectivities in her biography, *The Power and Passion of M. Carey Thomas* (New York: Knopf, 1994).

13. Chauncey, Jr., "From Sexual Inversion"; Carroll Smith-Rosenberg, *Disorderly Conduct: Visions of Gender in Victorian America* (New York: Knopf, 1985), 245–96; and Esther Newton, "The Mythic Mannish Lesbian: Radclyffe Hall and the New Woman," *Signs* 9(4) (1984): 557–75.

14. Horowitz, *Power and Passion;* and Duggan, "The Trials of Alice Mitchell."

15. MVW to parents, 10 October 1911, file 42 (misdated, probably 9 October 1911), MVW Papers; MVW, "Topical Syllabus No. 44(A) and No. 44(B) [for teachers], Psychology of Adolescence," 15 November 1911, Box 37, file 464, G. Stanley Hall Papers, Clark University, Worcester, Massachusetts.

16. MVW, "The Adolescent Girl among Primitive People," *Journal of Religious Psychology* 6(4) (1913): 375–421, and 7(1) (1914): 75–120 (esp. pt. 1, 377–78, and pt. 2, 102–5). Her advisor, Alexander Chamberlain, had been Franz Boas's first doctoral student at Clark.

17. MVW, "Adolescent Girl," pt. 2, 108–12.

18. MVW, *Youth in Conflict* (New York: New Republic, 1925), 35–36.

19. McDowell to MVW, 7 January 1949, file 201, MVW Papers. My emphasis.

20. John O'Connor, "Van Waters Rejects Inmate Sex Charge," *Boston Herald,* 1 January 1949, 1.

21. MVW, Boston University lecture transcript, 24 October 1951 (in possession of author).

22. Rumors about Van Waters's sexuality are discussed in MVW to Ethel Sturges Dummer, 26 September 1948, file 825, Ethel Sturges Dummer Papers, Schlesinger Library, Radcliffe College; and in letters from a former inmate to MVW, 1 June 1948, file 195, and from Harry R. Archibald to MVW, 7 February 1949, file 203, both in MVW Papers. For a full discussion of Van Waters's interpretation of lesbian identity and the political response to rumors of her own homosexuality, see Freedman, *Maternal Justice,* esp. chaps. 9, 12, 14, and 15.

23. MVW Journal, 30 March 1929, file 208, Gladding-MVW Papers. MVW's phrasing suggests an ambivalence about the experience of marriage and reproductive, as opposed to social, motherhood: Gordon, she wrote, might have been "anything—everything in fact but a stupid wife and mother—Wife she co[uld] have been and mother too."

24. When I began my research, the Schlesinger Library inventory listed only twelve volumes of these journals, from 1932 to 1959, with several gaps during the periods 1937–1938, 1939–1941, 1942–1945, and 1948–1951. Well into my first draft of the biography, a chance comment made by an archivist while I was arranging to deposit newly discovered materials alerted me to the fact that another box of her journals had never been inventoried because of a bureaucratic delay. In addition to the missing years, these journals included material from 1913–1916 and 1927–1930. I suspect that journals for intermediate years were lost when a fire destroyed Van Waters's residence in 1927.

25. See, for example, Geraldine Thompson (GT) to MVW, 31 October 1930, 4 November 1930, and 14 November 1930, file 261, Gladding-MVW Papers.

26. MVW Journal, 28 June 1928, file 206, Gladding-MVW Papers; compare Hans Weiss's (HW) sweet memory of "what you did for me when you had the tremendous courage of giving yourself to me." HW to MVW, 24 July 1930, file 279, Gladding-MVW Papers.

27. MVW Journal, 19 February 1928, 14 June 1928, file 206, and 23 November 1928, file 208; HW to MVW, 7 August 1930, file 280, all in Gladding-MVW Papers. For complex reasons, Van Waters refused to consider marrying Weiss. Aside from the emotional distance she kept, the formal obstacle to their marriage was his "tremendous longing for a home and for children." He accepted "the cruel reality" that he could not have this with her, for like many professional women, she had chosen career over marriage. Although some women reformers did try to combine the two, having a job and children would be too physically taxing for her and, given her history of tuberculosis, possibly life-threatening. HW to MVW, 19 January 1929, file 276, Gladding-MVW Papers.

28. MVW to Edna Mahan, 20 July 1930, file 253, Gladding-MVW Papers; and Katherine B. Davis, *Factors in the Sex Life of Twenty-Two Hundred Women* (New York: Harper and Row, 1929), 312, 295, 280. The data showed that 28 percent of the women's college graduates and 20 percent of those from coeducational schools recognized sexual components in their relations; in addition, almost equal numbers had enjoyed intense emotional attachments that involved kissing and hugging.

29. GT to MVW, 31 October 1930, file 261, 10 November and 6 November 1930, file 262, all in Gladding-MVW Papers; MVW Journal, 27 September 1930, and 11 June 1931, file 211, Gladding-MVW Papers. On self-discipline in women's erotic relationships, see Martha Vicinus, "Distance and Desire: English Boarding-School Friendships," *Signs* 9(4) (1984): 600–22. On the erotic content of Van Waters's dreams, see Freedman, *Maternal Justice,* chap. 12.

30. MVW Journal, 27 September 1930, and GT to MVW, 13 November 1930, file 262, both in Gladding-MVW Papers.

31. On Rorschach see, for example, Inmate Record, 21 February 1949, file 251, MVW Journal, 11 June 1938, 213v, Gladding-MVW Papers; MVW Journal, vol. 5, 26 June 1938, MVW Papers.

32. Eleanor Roosevelt (ER) letter, 19 December 1948, file 200; GT to Dorothy Kirchwey Bowen, 4 January 1949; ER to GT, n.d., in response to an enclosed letter from GT dated 5 January 1949, all in Box 3820, ER Papers. ER to GT, 13 January 1949, file 8, Friends of Framington Papers (hereafter FOF Papers), Schlesinger Library, Cambridge Massachusetts; Miriam Clark Nichols to ER, 18 January 1949, file 8, FOF Papers (the letter was reprinted in *The Civil Service Reporter* [8 February 1949]; 5); George Hooper to Friends of Framingham,

1 January 1949, file 8, FOF Papers.

33. SAC, Boston (100–15782) to Director, FBI (100–206852), "Office Memorandum," Re; Helen Reid Bryan, 20 January 1954, declassified 12 April 1994 pursuant to Freedom of Information Act Request (emphasis in original).

34. Telephone interview with Geraldine Boone, 17 February 1995; and Boone to author, 6 March 1995. Although we disagreed on other points of interpretation of her grandmother, I gained invaluable insights from Boone's observations.

6

Paula Snelling

A Significant Other

MARGARET ROSE GLADNEY

ON New Year's Day, 1994, my lover and I took the blue and red highways east from our home in west Alabama into middle-south Georgia to visit the grave of Paula Snelling. Stopping at the exit off Interstate 85 South a few miles outside Pinehurst, we asked directions to the cemetery. It wasn't difficult, the store owner said. Just follow the road into town and take a right. Driving past flat sandy fields and pecan groves, a few large brick homes, more smaller rundown frame homes, into the town itself, I thought: No wonder she preferred the mountains of north Georgia. We found her grave covered with a large white slab, on which was written only her name and the dates: January 1, 1899–February 22, 1985. No words, no epitaph described her character or place in that town or state or nation; nothing acknowledged her relationship of over forty years with the well-known writer Lillian Smith. I had not brought flowers, though Paula loved flowers. I had brought a dust cover of my book *How Am I to Be Heard? Letters of Lillian Smith;* and I left it there, held down by a small stone on the white marble slab.

I have often wondered whether anyone ever found that dust cover and read the words linking the lives of Paula Snelling and Lillian Smith. Odds are that the winter rains and wind left the white marble slab as clean as I had found it, but public knowledge of the significance of their relationship should not be left to chance. In the story of their lives we find two of the many and varied voices whose narratives combine to create modern lesbian, bisexual, and gay history. Of the two, only Snelling acknowledged the intimate sexual nature of their relationship and only Snelling claimed a lesbian identity; yet, because of Lillian Smith's established place in American social and literary history, it is her voice that has been heard. We know of Snelling primarily because of her relationship with Smith. Significantly, it seems, that is exactly how Snelling wanted to be known.

Considered by many the foremost white Southern liberal writer of the mid-twentieth century, Lillian Smith devoted her life to challenging her culture's fundamental assumptions: that by divine decree whites are superior to blacks and males are superior to females, that a racially segregated political and economic power structure must be maintained at all cost, and that nothing about the system of segregation should be questioned. Throughout the 1940s and early 1950s when even those whites working for social change in the South, such as leaders in the Southern Regional Council and the so-called liberal journalists Ralph McGill and Hodding Carter, could speak only of improving race relations on a separate but equal basis, Smith boldly and persistently called for an end to segregation. For such boldness she was often scorned by both moderate and conservative Southerners and threatened by arsonists, and was denied the critical attention she deserved as a writer. Yet she continued to write and speak for improved human relations and social justice throughout her life.

Born December 12, 1897, Lillian Smith grew up in Jasper, Florida, where her father was a prominent business and civic leader. Her life as a daughter of upper-class whites in the small-town Deep South changed abruptly when her father lost his turpentine mills in 1915 and moved the family to their summer home in the mountains of Clayton, Georgia. Financially on her own, Smith attended nearby Piedmont College for one year, helped her parents manage a hotel, and taught in two mountain schools before she was able to pursue her chosen career in music at the Peabody Conservatory in Baltimore. In 1922 she accepted a three-year position as director of music at a Methodist school for girls in Huchow (now Wu-shing), China. But her ambitions for a career in music ended when her parents, in ill health, asked her to return to direct the summer camp for girls begun by her father in 1920.

Under her direction from 1925 through 1948, Laurel Falls Camp became a highly popular innovative educational institution, known for its instruction in the arts, music, dramatics, and modern psychology. Through her work with the young women of Laurel Falls Camp, Smith found emotional access to her own childhood and awareness of the socialization process so crucial to understanding herself as a white Southern female and to her strength as a writer. There she began systematically to examine and then confront her society's concepts of race and gender. There also she came close to creating the world she wanted to live in, a world where every child could experience esteem, where individual creativity could be encouraged by a supportive community, where old ideas were questioned and new ones explored, and where differences could be appreciated. Encouraging emotional and psychological as well as physical development, Smith helped the daughters of upper-class white Southerners question the world they lived in and begin to envision the possibility of change in that world. Thus the camp became a laboratory for many of the ideas informing Smith's analysis of Southern culture, especially her understanding of the effects of child-rearing practices on adult racial and sexual relationships. Through the camp Smith also met Paula Snelling and began the lifelong relationship that encouraged and sustained her writing career.[1]

They met first in the summer of 1921 when Lillian Smith's father hired Snelling to work in the camp's athletic department. Snelling had helped pay her way through

Wesleyan College in Macon, Georgia, by teaching swimming and was known for her expertise in tennis and horseback riding, but when she first heard about Laurel Falls Camp she was teaching high school math in Americus, Georgia. Struggling to finance her studies at the Peabody Conservatory, Lillian Smith worked for her father during the summer as camp music counselor. Although Paula and Lillian were on the camp staff in the summers of 1921 and 1922, they did not begin to know each other very well until they sat together on the train to Clayton in July 1925, when Smith was returning from three years in China. In the intervening years Snelling had taught high school math for two years in Athens, Georgia, returning each summer to Laurel Falls Camp, and had spent the 1924–1925 school year at Columbia University, where she had earned a master's degree in psychology with a minor in English literature. Snelling remembered that conversation with Smith on the train the opening day of camp in July 1925 as the real beginning of their friendship, the first time they had talked "as two human beings who had something to say to each other" apart from their separate interests in sports and music. At the close of the 1925 camp season, Snelling was one of four staff members whom Smith retained. In the summer of 1926 Snelling was put in charge of athletics, and in 1928 when Smith bought the camp from her father, she named Snelling assistant director.[2]

That Snelling remembered the beginning of their friendship as a conversation about something more than their camp interests is significant. Both women were intellectuals, and their relationship grew beyond their work at camp as they pursued mutual interests in psychology and literature, in people and ideas. After Smith's father died in 1930, her mother spent several winters with her sister in Miami. On those occasions, Smith shared an apartment with Snelling, who since 1925 had been teaching high school math in Macon, Georgia. Of Snelling's influence in their early years together, Smith wrote: "She was intensely interested in books and poetry. We read together, we discussed literature a great deal, and it was through those discussions that I began to turn my creativity toward writing instead of music. . . . I began writing little clumsy things in 1930. . . . Without her encouragement I doubt I would have had the courage to go through those first four or five years of groping."[3]

Significantly, during those first "years of groping" between 1932 and 1934, Smith wrote a novella called at first "Walls" and then "And the Waters Flow On," which she later described as "A love letter to China . . . about six lonely white women (missionaries all from the arid South, U.S.A., who thought they had something to give China simply because they were Western and white) . . . I remembered the shadowy relationships, intense, passionate, but unnamed between some of these women and some of the Chinese girls. I wrote about this China. . . . It was soft, warm, passionate, vivid, naked, honest, lyrical and it scared the publishers to death. I laid it aside knowing I might never write so personal, so terribly honest a book again."[4]

While sharing Snelling's apartment in Macon, Smith became an active member of the city's intellectual community. She had been elected to the socially prestigious role of president of the Macon Writers Club when, in the spring of 1935, family responsibilities once again intervened to change her life. That spring, while vacationing in Florida, Smith's mother suffered a severe heart attack. Smith left the apartment in Macon and returned permanently to the summer home on Screamer Mountain to care for her mother.[5]

Looking back on the year 1935, Smith understandably called it a "mean" year but also "a transition year when [she and Snelling] were breaking away from the past, or from much in our lives." The breaking away was further precipitated when, on July 4, in a freak accident with one of the camp horses, Paula Snelling was knocked unconscious and nearly dragged to death, her throat split within a hair's breadth of the jugular vein, her face covered with hoofprints, and her ribs and teeth broken. While recuperating, Snelling took a year's leave from teaching and stayed on the mountain with Smith and her mother. Although she healed physically within a few months, her emotional and psychic recovery proved more difficult.[6]

Feeling the stress of daily care for her invalid mother and confinement to the small mountain cottage, Smith suggested in January 1936 that they start a literary magazine. Snelling remained on the mountain with Smith and never returned to her teaching position in Macon; for, as she later recalled, "Who would give up something as interesting as the magazine to teach high school geometry? . . . When we started the magazine, I felt now this is something I can really grow with and express myself through."[7]

Initially Snelling was editor, Smith associate editor. Smith hoped that taking responsibility for the magazine would help Snelling regain some of the self-confidence she had lost in her nearly fatal accident with the camp horse. From the beginning, however, Smith assumed major responsibility for the magazine, and after the first year her name appeared above Snelling's on the editorial page. To finance the venture, the two women sent "birth announcements" of the forthcoming *Pseudopodia* to about thirty friends, boldly proclaiming the editors' commitment to "difference" and to individuality of viewpoint. Snelling would later describe their original goals as "to find the creative forces at work in the South; to tell 'the honest truth' about everything (impossible of course); to write as beautifully as we could." Twenty-four subscriptions financed the first issue, in which the editors clearly opposed the Vanderbilt Agrarian school of literary criticism. Their magazine would concern itself with the South: with whatever seemed to them "artistic, vital, and significant," not to perpetuate "that sterile fetishism of the Old South" but to "expose rather than gloss over vapidness, dishonesty, cruelty, stupidity."[8] Published in the spring of 1936, *Pseudopodia* became the *North Georgia Review* (Spring 1937–Winter 1941) and finally *South Today* (Spring 1942–Winter 1945). Reviewing and publishing the work of black as well as white authors and openly attacking racial segregation (a first among white literary magazines published below the Mason-Dixon line), the magazine quickly achieved acclaim as a forum for liberal thought in the region.[9] "Within a year,"

Snelling remembered, "it was known widely over the U.S. and in parts of Europe. It got enormous publicity and editorial comment. Henry Mencken enjoyed it, Bernard De Voto loved it, Mrs. Roosevelt thought it amazing, Dr. Karl Menninger thought our psychological insights tremendous."[10]

What had begun as a psychological diversion soon became a major focus in their lives, individually and together, providing each an outlet for her particular skills and interests: Smith, in fiction and editorial commentary; Snelling, in book reviews and longer critical essays. Despite constant financial struggles, the ten years during which they coedited the magazine and ran the camp were probably the most enjoyable in their lives. To enliven their social life and in lieu of monetary payment for contributions to the magazine, the editors established a tradition of inviting contributors to spend a few days as their guests at the camp. Their guest lists expanded through the years to include a variety of people—editors, journalists, educators, political activists—mostly Southerners, whom Smith and Snelling thought would be interesting to know and whom they viewed as being involved in "changing the South." They had their first biracial dinner party with guests from Atlanta in the fall of 1936. Sometimes the gatherings consisted of students from nearby universities or colleges invited to the camp for a weekend. At other times guests came for four or five days. Always the occasions were designed to encourage stimulating conversation and the exchange of provocative ideas. Such house parties were not merely social functions; they were also, in the tradition of intellectual salons, important political activities. Through the magazine and their house parties, Smith and Snelling created, at least periodically, an aspect of the South in which they wanted to live: a place where intellectuals and artists could gather to exchange ideas, to examine their society, and to find ways to influence the development and direction of its future.[11]

About the same time they began the magazine, Smith also began writing *Strange Fruit,* the novel that would bring her international acclaim, and which she dedicated "to Paula." Even before the publication of her novel, however, the magazine's increasingly bold stands against racial segregation in 1942 and 1943 inevitably pushed Smith more into the public arena. Such boldness in the 1940s brought censure and censorship along with fame. First, an unsuccessful attempt was made in 1943 to ban *South Today* from the U.S. mails. Then, less than a month after it was published in the spring of 1944, *Strange Fruit,* which chronicled the emotional and social upheaval surrounding a biracial love affair in the 1920s Deep South, was banned in Boston and later temporarily banned from the U.S. mails.[12]

The notoriety surrounding the novel's banning and the subsequent production of the Broadway play brought additional demands on Smith as a public speaker and writer. With a subscription list of ten thousand, Smith felt that the magazine's growth severely hampered her writing of books and wanted Snelling to take over as full-time editor of *South Today,* but Snelling felt she lacked the energy and talent for what had become an enormous undertaking. "I could never have come up with the ideas for the magazine or written the bulk of what was published in it—as Lil did," she said. Consequently, they ceased publication of the magazine in 1946.[13]

Despite the notoriety of *Strange Fruit,* Smith and Snelling continued to operate Laurel Falls Camp through the summer of 1948. But the strain of two years of celebrity status and the failure of the Broadway production of *Strange Fruit* took their toll on Smith's physical health, and Smith correctly anticipated an even harsher reaction to the publication of *Killers of the Dream.* With its unequivocal denunciation of racial segregation including her bold discussion of its sexual implications, Smith also feared her autobiographical critique of Southern culture might be more than her camp patrons could tolerate. Early in 1949, knowing that she could not meet the publication deadline for *Killers* and also open the camp, Smith made the difficult decision to close the camp to devote her full energies to writing.[14]

Ironically, Smith's freedom to write came at the expense of psychic and emotional security. In abandoning the roles of magazine editor and camp director—socially appropriate activities for an unmarried intellectual woman—Smith lost the security of an acceptable gender role for her time and place. Whereas before she closed the camp her personal relationship with Snelling had been protected because it could be viewed as a friendly business partnership, with neither the camp nor the magazine to employ Snelling, Smith found it difficult to justify their living arrangements and to maintain their relationship as one of equals. Although she valued her partner's emotional and intellectual support, Smith grew increasingly frustrated that Snelling did not have her own work. In the early 1950s the two women collaborated on plans for an anthology about research relating to mental, emotional, and physical disabilities, but much of Smith's part of the project evolved into her second book of autobiographical essays, *The Journey* (1954), and the anthology was never completed. While Snelling seemed content to write an occasional book review and serve primarily as Smith's secretary, bookkeeper, and most respected critical audience, Smith feared that her own success as a writer had stifled Snelling's creativity.[15]

The few surviving letters between Smith and Snelling reflect Smith's ongoing struggle with her need for psychic space, her need for Snelling's companionship, and, especially after Smith was diagnosed with cancer in 1953, their increasing financial needs. Writing from her apartment in the Hotel Margaret, Brooklyn, where she spent much of the fall and winter of 1945–1946, during the production and then closing of *Strange Fruit,* Smith alternately acknowledged her dependency on Paula—"You know I love you and need you and depend on you in a thousand ways"—and protested Paula's dependency "solely on me and my friends for your life. . . . If you had one interest that was not mine I would feel better about it."[16] Only two weeks later, however, Smith closed a letter to Snelling with a somewhat different perspective on their relationship:

> It is good to be writing to you. You think I stopped because I stopped loving you. I think I stopped years ago because if I write you I won't write books. I am afraid of not having enough libido for both. And remember when I am wholly in love I can't write a line! So there!
>
> But I could do with a little loving for a change. Oh darling, if our full spirits and bodies could effect the marriage that our minds have always had—And that our integrity of spirit has had! Maybe the old wonderful Paula will come back too—the one so rich in ideas and feelings and inner vitality. The one who helped me through so many bad spots—so patiently and gently. Though you've never stopped helping me. I'd love to feel your lips on mine . . . and I can imagine other feelings too. Better guard these letters.[17]

The letters were guarded well, and we understand why in a homophobic culture Smith would feel the necessity to protect such evidence of the intimate nature of their relationship. Yet, a June 19, 1952, letter to Paula reveals that Smith struggled with more than her resentment of Paula's dependency in their relationship. Referring to a picture of the young Snelling, Smith commented on her "bi-sexual charm which no one dares admit is seductive—except in real life" and then confessed: "I am sorry my letters are burned, that is my ambivalence. My shame about something different and completely good. It has been that shame that has destroyed the keen edge of a pattern of love that was creative and good. Blurring it, dulling it. . . ." Then, ironically, after again expressing concern that Paula's creativity and individuality had been stifled in their relationship, Smith suggested that at the next opportunity, after they had finished work on the anthology, Snelling should write about their relationship: "However esoteric or strange or special, you should put down your feelings about you and me and life. What it has meant to you. What this relationship has meant. *It* might be *the* masterpiece, not my poor little attempts to tell the world how to be good."[18]

Although Snelling did not write a book about their relationship, in correspondence to Smith and later to others about their relationship she expressed no ambivalence about her role in Smith's life. While visiting her mother in Pinehurst in December 1943 and January 1944, Snelling wrote Smith: "While I know that my potentialities are not such that ours can be a 50–50 relationship, there is no reason why it can't be a mature one in which my percentage, whatever its numerical value, is indispensable and invaluable. It would make me happy to know I had made it so."[19] A few days later, after receiving a letter in which Smith confessed she had been unable to write because of her feelings of conflict about her relationship with another woman, Snelling wrote in no uncertain terms:

> There is one thing I want you to get straight: nothing about you and R. could bother me as much as the knowledge that the conflict interferes with your writing. So far as I am concerned there is no need for you to feel any deep conflict. For my favorite "image ideal" of myself is as aide to you in your writing, i.e. as background and stimulus for it—as a person who so fills your needs and appreciates your talents

> that you are in the maximum emotional and intellectual state for writing. And second, I really know that one can care for two people simultaneously. No "explaining" is needed on that scene. I haven't been basically hurt by it, except when for a while in Aug.–Sept. when I was not sure that *you* knew one could!
>
> Besides, whatever 'debts' you owe me have been overpaid (spiritually no less than financially) day by day through the years, and there are no obligations regarding the future. It is only so far as I essentially am continuing to meet your needs that you continue owing me anything. And I am unhappy only when it appears that my personality defects outweigh what I am still confident are my unique personality assets. For I, along with everyone else but perhaps more than most, function best when I feel prized. Whatever may come of the R. situation, I can adjust to it so long as I feel that I myself am invaluable and irreplaceable. I know that in many ways I fall short quantitatively; but I do not believe you could get along very well without certain qualities which I have and no one else could duplicate. As long as you feel the same way, other things can fall into focus. So don't waste any time 'conflicting' on that score.[20]

More than twenty years later, in a letter to Louise Blackwell and Frances Clay, Smith's first biographers, Snelling dismissed as "completely false" the "silly, envious rumors that [she] 'helped Lil write her books'" and concluded that

> whatever contribution I may have made to Lil's career has come through my faith in her, and my unwavering belief in my own ability to recognize greatness of spirit, mind and creativity when I encounter it, whether in person, in the printed book, or in manuscript. She has often said that she could not have endured the pain and humiliations that have come her way without my love and faith. Our friendship is so subtle, complex, deep and beautiful that neither of us likes to talk about it much. Nor to hear it talked about on the basis of rumor or third-hand gossip. . . . My talents lie in the field of criticism; within limits, I know the real from the phony, the important from the trivial. I think I know what to cherish and what to be indifferent to. On rare occasions I can get this down on paper. But I am not gifted with the ability to 'create'—if I were, I'd do it on my own, under my own name.[21]

When I asked Snelling about the nature of her relationship with Smith, she replied: "We cared very deeply for each other and sometimes it was expressed physically." Identifying herself as "the homosexual one," Snelling insisted that Smith should not be considered a lesbian because "Lil could have been happily married had she found the right man." While Smith had several close relationships with men, Snelling "never had the feelings for a man or men which would be necessary for a satisfactory marriage." As an adolescent, she said, she realized her feelings and broke off the one relationship with a boy in her home town who wanted to marry her. Snelling clearly accepted her lesbian sexuality, defining it as an abnormality of her genes, but not a sin and not a source of shame. She said she felt Smith hid their relationship, not to deny it but to protect it.[22]

Clearly, Paula Snelling's quiet confidence in herself and in her own ability to discern "the important from the trivial" was critical not only to Smith's development as a writer and to the quality of their relationship, but also to our understanding of lesbian, bisexual, and gay history. In their relationship we see both the effect of the closet and the quiet triumph of love that outlives the closet. In Snelling's confidence we see that it was possible to be born into a Southern, white, middle-class family in 1899 and grow up neither traumatized nor ashamed by the knowledge that one was a lesbian. Although that knowledge did not become for Snelling a public affirmation of lesbian identity, it remains valuable knowledge for us. Paula Snelling lived her commitment and Lillian Smith achieved her desire to be heard in part because Snelling kept her faith not only in Smith, but also in herself, in her own judgment and its worth in the world. Our world is richer for the gift of this significant other.

Notes

1. The previous three paragraphs appeared in another form in Margaret Rose Gladney, "Introduction to the 1994 Edition," Lillian Smith, *Killers of the Dream* (New York: W. W. Norton, 1994).
2. Margaret Rose Gladney, ed., *How Am I to Be Heard? Letters of Lillian Smith* (Chapel Hill: University of North Carolina Press, 1993), 5–6.
3. Ibid., 9.
4. Ibid., 9–10.
5. Ibid., 11.
6. Ibid., 11–12.
7. Ibid., 12.
8. Ibid., 23–24.
9. Margaret Sullivan, "A Bibliography of Lillian Smith and Paula Snelling," *Bulletin of the Mississippi Valley Collection* 4 (Spring 1971): 12.
10. Paula Snelling to Louise Blackwell and Frances Clay, 27 August 1966, Lillian Smith Collection, #1283A, Hargrett Rare Books and Manuscript Library, University of Georgia Libraries (UGA), Athens, Georgia.
11. Gladney, ed., *How Am I to Be Heard?*, 12–13.
12. Margaret Rose Gladney, "Introduction," Lillian Smith, *One Hour* (Chapel Hill: University of North Carolina Press, 1994), viii.
13. Gladney, ed., *How Am I to Be Heard?*, 13.
14. Ibid., 13–14.
15. Ibid., 14.
16. Ibid., 97.
17. Ibid., 100–01.
18. Ibid., 136–37. Emphasis in original.
19. Lillian Smith Collection, #2337, UGA.
20. Ibid.

21. Lillian Smith Collection, #1283A, UGA.

22. Paula Snelling, personal interview, 14 December 1981. For another account of this interview, see also Margaret Rose Gladney, "Personalizing the Political, Politicizing the Personal," in *Carryin' On in the Lesbian and Gay South,* ed. John Howard (New York: New York University Press, 1997), 99–100.

7

Homophobia and the Trajectory of Postwar American Radicalism

The Career of Bayard Rustin

JOHN D'EMILIO

OVER the last decade and a half, gay and lesbian history has emerged as a vibrant area of scholarship. Although the better part of our work is still ahead of us, enough has been done to give us a heady sense of accomplishment. There are monographs, scholarly articles, collections of documents, oral history anthologies, and important efforts at constructing theory. Unlike the situation that prevailed twenty years ago, when I write today about gay and lesbian history, I am not uttering an oxymoron.[1]

While lesbian history has forged strong intellectual ties with women's history and thus travels across the broad terrain mapped by gender studies, the historical literature on male homosexuality, at least that written about the United States, has for the most part remained curiously centered on itself. Not only is it, as one would expect, primarily about men whose erotic desire draws them toward other men, but it also focuses relentlessly upon those aspects of their lives in which gayness is central—on the construction of identity, the evolution of urban subcultures and communities, the forging of a political emancipation movement. When the literature moves beyond these topics, into areas such as cultural representation and the construction of hegemonic discourses, the point has generally been to assess how these men have been oppressed.[2]

To characterize gay American history in this way is not to fault it. For one, I have just described the largest part of my own work. And, besides, it is difficult to imagine the field developing in any other way. But it is also true that the steady focus on gayness—either gay life or gay oppression—threatens to obscure the bulk of gay historical experience. Most men who desire men have not led gay-centered social lives, and even those who do will have passed much of their time—in work, politics, worship, voluntary associations, and civic affairs—in non-gay contexts. How do we draw this experience into the orbit of gay history? How do we avoid writing a history of marginalized men that reproduces the marginalization gay oppression attempts to enforce?

My current project, a biography of Bayard Rustin, did not begin as an exploration in gay history. Rather, I wanted to study the 1960s. Personally, those times still resonate emotionally for me. Intellectually, as someone who regularly teaches courses on the 1960s, I have felt stymied by the response of my students to the decade. Initially excited by the optimism, idealism, and power of the civil rights and student movements, they are ultimately disturbed by what they see as the outcome: a nation spinning out of control, cynical, disillusioned, and fractured into separate identity movements. The sense that I carried away from those years—of a revolutionary moment greater than the sum of its individual parts—seems lost a generation later to young readers of the historical literature.

Rustin's career, which has not received much play in the writing about post–World War II struggles for peace and justice, caught my attention for a number of reasons. For one, the broad range of his interests offered an opportunity to explore the connections between several movements. Through his work with the Congress of Racial Equality, with A. Philip Randolph and Martin Luther King, Jr., Rustin was certainly as responsible as anyone for injecting Gandhian nonviolence into the heart of the struggle for racial equality. He was also at the center of the pacifist circles which kept alive a critique of Cold War militarism, sparked the first demonstrations against the nuclear arms race, and stood ready to mobilize as the Johnson administration escalated the war in Vietnam. Rustin was fiercely internationalist as well. He worked closely with European pacifists, such as those in the Campaign for Nuclear Disarmament in Britain, and, keenly attuned to the historic significance of decolonization, with African liberation leaders such as Nkrumah, Azikiwe, and Kaunda. To all these efforts, Rustin brought the skills of a master strategist and tactician as well as a vision of revolutionary change. It would not be an exaggeration to claim that more than anyone else in the postwar era, he was a bridge linking the African-American freedom struggle, peace campaigns, and a socialist vision of economic democracy.

Rustin's career also intrigued me because, in the mid-1960s, he proposed a road not taken. During the critical years from 1963 to 1966, as the force of the civil rights movement provoked a wave of support for social and economic reforms not seen since the mid-1930s, Rustin argued that radicals had to engage directly the political process. Just when the line between radical and liberal was opening into an unbridgeable chasm, just when many student radicals were embarking on an eternal romance with street action, Rustin urged a transition "from protest to politics."[3] At the time, militants tended to scorn Rustin's ideas. Many of his longtime associates argued then—and have continued to claim—that Rustin's strategic call was simply one manifestation of a more generalized turn to the right. In retrospect, with our ability to see how the radical war on liberalism helped to usher in a generation-long conservative hegemony in American politics, his approach seems less suspect. Thus, Rustin's career appeared as a promising vehicle for exploring afresh the achievements and failures of the 1960s.

That Rustin was also a gay man, and publicly identified as such in an era when the stigma attached to homosexuality was heavy, was a bonus. But I imagined his sexuality contained in the corner labeled "personal life" and saw it raising interesting, but secondary, questions that were not essential to the story of politics I wished to tell.

As my research has progressed, Rustin's sexuality has resisted this ghettoization. It appears, increasingly, inescapable, injecting itself everywhere. I am coming to believe that it molded his public life and shaped as well the response of others to him and to his ideas. In other words, it occupies not a peripheral but a critical place in Rustin's biography and, by extension, in the history of the 1960s.

In the rest of this essay, I will trace in broad outline Rustin's life and career. Along the way, I will pause to consider the moments when his sexual identity erupted into public view. Finally, I will speculate about the ways that I think his homosexuality shaped his strategic thinking in the mid-1960s, conditioned the reactions of others to him, and propelled, eventually, his alleged turn to the right.

BAYARD Rustin was born in 1912 into an African-American family in West Chester, Pennsylvania, a Quaker-settled area that had been a stop on the underground railroad for runaway slaves. His grandmother, Julia, who raised Bayard as her own child, was an early member of the NAACP. Rustin excelled in high school as a scholar, athlete, and singer, and he also displayed a willingness early on to challenge racial discrimination. In the mid-1930s, he made his way to New York City, which remained his home for the rest of his life.[4]

Living in Harlem and attending City College, Rustin found himself in the midst of the unruly politics of Depression-era New York. Along with many Americans of conscience in the 1930s, he was drawn to the Communist Party. Rustin's Quaker beliefs, expressed during these years by participation in work-study projects of the American Friends Service Committee (AFSC), only added to the attractiveness of the communist movement, for during the Popular Front period the party seemed to be against both war and fascism. Rustin joined the Young Communist League (YCL) and was active in the American Student Union, a major campus-based organization in which communists were influential. Yet, like many others, he eventually found himself alienated by the party's subservience to Moscow. After Hitler's invasion of the Soviet Union in June 1941, YCL leaders told Rustin to stop his activities for racial justice. Rustin broke with the party and remained deeply distrustful of it for the rest of his life.[5]

In the months before his split with the party, Rustin embarked on two critical political relationships. Earlier in 1941, he had met A. Philip Randolph, the black socialist labor leader who had just called for an African-American march on Washington. With Randolph leading a charge of the black masses, Rustin was naturally attracted to the older, more experienced leader, and began working in the youth section of the organization. A. J. Muste was the other older radical to whom Rustin was drawn. Muste, whose background included years at Brookwood Labor College and involvement with the American Trotskyist movement, had recently become director of the Fellowship of Reconciliation (FOR), the leading Christian-pacifist organization in the United States. He believed pacifists must engage in more than moral witness against injustice; they had to build a movement for permanent change. At Muste's invitation, Rustin joined the FOR's staff in September 1941 and stayed for the next twelve years.[6]

It may seem odd to describe the war years as an exciting moment for American pacifists, but such was their characterization of the times. The worldwide conflagration created an élan, an intense solidarity that drove the truest believers to ever greater sacrifices of time and energy. Rustin traveled across the country speaking to church and student groups, signing up new members, and visiting the relocation camps where Japanese Americans were incarcerated.[7] For Rustin, a good bit of the promise of this first paying job as an agent of social change came from the knowledge that he was breaking new ground. Along with James Farmer and George Houser, two other young staff members of the FOR, Rustin was expanding the group's mission into the field of race relations. They were building a new interracial organization, the Congress of Racial Equality (CORE), dedicated to the application of Gandhian techniques to the struggle for racial equality. During the 1940s, they conducted training workshops and embarked on action projects, desegregating restaurants, drugstore lunch counters, skating rinks, and theaters.[8] Rustin also served as the FOR's liaison to Randolph's March on Washington organization. Here was an authentic working-class vehicle, and Rustin strove to inject Gandhian nonviolence into this urban mass movement. After one of its major conferences, Rustin wrote enthusiastically to Muste that "Randolph really 'hit the gong.' We had a superb meeting. . . . He spoke in a way that convinced me that he is really concerned to develop an understanding and use of non-violence by the American Negro."[9]

Early in 1944, Rustin was jailed for refusing induction into the military. He entered a federal prison system that had been flooded by conscientious objectors whose hunger strikes and work stoppages were disrupting the routines of guards and inmates alike. Rustin plunged into these activities, challenging segregation and mail censorship, fomenting strikes among the prisoners and, in the process, deepening his commitment to a hybrid of Gandhian, Quaker, and Marxist teachings. The prison years convinced Rustin that Gandhianism was the gospel of the future, and that the postwar years would require a steel-like commitment to militant action.[10]

By the time he was released from prison in June 1946, the Cold War was becoming national dogma. Pacifists found themselves increasingly isolated and were forced into symbolic forms of protest. Race relations, on the other hand, seemed to offer a more promising field of action. In 1947, Rustin and George Houser, acting through CORE, organized a test of bus company compliance with a Supreme Court decision banning segregated seating in interstate travel. Riding through the upper South, the members of the "Journey of Reconciliation" used Gandhian techniques and rallied black communities wherever they traveled. Rustin and three others also faced arrest and conviction, leading to another prison sentence for Rustin.[11] In 1948, pacifists joined forces once again with Randolph, who was mobilizing against military segregation. Under prodding from Rustin, Randolph promised a campaign of civil disobedience, which opened new opportunities for Rustin's message of nonviolent resistance to sink roots into African-American communities.[12] Meanwhile, Rustin spent much of his time on the road leading workshops in which participants not only studied Gandhianism, but also exposed discrimination and instigated direct action campaigns.[13]

Because of the leadership qualities he displayed, Rustin attracted notice. Muste consciously mentored him and strategized his development as a leader. The FOR sent him to meet with European pacifist leaders and to confer with Gandhi's followers in India. The peers with whom he worked remember the Rustin of the 1940s vividly. They were awed by the personal courage of a man who, in his solitary travels, regularly refused to comply with segregation and received beatings and jail sentences because of it. In my interviews with pacifists from this era, the two words that recurred most frequently in their descriptions of Rustin were "prophetic" and "charismatic." Possessing a beautiful tenor voice, he could shift easily between speech and song, and moved audiences to tears with his renditions of Negro spirituals. Rustin made an indelible impression wherever he traveled. In the eyes of one associate, Bayard was "a shining star." Another remembered "the magic about him." To many, he seemed destined to become an American Gandhi.[14]

By the early 1950s, opportunities for radical activity, even in the area of race relations, were vanishing. Aware of the rising agitation throughout Africa for independence, Rustin proposed shifting the FOR's focus to support for decolonization. The strategy was to inject nonviolent methods into the independence movements; the larger goal was to open a new space for agitation that might eventually loosen the Cold War grip on politics at home. After extended travels in Africa in 1952, Rustin returned home enthusiastic about the possibilities, and the FOR began raising money for his plans.[15]

And then the roof caved in. In January 1953, while on a speaking tour to promote his African plans, Rustin was arrested in Pasadena, California. Discovered in a parked car with two other men, he was convicted of violating California's lewd-vagrancy law and sentenced to sixty days. The *Los Angeles Times* reported the incident and, since Rustin's lectures on the West Coast had to be canceled abruptly, word spread quickly through pacifist circles.[16]

The Pasadena arrest was not the first time that Rustin's homosexuality was subjected to scrutiny. Sometime early in his tenure at the FOR, he and Muste discussed it. Whether Rustin raised the issue himself or whether Muste initiated the dialogue is uncertain, and the circumstances and content of these early talks have eluded me. Rustin's primary erotic interest was young white men in their late teens and early twenties, with whom he had ample opportunity for contact through his work. Perhaps rumors about Rustin's approaches had reached Muste. Or, the quick intense bond that A. J. and Bayard formed (almost everyone who knew them during the 1940s referred to it as a father-son relationship characterized by mutual affection and respect) may have impelled Rustin to turn to Muste for guidance. In any case, Rustin's sexuality was grist for gossip among female staffers at the FOR, some of whom were smitten by his charm and good looks. Moreover, by 1943 Bayard was in a relationship with Davis Platt, a nineteen-year-old whom he had met at a conference, and Platt was now a Columbia student, visiting Rustin frequently at the FOR offices across the street from the campus. Platt does not recall having to hide their intimacy from Muste and the rest of the staff, and so, before Rustin went off to federal prison in 1944, sexual matters had certainly surfaced.[17]

Incarceration sharpened the issue. In the confined atmosphere of jail, the boundary between public role and private desire collapsed. On the eve of a prisoner strike that Rustin was organizing, he found himself accused by the warden of sexual misconduct and was placed in solitary. Rustin lied to his fellow inmates about the reasons for his punishment, and the incident provoked a deeply wrenching, many-layered crisis—with his fellow inmates, with Muste, and with himself. Bayard debated what course his sexual life should take: the way offered by "Marie," a code name he employed for Platt to circumvent the prison censors, or the "challenge" offered by Helen, a Quaker woman in love with Rustin. In letters written to Platt but also intended for Muste's reading, Rustin agonized over his future:

> I must pray, trust, experience, dream, hope and all else possible until I know clearly in my own mind and spirit that I have failed [to become heterosexual], if I must fail, not because of a faint heart, or for lack of confidence in my true self, or for pride, or for emotional instability, or for moral lethargy, or any other character fault, but rather, because I come to see after the most complete searching that the best for me lies elsewhere.[18]

Two weeks later, he was still in struggle. "Is celibacy the answer?" he wrote. "If so how can I develop an inner desire for it? I have a real desire for following another way but I have never had a desire to completely remove sex from my mind. What can celibacy become without such an inner desire? Does not holding M[arie] before me as an object toward whom I project these terrific impulses stifle the beam of light I saw when I spoke with H[elen]?[19]

Muste, meanwhile, wrote back, debating with Bayard the ethics of homosexual relationships. His letters were tender and affectionate, but also blunt. The issue for Muste was not the morality of homosexuality in the abstract. "On the question of a-typical relationships my position has not changed. I insist people must be understood and loved. I keep my mind open." Instead, the older man argued that everything Bayard had confided about his sexual life suggested the conflation of homosexuality and promiscuity, which for Muste represented "the travesty and denial of love . . . an impulse to use and exploit." Muste questioned whether Bayard could play a prominent role in a pacifist movement grounded in Christian ethics while leading an ethically degraded life. "Oh, Bayard, Bayard," he wrote. "No one, *no one,* has any business being self-righteous—but to *ourselves* we do apply standards and there are *some limits* to self-indulgence, to lying, to being the play-boy, for those who undertake to arouse their fellows to moral issues." He made it clear to his protégé that he would take action to protect the movement's reputation should Rustin's actions threaten its integrity. To Rustin, he urged "discontinuance of a certain type of relationship." As he put it in one of his letters, "if thy right hand offend thee, cut it off."[20]

The jail correspondence, and the clarity with which Muste sketched his position, locked Rustin into a duplicitous existence. After his release from prison in 1946, he neither pretended nor claimed to be heterosexual. But his homosexuality remained something apart, and he sought satisfaction in the ways available to gay men who did not immerse themselves in a homosexual social world—through cruising in public places. In October 1946, he was arrested on Morningside Heights for soliciting to commit an indecent act. Interviews with Rustin's associates from these years hint at other incidents, though I have been unable independently to confirm any of them. At some point, Bayard sought psychiatric help, and Muste raised money through pacifist circles to finance Rustin's therapy. Muste was led to believe that "the problem" was under control. But rumors concerning Rustin's sexuality continued to surface, and it is a measure of A. J.'s attachment to Bayard that a final crisis was always averted.[21]

Not so after Pasadena. The FOR executive board quickly issued a statement providing details of the arrest, tracing the history of the FOR's engagement with Rustin on the issue and announcing that he was no longer on staff. The statement was distributed widely to pacifist organizations and leaders, provoking a debate not only about Rustin but about homosexuality as well.[22]

Rustin was devastated. His correspondence from this time suggests an effort to deflect criticism away from his sexuality. As he wrote to one of his associates, "I have gone deeper in the past six weeks than ever before and feel that I have at last seen my real problem. It has been pride. . . . While sex is a very real problem and while it has colored my personality, I now see that it has never been my basic problem." But, however he might interpret it, the fact remained that he had been branded and cut adrift by the world that had sustained him for twelve years. Without a discourse of homosexual affirmation and oppression, he could only attribute his predicament to personal failing. As a leader in a movement grounded in rigorous self-discipline, Rustin absorbed the blame into himself.[23]

Rustin's journey out of the wilderness began with the aid of another pacifist organization, the War Resisters League (WRL). Secular rather than religious, the WRL saw him as a skilled organizer rather than as a morally compromised soul. Despite efforts by Muste to prevent Rustin's hiring, Rustin joined the staff six months after he returned to New York and remained there for more than a decade.[24]

Rustin and his associates worked as best they could through these reactionary times. In 1955 the WRL and other peace groups initiated a public refusal to participate in civilian defense drills. By the beginning of the 1960s, they were being joined by several thousand until New York State abandoned the program. Also in 1955, Rustin and a few others launched a new independent radical magazine. Grounding itself in a critique of both liberalism and classical Marxism, *Liberation* magazine was committed to economic and social justice under the banner of nonviolent revolution. It exerted an enormous influence on the American New Left, floating ideas that became hallmarks of New Left thinking and raising issues around which the young would rally.[25]

The brightest beacon in these years came from the South. Blacks in Montgomery, Alabama, were engaged in a community-wide mobilization against segregated city buses, and the leaders had stumbled upon nonviolent action as their method. One could say that this was the event for which Rustin had been waiting half a lifetime. In February 1956, as the boycott was reaching a critical juncture, Rustin went to Montgomery. In obvious ways, he was an ideal emissary: the leading African-American Gandhian in the nation, whose career testified to his commitment.[26]

But Rustin's trip south was no easy matter. In a cloak-and-dagger scenario whose details remain obscure, pacifists and civil rights leaders in New York met, telephoned, and dispatched letters with dizzying speed. Rustin, they argued, was a danger to the movement. It was not only, or even primarily, that he was a New Yorker who had once been associated with the Communist Party. Rather, his arrest in Pasadena, still a vivid memory to his associates, would compromise his effectiveness and subject the Montgomery movement to serious peril. The FOR's southern field secretary, Glenn Smiley, was ordered to avoid any contact with Rustin, and then upbraided when he revealed that their paths had unwittingly crossed. Randolph, Muste, and Norman Thomas, the head of the Socialist Party, were adamant that Rustin should return home.[27]

It is a tribute to Rustin's personal charm, charisma, and skill as a strategist that he survived these machinations and emerged as King's closest adviser. King was not in any sense a committed Gandhian when Rustin arrived. There were guns in his home, and the men who were guarding his house were armed. Rustin initiated the process that transformed King into the most illustrious proponent of nonviolence in the world. He also busied himself with the work of mobilizing support for the boycott, raising funds, organizing rallies, and winning labor union assistance.[28]

Rustin worked with King throughout the 1950s. He devised the plans for what became the Southern Christian Leadership Conference (SCLC), King's organizational vehicle and the means by which Rustin believed a southwide nonviolent movement would be created. Rustin devoted himself to King's emergence as a national leader. As he wrote to King in 1957, "Actually, Martin, the question of where you move next is more important than any other question Negroes face today."[29] He deliberately midwived a relationship between King and Randolph who, by this time, was the elder statesman of the black struggle. Using Randolph's stature as a legitimizing tool, Rustin organized a Prayer Pilgrimage to Washington in May 1957—at which King gave his first speech to a national audience—and two youth marches for integrated schools, in 1958 and 1959. These demonstrations gave King and the civil rights movement a national platform and forced the Eisenhower administration finally to meet with civil rights leaders.[30]

Two aspects of Rustin's work in these years deserve comment, one relating to method and the other to strategic vision. Throughout this period, King rarely made a decision of any consequence without consulting him. Rustin orchestrated much of what unfolded. Yet he appeared at the time, and in subsequent historical accounts, as a shadowy figure, someone deep in the background. Some of this is attributable to a leadership style, long cultivated by Rustin, that fused Quaker and Gandhian influences into a seamless modesty that never drew attention to himself. Some of this was forced upon him by his sexual identity. The Baptist ministers in the SCLC did not want Rustin as director of the organization; instead, he was a "special assistant" working in New York. But I wonder to what degree his self-effacement was, all along, an adaptation to the stigma of homosexuality—a concession to the dangers to which it made him, and the causes with which he was associated, susceptible. Rustin, in other words, affected a pose—his own version of the mask that gay men of the era wore—and his dissembling fooled contemporary observers and historians alike.

Rustin's thinking in these years also took on the coloration that defined it for the next decade. Even as he immersed himself in direct action protest—and thus by the standards of the time was deviant, marginal, radical—he conceptualized it as *leading somewhere.* Protest existed not as an end in itself, but as a means to power and influence. Again and again, in his comments on the work of both the peace and the civil rights movement, Rustin called attention to the lack of a political vehicle to move beyond protest. He described the problem in different ways—as the "absence of a vital socialist movement" or, more vaguely, as the need for "a political form."[31] But what it meant for him was that protest alone would never translate into the ability directly to shape foreign and domestic policy.

In the wake of his experience in Montgomery, he came to see the outlines of a solution. "The Democratic Party," he argued, "has to remake itself radically or fall apart." If a revitalized Socialist Party was not on the horizon, at least the civil rights movement might provoke a political realignment. Injecting the issue directly into the Democratic Party might force a defection of white Southerners, breaking their stranglehold not only over the national party but over key congressional committees as well. The best-case scenario might lead to a thoroughly reconstituted Democratic Party, beholden to a progressive constituency.[32]

With this in mind, Rustin proposed to Randolph a major election-year project for 1960, with massive demonstrations outside the Democratic Party convention in Los Angeles and concerted efforts to shape the party's platform. King, who figured prominently in Rustin's calculations, was drawn into the scheme. Rustin's centrality to the project can be gleaned from the reaction of Randolph when a Rustin visit to West Africa to protest French nuclear testing dragged out longer than expected. Through an associate he communicated to Rustin "your indispensability for ALL non-violent action projects" and urged his immediate return to the States. The eruption of a sit-in movement among Southern black students in the winter of 1960, which pushed civil rights to the front page of the nation's newspapers, promised to make the work a resounding success.[33]

But Rustin's plans and influence were derailed again, this time through the manipulation of the gay issue by another African-American leader. Adam Clayton Powell, the congressman from Harlem who fancied himself the black power broker in the Democratic Party, was not prepared to have a queer radical usurp his role. In June 1960, as Rustin's convention plans shifted into high gear, Powell publicly decried the sinister hidden forces who were holding civil rights leaders "captive," and mentioned Rustin by name. Privately he warned King that unless he abandoned the convention project and dismissed Rustin, Powell would charge that the two were having a homosexual affair. Rustin offered to resign as King's special assistant, expecting King to reject the maneuver. But King had panicked, and Rustin again found himself in the cold.[34]

In important ways this incident was far more crushing than the Pasadena arrest. Dave McReynolds, who worked alongside Rustin every day at the WRL and who was himself gay, remembered that "Bayard spent the most miserable time I have ever seen during those months. He was completely demoralized . . . absolutely broken. I hadn't seen Bayard, except in the [Pasadena] jail period, so destroyed. Here was a chance of a lifetime to . . . realign the political process . . . and he was paralyzed."[35] Rustin had fought his way back from pariah status, had shaped and nurtured King's career, had been the invisible guiding hand behind many civil rights initiatives for years, and yet, again, he was being discarded, this time for something that had never happened—indeed, for something that went unnamed. Interestingly, the only public criticism of King's actions that I have encountered came from James Baldwin, the African-American novelist and essayist whose work addressed gay issues openly and who also was familiar with exile.[36]

Rustin returned to his peace work. It was not a completely unsatisfying alternative, since dissent from the nuclear arms race was reviving and Rustin had helped provoke the change in political climate. In the early 1960s he spent much time in Europe, working on anti-nuclear campaigns, and in Africa, assisting the Zambian independence struggle by setting up training centers for Gandhian-style resistance. But these were also the years of the civil rights movement's greatest growth, which Rustin had to watch from the sidelines.[37]

Early in 1963, Rustin and Randolph discussed a mass march on Washington for jobs and freedom. At first, their idea roused little interest among other civil rights leaders, but by late spring the situation had changed dramatically. King's Birmingham protests had gripped the nation, and Rustin apprehended a significance to them beyond the outrage that electric cattle prods had incited. In Birmingham, the black community raised the issue of jobs; they were moving, in other words, beyond civil rights. Birmingham also unleashed a torrent of protest. Through the spring and summer of 1963, the FBI counted over fifteen hundred demonstrations in thirty-eight states; it estimated that 40 percent of African Americans had participated. And Birmingham had also stoked a panic within the Kennedy administration, which finally made civil rights a priority. In June, Kennedy addressed the nation on civil rights and proposed major federal civil rights legislation.[38]

Randolph and Rustin kept pressing the march. King lined up behind it, and moderate organizations acquiesced. Early in July, at a planning meeting, Roy Wilkins of the NAACP tried to veto Rustin's role as director, dragging out, once again, the Pasadena arrest. But Randolph finessed the move by accepting the role of director on condition that he choose his own assistants. He promptly named Rustin his deputy and turned over the organizing to him.[39]

Rustin was by no means out of the woods. For years J. Edgar Hoover had kept an eye on the civil rights movement, secretly feeding damaging information to key segregationists. Now the FBI worked overtime, scrutinizing the Washington march as they looked for subversive connections. Early in August, Senator Strom Thurmond of South Carolina, a rabid segregationist, addressed the issue of communist links and placed information into the *Congressional Record*. But most of it was old news and generated little interest, though it did spark worry in civil rights circles. On August 13, Thurmond tried again, this time targeting Rustin, who by then had been dubbed "Mr. March-on-Washington" by the press. He raised the issue of Rustin's old communist ties and, more explosively, his conviction on "sex perversion" charges. Thurmond placed into the *Congressional Record* not only press clippings about the Pasadena incident, but also a copy of the police booking slip. Since such a document was not easily available, and since Hoover had ordered a comprehensive probe of Rustin in mid-July, Thurmond's source seems obvious.[40]

By this time one might think that Rustin was inoculated against feeling on this issue. Yet Thurmond's charges represented something new. In 1953, pacifists had been made privy to Rustin's arrest, but the event was a throwaway item in local papers. In 1960, the conflict with Powell rippled through the nation's press, but the substance remained unnamed. Now the labeling process was clear and ubiquitous. Rustin was named a pervert before an audience of tens of millions.

The outcome was also unique. Because the accusation was so public, because it was leveled by a segregationist, and because it came just two weeks before an event on which the movement was banking so much, civil rights leaders had to rally to Rustin's defense. Addressing a major press conference, Randolph declared that "I am sure I speak for the combined Negro leadership in voicing my complete confidence in Bayard Rustin's character, integrity, and extraordinary ability. . . . I am dismayed that there are in this country men who, wrapping themselves in the mantle of Christian morality, would mutilate the most elementary conceptions of human decency, privacy and humility in order to persecute other men." With the elderly, dignified Randolph as spokesman, journalists did not ask probing questions about perversions.[41]

The March on Washington remains enshrined in popular memory as a glorious instant in time. Coming before the assassination of Kennedy, before ghetto uprisings, separatist rhetoric, campus rebellions, and government violence ripped the country into discordant parts, it stands as a symbol of unity, hope, and confidence. Twenty years later, James Baldwin eloquently recalled it as a moment when "it almost seemed that we stood on a height, and could see our inheritance; perhaps we could make the kingdom real, perhaps the beloved community would not forever remain that dream one dreamed in agony."[42] For Rustin, the march was the event that legitimated mass nonviolent protest. In the course of two months the Kennedys had shifted from hostility to endorsement. Members of Congress, who had initially rejected invitations to participate, ended by clamoring for a place on the platform. Labor and church groups had signed on to the cause, and all the major civil rights organizations, including the most conservative, had maintained a united front and thus explicitly had lined up behind mass action.[43]

The success of the march also transformed Rustin's persona. He was now a leader with a media profile and public recognition. He received a steady stream of interviews, invitations to speak, and opportunities to address major gatherings. The relationship with King was repaired for a time, and he was drawn back into King's inner circle. In other words, the perversion card had been played—and finally, so it seemed, trumped.[44]

In the succeeding months, Rustin was a man in motion. Early in 1964, he orchestrated a boycott of New York City's public schools; 45 percent of the system's pupils stayed home, making it the largest civil rights protest in history. He also pulled together a coalition of community, labor, and church groups to march on the New York State capitol and to lobby legislators for increases in the minimum wage, funding for public employment, and expansion of job-training programs.

Rustin was arrested at the opening of the New York World's Fair in a protest against racial bias in hiring. Later in 1964, he organized for A. Philip Randolph a "state of the race" conference in New York City, bringing together leading activists from around the country. In 1965 and 1966, he coordinated an effort to mobilize behind a comprehensive "Freedom Budget," a progressive alternative to the more modest War on Poverty. And, as American involvement in Vietnam deepened in 1964 and 1965, Rustin appeared at rallies and strategized how Martin Luther King might effectively deploy his influence.[45]

Rustin's evolving strategic vision played itself out in some other political choices that puzzled his associates. In July 1964, after Goldwater's nomination as the Republican presidential candidate, Rustin engineered a call for a moratorium on civil rights demonstrations until after the November election. The following month, at the Democratic National Convention, Rustin forcefully urged the Mississippi Freedom Democrats to accept the compromise offered by Lyndon Johnson. The compromise was rejected, and writers ever since have identified this as the moment when young radicals came to specify liberalism as the enemy. And, as agitation against the Vietnam War grew, Rustin criticized the antiwar movement—for its failure to exclude communists, for its glorification of violence, and for its anti-American rhetoric.[46]

Several common themes can be found in his actions, his speeches, and his published writing during this three-year period. One is that the Negro struggle had to move beyond civil rights. Jim Crow lunch counters were anachronisms in an advanced capitalist society, and they could be abolished by the deployment of black bodies. By contrast, structural unemployment, crumbling ghetto schools, and slum housing required the transformation of the political economy. The struggle for black equality, in other words, demanded revolutionary changes. Second, Rustin argued that African Americans could not do this by themselves. They needed coalitions. This required not only the articulation of a full social and economic program, but also action to make progressive forces the effective political majority in the United States. In the short and medium term, this was likely to happen only through the Democratic Party. Finally, Rustin believed that direct action had to be not abandoned, but tactically deployed as part of a larger political strategy.

Rustin articulated his overall perspective most succinctly in an article, "From Protest to Politics," that appeared in February 1965.[47] Even today, a generation later, it stands up well as a cogent discussion of American politics with continuing relevance. And yet "From Protest to Politics" initiated a process by which Rustin was attacked by his fellow radicals—not for his sexual identity but for a turn to the Right—and steadily isolated from the circles in which he had traveled for two decades.

Two examples capture the Left's transformation of Rustin from exemplary organizer to enemy collaborator. Stokely Carmichael, who was widely credited with coining the slogan "Black Power," considered Rustin in the 1950s to be "the revolution itself, the most revolutionary of men." By 1965 and 1966, he saw Rustin as sad and pathetic, an Uncle Tom whose true colors had been revealed, and in public debates fiercely criticized his former mentor. Meanwhile, in the pages of *Liberation,* the magazine Rustin had helped found, the young radical historian Staughton Lynd leveled blistering charges at Rustin. He accused Rustin of advocating "coalition with the marines," of embracing "elitism," and—the most damaging description of all on the Left—of serving as a "labor lieutenant of capitalism."[48]

The critique of Rustin that was made then, and repeated since, can be neatly contained within the categories of left-wing political discourse. What, then, do Rustin's ideas and actions in the post–March on Washington, post–stigmatized-pervert period, have to do with gay history? A great deal, I think. Something more was happening here, and to speculate about it admittedly involves reaching beyond a hard base of evidence. But let me suggest some connections.

First, Rustin's political perspective was unique among those who had shared his political history in the peace and nonviolent direct-action movements—those, in other words, who were self-consciously radical and who occupied a place marginal to the American political system. For instance, in the same article in which Staughton Lynd criticized Rustin for coalition politics, his own more typical "radical" proposal was to convene a people's "continental congress." Rustin, I believe, grasped the bankruptcy of radical marginality in a way that few of his peers did. Having repeatedly suffered from the stigma of the sexual-pervert label, he had lost all attachment to left-wing romanticism. His colleagues may also have been marginal to the political system, but many of them returned home at night to intentional communities grounded in heterosexual patterns of familial sociability. Not Rustin. In 1963, he was fifty-one years old, without a long-term intimate relationship, and, at least politically, he was searching for something more than a place at the periphery.

Secondly, Rustin argued for his political strategy without an institutional base. For years, the WRL had generously lent Rustin, its executive secretary, to the civil rights movement. But, after the March on Washington, Rustin was drawn more and more toward issues of race and economic justice, and as peace activities intensified, the WRL needed a full-time leader. Rustin was thus moving from one short-term, insecure job to another. He and Randolph tried to convert the March on Washington coalition into a permanent organization, but those plans fell victim to organizational rivalries and battles over turf.[49]

Given his level of skill and accomplishment, Rustin's free-floating status can only be attributed to the continuing stigma of his sexual identity. Even though the overt gay-baiting seemed finally to have been resolved on the eve of the March on Washington, the discomfort with Rustin's sexuality lingered. For instance, throughout late 1963 and early 1964, Martin Luther King debated with his advisers—men with whom Rustin was closely associated—whether it was now safe to bring Rustin onto the staff. One senses that King wanted to retain Rustin. But in the end he backed away, and he did so by revising his own history on the issue. In these private conversations, King explained his 1960 dismissal of Rustin not as caving in to Powell's threats, but as a response to Rustin's unrestrained sexual behavior. As King explained to one associate, "I think he controls himself pretty well until he gets to drinking and he would approach these students and they started talking with people about it and there was something of a reflection on me so that was really the main problem."[50] The outcome left Rustin without an institutional home. And his lack of organizational roots made him vulnerable; it made it harder for him to implement his ideas and easier for others to dismiss him.

Third, even when one acknowledges the sharp language of leftist debates, there was a level of invective, a tone of scorn, directed at Rustin that went beyond political disagreement. An example: In September 1963, Stanley Levison discussed with his brother the state of black politics. Levison was a former communist, a friend of Rustin, and a very close adviser to King, a relationship that they owed to Bayard. Levison's communist past was regularly invoked by J. Edgar Hoover and the Kennedy brothers to subvert King's effectiveness. In the conversation, Levison grouped James Baldwin and Rustin together and said that "the two were better qualified to lead a homo-sexual movement than a civil rights movement." A few days later, to a business associate, he described Rustin as "a shrieker," a word that, to me, connotes a gay queen.[51] Coming as these remarks did just a month after Rustin's Washington triumph and from someone best described as an armchair radical, the statements let us see the hidden homophobia in Rustin's world.

Finally, Rustin does, eventually, turn to the Right. Without a base, and indeed, without a job, he accepted the offer of Randolph to head a new institute that the elder leader proposed to create specifically for Rustin. The A. Philip Randolph Institute, devoted to the building of effective alliances between labor and the civil rights movement, remained Rustin's work venue for the rest of his life. But, funded as it was by the AFL-CIO, the institute was necessarily constrained in its ability to dissent from the liberal center of the Democratic Party. During the Vietnam era, this involved fateful compromises, which Rustin made. The war, whose effect on the nation and on the Left began to be felt just as the institute was being founded, would shrink the political ground that Rustin proposed to occupy, and he sought secure footing by moving to the Right, not the Left.

There was an element of resignation, perhaps even cynicism, in these final choices that sits uneasily alongside the profile of the younger Rustin. Shizu Proctor, who worked with Rustin at the FOR in the 1940s, remembers encountering him on the streets of New York about this time and questioning him. "You get tired after a while," he told her, "and you have to come home to something comfortable and something you can count on."[52] Should this response surprise us? For instance, late in 1964, Rustin supervised the arrangements for King's trip to Europe to accept the Nobel Peace Prize. Upon his return, he described to two friends an incident in Oslo.

One morning in the wee hours, Rustin was called by hotel security to deal with a potentially ugly situation. Apparently, Norwegian prostitutes were running naked through the halls, in and out of the rooms of King's brother and other members of the entourage. Rustin succeeded in keeping these events out of the papers, but what must have run through the mind of this man, whose sexuality had so often been used against him? The homophobia of American society and the response of his associates to Rustin's gay identity are deeply implicated in the political choices he made during these years.[53]

In the end, I think we can fathom at least two layers of gay meaning to Rustin's story. The first is a relatively poignant tale of one man's life and the ever widening circle of disclosure about his identity, stretching from the 1940s through the 1960s. Rustin's identity provoked a series of confrontations within the American Left about homosexuality that can be characterized—at least in its *public* manifestations—as a movement from ostracism to acceptance. In that regard, the debate about Rustin foreshadowed developments within American society as a whole.

But Rustin's career offers us a story of much broader significance, a story still gay in its meanings, a story of political alternatives proposed and then abandoned. Rustin's move from margin to center—and then back again—is a tale of gay oppression whose consequences have reverberated loudly in American politics from then until now.

Notes

1. See Jonathan Katz, *Gay American History* (New York: Thomas Crowell, 1976); *Gay/Lesbian Almanac* (New York: Harper and Row, 1983); John D'Emilio, *Sexual Politics, Sexual Communities: The Making of a Homosexual Minority in the United States, 1940–1970* (Chicago: University of Chicago Press, 1983); Martin Duberman, Martha Vicinus, and George Chauncey, eds., *Hidden from History: Reclaiming the Gay and Lesbian Past* (New York: New American Library, 1989); Allan Berube, *Coming Out Under Fire: The History of Gay Men and Women in World War II* (New York: Free Press, 1990); Lillian Faderman, *Odd Girls and Twilight Lovers: A History of Lesbian Life in Twentieth-Century America* (New York: Columbia University Press, 1991); Martin Duberman, *About Time: Exploring the Gay Past* (New York: Penguin, 1991); *Stonewall* (New York: Dutton, 1993); Elizabeth Lapovsky Kennedy and Madeline D. Davis, *Boots of Leather, Slippers of Gold: The History of a Lesbian Community* (New York: Routledge, 1993); Esther Newton, *Cherry Grove, Fire Island: Sixty Years in America's First Gay and Lesbian Town* (Boston: Beacon Press, 1993); and George Chauncey, *Gay New York: Gender, Urban Culture, and the Making of the Gay Male World, 1890–1940* (New York: Basic Books, 1994). There are also a significant number of gay and lesbian history articles in Kathy Peiss and Christina Simmons, eds., *Passion and Power: Sexuality in History* (Philadelphia: Temple University Press, 1989).

2. Of the books cited above, Berube's is least characterized by this gay focus, studying as it does the interaction of gays, the military, and psychiatry.

3. Bayard Rustin, "From Protest to Politics," *Commentary,* 39 (February 1965): 25–31.

4. Material on Rustin's first twenty-nine years, until he joined the staff of the Fellowship of Reconciliation (FOR) in 1941, is sparse. For information about his years in West Chester, see Rustin interview, Columbia University Oral History Project (hereafter CUOHP). See also the following material in the Chester County Historical Society collections, in West Chester, Pennsylvania: Rustin Family file in clippings collection; issues of *The Garnet and White,* the yearbook of West Chester High School, 1930–1932; and coverage of athletic events and commencement exercises in the West Chester *Daily Local News,* 1930–1932. The only significant biographical account of Rustin in print can be found in Milton Viorst, *Fire in the Streets: America in the 1960s* (New York: Simon and Schuster, 1979), 197–231. A full biography of Rustin by Jervis Anderson is currently near completion.

5. For contextual information on the Communist Party and on the student movement of the 1930s, see Mark Naison, *Communists in Harlem during the Depression* (Urbana: University of Illinois Press, 1983), and Robert Cohen, *When the Old Left Was Young: Student Radicals and America's First Mass Student Movement, 1929–1941* (New York: Oxford University Press, 1993). On his work with the American Friends Service Committee (AFSC), see "Peace Section Institutes. 1929–37," and "Peace Section. Mexico and Puerto Rico, 1939–41," in AFSC Archives, Philadelphia.

6. Rustin discusses his initial contacts with Randolph in his oral history at Columbia. The circumstances under which he met Muste remain unknown to me, but by the summer of 1941 they were corresponding, and arrangements had been made for Rustin to begin working at the FOR. See Muste to Rustin, July 29, 1941, and Rustin to Muste, August 5, 1941, in Fellowship of Reconciliation Papers, Document Group 13, Series D, Box 21, Puerto Rico Folder, Swarthmore College Peace Collection (hereafter SCPC). On Randolph's career, see Jervis Anderson, *A. Philip Randolph: A Biographical Portrait* (New York: Harcourt Brace Jovanovich, 1973); William H. Harris, *Keeping the Faith: A. Philip Randolph, Milton P. Webster, and the Brotherhood of Sleeping Car Porters, 1925–37* (Urbana: University of Illinois Press, 1977); and Paula F. Pfeffer, *A. Philip Randolph: Pioneer of the Civil Rights Movement* (Baton Rouge: Louisiana State University Press, 1990). On Muste, see Jo Ann Ooiman Robinson, *Abraham Went Out: A Biography of A. J. Muste* (Philadelphia: Temple University Press, 1981), and Nat Hentoff, *Peace Agitator: The Story of A. J. Muste* (New York: Macmillan, 1963).

7. On Rustin's activities, see FOR Papers, DG 13, Box 3, Executive Committee Meeting Minutes; Box 3, Reports; Box 10, Rustin Folder; and Series D, Box 1, Writings and Speeches, all in SCPC. On the peace movement, see Lawrence J. Wittner, *Rebels Against War: The American Peace Movement, 1933–1983* (Philadelphia: Temple University Press, 1984), esp. chap. 2.

8. On the early years of CORE, see August Meier and Elliott Rudwick, *CORE: A Study in the Civil Rights Movement, 1942–1968* (Urbana: University of Illinois Press, 1975), chap. 1, and James Farmer, *Lay Bare the Heart: An Autobiography of the Civil Rights Movement* (New York: Penguin, 1985).

9. Rustin to Muste, February 22, 1943, in FOR Papers, DG 13, Box 10, Rustin Folder, SCPC.

10. Material on Rustin's time in federal prison may be found in the file of his letters to Davis Platt, in Platt's possession, New York City, and in General Correspondence, 1944–1945,

Reel 20, Bayard Rustin Papers, UPA Microfilms (1988). For other discussions of conscientious objectors in prison during World War II, see James Tracy, "Forging Dissent in an Age of Consensus: Radical Pacifism in America, 1940–1970," Ph.D. diss., Stanford University, 1992, and David Dellinger, *From Yale to Jail: The Life Story of a Moral Dissenter* (New York: Pantheon, 1993).

11. Detailed accounts of the Journey of Reconciliation may be found in the "Log of the Journey" and in "Journey of Reconciliation: A Report by George Houser and Bayard Rustin," both in FOR Papers, DG 13, Series D, Box 1, SCPC. See also the brief account in Meier and Rudwick, *CORE,* 33–40. Rustin wrote a report on jail conditions in North Carolina, where he was sentenced, in which he discussed the subject of homosexuality in prison. See Rustin, "A Report on Twenty-Two Days on the Chain Gang at Roxboro, North Carolina," typescript, 1949, in Rustin File, CDG-A, SCPC.

12. On the campaign to end segregation in the military, see the material in A. Philip Randolph Papers, Boxes 15 and 16, Library of Congress (hereafter LC).

13. See, for example, the account of a month-long campaign in Washington, D.C., during July 1947: "The Interracial Workshop: A Report by George Houser and Bayard Rustin," in FOR Papers, DG 13, Series D, Box 1, SCPC.

14. Quotations are from my interviews with Roy Finch, March 8, 1993, and Glenn Smiley, November 14, 1992. For one account of Rustin's courage under pressure see "Non-Violence vs. Jim Crow," *Fellowship,* July 1942, p. 120.

15. On Rustin's thinking about Africa, see "Report on Trip to Africa," October 20, 1952, in FOR Papers, DG 13, Series D, Box 1, SCPC; and Rustin to Muste, November 30, 1952, in War Resisters League Papers, DG 40, Series B, Box 18, SCPC.

16. "Lecturer Jailed on Morals Charge," *Los Angeles Times,* January 22, 1953, and "Lecturer Sentenced to Jail on Morals Charge," *Los Angeles Times,* January 23, 1953, both in *Congressional Record,* Senate, August 13, 1963, p. 14837.

17. Information in this paragraph comes from the following interviews: Davis Platt, July 17, 1992, and December 14, 1993; Shizu Proctor, October 10, 1993; John Swomley, November 18, 1993; and Doris Grotewohl Baker, June 19, 1994.

18. Rustin to Platt, April 5, 1945, correspondence in the possession of Davis Platt.

19. Rustin to Platt, April 20, 1945, correspondence in the possession of Davis Platt.

20. Muste to Rustin, June 18, 1945, and July 4, 1945, both in Bayard Rustin Papers, Reel 20, Correspondence—1945, UPA Microfilms.

21. Information on the 1946 incident comes from a lengthy FBI memorandum on Rustin dated August 16, 1963, detailing his political affiliations, record of arrests, and foreign travel, obtained by the author through a Freedom of Information Act request. With regard to other incidents, see Rustin to Judge James Lanzetta, October 28, 1947, and Rustin to Dear Friend, October 10, 1947, both in FOR Papers, DG 13, Series D, Box 1, SCPC; additional information came from the author's interviews with John Swomley and Glenn Smiley.

22. FOR statement, adopted January 28, 1953, in FOR Papers, DG 13, Series D, Box 1, SCPC. For reactions to it, see the correspondence in General Administration, Individuals—Bayard Rustin, 1953, AFSC Archives; and the two memos of Roy Finch to the Executive Committee and National Advisory Committee of the War Resisters League, one from August 25, 1953, and the other undated, in WRL Papers, DG 40, Series B, Box 1, SCPC.

23. Rustin to Swomley, March 8, 1953, in FOR Papers, DG 13, Swomley Collection, Box 2, Rustin Folder, SCPC. Ironically, Rustin's arrest occurred at a moment when the Mattachine Society was growing rapidly in Los Angeles because of the group's challenge to police entrapment practices. Gerry Brissette, a young pacifist from northern California, heard of Rustin's arrest, wrote to the Mattachine Society, and proceeded to organize the first chapter of the Mattachine in the Bay Area. See Brissette to Mattachine Foundation, February 15, 1953, and Freeman to Brissette, February 23, 1953, in James Kepner Papers, Los Angeles.

24. See the memos of Roy Finch to the Executive Committee and National Advisory Committee of the War Resisters League, one from August 25, 1953 and the other undated, in WRL Papers, DG 40, Series B, Box 1, SCPC.

25. For a discussion of both initiatives, see Maurice Isserman, *If I Had a Hammer: The Death of the Old Left and the Birth of the New Left* (1987; repr. Urbana: University of Illinois Press, 1993), chap. 4.

26. Two important accounts of the Montgomery bus boycott, King's career, and Rustin's relationship with King are David J. Garrow, *Bearing the Cross: Martin Luther King, Jr., and the Southern Christian Leadership Conference* (New York: William Morrow, 1986), and Taylor Branch, *Parting the Waters: America in the King Years, 1954–63* (New York: Simon and Schuster, 1988).

27. For reactions to Rustin's trip to Montgomery, see Smiley to Swomley, February 29, 1956; Swomley to Riles, February 21, 1956; Swomley to Smiley, February 29, 1956 (three letters), and March 1, 1956, all in Swomley Papers, Box 2, SCPC. See also Swomley to Walker, n.d., Rustin Papers, Reel 4; and James Farmer Interview, CUOHP.

28. On Rustin's role in Montgomery and his early work with Martin Luther King, see Rustin to Brown, February 23, 1956, and Rustin to Brown and DiGia, both in CDG-A, Rustin file, SCPC; Rustin to King, May 9, 1956, and King to Rustin, September 20, 1956, both in Rustin Papers, Reel 3; Homer Jack Memo, March 9, 1956, in Rustin Papers, Reel 4; Rustin to King, March 8, 1956, Box 5, Folder 29, and Rustin to King, October 18, 1956, Box 64A, Folder 22, both in King Papers, Boston University. Rustin published an account of his first trip to Montgomery. See "Montgomery Diary," *Liberation* (April 1956): 7–10.

29. Rustin to King, May 10, 1957, in King Papers, Box 34, Folder 35, Boston University.

30. For information on the Prayer Pilgrimage and the youth marches, see the material in Rustin Papers, Reels 4 and 6, UPA Microfilms; and Randolph Papers, Boxes 30, 33, and 34, LC.

31. See, for example, his article, "To the Finland Station," *Liberation* (June 1958): 9–10.

32. Rustin, "New South, Old Politics," *Liberation* (October 1956): 23–26; emphasis in original. Rustin's thinking in this area bears a similarity to ideas associated with Max Shachtman, a Trotskyist active in the anti-Stalinist Left in New York. From the late 1950s onward, two of Rustin's closest associates were Tom Kahn, who became his lover for a time, and Rachelle Horowitz. Both were members of the Young People's Socialist League, and both were close to Shachtman. Whether Rustin's thinking about political realignment, already evident by 1956, influenced Shachtman and his followers, or whether the intellectual influence flowed in the other direction, is still unclear to me and requires further investigation. For a discussion of Shachtman and his influence on the Left in the 1950s and 1960s, see Isserman, *If I Had a Hammer,* chaps. 2 and 5.

33. Peck to Rustin, November 16, 1959, in Committee for Nonviolent Action Papers, DG 17, Box 13, Sahara Correspondence, SCPC. For more on the 1960 project see material in Rustin papers, Reel 1, "Election—1960" folder; CDG-A, Rustin folder, SCPC; and SNCC Papers, Subgroup A, Series I, Box 1, Folder 20, Martin Luther King Center Archives, Atlanta.

34. On the Powell incident, see *Pittsburgh Courier,* June 25, 1960, p. 3, and July 9, 1960, p. 2; the press release announcing Rustin's resignation, June 27, 1960, in CDG-A, Rustin file, SCPC; Rustin interview, CUOHP; and the accounts in Garrow, *Bearing the Cross,* 138–40, and Branch, *Parting the Waters,* 314–18.

35. Interview with David McReynolds, March 5, 1993.

36. See James Baldwin, "The Dangerous Road before Martin Luther King," *Harper's Magazine,* February 1961, pp. 33–42.

37. On Rustin's European work see CNVA Papers, Series VI, Boxes 14–16, "San Francisco to Moscow Peace Work," SCPC. On his African work see A. J. Muste Papers, Box 40, Folder 6, SCPC.

38. Material on the Birmingham demonstrations and on the March on Washington is voluminous. See the accounts in Garrow and Branch, previously cited in note 34. For Rustin's analysis of Birmingham see Rustin, "The Meaning of Birmingham," *Liberation* (June 1963): 7–9.

39. For accounts of the meeting, see Rustin Interview, CUOHP, and Milton Viorst's interview with John Lewis, 1976, in Howard University Civil Rights Collection.

40. See *Congressional Record,* Senate, August 2, 1963, pp. 13968–75; August 7, pp. 14454–63; and August 13, 14836–44. The designation of "Mr. March-on-Washington" comes from the *Washington Post,* August 11, 1963, p. A6. For concerns about Rustin, see the FBI memo dated August 11, 1963, reporting on a conversation between Martin Luther King and Ted Brown, obtained through Freedom of Information Act request. For discussions of the FBI and the civil rights movement, see David J. Garrow, *The FBI and Martin Luther King, Jr.* (New York: Penguin, 1983), and Kenneth O'Reilly, *"Racial Matters": The FBI's Secret File on Black America, 1960–1972* (New York: Free Press, 1989).

41. *Philadelphia Sunday Bulletin,* August 18, 1963, p. 1.

42. *Philadelphia Inquirer,* August 27, 1983, clipping in Chester County Historical Society.

43. See Bayard Rustin, "The Meaning of the March," *Liberation* (October 1963): 11–13.

44. *Life* magazine, for its issue of September 6, 1963, used for its cover a photo of Randolph and Rustin in front of the Lincoln Memorial. Newsweek captioned a photo of Rustin "Out of the Shadows," September 2, 1963, p. 18. King and his associates began discussing whether to invite Rustin to work for the Southern Christian Leadership Conference as early as September 10, 1963. See FBI Memo, New York Office, Bureau File 100-106670, September 11, 1963. One unwelcome sign of Rustin's newly acquired prominence is that the FBI decided, in the fall of 1963, to place him under electronic surveillance.

45. For information on these aspects of Rustin's work, see the following: on the school boycott, Rustin Papers, Reels 11 and 12, LC; on the Albany march, Rustin Papers, Reel 3, LC; on the Freedom Budget, Rustin Papers, Reels 13 and 14, LC; on the "State of the Race" Conference, Randolph Papers, Box 31, LC; on King and Vietnam, see King Papers, Series I, Boxes 29 and 31, King Center, Atlanta. There is also a great deal of information about Vietnam scattered through Rustin's FBI file.

46. Information on Rustin's role in the call for a moratorium and at Atlantic City comes from the almost daily FBI reports filed on Rustin during the summer of 1964. On Rustin's criticisms of the antiwar movement see Rustin Papers, Reel 6, War Resisters League File, LC.

47. Rustin, "From Protest to Politics," *Commentary* 39 (February 1965): 25–31. The choice of *Commentary* as a venue for his ideas was itself significant. Most of Rustin's writing in the previous half-dozen years had appeared in the self-consciously radical *Liberation; Commentary* in the 1950s and 1960s addressed an audience of Cold War liberals.

48. For Carmichael's comments, see Milton Viorst, *Fire in the Streets,* 350, 355. See also Staughton Lynd, "Coalition Politics or Nonviolent Revolution?", *Liberation* (June–July 1965): 18–21. David Dellinger was also sharply critical of Rustin. See David Dellinger, "The March on Washington and Its Critics," *Liberation* (May 1965): 6–7. The edge to these articles was so sharp that it provoked a defense of Rustin by David McReynolds: "Transition: Personal and Political Notes," *Liberation* (August 1965): 5–10.

49. On the conflicts over the March on Washington organization, see, for instance, Betti Whaley to Whitney Young, September 27, 1963, and Young to Randolph, January 29, 1964, both in National Urban League Papers, Part II, Series I, Box 25, LC.

50. FBI Memo, New York Office, August 11, 1963, Bureau File 100–106670.

51. Special Agent in Charge, New York, to Director, FBI, Air Telegram, September 23, 1963, in King and Levison FBI File, Box 8, Section 10, King Center, Atlanta. On the Levison-King relationship, see Garrow, *The FBI and Martin Luther King, Jr.*

52. Interview with Shizu Proctor, October 10, 1993.

53. Baumgardner to Sullivan, December 17, 1964, FBI Memo, Subject: Martin Luther King, Jr.

Part Three

Science, Fictions

8

Perverting the Diagnosis

The Lesbian and the Scientific Basis of Stigma

ALLIDA M. BLACK

SEXOLOGISTS have always equated female homosexuality with female neurosis; thus, they have never been able to recognize any difference between the two behaviors. Indeed, the more they try to analyze the two, the more confused sexologists become. Whether they are overtly critical of "sexual nervousness," condescendingly sympathetic with congenital "inversion," or painstakingly endorsing the "masculinity complex," the sexologists of the late nineteenth and early twentieth centuries never could transcend the physical and mental boundaries they sometimes criticized their neurological colleagues for adopting. Consequently, while sexologists and psychoanalysts from Carl Westphal to Sigmund Freud to Irving Bieber may differ on the extent to which sexual behavior is genetically determined, all agree that when female homosexuality is the subject, to a great extent, biology is destiny.[1]

Such eager acceptance of sexual neurosis as the defining characteristic of lesbianism not only shaped the way the mental health community viewed lesbians throughout the twentieth century, but also encouraged a diagnostic protocol that encouraged lesbians to see their behavior as diseased and dangerous. Once lesbians internalized this self-deprecating analysis, it became increasingly difficult for them to reconcile their sexuality with their humanity.

Implicit acceptance of neurasthenia is central to the sexological interpretation. Popularized in the late nineteenth century by physician George Beard, neurasthenics argued that "the body is a bundle of reflex actions" that if irritated "in one place will produce an irritation in another." Sexual desire was of particular interest to neurasthenics, who proclaimed that any extension of the brain or reproductive system could, without warning, inspire "a chronic functional disease of the nervous system" that could promote "hysteria or sexual perversion."[2]

Just as American physicians and gynecologists argued that neurasthenia was a natural physical response to unnatural sexual and intellectual activity, European sexologists preached that a genetic "taint" predisposed women to act in a sexually "abnormal" way. Taking the argument one step further, sexologists diligently tried to promote a delicate sexual balance among sexually active Victorian women that promoted marital intercourse as a moral and social obligation while condemning nonreproductive sexual gratification as selfish, nymphomaniacal excess.

Not only did they believe earlier claims that neuro-uterine dysfunction adversely shaped female sexuality, but they also argued that the appearance of a strange androgynous gene dominated some women's sexual development so strongly that it inverted their sexual identity. To Edward Carpenter, this genetic strain created a new androgynous "intermediate sex," neither male nor female. To Carl Ulrichs, it neurologically constructed a distinct "third sex." Even Havelock Ellis, who thought the third-sex metaphor excessive, nevertheless conceded that "a more or less distinct trace of masculinity" spurred "the girl who is congenitally predisposed to homosexuality."[3]

Such unquestioning allegiance to sexual predestination fostered a diagnostic framework that was both superficial and restrictive: superficial because the sexologists never wondered whether homosexuals could be responding to forces other than their own genetic composition, and restrictive because they refused to examine nonbiological influences on sexual conduct. Consequently, by eliminating all other avenues of investigation, the test group became no different from the control group and the results of the sexologists' investigation were predictable. As the historian Jeffrey Weeks astutely observed, when biology is the "avenue into the mysteries of Nature, . . . what existed 'in Nature' derived evidence for what was human."[4]

This climate of sexual Darwinism defined the terms of the debate over female sexuality in general, and lesbian sexuality in particular. Ironically, while most of the sexologists discussed in this essay thought they presented a rational plea for tolerance, what they in fact proposed was a one-dimensional portrait of lesbian sexual conduct, which argued that lesbianism was simultaneously perverse and uncontrollable. This diagnosis fed into the cultural schizophrenia that characterized Victorian heterosexuality. Moreover, it reinforced common support for what contemporary historians have labeled "shattered nerves" and promoted a diagnostic framework that refused to differentiate between sex and society, lesbianism and pathology.[5]

Such tacit acceptance of this neurological framework by medical and mental health professionals had dramatic consequences for both mental health professionals and lesbians. First, it fostered a subconscious bias against lesbians that dominated the way lesbians were viewed by these "experts" for the next century. As Lillian Faderman has thoroughly documented, it promoted "the morbidification of love between women." Second, as Andrea Dworkin has argued, the initial sexological tomes, especially Havelock Ellis's *Studies in the Psychology of Sex,* provided the evidence necessary to codify male sexual values. Third, it created a climate that encouraged sexologists and mental health professionals to view lesbianism as the manifestation of women who were trapped in roles that confused love with pain.

Lastly, by agreeing with Magnus Hirschfeld that "a sexual ethics based on science is the only sound system of ethics," the sexologists adopted a condescendingly moral tone, which implied that lesbianism was an amoral neurosis.[6]

Although the early sexologists believed that they were transcending the moral trappings that dominated the views of physicians who saw women's sexual activity as a dangerous neurological malfunction, the sexologists only deluded themselves. Sexologists did not bypass contemporary social mores in their assessment of lesbianism. Rather, their protestations to the contrary, the early sexologists merely replaced neurasthenic and other pseudoneurological classifications with a prescription even more detrimental to lesbian health. When sexologists and their colleagues combined what historian Janet Oppenheim has called "the power of positive thinking with the influence of a father confessor" and praised only the lesbian who refused to act out her emotional and sexual feelings, their insistent praise of abstinence effectively condemned all other actions and expressions. While they claimed to believe that the lesbian was not to blame because she could not help herself, the sexologists nevertheless defended only those lesbians who refused to act out their emotional and sexual desires. As Alfred Kinsey caustically noted almost half a century later, when his precursors pleaded for toleration of sexual deviation as a medical condition, they only served to reinforce "scientific classifications . . . [which were] nearly identical with theologic classifications and with the moral pronouncements of the English common law."[7]

Consequently, as the following brief overview demonstrates, sexologists and their colleagues encouraged the lesbian not only to see herself as both a blemished personality and threat to society, but also to believe that happiness and lesbian sexuality were mutually exclusive. This attitude, in turn, created a climate within the lesbian population that perpetuated the stigma the sexologists claimed to want to erase and that formed the foundation psychoanalysts investigating lesbianism would adopt throughout the next century.

As the first sexologist to use the case study method to examine lesbian activity, Carl Westphal applied George Beard's concept of sexual nervousness to paint a portrait of the lesbian as one who succumbed to a "contrary sexual feeling," which was inspired by an "inherited diseased condition of the central nervous system." Yet despite Westphal's emphasis on neurological causation, a profound moral ambivalence characterizes his depiction of his patient. Although he acknowledged that women who loved other women and who wanted to act out this affection in a sexual manner were responding to "cerebral abnormalities," he also portrayed this affection as a "functional sign of degeneration." Trapped in behavior they were helpless to change, Westphal's lesbians were nevertheless tainted by the "abnormality" of their congenital desire. Legally sane, but morally tarnished, these women were relegated to a category that emphasized the schizophrenic and oxymoronic nature of their "affliction."[8]

Once Westphal introduced this image, it ricocheted throughout the sexological, medical, and psychological communities with such rapidity that it became accepted as fact, rather than examined as theory. Indeed, those interested in regulating sexuality by shaping public opinion were so eager to have "scientific" data as proof positive of their argument that they pounced on any theory that could lend credence to their own argument. As a review of the works of Richard von Krafft-Ebing, Edward Carpenter, Havelock Ellis, Magnus Hirschfeld, and their contemporaries reveals, no matter what weight sexologists gave to different specific neurological impulses, they all agreed that lesbian activity revealed a predisposed biological and emotional pseudomasculinity. This widespread stereotype, in turn, reinforced the popular perception that any deviation from the sexual norm was in fact both "neurological" and "neurotic." By failing to distinguish between the two, the sexologists not only tainted their subjects in the public eye, but infantilized them by proclaiming that even if they wanted to, lesbians could not control their hearts and minds.

Consequently, despite their avowed intent of destigmatizing homosexuality, when the sexologists discussed homosexuality among women, the neurasthenic gender parallel held: Just as the neurological stimulus for masturbation created a climate that left neurasthenic women short-circuited and depleted, the somatic impulse to homosexual activity left women nervous, sick, and perverse. Even medico-legal experts committed to reforming sexual statutes and physicians seeking neurological cures for this predisposition agreed that there was no possible alternative. The situation was critical, Krafft-Ebing asserted. Unless the medical community intervened, Nature would rise "in her power and lead . . . the helpless, unprotected [invert] into dangerous by-paths" associated with her "antipathic sexual instinct."[9]

In short, by defining lesbian sexuality as a neurological malfunction inspired by a genetic quirk, and by refusing to reject categorically the neurasthenic model in the process, sexologists unwittingly abetted the construction of a social attitude that promoted viewpoints undercutting their own pleas for tolerance and compassion. Moreover, as Lillian Faderman argues, and as a close reading of late-nineteenth- and early-twentieth-century sexologists reveal, while all sexologists, whether they be heterosexual or homosexual, unite in their pleas for understanding of male homosexuals, they are deliberately hostile toward lesbian conduct, labeling lesbianism a "spurious imitation" of heterosexual love.[10]

If neurasthenia was the central medical component in the sexologists' diagnosis, they believed the lesbian's predominant identification with masculine sexualness was the core of her sexual activity. Adamant in their conviction that each sex had personality traits specific to its gender, sexologists emphasized the dominant nature of masculinity and its widespread effect on the lesbian personality. The "scientific" case studies that they so prominently presented in their discussions reinforced the image of a woman trying to live like a man. To Westphal and his followers, the sexually active lesbian was a woman who thought like a man, desired and masturbated like a man, and had sex like a man. Carpenter's "homogenic woman" lived in a body "thoroughly feminine and gracious . . . , but in which the inner nature is to [such] a great extent masculine" that it promoted a "fiery, active, bold" sexuality often boardering on "brusqueness and coarseness." Krafft-Ebing described the typical female invert as a "masculine soul, heaving in the female bosom," who found "pleasure in the pursuit of manly sports, and in manifestations of courage and bravado" and who had a "strong desire to imitate the male fashion in dressing the hair and in general style." Havelock Ellis, ever the popularizer of theories promoted by his contemporaries, produced a myriad of case studies to substantiate this claim. Therefore, he could rely on Westphal, Krafft-Ebing, and Carpenter to argue, first, that there was some, albeit not much, variety in the way lesbians had sex, and second, that because they were unable to control these sexually aggressive instincts, lesbians were predisposed to violence.[11]

Striking visual imagery accompanies this image of the lesbian as a woman who wished to behave in a traditionally masculine way. According to the studies presented in sexological tracts, lesbians suffered from elongated clitorises or hermaphrodism, a desire for penal substitutes, and the constant urge to cross-dress or masturbate. Unable to reconcile the image of female tenderness with lesbian sex, sexologists presented portraits of lesbianism that focused more on deviation than tenderness. For example, while Ellis began his summation of lesbian sex by declaring that "homosexual passion in women finds more or less complete expression in kissing, sleeping together, and close embraces," he concluded his overview by discussing cunnilingus and the "by no means uncommon and very widespread use" of an "artificial penis." Consequently, their claims to the contrary, the Founding Fathers of Sexology promoted an image of the lesbian that only the most tolerant and empathetic segments of the population could support.[12]

Such conflicting oxymoronic assessments placed lesbians in a psychological dilemma. Implicit in this diagnosis was the sexologists' message that while lesbians had a legal right to pursue their predisposition, happiness and inversion were mutually exclusive. Nowhere is this more clearly illustrated than in the most often quoted passage of *Sexual Inversion in Women,* Ellis's description of Patient XXXVI, a woman who

> finds sexual satisfaction in tenderly touching, caressing, and kissing the loved one's body. . . . She believes that homosexual love is morally right when it is really part of a person's nature, and provided that the nature of homosexual love is always made plain to the object of such affection. She does not approve of it as a mere makeshift, or the expression of sensuality. . . . She has sometimes resisted the sexual expression of her feelings, once for years at a time, but always in vain. The effect of her loving women is distinctly good, she asserts, both spiritually and physically, while repression leads to morbidity and hysteria.[13]

Yet immediately after recording her views, Ellis brusquely dismissed them. Patient XXXVI "has suffered much from neurasthenia at various periods" and "the inverted instinct is too deeply rooted to eradicate."[14] But when the identity of Patient XXXVI is revealed, Ellis's underlying motivations for discounting her pleasure become apparent. Miss H., or Patient XXXVI, was Edith Lees, Ellis's wife. And while Ellis could espouse commitment to sexual freedom within marriage, when his wife had a passionate affair with "Claire" the year after their marriage, Ellis, while philosophically agreeing that other emotional involvements were acceptable, was disconsolate that Edith's new partner was a woman. Consequently, for years Ellis strove to rationalize their asexual commitment to one another. Discounting his own obsession with undinism, or watching women urinate, as well as his own virginity, Ellis later recalled:

> Even my strong sense of justice could scarcely have tolerated so one-sided a sexual freedom in marriage. It might be true that I was exclusively heterosexual and she was not, and that therefore there was no demand for me to go outside marriage for love. But it was also true that the very qualities in her nature which made her largely homosexual were qualities which fortifying as they might be to our comradeship, were inimical to the purely feminine qualities of sweetness and repose which a man seeks in woman.[15]

Sigmund Freud agreed. Picking up where the sexologists left off, the father of psychoanalysis expanded the areas under investigation only to reach the same conclusion. According to this new viewpoint, the lesbian suffered not only from an abnormal physical development and a strong sexual identification with masculine aggression, but also from an unrestrained love-hate relationship with her father. This incestuous fixation, which Freud labeled the Electra complex, combined with a "physical and psychical hermaphroditism" to promote a "strongly marked 'masculinity complex'." Consequently, once again the lesbian had no choice but to follow her own "perversion."[16]

Why did the great analyst reach these conclusions? Because like Ellis, Freud believed that the characteristics associated with male-female camaraderie were in fact detrimental to heterosexual sexual relationships. The lesbian "had developed a pronounced envy for the penis, and the thoughts she derived from this envy still continued to fill her mind." This jealousy arrested her "normal" development and she "changed into a man . . . [who] took her mother in place of her father as the object of her love."[17]

Like his sexological predecessors, Freud believed that he was being supportive of his client. He carefully noted her positive character traits, such as her "masculine . . . acuteness of comprehension and lucid objectivity." Nevertheless, Freud concluded that his patient was in fact diseased. She had succumbed to a masculine object-choice, adopted a "masculine sexual attitude," and followed the innate desires of her physical hermaphroditism. Because this woman was unrepentant in her desire to love women—"She was in fact a feminist . . . and rebelled against the lot of women in general"—the analysis did not achieve the results that Freud intended. Reflecting on this case years later, Freud wrote that his failure to "cure" this woman's "desires" led him to conclude that "it was not for psychoanalysts to solve the *problem* of homosexuality."[18]

This admission of analytic limitations did not stop Freud's followers from trying to prove their mentor wrong. As Vern Bullough painstakingly proves, no profession spent more time trying to trace the causes of and develop a cure for homosexuality than psychiatry. From the 1930s through the 1970s, such renowned analysts as Helen Deutsch, Sandor Rado, and Charles Socarides never doubted Irving Bieber's contention that "homosexuality is psychopathologic." Indeed, as Ronald Bayer declared in *Homosexuality and Psychiatry,* "for almost forty years . . . the psychoanalytic movement . . . held that homosexuality was an irreversible abnormality" that had both somatic and neurotic origins. Instead the issue the neo-Freudians tackled the most became not whether lesbianism was a perversion, but only what type of perversion it was. Was it purely neurological? Was it both psychosomatic and psychologic? Was it merely an abnormal manifestation of arrested normal sexual desire? Or was it a desperate attempt of frustrated women to overcompensate for their lack of status within their own families and in society at large?[19]

Consider the reaction of one of Freud's star pupils, Helen Deutsch, when one of her clients was cured of depression and suicidal tendencies only after she embraced her lesbianism. Deutsch worried how her mentor and other colleagues would react to this development. Indeed Deutsch was so distressed over this client's enthusiastic acceptance of lesbianism that she refused to accept her mentor's praise, tersely dismissing Freud's congratulations with "but she's still a lesbian."[20] Ten years after this therapeutic relationship had terminated, Deutsch's dissatisfaction with this client was still apparent. Writing about lesbians in her opus magnum *The Psychology of Women,* Deutsch concluded that since lesbian sex was really displaced daughter-mother sexual gratification, there must have been overwhelming psychological reasons why she was unable to correct such "perversion."

> This relationship had a form that was unmistakably connected with early childhood functions. . . . [The patient's mother had tied her hands to the bed post when she was a child to keep her from masturbating and told the child that her activity was sinful.] With conscious understanding of their situation, the two women encountered a mother-child relation. . . . One had the impression that the feeling of happiness lay in the possibility of being able to play both roles. . . . It goes without saying that the experience fell far below what psychoanalysis demands of an adult personality; on the contrary in such infantile substitutes for sexual gratifications analysis sees the danger of and not the cure for neurotic illness. But sometimes the therapeutic goal can be achieved only through a compromise. In this case, analytic treatment did not lead to the patient's renouncing homosexuality and turning toward men;

> thus its real task was not fulfilled. But it succeeded in bringing the unhappy woman who was constantly on the verge of suicide to the point where . . . she could achieve tenderness and sexual gratification. A better solution of the fatal mother tie proved impossible.[21]

However, the remorse that Deutsch expressed over this "fatal tie" paled in comparison to the overt hostility her fellow neo-Freudians Alfred Adler, Edmund Bergler, and Otto Fenichel displayed toward lesbianism. Reverting to the obsession with male genitalia and masculine aggression that Freud believed inspired lesbian development, these three men argued in strident language that lesbians were women who despised men as individuals while coveting the power they associated with male social roles. To them, the lesbian was a woman who refused to resign herself to her "castrated" status, who subconsciously denied her penis envy, and who became a lesbian only after her "normal" development was "arrested." Having been deprived of the gratification she initially sought in life, these dissatisfied, embittered women "overcompensated" and turned toward other women for gratification. But, as Bergler repeatedly asserted, this could only lead to disappointment and further frustration, because happiness and lesbianism were mutually exclusive. "Even if the world left them in peace," lesbians would suffer because they "unconsciously want to be disappointed." After all, the analyst declared, "the amount of conflicts, of jealousy . . . between homosexuals surpasses everything known in bad heterosexual relationships."[22]

Since lesbians did not live apart from the heterosexual community, they repeatedly faced a mixed message. While on the one hand they could be excused because they could not choose another sexuality, on the other hand they must be castigated for the behavioral taint this predisposition caused. By championing this "damned if you do, damned if you don't" dichotomy, the early sexologists and psychoanalysts defined the debate over female homosexuality in terms that forced the women to see themselves as blemished and diseased.

While Lillian Faderman is correct in her assertions that the bias inherent in the early sexological assessment of lesbians gave great impetus to the psychoanalytic "morbidification" of lesbianism, that is only half the story. The double message sexologists and analysts sent to the lesbian population was, in the long run, much more destructive. Even if the neurasthenic malfunctions could be tamed and the sexual urges controlled, lesbians would be only "half-cured." For the inversion to be completely eliminated, the emotional and moral manifestations of lesbianism must be purged as well. Love and desire were just as dangerous and just as perverse as tribadism and lesbian sex. To be healthy, lesbians must understand that what they thought in their minds was just as diseased as what they felt inside their bodies.

This created a social and psychological atmosphere in which lesbians were helpless to change because of their genetic composition and arrested psychological development. This then encouraged lesbians to despise themselves because their advocates within the scientific community concluded that the conduct to which lesbians were genetically and affectionally predisposed was inherently inverted and perverse. In contemporary terms, the theory promoted by the sexologists encouraged the lesbians to blame themselves and to adopt society's heterosexual mores. This internalized homophobia in turn spurred self-deprecating and self-loathing behavior, which the analysts then argued was the cause rather than the result of social disapproval.

As John D'Emilio and Estelle Freedman argue, by the early 1920s "evidence abounded that women were internalizing" the sexologists' message. Studies of lesbian couples during that decade confirm D'Emilio and Freedman's assessment. Lesbians interviewed by Katherine Davis in the mid-1920s began to redefine their relationships in terms that clearly revealed how much they internalized the prevailing psychoanalytic assessment of lesbianism. Many women who believed that their relationships were nurturing and caring nevertheless categorized them as perverse, "abnormal," or "unnatural." Indeed these women believed the psychoanalytic influence on society's opinion of lesbians to be so strong that one woman pronounced that women who loved other women would be soon declared "pariahs, dirty evil things."[23]

Nor was this fear disclosed only behind the safety of physicians' walls. Radclyffe Hall, arguably the world's most famous lesbian, created Stephen Gordon, the lead character of her lesbian epic *The Well of Loneliness,* to reflect these concerns. Gordon was not only the quintessential masculine prototype who believed that she was unjustly trapped in a man's body, but also the sexually aggressive lesbian who finally acknowledged the futility of trying to maintain a lesbian relationship in a heterosexual world. Hall continued this theme in her prose as well. Indeed Hall believed so strongly that she was trapped in psychobiological purgatory that she reorganized her autobiography to reflect "the third sex" theory advocated by Ellis and his contemporaries.[24]

Even lesbians who disagreed with Hall's assessment and who were mortified by her depiction of lesbian life nevertheless admitted that they knew Ellis's and Freud's theories and spent a great deal of time refuting them when questioned about their sexuality. As a group of lesbians confided to an unnamed friend, who bequeathed this record to her niece, historian Bonnie Bullough, while they all conceded that society viewed them as pariahs, none of them admitted that any of the circle saw themselves as deviant or a threat to society. However, they never disclosed their sexuality to anyone outside their own circle for fear of retaliation and rejection, and they repeatedly praised the rational and responsible way in which they guarded their privacy.[25]

The responses to the questionnaire read like an earlier version of today's "don't ask, don't tell" military guidelines. All concealed their lesbianism, disdained masturbation, and abhorred public displays of affection; no one had ever been in analysis; only one had attempted suicide; and all held successful positions within the community. Yet a closer reading of these interviews reveals how much they internalized society's assessment and tried to police lesbian conduct. Consider, for example, the physical education instructor who was unabashedly respected for her strict disciplinarian nature, her ferreting out "unwholesome sexual relationships among her [female] students," and her unceasing desire to correct "the abominable habit [of masturbation]." One could easily speculate that it would be very hard to find a more perfect example of what Adrienne Rich would later label "compulsory heterosexuality and lesbian existence."[26]

If any lesbians entered the twentieth century hopeful that science would become their ally in their quest for understanding, tolerance, and serenity, they were sorely disappointed. Rather, they soon understood that instead of becoming their champions, sexologists and analysts promoted a system that introduced new ways to stigmatize lesbian behavior. As Simone de Beauvoir noted, psychoanalysts "through moralistic conformity . . . never [regarded lesbianism as] other than an unauthentic attitude." The lesbian immediately recognized this and began to "see herself and her kind as prey."[27]

Consequently, lesbians were very careful to conceal their identity as the most basic form of self-preservation. This concealment only reinforced analysts' assumptions that lesbians were not as prevalent a population as male homosexuals. That conclusion then served to reinforce their tendency to study a more easily observable population: male homosexuals. After being so thoroughly stigmatized as perverse and abnormal, many lesbians were more than willing to take a backseat in sexuality research and to let the hostility that the medical community brought to lesbians be applied to their male counterparts.

EVEN though few sexologists still dare to address the doctrine of masculine and/or somatic perversity that characterizes the standard psychoanalytic definition of lesbianism, the debate over the causes of homosexuality continues to generate passionate discussion within the genetics and psychological communities. Yet, just as the early sexologists focused on male homosexuality and then struggled to make lesbians fit into a pattern designed for men, contemporary geneticists continue to concentrate on gay men and then stretch to apply their conclusions to lesbians, if they discuss lesbians at all. Moreover, just as the early neurasthenists strove to argue that nerves dictate behavior, many contemporary psychiatrists refuse to consider that there may be social influences that serve as co-factors in the development of sexual identity. By refusing to expand the focus of the investigation, by limiting the range of the study of sexuality, historians, activists, and medical researchers are further polarizing the debate rather than searching for answers.[28]

In 1988, the National Lesbian and Gay Health Foundation published the only nationwide study of lesbian health concerns. Directed toward physicians who treat lesbian patients as well as the lesbian population at large, the study revealed that all lesbians struggled as much against a strong negative image of themselves as they did against physical illness and social stigma. Yet rather than question the goals of a society that increasingly preached tolerance rather than acceptance, the respondents questioned their own sense of self-worth. Even a majority of those women who had been sexually assaulted or physically beaten refused to discount completely that they deserved the abuse because they were not sexually "normal."[29]

The implications of these testimonies are just as startling as the sexologists' emphasis on psychosomatic and neurasthenic illnesses and the analysts' obsession with arrested development and penis envy. Repeatedly, the respondents reveal their painful struggle to balance their physical health and their psychological well-being. Many have incorporated the uneasiness characteristic of the analytic community's attitude toward lesbianism into their own lives. Historians must not fall into the same trap. Rather than perpetuate this either-or dichotomy by treating these findings as separate and distinct theories, historians must help frame the scope of the investigation by connecting sex to society in ways that show, first, that sex and nature are not mutually exclusive terms, and second, that science and society have historically treated and valued women differently from men.

As historians expand the areas of their discipline and begin to apply their unique skills to areas of history that have been ignored by their predecessors, they must exercise panoramic vision. If they truly want to understand the complex nature of sexuality, historians of sex, historians of lesbian and gay experience, and lesbian and gay historians themselves must redefine their investigative questions. They must learn from other disciplines and other cultures. They must ask, in the words of the philosopher Sandra Harding, "whose science, whose knowledge?" They must understand that "science produces information, but it also produces meanings" and that there are no meanings about individual behavior apart from the culture in which the individual lives. Furthermore, historians must confront the tensions inherent in analyzing so volatile a topic and to be aware of the influence of their own biases on their investigative framework. To do otherwise is to capitulate to the model that the early sexologists set for one another. It is to ask the same questions over and over again, to conflate culture with science, and to abandon inquiry for politics.[30]

Notes

1. George M. Beard, *American Nervousness, Its Causes and Consequences: A Supplement to Nervous Exhaustion* (1881; repr. New York: Ayer Company, 1972), especially 41–46; and *Sexual Neurasthenia, Its Hygiene, Causes, Symptoms and Treatment with a Chapter on Diet for the Nervous* (1898; repr. New York: Ayer Company Publishers, 1972).
2. Beard, *Sexual Nervousness*, 41–42, 75.

3. Elaine Showalter, *The Female Malady: Women, Madness and English Culture, 1930–1980* (New York: Alfred Knopf, 1987) 121–44; Edward Carpenter, "The Intermediate Sex," in *Selected Writings, Volume I: Sex* GMP, 1912, 1984), 184–244; Karl Ulrichs, *Forschungen uber das Ratsel der Mann Mannlichen Liebe* (1898; repr. New York: Arno Press, 1975); and Havelock Ellis, "Sexual Inversion in Women," in *Studies in the Psychology of Sex—Volume II* (1915; repr. New York: Random House, 1945), 222.

4. Jeffrey Weeks, *Sexuality and Its Discontents* (London: Routledge and Kegan Paul, 1985), 67.

5. Janet Oppenheim, *Shattered Nerves* (New York: Oxford University Press, 1991), 204–08.

6. Margaret Jackson, "Sexual Liberation or Social Control: Some Aspects of the Relationship between Feminism and the Social Construction of Sexual Knowledge in the Early Twentieth Century," *Women's Studies International Forum,* 6(1) (1983): 1–17; Lillian Faderman, "The Morbidification of Love between Women by 19th Century Sexologists," *Journal of Homosexuality,* 4(1) (Fall 1978): 73–88; Andrea Dworkin, *Pornography: Men Possessing Women* (London: The Women's Press, 1981); Ellis, *Studies in the Psychology of Sex, Vol. III,* 32–35; and Magnus Hirschfeld, Address to 1929 Congress of World League of Sex Reform, quoted in Jeffrey Weeks, "Invented Moralities," *History Workshop* 32 (Autumn 1991): 154.

7. Indeed, mental health professionals were very conscious of their authority and did not hesitate to impose it on their patients. See Janet Oppenheim, "The Diagnosis and Treatment of Nervous Breakdown," in *The Political Culture of Modern Britain,* ed. J. M. W. Bean (London: Hamilton Hamish, 1987), 83–84; and Alfred Kinsey, William B. Pomeroy, and Clyde E. Martin, *Sexual Behavior in the Human Male* (Philadelphia: W. B. Saunders, 1948), 202.

8. Carl Westphal, "Die Contrare Sexualempfindung," *Archiv fur Psychiatrie,* 11 (1870): 73–108. See also Richard von Krafft-Ebing, *Psychopathia Sexualis* (1906; repr. Brooklyn: Physicians and Surgeons Book Company, 1934), 395–97.

9. Beard, *Sexual Neurasthenia,* 200–06; and Krafft-Ebing, *Psychopathia Sexualis,* 397.

10. Faderman has a much more positive interpretation of the sexological labeling than I do. Indeed, she argues in *Odd Girls and Twilight Lovers* that the sexologists acted as "midwives" to a lesbian subculture and "crystallized possibilities for young women that they would have had difficulty conceptualizing on their own." Lillian Faderman, *Odd Girls and Twilight Lovers: A History of Lesbian Life in Twentieth Century America* (New York: Columbia University Press, 1991), 60. See also Lillian Faderman, "The Morbidification of Love between Women by 19th Century Sexologists," *Journal of Homosexuality,* 4(1) (Fall 1978): 73–88.

11. Carpenter, "Intermediate Sex," 194; Krafft-Ebing, *Psychopathia Sexualis,* 399; and Ellis, *Studies in the Psychology of Sex,* 201, 219–20, 222.

12. Ellis, *Studies in the Psychology of Sex,* 258. The quotation has been inverted for stylistic reasons.

13. Ibid., 226.

14. Ibid.

15. Ibid.; Havelock Ellis, *My Life* (London: Heinemann, 1940), 264. For accounts of Edith Lees's lesbianism and Ellis's response, see Phyllis Grosskurth, *Havelock Ellis: A Biography* (New York: New York University Press, 1985), 154–58; and Ruth Brandon, *The New Women and the Old Men: Love, Sex and the Woman Question* (New York: Norton, 1990), 114–22, 239–42.

16. Sigmund Freud, "Psychogenesis of a Case of Female Homosexuality," in *Freud on Women*, ed. Elizabeth Young-Bruehl (New York: Norton, 1990), 245–46, 249, and 253–55. Although students of male homosexual analytical theory have been generally supportive of Freud's theory of bisexuality, when Freud's writings about lesbians are analyzed a different attitude emerges. For a differing interpretation of Freud that is supportive of his diagnosis see George Chauncy, "From Sexual Inversion to Homosexuality: Medicine and the Changing Concept of Female Deviance," *Salmagundi*, 58–59 (Fall 1982): 115–46.

17. Freud, like Ulrichs and Krafft-Ebing, was greatly influenced when he learned that vertebrate embryos have both masculine and feminine sex organs, one of which disappears during growth. The analysts incorporated this finding into his psychoanalytic theory to argue that all humans were bisexual at one point in their lives. For example, Freud believed that a newborn child has no specific sexuality because it has no one specific source of tactical or sexual pleasure. Only after the child physically matures does the sexual drive find specific sources of gratification. Each stage in the child's physical development corresponds with a choice of a new love object, which in the course of "normal" development progresses from the self to the mother to the father to a person of the opposite sex. But homosexual affiliation is never completely erased during development. Consequently, historian David Greenberg can declare:

> It is fundamental to Freudian theory that, even though unacceptable impulses can be repressed so that they never come to consciousness, they can nevertheless continue to exercise a potent influence on mental process. Thus someone can be a "latent" homosexual without ever having been aware of homosexual desires.

See David F. Greenberg, *The Construction of Homosexuality* (Chicago: University of Chicago Press, 1988), 424–25.

Anna Freud seconded her father's opinion and repeatedly argued that "sexuality repressed or denied can be recovered symbolically or vicariously in a relationship of complementarity." Moreover, as her biographer Elisabeth Young-Bruehl notes, Freud was "eager not to have her new life [with companion Dorothy Burlingham] misconstrued or labelled homosexual." Elisabeth Young-Bruehl, *Anna Freud: A Biography* (New York: Summit Books, 1988), 138, 196.

18. Freud, "Psychogenesis of a Case of Female Homosexuality," 249, 253, 265. My emphasis.

19. Vern Bullough, "Challenges to Societal Attitudes toward Homosexuality in the Late Nineteenth and Early Twentieth Centuries," *Social Science Quarterly*, 58(1) (June 1977): 29–44; Irving Bieber, *Homosexuality: A Psychoanalytic Study* (Norvale, N.J.: Jason Aronson, Inc., 1962; repr. New York: Basic Books, 1988), 303–19; and Ronald Bayer, *Homosexuality and American Psychiatry: The Politics of Diagnosis* (Princeton: Princeton University Press, 1987), 30.

20. E. Bergler, "The Respective Importance of Reality and Fantasy in the Genesis of Female Homosexuality," *Journal of Criminal Psychopathology* 6 (1943): no pagination.

21. Helen Deutsch, *The Psychology of Women* (Bantam Books: New York, 1973) 353–54; and Jonathan Katz, *Gay American History* (New York: Harper and Row, 1976), 161.

22. Frank Caprio, *Female Homosexuality: A Psychodynamic Study of Lesbianism* (New York: Citadel Press, 1954) 112–17; E. Bergler, "The Respective Importance of Reality and Fantasy in the Genesis of Female Homosexuality," *Journal of Criminal Psychopathology* 6 (1943):

no pagination; "Differential Diagnosis between Spurious Homosexuality and Perversion Homosexuality," *Psychiatric Quarterly,* 21 (July 1947): 299–409; *Neurotic Counter-feit Sex: Impotence, Frigidity, "Mechanical" and Pseudosexuality, Homosexuality* (New York: Grune and Stratton, 1951); and Otto Fenichel, *The Psychoanalytic Theory of Neurosis* (New York: Norton, 1945), 338–44.

23. John D'Emilio and Estelle B. Freedman, *Intimate Matters: A History of Sexuality in America* (New York: Oxford University Press, 1988), 193–94; and Katherine B. Davis, *Factors in the Sex Life of Twenty-Two Hundred Women* (New York, Harper & Row, 1929), 260, 270–71.

24. Radclyffe Hall, *The Well of Loneliness* (New York: Avon Books, 1981); and Greenberg, *The Construction of Homosexuality,* 425.

25. Vern and Bonnie Bullough, "Lesbianism in the 1920s and 1930s: A Newfound Study," *Signs* (Summer 1977): 895–904.

26. Adrienne Rich, "Compulsory Heterosexuality and Lesbian Existence," *Signs* (Summer 1980): 631–61.

27. Simone de Beauvoir, *The Second Sex* (New York: Knopf, 1968), 383–83. For an interesting discussion of how lesbians viewed their sexuality as a disease and internalized homophobia in the 1950s and 1960s, see Kristin Gay Esterberg, "From Illness to Action: Conceptions of Homosexuality in the Ladder, 1956–1965," *Journal of Sex Research,* 27 (February 1990): 65–80.

28. For excellent histories of psychoanalysis and male homosexuality, see Bayer, *Homosexuality and Psychoanalysis;* Greenberg, *The Construction of Homosexuality;* and Kenneth Lewes, *The Psychoanalytic History of Male Homosexuality* (New York: Basic Books, 1989). For samples of contemporary research methodologies, see "Is This Child Gay? Born or Bred: The Origins of Homosexuality," *Newsweek* 119(8) (February 24, 1992); Natalie Angier, "Report Suggests Homosexuality Is Linked to Genes," *New York Times,* July 16, 1993; and J. Michael Bailey and Richard C. Pillard, "A Genetic Study of Male Sexual Orientation," *Archives of General Psychiatry* 48 (December 1991): 1089–96.

29. Caitlin Conor Ryan and Judith Bradford, *National Lesbian Health Care Survey* (Washington, D.C.: National Lesbian and Gay Health Foundation, 1988).

30. Margaret Jackson, "Sexual Liberation or Social Control: Some Aspects of the Relationship between Feminism and the Social Construction of Sexual Knowledge in the Early Twentieth Century," *Women's Studies International Forum,* 6(1) (1983): 1–17; Lillian Faderman, "The Morbidification of Love between Women by 19th Century Sexologists," *Journal of Homosexuality,* 4(1) (Fall 1978): 73–88; Andrea Dworkin, *Pornography: Men Possessing Women* (London: The Women's Press, 1981); Ellis, *Studies in the Psychology of Sex, Vol. III,* 32–35; and Hirschfeld, Address to 1929 Congress of World League of Sex Reform, in Weeks, "Invented Moralities," 154.

9

"A Thought a Mother Can Hardly Face"

Sissy Boys, Parents, and Professionals in Mid-Twentieth-Century America

JULIA GRANT

WRITING in 1957 to a newspaper advice column for parents, a mother wondered about the meaning of her seven-year-old son's preference for quiet play with girls rather than sports and roughhousing: "Does it mean that he's growing up to be a sissy or effeminate because he is not a mean and rough boy like so many of them are and that I'm not doing the right thing to make him more masculine or should I respect his personality—that he'll never be one of those rough boys and let him hang around girls and do what he wants?"[1] This mother was clearly worried that her son was at risk for being labeled with the terms "sissy" and "effeminate"—labels designed to stigmatize boys who did not conform to cultural norms of behavior. Yet the mother's sympathy for her young son is suggested by the fact that she deems normal boys "mean and rough" and wonders whether she should "respect his personality" rather than seek to "make him more masculine." The competing ideas expressed in the mother's query mirrored two streams of discourse about the socialization of children into their gender roles during the 1940s and 1950s—one that focused on the need to respect children's individual temperaments, and another that stressed the responsibility of parents to raise masculine boys and feminine girls.

In her response to the mother, psychologist Louise Bates Ames argued that parents were largely unable to alter children's individual temperaments: "It is most difficult to make a boy more masculine than he actually is. To a large extent, this kind of thing is, in our opinion, inborn." Influenced by the work of William Sheldon, whose writings on the relationship between body type and temperament were quite influential, Ames believed that children's personalities were largely determined by their bodies rather than by their relationship with their parents.[2] The view that the degree of masculinity and femininity that a person exhibited was largely dependent on constitutional factors represented an influential strand of discourse in mid-twentieth-century America. While theorists differed in their opinions as to whether boys with less than masculine body builds and personalities were "deviant" or "normal," Ames contended that there were many varieties of constitutions and temperaments within each gender—most of which could be subsumed under the category of "normal."

Ames's use of biology to defend sissy boys put her at odds with many of her peers in the psychological profession and the parental advice industry who professed that children who violated gender norms were the victims of bad parenting. In his infamous *Baby and Child Care,* first published in 1946, Benjamin Spock offered the more conventional analysis of boys who departed from gender norms in his chapter on fatherless boys: "The temptation of the mother who has no other equally strong ties is to make him [her son] her closest spiritual companion, getting him interested in clothes and interior decoration, in her opinions and feelings about people, in the books and other recreations she enjoys. If she succeeds in making her world more appealing to him, easier to get along in, then he may grow up to be precocious and effeminate."[3] Spock's explanation of the sissy boy—overprotected by a mother whose son is her major confidant—was a staple of the era's psychological thinking and popular culture. The theory of the overprotective mom who emasculated her sons informed a spate of popular psychological works published within a few years of each other, including Edward Strecker's explanation of shell-shocked veterans, *Their Mother's Sons* (1946); Philip Wylie's jeremiad about the dangers to American civilization of a mollycoddled generation of men, *Generation of Vipers* (1942); and David Levy's psychoanalytic account of the dangers of mother love, *Maternal Overprotection* (1943). The fear that the nation's moms might be producing "pansies" incapable of defending American democracy continued to be salient throughout the postwar era. The power of these popular writings has permeated historical analyses of the period, leading us to overlook less sensational discussions of gender roles during this era.[4] Yet Ames's plea for tolerance of individual differences among boys also had adherents in popular and professional circles.

Why was the sissy boy subjected to such psychological scrutiny during this period? The sissy, effeminate boy posed a threat to the image of a strong, masculine, and virile America, untainted by feminine influences and able to stand up to Nazis and Communists alike. Psychiatrists played a major role in World War II, and diagnosing and studying homosexuals was no small part of their work. Their work held homosexuals up to public scrutiny, even while the barracks themselves provided new arenas for the creation of homosexual communities.[5] According to Geoffrey Smith, during the Cold War notions of effeminacy and sexual deviancy were intertwined, and the purging of homosexuals from the FBI and the armed forces was predicated upon the idea of both ridding these institutions of the disease of homosexuality and reinforcing stringent gender classifications.[6]

Popular social-scientific writings helped to establish the connection between sissy boys and the despised homosexuals who seemed increasingly to populate the armed forces and urban centers. For instance, an article in *Science Digest* entitled "Homosexuals Didn't Play Baseball" (1956) reported the results of a study of male homosexuals who tended to play with dolls as young boys and—to the amazement of the reporter—weren't particularly keen on baseball.[7]

In parental advice literature, the connections between sissy boys and homosexuality were less explicit. However, the language of dread, disappointment, and revulsion that surrounded discussions of sissy boys suggests that popular advice writers and parents were all too conscious that girlish boys might grow up to choose other boys as sexual partners. Anthropologist Geoffrey Gorer insisted in 1956 that the fact that American parents were raising a crop of sissies was "the overriding fear of every American parent." A mother writing for *Parents' Magazine* in 1951 confessed that the realization that there was something "sissy" and "downright girlish" about her seven-year-old son was a thought that "a mother can hardly face." Why would a boy who liked to play with dolls cause thoughts that "a mother can hardly face," unless she was imagining her son's possible fate as a social and sexual deviant?[8]

In addition to a growing consciousness of the presence of a homosexual culture, there are other possible explanations for concerns about sissy boys during the 1940s and 1950s. Men's work roles, especially among the middle class, were less likely than in the past to allow them to exercise the traditional masculine virtues of strength, courage, and decision-making. Instead they were urged to cultivate their masculine virtues in their roles as fathers and husbands in the home, a traditionally feminine venue.[9] Thus men's roles themselves were in the process of being "feminized," leaving them less able to raise "manly" sons than in the past. Researchers also were influenced by Freudian theories of identification, which suggested that young boys must engage in the complex process of shifting their early identification with the mother to that of the more distant father. The fact that many fathers were absent from the home, either literally or symbolically, made it difficult for young boys to form an appropriate sex identification, according to the theory. Researchers also worried that domineering mothers were acculturating young boys to female values in the home. Thus many hypothesized that the typical configuration of the American home put boys at risk for becoming the dreaded sissy.[10]

Of course, it was not only boys who aroused alarm about deviations from traditional gender norms. While the postwar era is often remembered for its conservative conception of the family, many who lived during that time felt that they were witnessing dramatic changes in many areas, including sex roles. In a 1957 *New York Times* article entitled "Trousered Mothers and Dishwashing Dads," Dorothy Barclay explored the difficulty of transmitting traditional gender roles to children in an era of change: "The little boy today can see little that obviously differentiates young males and young females. Little girls not too many years ago wore dresses consistently, played quiet games and were repeatedly reminded to behave like little ladies. Today in some circles the tree-climbing, marble-playing, ball-batting boy is just as likely to find a short-haired and betrousered girl beside him as another lad."[11] Among many of her psychoanalytic peers, Irene Jossely worried that "we are drifting toward a social structure made up of he-women and she-men" and became determined to take action to reverse what she saw as a dangerous trend toward androgyny.[12] The fear that children were not being adequately socialized into their appropriate sex roles was manifested in many studies of young children, including one of five-year-olds, published in 1956, which stated that the middle class lacks "clear definition of adult roles," resulting in the "inability of this group [of young children] to discriminate the role which is appropriate for his sex, and to adapt his behavior accordingly."[13] In the infamous *Modern Woman: The Lost Sex* (1947), psychologists Ferdinand Lundberg and Marynia Farnham argued that feminism had triumphed and gender roles had been extinguished to the detriment of society as a whole.[14] It was assumed, however, that girls' deviations from traditional gender norms were more likely related to the fact that they wished to identify themselves with the status of the dominant gender rather than as necessary indications of future homosexuality.

The fact that children's sex roles appeared to be in flux caused consternation to many who sought to ensure that children adopt traditional sex-role characteristics. But there was a sizeable contingent of thinkers who argued that children's individual differences should take precedence over gender conformity and who feared the consequences of an overemphasis on differentiations between boys and girls. At a 1957 conference of parent educators, "The Male Role in the Family," a vocal group "acknowledged no stereotypes of 'maleness' and 'femaleness' and suggested that it would be not only useless but dangerous to set them up. They held it more important that each individual—regardless of sex—have instead the freedom to become his or her own best self."[15] In that same vein, an article in *Parents' Magazine,* with the ironic title "That's What Little Boys Are Like!" (1951), included the caption "Nobody spoiled this cowboy's fun by saying boys don't play with dolls. He knows they do, and girls play cowboys, too." Writer Doris Guilford argued that "little boys have the same natural interest and curiosity concerning the routines of household, family and neighborhood living that small girls do. . . . If we become too intent on our small sons being 'all boy,' we may deny them some of the tenderness and the help that they need in these early years."[16]

Researchers on both sides of the debate were influenced by advances in embryology, which indicated that maleness and femaleness were not as distinct as was once thought. George Henry's *All the Sexes: A Study of Masculinity and Femininity* (1955) demonstrates some of the contradictions in the era's thinking. Henry was vehemently homophobic and recommended that "sex variants" be kept under psychiatric supervision. However, the title of his book, he explained, "attempts to convey the idea of gradation from masculinity and femininity," and he admitted that "it is scientifically inaccurate to classify persons as fully male or female."[17] Eminent psychologist Lewis Terman observed in 1946 that all men secrete estrogens and women secrete androgens, and he provocatively stated: "There are no men, there are no women; there are only sexual majorities."[18] Similarly, Alfred Kinsey's widely publicized studies of male sexuality (1948) suggested that many "normal" heterosexual men had engaged in "deviant" homosexual behaviors.[19] If indeed sexuality was as unstable a category as some of this research seemed to suggest, then social science had its work cut out for it in seeking to forge a science that could control the social and sexual behavior of men and women.

Thus the burgeoning of sex-role development research in the 1940s and 1950s was closely tied to concerns about American society's inability to correctly socialize children into their gender roles. Psychologists Lewis Terman and Catherine Cox Miles's studies of masculinity and femininity, first published in 1936, provided the underpinning for many future studies of children's sex-role development. Terman and Miles sought to rate the masculinity and femininity of men and women using what was termed an "M-F" (masculinity-femininity) scale, which was widely replicated and elaborated upon in succeeding decades.[20] The creation of the scale suggested researchers' awareness of the variability in the degree to which men and women exhibited gender-appropriate behavior, as well as their desire to use science to diagnose and treat gender deviations. Respondents were asked to answer a number of questions about their personality and interests in order to rate their degree of masculinity and femininity. Positive responses to such questions as whether you "nearly always prefer someone else to take the lead" or whether you are "extremely careful about your manner of dress" gave the respondent femininity points. The researchers chose a group of homosexuals to test, hoping to find conformation of their thesis that homosexuality and gender deviancy were related. However, they were forced to divide the group into "active" and "passive" homosexuals because the active group was too masculine and disproved their thesis. The passive group, on the other hand, had many personality characteristics similar to females and were more enthusiastic about playing "house" as children than any other male group. These findings led the researchers to hope that such childhood "clues" might lead to better efforts to prevent the onset of homosexuality. At the conclusion of the published results, the authors provided a "formula" for homosexuality: "too demonstrative affection from an excessively emotional mother . . . a father who is unsympathetic, autocratic, brutal, much away from home, or deceased . . . treatment of the child as a girl, coupled with lack of encouragement or opportunity to associate with boys and to take part in the rougher masculine activities; overemphasis of neatness, niceness, and spirituality."[21] Terman and Miles's research in masculinity and femininity, therefore, had as its underlying aim that of seeking to find ways of locating and correcting those who most flagrantly deviated from gender norms: homosexuals.

In the 1940s and 1950s, researchers built on Terman and Miles by studying the degree and speed with which young children acquired sex roles. Many were influenced by Margaret Mead's work, which suggested that masculinity and femininity were differently defined across cultures, and by Alfred Kinsey's studies of human sexual behavior, which theorized that individuals of different social classes exhibited varying patterns of sexual behavior.[22] While many researchers were influenced by Freudian theories of sexuality, most useful for their purposes was the concept of identification with the same-sex parent, which many social scientists combined with an interest in what they termed "social learning." The idea that children learn sex roles from their interactions with parents and peers was much easier to test than the theories of the unconscious on which most Freudian theories rested. Although many case studies existed of adults who had developed gender disturbances or who were homosexual, these were retrospective, anecdotal, and did not meet the requirements of objective social science. Most social scientists accepted the cultural basis of sex roles, but they clung to the notion that social cohesion required that children adapt to the cultural pattern. Those who did not conform to this cultural pattern would be labeled deviant and were at risk for adopting deviant—a codeword for homosexual—lifestyles.

A series of tests were devised to evaluate the extent to which young children identified themselves with the gender role to which they had been assigned. Tests commonly involved surveys of toy preferences, doll play, stick drawings, and reported behaviors, characteristics, and interests of children secured through interviews and observations by parents and teachers.[23] One example of the stick-drawing test provided the child with a drawing and then the test-giver stated: "This boy (or girl) is playing with his toy trucks. You see, he has a truck in each hand. And his mother and father are watching him as he plays. Here the boy (or girl) is playing cooking. . . . His mother and daddy are watching him as he plays cooking." The child was then asked what his or her own choice of activity was, and which activities his parents would prefer him or her to be engaged in. The stick-drawing test thus evaluated both the child's gender identification and the extent to which the child's parents were reinforcing gender-appropriate behavior.[24] The toy-preference test had children choose their preferred toys, and their choices were measured against norms that had been set up by a "typical" sample of boys and girls. Children who chose toys that were not typically selected by children of their own gender were likely to be diagnosed as gender deviant.[25] With doll-play tests, researchers examined the ways in which children played with dolls, whether they occupied the male or female role with their dolls, and how dolls of different genders behaved. One widely reported finding was that boys from father-absent homes were less aggressive in their doll play; the implication was that they did not have a masculine role model from whom to learn aggression.[26] The description of girls who played aggressively with dolls also took its bearing from social learning and identification theories: "For girls, however, the appropriate sex role model is normally nonaggressive. Only when the particular model most visible to the girl (her mother) is especially aggressive does the girl adopt an aggressive way of behaving."[27] These studies made clear the connection between identification and social learning; children must identify with the same-sex parent in order to learn their roles properly. However, if the same-sex (or opposite sex) parent behaved outside of traditional gender norms, gender deviant behavior could be expected from the child.

In contrast to the speculations of those who feared that children were not learning gender-appropriate behavior, many studies conceded that by five years of age, the majority of children were quite clear about the activities, toy preferences, and personal characteristics most suitable for a child of their gender. Significant class differences were discovered, however, with working-class children acquiring more definitive sex roles at an earlier age than their middle-class counterparts. Many studies observed that girls continued to play both boys' and girls' games up through the age seven or eight, while most boys abandoned girls' games fairly early on. Researchers concluded that this was due to the prestige granted the male role and the fact that boys were taught to disparage traditional female activities. Yet when boys did veer from their expected sex roles, they were found to veer more dramatically than girls, and researchers engaged in more sustained commentary, with some claiming that the degree and consequences of their gender-deviant behavior were more severe than for girls.[28]

What about those boys whose tests indicated that they were failing to acquire the trappings of the typical male role? Overprotecting mothers and absentee fathers were an obvious culprit, but so too were parents who failed to provide explicit instruction in gender-appropriate behavior.[29] Psychologist Meyer Rabban theorized that the combination of father absence and a permissive attitude on the part of mothers toward gender roles could result in an effeminate boy. For instance, five-year-old Norman chose girls' toys over boys' and "would just as soon cook as carpentry." His mother remarked that he "doesn't seem to recognize boy and girl differences in activities." What was worse, however, was that she was unconcerned with Norman's preference for girls' activities. Rabban's assessment of the matter was that Norman's low masculinity score was due to "considerable father absence with only a minimal sense of identification" combined with "parents who are not concerned with early or strict definitions of sex-appropriate behavior."[30] On the other hand, four-year-old Danny was quite conscious of the difference between boys' toys and girls'. When the mother was asked what she would do if her son wanted to play girls' games, she claimed that she would tell him: "Dolls are for girls, not for boys. Everybody will think you are a sissy. You should play with cars and trucks."[31] Such findings led Rabban and many others to ascribe a great deal to social learning in children's acquisition of sex roles.

Although social learning theorists were predominant in explaining children's sex role development, constitutional psychologists claimed that biological factors predisposed boys to be either more or less "manly." In William Sheldon's work on the ectomorph, mesomorph, and endodorph physiques, published in the early 1940s, he sought to prove that body type was directly related to an individual's masculinity or femininity, which provoked a number of studies seeking to replicate his findings.

Carl Seltzer's 1948 study of Harvard college students, who were photographed in the nude, argued that less masculine body types had "an aversion to strenuous exercise and sports," were "low in physical fitness . . . frequently sensitive . . . inclined toward creative and intuitive traits." He concluded that "leadership qualities of the type required for combat officership is noticeably lacking in this group."[32] Child psychologist Nancy Bayley evaluated the physiques of girls and boys in 1951 and found very little to substantiate the notion that there was a correspondence between body build and masculinity and femininity. However, she clearly believed that certain body builds were gender-deviant and bound to generate psychological conflict. She contended, "Some of the bisexual [meaning having builds with both masculine and feminine qualities] girls accept their builds and develop congruent interests, while others reject them and compensate with feminine interests." She also claimed that several girls in the study had "emotional difficulties which are associated in part with their deviant physiques."[33] While the study of masculine and feminine body types was largely inconclusive, the concept lingered that there were physical correlates of deviations from gender norms, with some arguing that parents must make special efforts to inculcate appropriate sex roles in children with "deviant" body builds.[34]

Margaret Mead attacked the propensity to equate certain body types and temperaments with masculinity and femininity in her book *Male and Female,* published in 1949. She was concerned about the propensity to label certain behavioral traits as belonging to one sex rather than the other, fearing that boys who were labeled as "feminine" because of their appearance or mannerisms might be led to take refuge in "explicit femininity," leading to social deviance. Mead subscribed, however, to the notion that temperaments and body types were related. In speaking of girls whose secondary sex characteristics were less marked than in other types of girls, she stated her desire that "these deviations would no longer be regarded as signs of greater or less femininity, but of different types of women, types so biologically rooted that all the apparatus of cultural conditioning is insufficient to mold them completely to the type which that particular culture has come to regard as really feminine or masculine."[35] Thus, Mead yearned for a culture in which a wider spectrum of bodies, temperaments, and interests were acceptable for both genders, while simultaneously urging that a greater social tolerance of such differences might help to avert the "homosexual menace."

Mead was not the only one who worried about the sissy and effeminate boy who might be led down the path of homosexuality by a culture unwilling to accept less masculine boys into the ranks of the heterosexuals. Indeed, during the 1950s adolescent medical specialists emerged to help address the concerns of anxious parents about undeveloped boys and girls with little interest in the opposite sex. For instance, historian Heather Munro Prescott tells the story of a patient in an adolescent health clinic with a "small, slight figure" and a "waltzing, mincing manner." The doctor's treatment included two years of androgen supplements combined with psychotherapy to address the problems of an "oversolicitous mother."[36] The doctors believed that even "feminine-looking" boys could be "steered along the correct path to masculinity" if caught in time. Unfortunately, some effeminate boys did not benefit from the doctor's guidance. Rejected by their peers, they were "forced to fill . . . needs for companionship by associating with those who have no other friends—perhaps true homosexuals."[37] Thus the physicians Prescott examined felt, like Mead, that it was in society's best interests to be less rigid in their expectations of masculine behavior as a means of lessening the attractions of homosexuality.

Even those engaged in rating and diagnosing children's sex roles balked at times at the implications of their studies. Following a comprehensive study of the acquisition of children's sex roles, Rabban wondered "whether the pressure to conform to the defined appropriate sex-role pattern is conducive to optimum expression of the individual personality." Psychologist Ruth Hartley, who conducted several studies of children's sex roles, was critical of the era's preoccupation with steering boys into a masculine direction at an early age. She noted as well that it was problematic to ask young boys—who were being raised by women—to define themselves in opposition to females: "On the one hand, he is told that he is supposed to be rugged, independent, able to take care of himself, and to disdain 'sissies.' On the other, he is forced into close contact with the epitome of all sissy-things—women—for most of his day. . . . In other words, he is compelled to knuckle under to that which he has been taught to despise."[38]

It is difficult to ascertain to what extent social scientists were reflecting widespread social attitudes and concerns or whether they were effective salespersons for their ideas in the larger public—probably both. But researchers' concerns were surely mirrored in the concerns of parents, who labored to raise their boys in the context of a discourse that posed as problematic the acquisition of appropriate sex roles.

As Robert Sears showed in his study of parenting practices, *Patterns of Child Rearing* (1957), mothers varied in the degree to which they sought to induce gender conformity in their young children. Even mothers who were insistent about the necessity of raising boys who would not be sissies, however, shared the view that boys did not become boys by nature alone. Sears asked mothers of preschoolers if they were interested in raising their boys to be "real boys." Their responses illuminate this point: "I think he should be a real boy—and then again I think it is up to the father to help him become a real boy. I don't think a mother can help a boy to become a real boy." A real boy, it would seem, is defined by his participation in different masculine activities, such as hunting and baseball, as she explained later in the interview. The idea that one *becomes* a boy is evident as well in the following statement: "I would want him to be a real boy. . . . Last week he came home and climbed a fence and ripped a brand new pair of grey flannel pants. His father was very proud of him. He at last had become a boy." Another mother admitted that she wanted a "real boy" and not a "sissy." "I wouldn't want him otherwise—I would give him boxing lessons if I had to." Male role models and appropriate socialization experiences, such as boxing classes and Boy Scouts, were essential to the creation of a real boy.[39]

Mothers who failed at the task could end up with the dreaded "sissy," who had a sensitive temperament, liked to play with girls, and preferred quiet activities. For instance, eleven year-old Alan refused to join the Boy Scouts and was uninterested in fishing, sports, models, engines, chemistry sets, and tools. Instead, he enjoyed reading, drawing, and listening to the radio, all of which his mother claimed were "sedentary, passive, not active or the participating kind of interest which most boys have." In a letter to Ames, the mother wondered whether the behavior was "a natural things for boys of Alan's type? Should we simply ignore it and let him go his happy, unstimulated way without any effort to help him fit himself into a tough masculine world? Or should we suggest and then press until he does some of these things?" Although the mother's language suggests her preference that her boy be masculine, she was also aware that her son's behavior might be "normal" for his *type* of child. Some parents also drew the connections the experts did between "sissy" behaviors and homosexuality. One woman who wrote to Spock in a panic because she had found her eleven-year-old son engaged in sex play with another boy defended him in these terms: "He is all boy, with no trace whatever of feminine characteristics. He is interested in playing ball . . . comic books, television, rock 'n roll, etc."[40] Thus, this mother felt perplexed that a child who clearly preferred "boys'" activities would engage in sex play with another boy.

But some mothers were much more fluid in their expectations of the behavior of their children, especially younger children. They maintained that the play interests of preschool boys and girls were relatively indistinguishable and allowed their boys to play with dolls, believing that they would soon outgrow this interest. And some other mothers were more philosophically inclined to gender-neutrality. According to one mother cited in Sears's study, "I think that boys and girls have many similar likes and dislikes in play. . . . Oftentimes he plays house with her [his cousin], and she often plays cowboys with him. And I don't think there's too much difference in what boys and girls play at that age. And just to be a regular boy, because he is a boy, I don't think is all that important."[41] This mother's differentiation between the concept of the "regular boy" and her own child's sex membership suggests her awareness of the constructedness of the "regular boy" and her resistance to this cultural mandate. Another less articulate mother defended her parenting of five-year-old Sammy, whom daycare workers described as having "many effeminate mannerisms." According to Rabban, "He enjoys wearing his mother's apron and putting her kerchief on his head after he has put pin curls into his hair. His mother participates in his play." In response to a query from the researcher about how the mother felt about Sammy's play preferences, she said: "It's all right for him. Don't feel that way is bad. I am against guns, and no cowboy and robber play."[42]

This mother was quite clear about the superiority of her feminine sensibility and seemingly happy that her son shared her preferences.

There is suggestive evidence that some parents were uncomfortable with the masculine ethos that was being thrust upon their sons. Ames sparked a controversy and much correspondence from mothers when she published a letter critiquing fathers' harsh and critical treatment of their sons. One mother argued that the fear of the sissy was negatively impacting fathers' parenting practices: "I think there is a curious notion current among fathers that boys will grow up 'sissies' if they are comforted when they are unhappy or in pain, allowed to express themselves by crying or showing fear. I really think each of these men is betraying his own fear that he might . . . show feminine weaknesses in his own responses to life."[43] Not only was it difficult for women to bring up properly "manly" men, but many felt ambivalent about cooperating with a cultural mandate that posited that masculinity must be constructed in opposition to femininity, with a corresponding denigration of female values.

The contrast between these discussions about the difficulty of acquiring appropriate gender roles and today's assumptions about the immutability of sex-typed patterns of behaviors and interests among young children is striking. This analysis of the treatment of sissy boys at mid-twentieth century suggests the ambiguous legacy of biological explanations for our understanding of gender deviance and homosexuality. Both biological and environmental explanations of homosexuality and gender roles can be used to punish or to argue for greater social tolerance for those who stray from traditional norms of sexual and social behavior. While today we think of environmentalist explanations of gender roles as progressive, in mid-twentieth-century America many environmentalist social scientists tried to use their science to preserve the status quo, beginning with young children—some of whom were thought to be "at risk" for homosexuality and gender deviance. On the other hand, some who championed the biological point of view argued that there were a range of "normal" differences among children, some of which were inscribed upon the body, and that it was undemocratic to seek to eradicate those differences. It is perhaps more biologically deterministic to claim, as many now do, that boys will be boys, and girls girls, regardless of the method of socialization. This would have been news to Margaret Mead, Louise Bates Ames, and Alfred Kinsey, who could not help but notice that some—but not all—boys will be boys.

Notes

1. Mrs. N. N. of Raleigh, North Carolina to Louise Bates Ames, 9 December 1957, Parents Ask Letters, Louise Bates Ames Papers, Library of Congress.

2. Louise Bates Ames to Mrs. N. N. of Raleigh, North Carolina, 17 December 1959, Parents Ask Letters, Louise Bates Ames Papers, Library of Congress. For Sheldon's impact

on Ames and her colleague Frances Ilg, see Frances L. Ilg and Louise B. Ames, *Child Behavior* (New York: Harper, 1955); and Ilg and Ames, *Parents Ask* (New York: Harper, 1951). See also W. H. Sheldon, S. S. Stevens, and W. B. Tucker, *The Varieties of Human Physique* (New York: Harper, 1940); and William H. Sheldon, *Varieties of Temperament* (New York: Harper, 1942).

3. Benjamin Spock, *The Commonsense Book of Baby and Child Care* (New York: Duell, Sloan and Pearce, 1946), 492.

4. Edward A. Strecker, *Their Mothers' Sons: The Psychiatrist Examines an American Problem* (New York and Philadelphia: J. B. Lippincott, 1946); Philip Wylie, *Generation of Vipers* (New York: Farrar and Rinehart, 1942); David Levy, *Maternal Overprotection* (New York: Columbia University Press, 1943). The 1940s and 1950s are undergoing historical revision. Joanne Meyerowitz's "Beyond the Feminine Mystique: A Reassessment of Postwar Mass Culture, 1946–1958," *Journal of American History* 79 (March 1993): 1455–82, is a good example of recent efforts to challenge the notion that there was only one reigning ideology of thought around issues relating to gender during this era.

5. Allan Berube's chapter on psychiatrists and the gay GI is indispensable; *Coming Out Under Fire: The History of Gay Men and Women in World War II* (New York: Free Press, 1990), 149–74. See also Jennifer Terry, "'Momism' and the Making of Treasonous Homosexuals," in *Bad Mothers: The Politics of Blame in Twentieth-Century America,* ed. Molly Ladd-Taylor and Lauri Umansky (New York: New York University Press, 1998), 169–90; and Elaine Tyler May, *Homeward Bound: American Families in Cold War America* (New York: Basic Books, 1998).

6. Geoffrey S. Smith, "National Security and Personal Isolation: Sex, Gender, and Disease in the Cold-War United States," in *The International History Review* 14 (May 1992): 221–40.

7. "Homosexuals Didn't Play Baseball," *Science Digest* 40 (September 1956): 37. On this theme, see also John D'Emilio, "The Homosexual Menace: The Politics of Sexuality in Cold War America," in *Passion and Power: Sexuality in History,* ed. Kathy Peiss and Christina Simmons (Philadelphia: Temple University Press, 1989).

8. Quotation from Gorer is cited in Michael Kimmel, *Manhood in America: A Cultural History* (New York: The Free Press, 1996), 243; A Mother, "Was Our Boy a Sissy?" *Parents' Magazine* 26 (April 1951): 45.

9. Kimmel, *Manhood in American,* 205.

10. Joseph H. Pleck, "The Theory of Male Sex Role Identity," in Miriam Lewin, ed., *In the Shadow of the Past: Psychology Portrays the Sexes* (New York: Columbia University Press, 1984), 158–67; and Pleck, *The Myth of Masculinity* (Cambridge: MIT Press, 1981).

11. Dorothy Barclay, "Trousered Mothers and Dishwashing Dads," *New York Times Magazine,* April 28, 1957, p. 48.

12. Quoted in Barclay, "Trousered Mothers," 48.

13. Lydia Boyce Fauls and Walter D. Smith, "Sex-Role Learning of Five-Year-Olds," *Journal of Genetic Psychology* 89 (1956): 106. Marynia F. Farnham replicated this argument when she stated, "On the whole, the youngsters are brought up as though there were no fundamental differences between boys and girls"; see "Helping Boys to Be Boys . . . Girls to Be Girls," *Parents' Magazine* 28 (January 1953): 34.

14. Ferdinand Lundberg and Marynia F. Farnham, *Modern Woman: The Lost Sex* (New York: Harpers, 1947).

15. Barclay, "Trousered Mothers," 48.

16. Doris F. Guilford, "That's What Little Boys Are Like!" *Parents' Magazine* 26 (July 1951): 42–43.

17. George W. Henry, *All the Sexes: A Study of Masculinity and Femininity* (Toronto: Rinehart and Co., 1955) xiii, 584. Stephanie H. Kenen discusses the work of sex researcher Clifford Wright, who argued in the 1930s and 1940s that "all humans are bisexual . . . but in the homosexual the proper proportions are reversed"; in "Who Counts When You're Counting Homosexuals: Hormones and Homosexuality in Mid-Twentieth-Century America," *Science and Homosexualities,* ed. Vernon A. Rosario (New York: Routledge, 1997), 200.

18. Lewis M. Terman, W. B. Johnson, G. Kuznets, and Q. W. McNemar, "Psychological Sex Differences," in *Manual of Child Psychology,* ed. Leonard Carmichael (New York: Wiley, 1946), 955.

19. Alfred C. Kinsey, *Sexual Behavior in the Human Male* (Philadelphia: W. B. Saunders Co., 1948). On Kinsey's emphasis on variations in normal behavior, see James H. Jones, *Alfred C. Kinsey: A Public/Private Life* (New York: W. W. Norton, 1997), 54–55.

20. On the Terman studies, see especially Henry L. Minton, "Femininity in Men and Masculinity in Women: American Psychiatry and Psychology Portray Homosexuality in the 1930s," *Journal of Homosexuality* 1 (Fall 1986): 8–14; Miriam Lewin, "'Rather Worse Than Folly?': Psychology Measures Femininity and Masculinity," in *In the Shadow of the Past,* 1; Pleck, "The Theory of Male Sex Role Identity," 5–25; and Pleck, *The Myth of Masculinity.*

21. Catherine C. Miles and Lewis Terman, *Sex and Personality: Studies in Masculinity and Femininity* (New York: McGraw-Hill, 1936), 249, 320.

22. See Margaret Mead, *Sex and Temperament in Three Primitive Societies* (New York: W. Morrow & Co., 1935); and Mead, *Male and Female* (New York: William Morrow & Co., 1949). Kinsey, *Sexual Behavior in the Human Male.* Marjorie Hall and Robert A. Keith explicitly acknowledged their debt to both Mead and Kinsey in the opening of their article, "Sex-Role Preference Among Children of Upper and Lower Social Class," *Journal of Social Psychology* 62 (1964): 101–10.

23. For instance, Ruth Hartley's "Children's Concepts of Male and Female Roles" used a series of interviews where children were asked to tell visitors from Mars what girls (or boys) need to know and do. Interviewers also showed little girls pictures of their mothers going to work and asked them how they felt and how they thought their mother felt, in *Merrill Palmer Quarterly* (Winter 1959): 83–91.

24. Fauls and Smith, "Sex-Role Learning of Five-Year-Olds," 109–10.

25. Fauls and Smith, "Sex-Role Learning of Five-Year-Olds," 110; B. G. Rosenberg and B. Sutton-Smith, "The Measurement of Masculinity and Femininity in Children," *Child Development* 39 (1959): 372–80; Lenore A. DeLucia, "The Toy Preference Test: A Measure of Sex-Role Identification," *Child Development* 34 (1963): 107–17; D. G. Brown, "Sex-Role Preference in Young Children," *Psychological Monographs* 70 (1956).

26. Pauline S. Sears, "Doll Play Aggression in Normal Young Children: Influence of Sex, Age, Sibling Status, Father's Absence," *Psychological Monographs* 65 (1951). See also Margaret H. Pintler, Ruth Phillips, and Robert R. Sears, "Sex Differences in Projective Doll Play of Preschool Children," *Journal of Psychology* 21 (1946): 73–80.

27. Harry Levin and Robert R. Sears, "Identification with Parents as a Determinant of Doll Play Aggression," *Child Development* 27 (June 1956): 148.

28. Rosenberg and Sutton-Smith, "The Measurement of Masculinity and Femininity in Children"; DeLucia, "The Toy Preference Test"; Brown, "Sex-Role Preference in Young Children," *Psychological Monographs* 70 (1946).

29. Paul Mussen and Luther Distler, "Masculinity, Identification, and Father-Son Relationships," *Journal of Abnormal and Social Psychology* 59 (1959): 350–56.

30. Meyer Rabban, "Sex-Role Identification in Young Children in Two Diverse Social Groups," *Genetic Psychology Monographs* 42 (1950): 132.

31. Rabban, "Sex-Role Identification," 130–31.

32. Sheldon, *Varieties of Temperament*; Carl C. Seltzer, "The Relationship Between the Masculine Component and Personality," in *Personality,* ed. C. Kluckholn and H. A. Murray (New York: Knopf, 1948), 95–96. For a larger account of the Harvard study, which received major funding from the William T. Grant Foundation, see Earnest A. Hooton, *"Young Man, You Are Normal": Findings from a Study of Students* (New York: G. P. Putnam, 1945).

33. Nancy Bayley, "Some Psychological Correlates of Somatic Androgyny," *Child Development* 22 (March 1951): 56–57. See also Richard N. Walker, "Body Build and Behavior in Young Children: Body Build and Parents' Ratings," *Child Development* 34 (1963): 1–23.

34. Terman et al., "Psychological Sex Differences," 955. Other studies of the relationship of children's body builds to their masculinity-femininity include Nancy Bayley and Mary Cover Jones, "Some Personality Characteristics of Boys with Retarded Skeletal Maturity," *Psychological Bulletin* 38 (1941); W. A. Schoncence, "Deficient Development of Masculinity: Psychosomatic Problem of Adolescence," *American Journal of Diseases of Children* 79 (January 1950): 17–29; and "Inadequate Masculine Physique as a Factor in Personality Development of Adolescent Boys," *Psychosomatic Medicine* 12 (January–February 1950): 49–54.

35. Mead, *Male and Female,* 130, 136.

36. Heather Munro Prescott, *A Doctor of Their Own: The History of Adolescent Medicine* (Cambridge: Harvard University Press, 1998), 114–15.

37. Munro Prescott, *A Doctor of Their Own,* 114.

38. Ruth E. Hartley, "Sex-Role Pressures and the Socialization of the Male Child," *Psychological Reports* 5 (1959): 458.

39. Robert R. Sears, Eleanor E. Maccoby, and Harry Levin, *Patterns of Child Rearing* (Evanston, Ill.: Row, Peterson, and Co., 1957), 398, 404.

40. M. J. D. of Hamden, Connecticut, to Louise Bates Ames and Frances Ilg, 14 September 1955, Louise Bates Ames Archives, Syracuse University Libraries; Mrs. H. F. to Benjamin Spock, 21 August 1959, Box 4, Benjamin Spock Archives, Syracuse University Libraries.

41. Sears et al., *Patterns of Child Rearing,* 99.

42. Rabban, "Sex-Role Identification," 133.

43. C. C. B. to Benjamin Spock, December 1959, Box 5, Benjamin Spock Papers, Syracuse University Library, Syracuse, New York.

10

Something They Did in the Dark

Lesbian and Gay Novels in the United States, 1948–1973

CHRIS FREEMAN

CHANNEL surfing, I pause on the TV talk show *Leeza* where the topic is gay teenagers. Host Leeza Gibbons tells her audience that there are currently over thirty gay characters on television, and she suggests that gay teens can use that presence as an impetus for talking to their parents about sexuality, even about being gay. They can begin the complex and difficult coming-out process with the *help* of a medium like television. Twenty years ago, when I was a gay teenager, I spent lots of time looking for images of myself; I hardly ever found them. From time to time, *Donahue* would feature a show on transsexuals or on lesbians in small towns, but such occasions were rare and tended to be more like circus sideshows than opportunities to foster dialogue.[1] I remember reading the entry "Homosexuality" in my *World Book Encyclopedia* (1976 edition); it was hardly encouraging or affirming. I remember looking in the indexes of lots of books trying to find out about homosexuals, about myself. I remember being in a used bookstore looking at David Reuben's *Everything You Ever Wanted to Know about Sex but Were Afraid to Ask*. As you might expect, Dr. Reuben has a lot to say about homosexuality and homosexuals, but most of it is homophobic and inaccurate. It didn't help me very much, and I suspect that other young lesbian and gay readers have been harmed rather than helped by finding out things they never wanted to know about their sexuality from this unenlightened 1970 bestseller.

Two very different texts were catalysts in my coming-out process as a twenty-two-year-old graduate student: the film *Prick Up Your Ears* and the novel *Maurice*. *Prick Up Your Ears* is a biopic about gay English playwright Joe Orton and his lover, Kenneth Halliwell, who bludgeoned Orton to death with a hammer and then killed himself. Needless to say, this is hardly an uplifting gay film; nonetheless, it was a significant gay *event* for me. Someone from the lesbigay group on my campus was at the film handing out informational cards with the group's post office box and phone number. In some way, then, attending this gay film (which I did alone and with trepidation) helped me take steps in my own coming-out process.

I came to E. M. Forster's novel *Maurice* about three months later, just after I had attended my first meeting at the lesbigay group on campus, meetings that were held at a private, unadvertised location and that felt a little like what an AA meeting must feel like. *Maurice* was the focus of a book group on campus, and I read it cover to cover with little advanced knowledge about the text. I knew that it was a gay novel that had been written before World War I and that Forster suppressed its publication until after his death in 1970. Unlike *Prick Up Your Ears, Maurice* provided me with a wonderful depiction of love between men. Forster has said, in the book's Terminal Note (which he wrote in 1960), that a "happy ending was imperative. I shouldn't have bothered to write otherwise. I was determined that in fiction anyway two men should fall in love and remain in it for the ever and ever that fiction allows."[2]

In this essay, I am starting with the hypothesis that what we read, at least as gay and lesbian readers, can have a strong, perhaps unpredictable, impact on the formation and development of our identities, our senses of who we are and who our lesbian and gay antecedents are and what their lives might have been like. The ubiquitous lesbian and gay "Who's Who" that extends from Plato and Sappho to Michelangelo and Shakespeare, to Whitman and Wilde, to Stein and Woolf, to Martina Navratilova and Elton John, indicates to me that regardless of where we stand as historians or theorists, the people like us in history interest us, even as we spend lots of time and intellectual energy explaining the historical fallacies involved in talking about Sappho and Ellen Degeneres or Shakespeare and Harvey Fierstein in the same terms.

While I am not interested in rehearsing the essentialist/social constructionist debate here, I do want to spend some time talking about reading and identity—about queer reading and queer identification—as it has been articulated in queer theory and in its antecedents, feminist and reader-response theory. Feminist theory and reader-response theory, as they emerged in the 1970s and 1980s, were both concerned with the position of the reader vis-à-vis the text. As described and practiced by Stanley Fish, Janice Radway, and others, reader-response criticism empowers readers by suggesting that the text is produced in the interaction between reader and artifact. Cultural and historical context as well as individual subjectivity (or subject position) contributes to this active process of production.[3] Feminist theory is in part about empowering women as it critiques patriarchal structures and traditions, and it offers women, as subjects and as readers, not only a theoretical and historical account of oppression, but also the possibility for creating change and exercising agency.

The nexus of feminist and reader-response theory can be seen, for example, in Judith Fetterley's *The Resisting Reader* (1978) and in Radway's *Reading the Romance* (1984). In her introduction, entitled "On the Politics of Literature," Fetterley writes:

> Power is the issue in the politics of literature, as it is in the politics of anything else. To be excluded from a literature that claims to define one's identity is to experience a peculiar form of powerlessness—not simply the powerlessness which derives from not seeing one's experience articulated, clarified, and legitimized in art, but more significantly the powerlessness which results from the endless division of self against self.[4]

Exclusion is key here. The process of coming to an identification of self—to a self-understanding—requires recognition elsewhere, and a theoretical framework such as feminist theory can enable that process by situating the feminist reader to resist her (or his) erasure by patriarchal culture: as Fetterley would have it, "to become a resisting rather than an assenting reader."[5]

In her reader-response/feminist approach to romance fiction and its mostly female audience, Radway asks how one can resist the pervasive ideological power of mass culture. At the end of her study, she writes:

> In thus recalling the interactive character of operations like reading, we . . . increase our chances of sorting out or articulating the difference between the repressive imposition of ideology and oppositional practices that, though limited in their scope and effect, at least dispute or contest the control of ideological forms. If we can learn, then, to look at the ways in which various groups appropriate and use the mass-produced art of our culture, I suspect we may well begin to understand that although the ideological power of contemporary cultural forms is enormous, indeed sometimes even frightening, that power is not yet all-pervasive, totally vigilant, or complete.[6]

For our purposes, one of the "various groups" implied in Radway's hopeful conclusion is queer people—and queer theory, as it developed in the late 1980s and 1990s, is located at the critical juncture of feminist and reader-response theory.

Eve Kosofsky Sedgwick, whose work stands at the center of queer theory, has written about coming of age as a queer reader. In her book *Tendencies* (1993), Sedgwick's introductory essay "Queer and Now" contains a subsection called "Promising, Smuggling, Reading, Overreading" in which she talks about "queer survival" as "surviving *into* threat, stigma, and the spiraling violence of gay- and lesbian-bashing" but also as "surviv[ing] into a moment of unprecedented cultural richness, cohesion, and assertiveness for many lesbian and gay adults." Sedgwick and many others of us invested in this loosely defined discourse of gay/lesbian/bisexual/transgender studies are "trying, in our work, to keep faith with vividly remembered promises made to ourselves in childhood: promises to make invisible possibilities and desires visible . . . to smuggle queer representation in where it must be smuggled and, with the relative freedom of adulthood, to challenge queer-eradicating impulses frontally where they are to be challenged."[7]

Sedgwick, who describes herself as a "perverse reader," is an exemplary resisting reader.[8] To read in that mode is a survival strategy; it is an identificatory strategy; and it can be an empowering strategy. If we find ourselves in a text or a context rife with "queer eradicating impulses," how do we survive? How do we assert ourselves, claim our identities, create art and literature?

To address some of these questions, I will focus on the intersection of recent U.S. literary history and homosexuality, from the years immediately following World War II to the early 1970s, when the contemporary gay rights movement was beginning to flourish. My somewhat autobiographical approach follows the lead of an early nonfictional work in this period, Donald Webster Cory's *The Homosexual in America: A Subjective Approach* (1951).[9] In his preface, the pseudonymous Cory emphasizes the "subjective" nature of his book's subtitle, and his remarks indicate the discursive struggle regarding homosexuality at mid-century: "It is my belief that the observations and viewpoints *of the homosexual* are as essential as those of the psychiatrist, the jurist, or the churchman in arriving at any conclusions on homosexuality."[10] Cory attempts to add the testimonial voice of a gay man to the proscriptive voices of psychiatric, juridical, and religious discourses. Likewise, the authors I discuss below have contributed to the emerging voices of lesbians and gay men (usually through the veil of fiction) in their "subjective" depictions of gay lives and times.

In 1948, Dr. Alfred Kinsey and his colleagues published their study *Sexual Behavior in the Human Male*. This groundbreaking work included some information about homosexuality that was rather shocking to the American public. Chapter 21 of the Kinsey Report, titled "Homosexual Outlet," contains the following statistical bombshell: "In . . . terms of physical contact to the point of orgasm, the data in the present study indicate that at least 37 per cent of the male population has some homosexual experience between the beginning of adolescence and old age. . . . Among the males who remain unmarried until the age of 35, almost exactly 50 per cent have homosexual experience."[11] Virtually singlehandedly, the Kinsey Report transformed the social import of homosexuality from an obscure, highly marginalized behavior to an activity that many—if not most—men had participated in after adolescence. Whether Kinsey's numbers are absolutely accurate or not is less important than the impact of such statistical claims coming from such a reputable, "objective" source. My review and reading of lesbian and gay fiction from this period in U.S. history suggests that the Kinsey report more or less corresponds with an increase in the productivity of lesbian and gay writing; I would not necessarily claim that Kinsey's influence sparked this emergence of gay creativity, but certainly the public awareness and controversy surrounding Kinsey's findings and the increasing prominence of lesbian and gay fiction reflect the modest social change that helped usher in the beginnings of the gay rights movement in the 1950s and after.

Another 1948 landmark was twenty-one-year-old novelist Gore Vidal's *The City and the Pillar*. Vidal's novel made significant advances in extending the range of gay male character types. The protagonist, Jim Willard, is an athletic, handsome, rather conventionally masculine young man; one of his lovers, Ronald Shaw, is a closeted Hollywood star. In retrospect, one can see Shaw as a kind of Rock Hudson or Anthony Perkins figure. An exchange between Willard and his lover, writer Paul Sullivan, provides an excellent example of the issues Vidal addresses in his novel. In a discussion about hiding one's homosexuality, Paul says:

> There should be no need to hide . . . ; everything should be open and declared. . . . It's censured because the others are afraid, afraid for themselves. . . . As it is here in America we're sick with fear: sexual, professional, on the surface and beneath. We are very sick and frightened and we condemn what we don't understand or what we feel endangers us. The men cannot love women, cannot love one another, cannot love themselves. All they have left is hate; hate of the ones who try to love; hate of the few who succeed. No, we must declare ourselves, become known; allow the world to discover this subterranean life of ours which connects kings and farm boys, artists and clerks. Let them see that the important thing is not the object of love but the emotion itself. . . . As for homosexuality itself, it has always existed and always will and probably no explanation can be given for it.[12]

This passage contains an indictment of the fear and heartlessness endemic, as Paul and probably Vidal saw it at least, in post–World War II America—the same America in which Senator Joseph McCarthy spearheaded Communist and homosexual witch-hunts.

Vidal's novel ends with a drunken brawl between Jim and his boyhood friend Bob, whom Jim has always loved. Bob rebuffs Jim's advances, saying to him, "You're a queer . . . you're nothing but a damned queer."[13] Enraged, Jim fights Bob, finally choking him to death. And so, in spite of its "progressiveness," *The City and the Pillar* has the typical tragic ending that Forster was so insistent about avoiding. In 1965, though, Vidal revised the novel's conclusion. In this version, Jim and Bob fight; Jim subdues and rapes him. No happy ending here either, but a power struggle and a novel more about sexuality and honesty (or truth to oneself) than about murder. In "An Afterword" to the 1965 edition, Vidal says, "By the time I came to write *The City and the Pillar,* I was bored with playing it safe. I wanted to take risks, to try something no American had done before." He also points out that the Kinsey report came out a few months after his best seller was published, which made him feel "somewhat exonerated" for his frank treatment of homosexuality in the novel. Vidal reports having received "a nice letter from the good doctor [Kinsey], complimenting me on 'your work in the field.'"[14]

While a novel like Vidal's or a study like Kinsey's might seem to indicate a time of progress regarding homosexuality in the United States, that was not entirely the case. As I mentioned, the paradoxical postwar years seem to have become alarmingly similar to what Paul Sullivan describes in the above cited passage from *The City and the Pillar:* a climate of fear, paranoia, and backlash emerged. Historian John D'Emilio has shown that these years were crucial in crystallizing emerging communities of lesbians and gay men: "One can scarcely overestimate the significance of the 1940s in restructuring the social expression of same-sex eroticism. . . . A sexual and emotional life that gay men and women previously experienced mainly in individual terms suddenly became, for the war generation, a widely shared collective phenomenon."[15]

It is telling that D'Emilio's chapter on the 1950s is titled "The Bonds of Oppression: Gay Life in the 1950s." In the midst of the Red Scare—and what we also might call the Lavender Scare—the fledgling gay communities forged in the 1940s survived, wounded and defensive, but at least somewhat organized. In Los Angeles in 1950, Harry Hay and Bob Hull began to organize a secret group of gay men that would become the Mattachine Society, which started out as a discussion group and expanded into a kind of watchdog organization, keeping records of police harassment, surveying gay and lesbian literature, and reviewing research about homosexuality. In January of 1953, a few members of the Mattachine Society published the first issue of *ONE,* a "homophile" magazine. Very quickly, the magazine's monthly circulation surpassed two thousand copies, which "helped spread word that a homosexual emancipation organization had formed."[16] However, the cultural strains of McCarthyism hampered the organization, and after a few years the group's radicalism was severely curtailed, though *ONE* continued to forge ahead and even criticized the retreats of its brother organization.

In late 1955, Del Martin and Phyllis Lyon, a lesbian couple in San Francisco, organized a meeting of three other lesbian couples and formed the Daughters of Bilitis (DOB), which forged alliances with *ONE* and Mattachine in early 1956. DOB began publishing *The Ladder,* focusing on lesbian (and women's) concerns, in October of the same year. These organizations remained in a cooperative association for many years, and the DOB's focus on women's rights issues added feminism to the homosexual rights agenda.[17]

Clearly, then, gays and lesbians in the United States began to have a real sense of group identity and community in these years, in spite of—or perhaps because of—the social stigma associated with their very being. The literature of the 1950s and 1960s mirrors social realities: homosexuals were becoming visible, not just in urban centers or in news scandals, but also in magazines and books. They were beginning to speak for themselves and about themselves.[18] This self-articulation was, naturally, not always what we might, half a century later, call affirmative; however, visibility—being able to read about oneself and others like you—must have been a profoundly important experience for lesbian and gay readers.

Obviously, I would therefore not assert that things have "gradually improved" since the 1940s. History is much more complicated than that, as is literature. What this overview of gay and lesbian representation attempts to show is how issues of concern for gay and lesbian writers and readers have developed and how visibility has shaped identity. It also seeks to show that gay and lesbian writing, which has often been marginalized by the critical establishment, has a significant place in post–World War II American literature and culture. It is not a matter of "two steps forward and one step back" or of slow but inevitable progress. Instead, my concern is to ask readers to think of their *own* responses to this literature, this culture, and this *anxiety* of process, progress, and social change.

What did lesbians and gay men have to read in these formative years? First, the women. In 1952, writing under the pseudonym Claire Morgan, Patricia Highsmith published *The Price of Salt* (also known as *Carol*). The author provided an afterword to the thirtieth anniversary republication of the novel in which she discussed its reception and its milieu: "When *The Price of Salt* was written, a few novels about homosexuality were raising their heads, somewhat timidly, though the publishers' jacket blurbs said 'daring'. . . . The homosexual novel then had to have a tragic ending. . . . *The Price of Salt* in 1952 was said to be the first gay book with a happy ending."[19] Note Highsmith's comments about book jackets; publishers relished sensationalizing lesbian and gay writing, fostering a pulp fiction market that flourished in the 1950s.

The Price of Salt, set primarily in New York, is a well-written novel about love at first sight between Therese, a young woman, and Carol, an older married woman in the process of getting a divorce. Carol has had one affair with a woman, her business partner Abby, and Carol and Therese go through a protracted flirtation that leads into a cross-country road trip. Blackmail, a real threat for lesbians and gays in this period, becomes an issue; Carol's husband has them followed by a private detective, and what he discovers—that they are lovers—costs Carol custody of her daughter in the divorce settlement. The novel almost ends tragically: it seems that Carol is going to freeze out Therese in the hope of salvaging visitation rights with her daughter. Instead, she defies her ex-husband and the law, and she and Therese come together in the closing moment of the novel, where Carol dines with a male friend and Therese watches them from the doorway:

> Carol raised her hand slowly and brushed her hair back, once on either side, and Therese smiled because the gesture was Carol, and it was Carol she loved and would always love. Oh in a different way now, because she was a different person, and it was like meeting Carol all over again, and it was still Carol and no one else. It would be Carol, in a thousand cities, a thousand houses, in foreign lands where they would go together, in heaven and hell. . . . Carol saw her, seemed to stare at her incredulously a moment while Therese watched the slow smile growing, before her arm lifted suddenly, her hand waved a quick eager greeting that Therese had never seen before. Therese walked toward her.[20]

Hardly a hot and heavy conclusion, though the novel does not shy away from depicting the women's passion. To a later audience, *The Price of Salt* will seem a bit like the film *Thelma and Louise* (1991) without the Grand Canyon but with more passion between the two protagonists.

Another major lesbian novelist from this period is Ann Bannon, who published a series of five popular novels between 1957 and 1962. *Odd Girl Out* (1957) is a love story concerning two young college friends, Laura and Beth. The novel has a similar structure to Radclyffe Hall's English lesbian classic *The Well of Loneliness* (1928). In both novels, the heroines leave their beloveds to the care of men who will undoubtedly not be adequate to the task. The whole of *Odd Girl Out* seems to resist Laura's strength, but she is redeemed because she is true to her "queer" self. In the closing scene, as she leaves Beth in the hands of Charlie, Laura says, "'I know what I am, and I can be honest with myself now. I'll live my life as honestly as I can, without ruining it. . . . I knew you weren't—queer—like I am. . . . Beth, you're meant for a man. Like Charlie. I'm not.'"[21] Laura goes off to find others of her kind in New York City, and Bannon's series continues, following these characters and introducing her most notorious creation, Beebo Brinker.

Bannon's next novel, *I Am a Woman* (1959), focuses on Laura's life in New York, where she meets Beebo and where she becomes close friends with Jack, a gay man who recognizes that she's a lesbian when the two are on a blind date together. Jack tells Laura that he always tries to pick out fellow homosexuals: "'You might say it's a hobby with me. I spot one and I think to myself, 'Another poor bastard like me.' It boosts my morale. I guess it's a case of misery loves company.'"[22] Laura's response to Jack, which indicates the emergence of a new discourse among homosexuals, shows that this novel is an important document of homosexual history: "'I never heard that word—gay—like you used it until our date Friday. Nobody ever called me 'gay' before. I didn't even know what it meant.'"[23] *I Am a Woman* is a sexy novel, an informative portrait of gay culture in Greenwich Village in the 1950s, and, most importantly, it is a narrative of queer alliance between a lesbian and a gay man, a situation parallel to the coming together of the Mattachine Society and Daughters of Bilitis on the other coast at the same time.

By the time of Bannon's *Women in the Shadows* (1959), these characters' lives have become bleak and rather dysfunctional. Laura and Beebo have been lovers for a couple of tumultuous years. This novel adds issues of race and of queer bashing in two subplots: Laura has a fling with Tish, a Native American who passes as white, and Beebo, in a particularly pathetic and self-loathing moment, fakes having been beaten up, claiming she's been recognized as a butch lesbian. Laura, who always seems to be seeking an easy way out of difficulty, marries Jack and, utilizing the technology of artificial insemination, becomes what must be the first lesbian mom in American fiction. The novel's concluding paragraphs show its normalizing impulse: "[Laura] wondered, in that violet twilight before sleep, how long it would take her to get used to this closeness with [Jack]. She was so comfortable . . . more comfortable, it seemed, and more safe than she ever had been. And they fell asleep together with the sigh of relief and hope that only the lost, who have found themselves, can feel."[24]

Journey to a Woman (1960) brings the newly separated Beth back into the picture; she returns hoping to find and reunite with Laura. Instead, she and Beebo become lovers. For our purposes, this novel contains a very interesting subplot: Beth reads lesbian fiction! In fact, she corresponds with and finally meets (and sleeps with) Nina Spicer, a lesbian novelist in New York, who eventually leads her to Laura and Beebo. It's a small world after all.[25]

Another major lesbian writer, whose career began a few years after Ann Bannon gave up writing and went underground, is Jane Rule. Her first novel, *Desert of the Heart* (1964), has become a lesbian classic, especially after it was made into a film by Donna Deitch in 1985. Rule's fiction is similar (at least in terms of plot) to Bannon's and Highsmith's in some ways; her protagonist, Evelyn, a professor of English, has come to Reno seeking a quick divorce. At a boardinghouse she meets the younger Ann, and the two quickly fall in love. Ann, who works at a casino, is really a political cartoonist, and Evelyn encourages her work. As in Highsmith's novel, the divorce process is complicated, and Evelyn fears that her lesbianism will be used against her. It is easy to see, considering plots like these, why lesbian concerns and women's rights intertwined. In a cautiously hopeful ending, Evelyn's divorce becomes final, and she and Ann decide to try continuing their lives together.

Rule has written several other notable works, including the novels *This Is Not for You* (1970), *Against the Season* (1971), and *Lesbian Images* (1975), the latter an informative and insightful collection of essays that includes discussions of Radclyffe Hall, Del Martin and Phyllis Lyon, and May Sarton. *This Is Not for You* is an astonishing book. Addressed to the narrator's ex-lover, who has become a nun, the book opens: "This is not a letter. I wrote you for the last time over a year ago to offer the little understanding I had, to say good-bye."[26] A novel filled with one-night stands and bitterness, *This Is Not for You* ends with an implicit message: this *is* for some, this is for me, not bitter, but resigned. The novel's last paragraph encapsulates its impulses: "I am not guilty, and Joyce is right: it is a limited way to live. Yet I don't see how I could have afforded any other. . . . If I have been incapable of loving you well enough, I've made a virtue of loving you badly. Pray for me if you will, Sister, beloved of God. This is not for you."[27]

Before shifting the focus of this discussion to gay male fiction from this period, I want to talk about one other very fine lesbian novel, Isabel Miller's *Patience and Sarah,* also known as *A Place for Us* (1969). Miller, whose real name is Alma Routsong, divorced her husband in 1962 and moved to New York City the following year, where she began writing *A Place for Us,* which would be her third novel but her first as "Isabel Miller" and her first lesbian work. In the late 1960s and early 1970s, Miller was a member of the Daughters of Bilitis and an active worker in the gay liberation movement. In 1971, *Patience and Sarah* won the first Gay Book Award given by the American Library Association for "present[ing] a positive image of homosexuals and their lifestyle."[28] That the American Library Association was giving such an award speaks volumes about the increased visibility of lesbian and gay culture. Can you imagine *The Price of Salt* being given such an award in 1952?

Patience and Sarah is a historical novel. Set in early- nineteenth-century New England, it tells the story of the love of two women, Patience White, a relatively wealthy painter, and Sarah (Sam) Dowling, a lower-class farm girl, her father's favorite "son." The novel is based on the lives of painter Mary Ann Willson and her companion, a Miss Bundidge, and Miller's afterword provides strands of historical evidence regarding the two women, which makes this novel part of an effort to reclaim lesbian herstory, an endeavor that Joan Nestle, Esther Newton, Lillian Faderman, Carroll Smith-Rosenberg, and others have continued.

Against all odds, and against Sarah's father's will, the two women go west, into upstate New York, and become frontier women. As they board a boat to take them to Hudson in the "Kaatskill," Patience tells us, "I held Sarah's hand and felt the ancient sea and the new wheels carry us to a life we had no pattern for, that no one we knew of had ever lived, that we must invent for ourselves on a razor's edge, and I tipped my head back and sang three hallelujahs."[29] This pioneering spirit is representative of the positive, affirming story of two strong, determined women living many years ahead of their time. To my mind, *Patience and Sarah* is the culmination of twenty years of burgeoning lesbian fiction in the United States.

Like their lesbian counterparts, gay male novelists writing during this period struggled toward self-representation. Many of their novels cannot be called affirming—many have tragic endings or are peopled by dreadfully sad, unfulfilled men—but some of the men are bold, some are resistant, and some have been able to love. As Ann Bannon's character Beth discovered from reading about homosexuality, regardless of the story these novels can provide security, solace, and companionship for their readers. To open my discussion of gay male writing in the 1950s, I want to focus on two very different writers, both of whom continued to work into the 1980s: James Baldwin, an expatriate African American, and Christopher Isherwood, an English-born naturalized American.

Baldwin's writing is centrally concerned with race and sexuality, issues so strong is his own life that they drove him into exile in France, where he wrote his first three novels. His autobiographical first novel, *Go Tell It on the Mountain* (1953), is the story of young John Grimes, a fourteen-year-old in Harlem who is in love with Elisha, a preacher three years his senior. Though not primarily a gay novel, *Go Tell It on the Mountain* is nuanced with John's desire for Elisha (and other boys) and the shame and guilt he associates with it:

> He had sinned. In spite of the saints, his mother and his father, the warnings he heard from his earliest beginnings, [John] had sinned with his hands a sin that was hard to forgive. In the school lavatory, alone, thinking of the boys, older, bigger, braver, who made bets with each other as to whose urine could arch higher, he had watched in himself a transformation of which he would never dare speak.[30]

John's spiritual life in conflict with his budding sexuality is suggestive of the pressures that Baldwin himself wrestled with in his own life and in much of his work.

The nature of authority—represented by the church and by his parents—weighs heavily on John, but he is unable to overcome those burdens, which is partly reflected in his inability to articulate his desires for Elisha. The novel's closing scene, depicting the parting of the two young men after a night of spiritual awakening in their church, characteristically disarticulates John's love:

> They were approaching [John's] house—his father's house. In a moment he must leave Elisha, step out from under his protecting arm, and walk alone into the house—alone with his mother and father. And he was afraid. He wanted to stop and turn to Elisha, and tell him . . . something for which he found no words. . . . John stood still watching him walk away. The sun had come fully awake. It was waking the streets. . . . It fell over Elisha like a golden robe, and struck John's forehead, where Elisha had kissed him, like a seal ineffaceable forever.[31]

The kiss may be "ineffaceable" here, but the love remains effaced until Baldwin's third novel, *Giovanni's Room* (1956).

A truly expatriate novel, *Giovanni's Room* is set in France and centers on David, a white American, and his lover, Giovanni, an Italian. Every bit as frank about homosexuality as Vidal's *The City and the Pillar, Giovanni's Room* shows Baldwin's courageousness as a gay writer, but it sparked a contentious relationship with critics that would be part of Baldwin's entire career. The novel is lyrically written; claustrophobia, as implied by the title, is the overwhelming sense it gives the reader. Unable to stay with his male lover, David goes back to Hella, his fiancée, leaving Giovanni to dissipate and turn to a life of crime, for which he is to be executed. In the scene where he and David finally separate, Giovanni's insights into David's character are sharp:

> You have never loved anyone. . . . You love your purity, you love your mirror—you are just like a little virgin. . . . You want to be *clean*. . . . You want to leave Giovanni because he makes you stink. You want to despise Giovanni because he is not afraid of the stink of love. You want to *kill* him in the name of all your little lying moralities. You are, by far, the most immoral man I have met in my life. Look, *look* what you have done to me. Do you think you could have done this if I did not love you? Is *this* what you should do to love?[32]

This novel's agony is clear in this passage, which undoubtedly represents a kind of self-loathing familiar to many gay men in the 1950s, surely a phenomenon not limited to that bleak decade.

Baldwin's most powerful novel, to my mind, is *Another Country* (1962), a book peopled with well-drawn black and white, male and female, and gay, bisexual, and straight characters. Sexuality is fluid in this novel, defying strict categorization. Much of the narrative is a paean to Rufus, a black bisexual jazz musician who dies early in the story. The most successful couple in the novel, Eric and Yves, give the book a hopeful ending. In the closing scene, Yves arrives from France to join Eric in New York: "Yves looked up joyously, unable to say anything. *Eric.* And all his fear left him, he was certain, now, that everything would be all right."[33]

The arrival of Yves to his life in "another country" is told in much the same way that Christopher Isherwood has written of his arrival in the United States at the end of his memoir, *Christopher and His Kind* (1976). Both Yves and Christopher arrive on the shore of the new world with great expectations. Isherwood, traveling with W. H. Auden, left England just before World War II began, and he became a U.S. citizen in 1946. Though much of Isherwood's early work contained elements of homosexuality, his earliest explicitly political handling of the topic comes in his novel *The World in the Evening* (1954), a narrative focusing on the bisexual protagonist, Stephen, his writer-wife Elizabeth Rydal, and a young American, Michael, who falls in love with Stephen. Much of Stephen's approach to his sexuality involves rationalization; however, in a subplot, he encounters a gay couple, Bob and Charles, who are forthright in their sexual politics. Stephen balks at Bob's confrontational attitude about being gay. Bob responds:

> Maybe we're too tactful. People just ignore us, most of the time, and we just let them. . . . So this whole business never gets discussed, and the laws never get changed.[34]

Bob's assessment of this vexing situation sounds a lot like Cory's in *The Homosexual in America* and Vidal's through the character of Paul Sullivan's in *The City and the Pillar;* however, one gets the idea that Bob is willing to become the martyr, to be the activist who risks his neck to incite social change.

Later in the novel, Bob gives a diatribe about the military's anti-gay policy, which has continued to be a political controversy even after the instigation of President Clinton's ineffectual "don't ask, don't tell" policy. Talking about Quakers and conscientious objectors, Bob exclaims:

> I can't be a [conscientious objector] because, if they declared war on the queers—tried to round us up and liquidate us, or something—I'd fight. I'd fight till I dropped. I know that. . . . Of course, I could have gotten out of this whole thing. I could have told the psychiatrist, when I had my medical examination. All you have to do is tell them you're queer, and you're out. I couldn't do that, though. Because they're claiming that us queers are unfit for their beautiful pure Army and Navy—when they ought to be glad to have us. . . . My God, look at all the big heroes in history.[35]

Bob is perhaps the first "militant homosexual" in American literature. He certainly recognizes that the social "problem" of homosexuals is not our problem, and he is willing to fight the system to protect himself and his kind.

Isherwood's most memorable gay character (aside from himself) is George, the protagonist of his 1964 novel, *A Single Man.* A parody of James Joyce's *Ulysses* and of Virginia Woolf's *Mrs. Dalloway, A Single Man* depicts one day in the life of an English professor whose lover has been killed in a car accident a few years earlier. Part of Isherwood's point in this novel is that George is different because he's gay, but he's not *that* different. This is not an assimilationist perspective but rather a statement about the importance of identity. The wandering George never fits into a community, though in striving for a connection, the novel makes it clear that the desiring gay male body is the central location for George's identity and community. In what appears to be a seduction scene, George and his student Kenny come very close to physical contact, but it fails to happen. Frustrated and somewhat angered, George lashes out at Kenny:

> You came here this evening to see me. . . . You want me to tell you what I know. . . . But I can't. I quite literally can't. Because, don't you see, what I know is what I am? . . . Instead of trying to know, you commit the inexcusable triviality of saying "he's a dirty old man," and turning this evening, which might be the most precious and unforgettable of your life, into a flirtation! . . . It's the enormous tragedy of everything nowadays: flirtation. Flirtation instead of fucking, if you'll pardon my coarseness.[36]

Flirtation excludes the body; it sanitizes the near connection back into a dialogue of separation. For Isherwood, the body's centrality is a metaphor for his own drive toward articulating himself as a gay man. In the 1970s, when Isherwood began giving interviews in the gay press and when he started talking about being gay outside of his books, he told a reporter from the *Los Angeles Times,* "I'm an advocate, but I wouldn't call myself an activist. I'm just an old and respectable man using his respectability as a weapon."[37] Isherwood wrote his way out of the closet, and his rhetoric here points toward a new era in gay fiction, a move beyond representation and into advocacy.[38]

The sexualized gay body has a rather different signification in the work of John Rechy. Rechy's work, like Isherwood's, tends to blur the lines between life and fiction. Rechy burst on the literary scene with *City of Night* in 1963. A pseudodocumentary, *City of Night* mines the homosexual underworld. Many interesting characters are described in great detail; some are desperate, some tragic, and some heroic. Rechy's writing style—in his privileging of the moment, the unpolished thought—is similar to that of some writers of the Beat movement. Like Bannon's account of the gay underworld in Greenwich Village in the 1960s, Rechy documents (without sensationalizing) many gay subcultures in this novel: hustlers, leathermen, drag queens, and fetishists of all sorts. In *City of Night* the hustler/narrator is unnamed, which graphically separates the reader from the character, signifying the separations pervasive in the world the novel depicts.

Rechy's follow-up novel, *Numbers* (1968), is a kind of sequel to *City of Night.* Johnny Rio, a former hustler, returns to his old haunts in Los Angeles seeking to reassert himself and to reaffirm his ego by being able to "score" thirty times in ten days. In this narrative of sexual compulsion and the disarticulation of homosexual desire, Johnny Rio fears losing self-control and losing his good looks. Time and again, Johnny looks at himself in a bathroom mirror in Griffith Park; sometimes he sees a sexy young man and sometimes a monster. This imagery recalls Oscar Wilde's novel, *The Picture of Dorian Gray* (1891), implying that Johnny's actions, though hidden in the bushes of the park and the balconies of movie houses, do have visible effects on him, body and soul.

In a dinner party scene, Johnny claims that he has given up his compulsive sexual behavior. Sebastian, a character based on Christopher Isherwood, whom Rechy knew, asks Johnny if he's sure he can quit cruising the park. Johnny replies:

> I'm sure. . . . Never, never again. Not in the Park, nor in any other park, nor in movie balconies. It'll be only with people with identity—men or women—with people I know, not people without names—not just "numbers." . . . [N]ow I can stay in control.[39]

Because Johnny Rio can't get a handle on his own identity, he cannot gain the control that he longs for. Rechy's books portray sexual obsession and narcissism, but they move beyond self-absorption and stand as documents of a myriad of behavior and character types whose lives have not otherwise been recorded in American literature.

The final pre-Stonewall novel I want to discuss brings us full circle, back to one of the pioneers, Gore Vidal. Returning the favor given him in the dedication of *A Single Man,* Vidal dedicated *Myra Breckinridge* to Isherwood. Wonderfully outrageous, especially when compared to the somber *City and the Pillar,* Vidal's 1968 novel is a campy pseudo-autobiography of the transsexual Myra Breckinridge.[40] Vidal published *Myron,* the pre-operative side of the story, in 1974, but *Myra* is the better novel. Addressing issues of gender, sexuality, and the origins of homosexuality, Vidal, like Baldwin in *Another Country,* takes the gay novel into territory that critics in the 1990s, in an effort to reclaim a formerly oppressive term, would call "queer," a realm in which gender and sexuality defy categories and move fluidly across a broad spectrum. *Myra* is a Hollywood insider novel; ironically, it was made into a classically dreadful film starring Raquel Welch and Mae West (as Myra) in 1970.[41]

In order to point to the post-Stonewall future of lesbian and gay fiction, I want to discuss briefly two novels from the early 1970s, one very well known and the other rather obscure. Rita Mae Brown's *Rubyfruit Jungle* (1973) is perhaps the best-selling lesbian novel of all time. Brown attended New York University in the mid-1960s; while there, she helped establish a lesbian/gay student group. Later, she was an early member of the National Organization of Women, though her lesbianism put her at odds with that group.

Rubyfruit Jungle is an autobiographical novel. Molly Bolt, the protagonist, knows she is attracted to girls at an early age. Growing up poor in Florida, Molly and her cousin Leroy talk a lot about their lives and desires, and the novel provides a fascinating portrait of the pressures on queer kids to grow up straight, as Leroy struggles to do. Molly, though, remains true to herself, gets kicked out of college for her lesbianism, and heads to New York City. She shares some characteristics with Bannon's Beebo, her rambunctious lesbian literary antecedent. Brown's novel is remarkable for its radical feminism, its strong heroine, and its confrontational, unapologetic depiction of a young woman who is proud of who she is and of what she has done. Molly takes ownership of her body and her life. As she tells her former lover, who's now married with children, "I love women. I'll never marry a man and I'll never marry a woman either. That's not my way. I'm a devil-may-care lesbian."[42]

The attitude of Daniel Curzon's hero Cole in his novel *Something You Do in the Dark* (1971) goes beyond devil-may-care, to say the least. Although Curzon claims that he had not heard of the Stonewall Rebellion when he wrote his novel, the book is filled with rage at the oppression gay people experience and at the outrageous barriers to our happiness. A revenge narrative, the plot focuses on Cole, who has just been released from prison having been busted by a plainclothes police officer for indecent exposure and lewd and lascivious behavior. Shame and anger combine in Cole, a troubled but somehow very likeable character. Cole attempts some political organizing and offers help to other men victimized by vice officers.

In a scene that exemplifies some of the frustration and desperation depicted in Curzon's novel, Cole meets Jerry, a teacher, and they go to the house where Cole's father, who is in ill health, lives. Cole and Jerry, in the course of their sexual repartee, parody some psychoanalytic stereotypes: "Those queers do lots of funny things. . . . They're merely compensating. . . . They're fixated orally—and sometimes even anally."[43] Predictably, given the run of Cole's bad luck, his father hears something and walks in to find his son with "warm semen spatter[ed] across his jaw."[44]

Cole literally becomes the martyr that Donald Cory noted would be necessary for gay liberation. In an act of suicidal defiance, he attempts to kill members of the vice squad who continue to make life miserable for gay men everywhere. Unfortunately, the attempt at heroism is botched and tragic, but it is certainly a different kind of tragedy than the earlier model from gay literature, in which the hero would have hanged himself in a closed room. Curzon's fated hero fights to the end, a martyr doing something desperate to fight oppression. Although its hero is finally defeated, Curzon's novel celebrates activism and queer visibility and documents a persecuted gay population with dark humor and rage.

In this essay, I have traced the development of lesbian and gay fiction in the United States over a period of approximately twenty-five years. I opened with discussion of a nonfiction study, Cory's "subjective" book *The Homosexual in America,* first published in 1951. The publication of *Lesbian/Woman* by Del Martin and Phyllis Lyon in 1972 is a powerful counterpoint to Cory's anonymous and apologist text. Where Cory is politely indirect, Martin and Lyon—using their real names—are defiant and forthright. Their book is virtually a how-to guide for lesbians. They end it strongly:

> The homophile community of fifteen years ago might have settled for "tolerance." But not today: no halfway measures will do. . . . [W]e want equal rights and full citizenship. . . . Today there are no pleas nor pleases—there are only demands. . . . No longer is toleration acceptable. The Lesbians, along with all oppressed people, want freedom—and we want it *now*![45]

It took pride and courage for Martin and Lyon to write those words; they had been fighting for gay and lesbian rights (and women's rights) since the mid-1950s when they founded the Daughters of Bilitis, so it is only fitting that their triumphant ending likewise close this history—but not quite yet, not without a little reflection on where we've been.

So, gentle reader, where is your story in all of this history? How does your identity figure into these? Imagine that it's 1972 and you live in Nashville. What would it have been like to walk down to Mill's Bookstore in Hillsboro Village and buy a $2.95 paperback titled *Lesbian/Woman*? How much harder would it have been to check out *The Homosexual in America* in 1952 from the Nashville Public Library, assuming that it was even available on those shelves? Surely it was easier in 1972, but how much? Several of the books I needed to read in order to write this essay were missing or lost at both public libraries and university libraries. Why? Because of fear, shame, guilt by association.

But it's the new millennium. More than thirty years have passed since the Stonewall Rebellion; Leeza Gibbons tells us that there are more than thirty out and proud gay and lesbian characters on television, and if we believe *Newsweek,* AIDS is all but a thing of the past, thanks to protease inhibitors and safer-sex campaigns. Vermont has done what Hawaii would not in terms of recognizing the legitimacy of our domestic partnerships.

So, now, when you shop at Barnes and Noble, do you unselfconsciously browse the "Lesbian/Gay Studies" section, or do you find yourself glancing over your shoulder to see who's around? How did you feel when you bought *Modern American Queer History,* or when you checked it out from your library? I'd be willing to bet that your heart rate increased (if only slightly) and your mouth may have become a little dry. If that, combined with what you've read about here, helps you empathize with lesbian and gay readers (and writers) of the past, then history has taught you an important lesson: it has shown you that you are part of something that need not be done in the dark any longer.

Notes

1. For more on the role of television talk shows and their depiction of homosexuality, see Joshua Gamson, *Freaks Talk Back: Tabloid Talk Shows and Sexual Nonconformity* (Chicago: University of Chicago Press, 1998).

2. E. M. Forster, "Terminal Note" in *Maurice* (1913; repr. New York: Norton, 1987), 250. Forster ends his "Terminal Note" with one paragraph under the heading "Homosexuality": "Since *Maurice* was written there has been a change in the public attitude [toward homosexuality] here: the change from ignorance and terror to familiarity and contempt. . . . We had not realized that what the public really loathes in homosexuality is not the thing itself but having to think about it" (255). Although Forster's words were written in England, attitudes in the United States were not much different, and his closing remarks here can be verified

by reading many contemporary reviews of the novels I will be discussing in this essay—or by reading almost any review of *Maurice*.

3. See, for example, Stanley Fish, *Is There a Text in this Class?* (Cambridge: Harvard University Press, 1980); and Janice A. Radway, *Reading the Romance* (Chapel Hill: University of North Carolina Press, 1984). See also Catherine Belsey, *Critical Practice* (London: Methuen, 1980). Belsey writes that "critical practice is seen as a process of releasing the positions from which the text is intelligible. Liberated from the fixity of the communication model, the text is available for production in the process of reading" (140).

4. Judith Fetterley, *The Resisting Reader* (Bloomington: Indiana University Press, 1978), xiii.

5. Ibid., xxii.

6. Radway, *Reading the Romance,* 221–22.

7. Eve Kosofsky Sedgwick, *Tendencies* (Durham: Duke University Press, 1993), 3.

8. Ibid., 4.

9. Donald Webster Cory (pseudonym of Edward Sagarin), *The Homosexual in America: A Subjective Approach* (1951; repr. New York: Arno, 1975). Byrne R. S. Fone, in his book *A Road to Stonewall: Male Homosexuality and Homophobia in English and American Literature, 1750–1969* (New York: Twayne, 1995), 254, reports that Cory's book went through six printings in its first five years and suggests that "perhaps its popularity encouraged writers." While Fone gives a rather positive reading of Cory's groundbreaking book, my reading of it is more ambivalent, especially taking into account the 1959 and 1975 prefaces included in the twenty-fifth anniversary Arno edition. In the 1975 preface, Cory refers to his book as a "museum piece," and he refutes his original implication that homosexuality is "an equally good way of life as heterosexuality." He says that he is "appalled at [my] suggestion that children should be raised to see homosexuality as an equally good alternate lifestyle, and I cannot believe that people who themselves have suffered so much would wish to inflict such sufferings on others" (9). While this later preface is highly problematic, the substance of Cory's book is a plea for social justice and understanding and must surely have been encouraging to lesbians and gay men who read it in the 1950s and after. Cory, it should be noted, published *The Lesbian in America* in 1965. For a fascinating essay on Cory's life, see Martin Duberman's "Dr. Sagarin and Mr. Cory: The 'Father' of the Homophile Movement," in *Harvard Gay and Lesbian Review* 4(4) (Fall 1997): 7–14.

10. Cory, *The Homosexual in America,* xiii. My emphasis.

11. Alfred Kinsey et al., *Sexual Behavior in the Human Male* (Philadelphia: Saunders, 1948), 623. Kinsey and his associates published the companion study *Sexual Behavior in the Human Female* in 1953. For his findings regarding lesbianism, see his "Homosexual Responses and Contacts" (chap. 11, 446–501). As Kinsey's findings indicate, "Homosexual contacts are highly effective in bringing the female to orgasm" (457). Gore Vidal provides some wonderful details about Kinsey and his milieu in his must-read memoir, *Palimpsest* (New York: Random House, 1995), esp. 102–05. For more on Kinsey's life and work, see James H. Jones, *Alfred Kinsey: A Public/Private Life* (New York: Norton, 1997).

12. Gore Vidal, *The City and the Pillar* (New York: Grosset and Dunlap, 1948), 140–41. Note that Paul doesn't concern himself with the causes or origins of homosexuality, which is somewhat surprising in this era of psychoanalytic hysteria. This exchange ends with Paul

saying that he doesn't have the courage to make these very declarations. Vidal thus locates the paradox of the need to be public and come out and the fear of doing so. Cory, in *The Homosexual in America,* discusses the same vexing problem: "The homosexual is thus locked in his present position. If he does not rise up and demand his rights, he will never get them, but until he gets those rights, he cannot be expected to expose himself to the martyrdom that would come if he should rise up and demand them. It is a vicious circle, and what the homosexual is seeking, first and foremost, is an answer to this dilemma" (228). Perhaps Vidal and others, even Cory, answer this dilemma by writing their way out of the closet and toward a resolution of this Catch-22. For a more detailed discussion of Vidal's novel, see Claude J. Summers, *Gay Fictions: Wilde to Stonewall* (New York: Continuum, 1990), 112–29; and Roger Austen, *Playing the Game: The Homosexual Novel in America* (Indianapolis: Bobbs-Merrill, 1977), 93–125, passim.

13. Vidal, *The City and the Pillar* (1948 ed.), 306.

14. Gore Vidal, *The City and the Pillar,* rev. ed. (New York: E. P. Dutton, 1965), 155, 157.

15. John D'Emilio, *Sexual Politics, Sexual Communities: The Making of a Homosexual Minority in the United States, 1940–1970* (Chicago: University of Chicago Press, 1983), 38. D'Emilio's study is essential in understanding twentieth-century lesbian/gay culture in the United States. On the significance of World War II and the forging of gay identities and communities, see also Allan Berube, *Coming Out Under Fire: The History of Gay Men and Women in World War Two* (New York: Free Press, 1990). For analysis of the period before the war, see George Chauncey, *Gay New York: Gender, Urban Culture, and the Making of the Gay Male World, 1890–1940* (New York: Basic Books, 1994). On lesbian history of the same period, see Lillian Faderman, *Odd Girls and Twilight Lovers: A History of Lesbian Life in Twentieth-Century America* (New York: Columbia University Press, 1991), esp. 118–245.

16. D'Emilio, *Sexual Politics, Sexual Communities,* 57–74.

17. For more on the Daughters of Bilitis, see D'Emilio, *Sexual Politics, Sexual Communities,* 92–107, and Del Martin and Phyllis Lyon, *Lesbian/Woman* (New York: Bantam, 1972), which I discuss at greater length below. Much of my discussion here is drawn from these two sources.

18. For more on the shift from the dismal 1950s to the more hopeful 1960s, see John D'Emilio, *Sexual Politics, Sexual Communities,* 129–48.

19. Patricia Highsmith (pseud. of Claire Morgan), *The Price of Salt* (1952; repr. Tallahassee: Naiad Press, 1991), 277. Primarily known as a crime novelist, Highsmith is the author of the homoerotic *Strangers on a Train* (1949), which was made into a film by Alfred Hitchcock and costarred gay actor Farley Granger. The film version of *The Talented Mr. Ripley* (1999) brought much recent attention to Highsmith, who died in Switzerland in 1995. *The Price of Salt* is the final novel discussed in Jeanette Foster's groundbreaking study of lesbianism in literature, *Sex Variant Women in Literature* (1958; repr. Tallahassee: Naiad, 1985), 339–41. Naiad's newer edition of Foster's work contains a useful bibliography of novels and critical works on lesbian literature through the mid-1970s.

20. Highsmith, *The Price of Salt,* 276.

21. Ann Bannon (pseud. of Ann Thayer), *Odd Girl Out* (1957; repr. New York: Arno, 1975), 191–92. For more on lesbian pulp fiction, see the fascinating *Forbidden Love: The*

Unashamed Stories of Lesbian Lives (1992), a quasi-documentary interwoven with a fictional lesbian love story in which Bannon is interviewed.

22. Ann Bannon, *I Am a Woman* (1959; repr. New York: Arno, 1975), 53. I think this is the most important (and most readable) of Bannon's books, in part because of the encouraging lesbian/gay male alliance. May Sarton's novel *Mrs. Stevens Hears the Mermaids Singing* (1965; repr. New York: Norton, 1974) also contains such an alliance. The older Hilary Stevens, a widowed writer, is clearly a lesbian, and she positions herself as a kind of artistic and personal mentor to a young gay man, Mar Hemmer. For more on Sarton, see the recent biography by Margot Peters, *May Sarton* (New York: Knopf, 1997).

23. Bannon, *I Am a Woman,* 53.

24. Ann Bannon, *Women in the Shadows* (1959; repr. New York: Arno, 1975), 176. It is unclear why Laura or Jack would "go straight"—other than the fact that their lovers, Beebo and Terry, are such mismatches for the two of them. From a contemporary point of view, this novel's lesbian parenting seems almost prescient.

25. Ann Bannon, *Journey to a Woman* (1960; repr. New York: Arno, 1975), 74: "To while away the hours, [Beth] read. On her shopping trips, she picked up books—every book she could find on the subject of homosexuality and Lesbianism. She read them with passionate interest, and found a release in them she had not expected. Most of them were novels with tragic endings. Some were even dull. . . . Some of them depressed her, but all of them interested her and she gained a feeling of companionship with some of the writers, which alleviated her solitude a little." I think we can take these remarks as a pretty reliable barometer of the status and uses of lesbian/gay writing in this period. I also can't help but read "Nina Spicer" as Ann Bannon. Imagine that Bannon got a letter from a fan, they met for dinner, and—. For the rest of the story, you have to read *Journey to a Woman.* In 1962, Bannon published one other novel, *Beebo Brinker,* in this series. It covers Beebo's youth and her move from the Midwest to Greenwich Village. For more on Bannon, see Sherrie A. Inness, "Ann Bannon," in *The Gay and Lesbian Literary Heritage,* ed. Claude J. Summers (New York: Henry Holt, 1995), 75. Some of my thoughts on Bannon are drawn from Inness's essay; Summers's book, which is essential for anyone interested in lesbian/gay literature, contains entries on many topics covered in this essay.

26. Jane Rule, *This Is Not for You* (1970; repr. Tallahassee: Naiad Press, 1982), 3. For more on Jane Rule and her work, see Margaret Soenser Breen, "Jane Rule," in Summers, *The Gay and Lesbian Literary Heritage,* 609–10; and Anna Klauda, "Jane Rule," in *Contemporary Lesbian Writers of the United States,* ed. Sandra Pollack and Denise D. Knight (Westport, Conn.: Greenwood Press, 1993), 468–75. Pollack and Knight's valuable book includes entries on many of the writers covered in this essay.

27. Rule, *This Is Not for You,* 284.

28. Quoted in Elizabeth M. Wavle, "Isabel Miller, pseud.," in Pollack and Knight, *Contemporary Lesbian Writers of the United States,* 354–60. Much of my account of Miller's life and career comes from Wavle's very informative essay.

29. Isabel Miller (pseud. of Alma Routsong), *Patience and Sarah* (1969; repr. New York: McGraw-Hill, 1972), 194. The spirit Patience exhibits here—of forging a new life in unchartered territory—is reminiscent of the life Maurice and Alec will live in the greenwood in E. M. Forster's novel. The original publication of *A Place for Us,* by Bleeker Street Press,

was a run of a thousand copies, which Miller paid for herself. Literary agent Charlotte Sheedy helped place Miller's novel at McGraw-Hill; Sheedy continues to be active in publishing and recently helped get lesbian writer Sapphire's first novel, *Push,* published by Knopf. A major change of the past twenty or thirty years, especially in terms of lesbian writers, has been the emergence of lesbian writing from small presses to major publishers, and agents like Sheedy have been central to getting lesbian fiction into mainstream publishing houses. For more on lesbian publishing, see Faderman, *Odd Girls,* 225. In *The Safe Sea of Women: Lesbian Fiction, 1969–1989* (Boston: Beacon Press, 1990), Bonnie Zimmerman discusses *A Place for Us* in the context of the history of lesbian fiction (xi–32). An operatic version of *Patience and Sarah* premiered at New York's Lincoln Center Festival in July 1998. Miller, who died in 1995, was supportive of the adaptation by Wende Persons and Paula M. Kimper. See "Time and Patience" by Cathy Che in *The Advocate* 759 (May 12, 1998): 73–74.

30. James Baldwin, *Go Tell It on the Mountain* (1953; repr. New York: Dial Press, 1963), 18. The end of this passage echoes Lord Alfred Douglas's poem about his relationship with Oscar Wilde: "The love that dare not speak its name."

31. Baldwin, *Go Tell It on the Mountain,* 250, 253; first ellipsis in original.

32. James Baldwin, *Giovanni's Room* (New York: Dell, 1956), 186–87; emphasis in original. For more on this novel, Baldwin's most famous gay work, see Stephen Adams, *The Homosexual as Hero in Contemporary Fiction* (New York: Barnes and Noble, 1980), 35–55; and Wilfred R. Kopenon, *Embracing a Gay Identity: Gay Novels as Guides* (Westport, Conn.: Bergin and Garvey, 1993), 53–71. On Baldwin, see the biography by David Leeming, *James Baldwin* (New York: Knopf, 1994). Adams and Kopenon cover a lot of useful material on gay writing from this period.

33. James Baldwin, *Another Country* (New York: Dell, 1962), 365–66; emphasis in original. Some of my views on Baldwin's work have been drawn from Emmanuel S. Nelson, "James Baldwin," in *Contemporary Gay American Novelists,* ed. Emmanuel S. Nelson (Westport, Conn.: Greenwood Press, 1993), 6–24. Nelson's volume is essential for students of gay literature.

34. Christopher Isherwood, *The World in the Evening* (New York: Farrar, Straus, and Giroux, 1954), 105. For a reading that puts this novel in the context of contemporary queer theory and that deals with other novels of this period (John Horne Burns's *The Gallery* from 1947, Robert Coates's *The Bitter Season* from 1947, and Isabel Bolton's *The Christmas Tree* from 1949), see Robert Caserio, "Queer Passions, Queer Citizenship: Some Novels about the State of the American Nation," *Modern Fiction Studies* 43(1) (Spring 1997): 170–205.

35. Isherwood, *The World in the Evening,* 281.

36. Christopher Isherwood, *A Single Man* (New York: Farrar, Straus, and Giroux, 1964), 175–76. Isherwood dedicated this novel to Gore Vidal. For more on Isherwood's life and career, see Claude J. Summers, *Christopher Isherwood* (New York: Ungar, 1980), and his *Gay Fictions,* 195–214. See also James Berg and Chris Freeman, eds., *The Isherwood Century: Essays on the Life and Work of Christopher Isherwood* (Madison: University of Wisconsin Press, 2000).

37. Quoted in Ben Reuven, "Christopher Isherwood: Reading the Sands of Time," *Los Angeles Times,* 5 December 1976, pp. 3, 16.

38. This move toward advocacy and activism can be seen in other figures, of course. Perhaps the most significant one is Beat poet Allen Ginsberg. Ginsberg (*Howl,* 1956) and William Burroughs (*Queer,* written in 1952 and published in 1985, and *Naked Lunch,* 1959)

contributed significantly to the body of gay literature beginning in the mid-1950s. With the death of both Ginsberg and Burroughs in 1997, one can't help but feel that a generation of gay American literature has been lost. For more on the Beats and gay literature, see Catherine R. Stimpson, "The Beat Generation and the Trials of Homosexual Liberation," *Salmagundi* 58–59 (1982–83): 373–92.

39. John Rechy, *Numbers* (New York: Grove, 1967), 235. Rechy is the son of a Scottish man and a Mexican woman, and much of his later work centers more on racial identity than on sexuality. For more on Rechy, see Gregory Bredbeck, "John Rechy," in Nelson, *Contemporary Gay American Novelists,* 340–51. See also James Levin, *The Gay Novel in America* (New York: Garland, 1991), 197–99, 223–25. Levin's book is a useful survey of virtually all works in American fiction with gay characters. In *The Homosexual as Hero,* Stephen Adams compares Rechy and Burroughs under the subhead "Terminal Sex" (83–105). A very interesting interview with Rechy, conducted by Richard Canning, appears in *The Gay and Lesbian Review* (formerly *Harvard Gay and Lesbian Review*), 7(2) (Spring 2000): 9–13.

40. For more on *Myra,* see James Levin, *The Gay Novel in America,* 226–28, from which some of my discussion is drawn. In praise of the novel, Levin writes, "No other American novel presents such a total protest of conventional Western cultural norms about gender and sexuality" (229).

41. Another landmark film, *Boys in the Band,* based on Mart Crowley's successful play, was released in 1970. For more on lesbians and gays in film, see Vito Russo, *Celluloid Closet: Homosexuality in the Movies* (New York: Harper and Row, 1981), and the excellent 1995 documentary based on Russo's book made by Rob Epstein and Jeffrey Friedman.

42. Rita Mae Brown, *Rubyfruit Jungle* (Plainfield, Vt.: DaughtersInc., 1973), 193. This sentiment, and the novel as a whole, echoes Miller and Bannon, but Brown's forthrightness is, for me, significant in getting at the radicalism available after Stonewall and after the first few years of Gay Pride marches. For more on Brown, see her memoir *Rita Will* (New York: Bantam, 1997).

43. Daniel Curzon, *Something You Do in the Dark* (New York: Putnam's, 1971), 296. For more on Curzon, see an essay written by his lover, John Gettys, "Daniel Curzon," in Nelson, *Contemporary Gay American Novelists,* 89–95, which influenced my views of this complex novel.

44. Curzon, *Something You Do in the Dark,* 299.

45. Del Martin and Phyllis Lyon, *Lesbian/Woman* (New York: Bantam, 1972), 309–10. Continuing in the tradition of 1950s pulp classics, the publishers put the following blurb on the front cover of the paperback: "The most complete and revealing book ever written about women who love other women." Like *Patience and Sarah* the year before, *Lesbian/Woman* won the American Library Association's Gay/Lesbian Book Award in 1972.

Part Four

Community, Institutions

11

Rizzo's Raiders, Beaten Beats, and Coffeehouse Culture in 1950s Philadelphia

MARC STEIN

"POLICE Raiders Break Up Chess Game, Seize Men in Beards, Girls in Tights," ran the outlandish headline in Philadelphia's *Evening Bulletin* on 12 February 1959. Below the headline, the story began in a tone that mocked the police: "There was last night at the Humoresque Coffeeshop, 2036 Sansom St., the playing of music and chess, the talking of talk, and, of course, the drinking of coffee. There was the growing of beards, the wearing of turtle-neck sweaters and tights and the smoking of pipes and cigarettes." For these crimes, the owner of the coffeehouse, twenty-three–year-old Melvin Heifetz, and thirty-four of his patrons were "hauled off" in police wagons.[1]

The *Bulletin* explained that two policemen from Captain Frank Rizzo's Center City precinct had gone to the Humoresque "because neighbors were telephoning that it was noisy." Describing what the policemen observed, the story returned to its original tone: "Crescendos of classical music. And when the music went diminuendo the rising babble of voices. Yeah, man! Every once in a while the policemen heard a curious shout, 'Check!'" Some of the men had facial hair, "the kind in which mustache and beard melt into a single composition." All seven "girls" had on "full length tights." The men wore "corduroy trousers, very tight pants," and some had "leather jackets, not the kind worn by rocks, but well-tailored jackets. . . . A number of chess games were in what is called progress. The talk was loud. The subjects were intellectual. [Officer] Powell distinctly heard the word 'art.'" At the police station at 12th and Pine, those patrons who were under the age of eighteen, "all seven girls and ten of the boys," were released into the custody of their parents. Heifetz was charged as the proprietor of a disorderly house, the other seventeen adult males with breach of peace. The next day, Heifetz was held on $300 bail; the other adults were each fined $12.50.

In part, the *Bulletin* offered a narrative of territorial conflict to account for the raid. According to Gertrude Fitzpatrick, a "neighbor of the Humoresque," patrons "parked their cars on her sidewalk and made so much noise in her back yard she couldn't sleep." When she complained, "all she got was 'a mouthful of sass.'" The patrons, reportedly from "various sections of the city," were represented as unwelcome outsiders.

The *Bulletin* also offered a narrative of cultural conflict. Enjoying elite music and effete games, the patrons were regarded as eccentric by the police. While the male patrons wore facial hair and leather jackets, the authenticity of their embodied masculinity was in question insofar as these were not the types of jackets worn by rock and rollers but were "well-tailored" outerwear, "worth maybe $50" each. The colors of the female patrons' tights, some black or red, none pink or orange, signified rejection of contemporary norms of femininity.[2] In contrast, the police, revealingly garbed in "plainclothes," were represented as working-class buffoons.

Over the course of the next several months, as attacks on the coffeehouse continued and coffeehouse defenders responded, media accounts changed in significant ways. Supplementing, grafting onto, and to some extent displacing the earlier narratives of territorial and cultural conflict were stories about drugs, interracial mixing, and same-sex sexualities. Whether this change was due to tactical shifts by coffeehouse opponents, who needed to rally support in the court of public opinion and in courts of law, or new media willingness to discuss these topics, the coffeehouse controversy proved to be a critical episode in the history of public discourse about same-sex sexualities in the "Private City."[3]

This essay, along with other new scholarship in lesbian and gay history, challenges the notion that a "conspiracy of silence" is the best way to characterize public discourse on same-sex sexualities in the middle decades of the twentieth century. It also suggests some of the ways that discourses of same-sex sexualities intersected with other discourses of "deviance" in this period. Critics, defenders, and other observers of Philadelphia's coffeehouses strategically deployed public representations of same-sex sexualities and other representations of "deviance" to advance their interests. Oral history narratives produced in the 1990s cast new light on the conflicts of the 1950s, but they confirm the public nature of discussions about same-sex sexualities in the coffeehouse controversy.

This essay also contributes to the project of exploring relationships between lesbian history and gay history. In Philadelphia in the 1940s, 1950s, and 1960s, public discussions about same-sex sexualities tended to focus on men and boys and tended to derive claims about female same-sex sexualities from male counterparts. In fact, same-sex sexualities were constructed in dominant discourse as more male than female. This was the case, for instance, in local media coverage of sex murders and crimes, police raids and arrests, sexual science and medicine, urban geographies and cultures, and controversies surrounding tennis-great Big Bill Tilden and the Walt Whitman Bridge. It was the case not only in Philadelphia's mass-circulation newspapers, but also in locally produced legal, medical, and social-scientific publications.

The focus on males did not occur because Philadelphia lacked dynamic and vibrant lesbian cultures. In these decades, lesbians concentrated residentially in three urban neighborhoods (Center City, West Philadelphia, and Germantown/Mount Airy); frequented dozens of predominantly lesbian and gay bars, clubs, restaurants, and other commercial establishments; and made themselves visible to one another on various streets, in various parks, and in various other public spaces. Significantly, while lesbian and gay geographies in Philadelphia diverged in important ways, they converged in the coffeehouses. In part, the focus of public discourse on men and boys reflected the fact that lesbian geographies were constituted as more "private" and gay geographies more "public." In part, it reflected the tendency of dominant discourse to focus on men and to conceive of sexual agency as male. While cultural links between same-sex sexualities (lesbian and gay) and gender inversion (female masculinity and male femininity) might have led dominant discourse to focus on lesbians as much as or more than on gay men, the primary determinant of public attention was sex (male/female), not gender (masculinity/femininity). What is particularly noteworthy about the coffeehouse controversy is that in this case public discourse not only strengthened links between same-sex sexualities and males, but suppressed and severed links between same-sex sexualities and females.

Raiding Representations

Four historical developments converged in 1959 to help transform a series of police raids into a major media story. The first was the emergence of the "beat generation" and "hipsters." Calling themselves beats, John D'Emilio and Estelle Freedman observe, a group of San Francisco poets and artists including Allen Ginsberg "broke sharply with the values of Cold War America by rejecting the ethos of career, marriage, and suburban consumerism." The beats achieved national recognition in 1957 with the publication of Jack Kerouac's *On the Road* and the arrest on obscenity charges of Lawrence Ferlinghetti, publisher of Ginsberg's homoerotic *Howl and Other Poems*. D'Emilio and Freedman also comment on the relationship between "beat," "hip," and "gay," noting that beats were inspired by "black hipster[s] of the northern ghettos who moved in a world of jazz, drugs, and sex" and that the beat subculture and gay world "overlapped."[4]

Heightened attention to juvenile delinquency was the second development that transformed the raids into a story. National concern about this problem soon led John F. Kennedy to create the President's Committee on Juvenile Delinquency and the U.S. Congress to pass the 1961 Juvenile Delinquency and Youth Offenses Control Act. Media coverage of the National Association of Secondary-School Principals' convention in Philadelphia in the days immediately surrounding the raids highlighted the problems of delinquency. Meanwhile, local officials reported that "juveniles under 18 accounted for nearly one-fourth of the 1958 city arrests for major crimes."[5]

If San Francisco beats found their worst enemy in Capt. William Hanrahan, Philadelphia's coffeehouse aficionados encountered their nemesis in Frank Rizzo, whose rise to power was the third development that made a story out of the raids. Born into an Italian-American Catholic family in 1920, Rizzo grew up in South Philly and joined the police force in 1943. In 1952, police commissioner Thomas Gibbons named Rizzo an acting captain, one result of the local Democratic revolution that put Joseph Clark in the mayor's office. After a brief assignment in West Philly, Rizzo began a seven-year career-making stint as a Center City captain. Rizzo was appointed acting police commissioner in 1966 and commissioner in 1967. According to one biographer, Rizzo then became the "first cop to run for mayor of a major American city." Winning two mayoral terms as a Democrat (but frequently flirting with Republicans such as President Richard Nixon), Rizzo served from 1972 to 1980.[6]

Rizzo's career was linked with key transformations in the relationship between law enforcement and electoral politics. As Frank Donner has argued, "While practices associated with the term *police state* abound in the United States . . . , beginning in the sixties, police state modes of governance emerged in ominous perspective in urban America. Among such subsequently disclosed police state patterns, Philadelphia's is outstanding. Not merely in a rhetorical sense, Philadelphia became a police city." Donner emphasizes the role played by the media in this process: "Rizzo instinctively knew that there was political gold in his blend of moralizing and law enforcement. But in order to extract it, he needed the help of the media." In Rizzo's city, Donner concludes, "the press was cast in the role of an enthusiastic collaborator in an arrangement by which a continuing supply of 'news' was exchanged for an equal amount of personal publicity."[7]

Rizzo's career was built on the tough reputation he acquired in the 1950s, a reputation that derived from the anti-vice image he cultivated with raids on bars, clubs, gambling dens, brothels, and strip joints. Pressed by the Greater Philadelphia Movement's campaign to rebuild downtown, the fourth development that turned the raids into a story, reformers were only too happy to have Rizzo celebrated for cleaning up a city voted "cleanest" in the nation while the coffeehouse controversy brewed and boiled over.[8]

Whether Rizzo was clean himself is widely debated. In a city W. E. B. Dubois had described as "one of the worst governed of America's badly governed cities" and Lincoln Steffens had called "corrupt and contented," Rizzo's rise took place in the aftermath of extraordinary revelations of municipal corruption. Police were implicated in these scandals most prominently in 1950, when Craig Ellis, head of the vice squad, and two other policemen committed suicide after U.S. Senator Estes Kefauver, the Senate Crime Investigating Committee, and a federal grand jury began examining Philadelphia. Kefauver concluded that "a paralyzing attitude of *laissez faire* seems to hang like an ether mist over the administration of the Philadelphia Police Department." In the next decade, Rizzo was accused of working with South Philly mob leaders and having an affair with stripper Blaze Starr, "Miss Spontaneous Combustion." In 1973, Jonathan Rubinstein's *City Police* described an extensive pattern of Philadelphia police payoffs by gambling, liquor, restaurant, and business interests during Rizzo's reign. In 1974, the Pennsylvania Crime Commission accused the Philadelphia police of "widespread, systematic" corruption. One of the commission's recommendations was that police resources should no longer be used to "curb prostitution and homosexuality," since this was "ineffective" and produced "a greater moral problem than the one it is seeking to cure, namely corruption."[9]

Although some payoffs protected businesses that served lesbians and gay men, for Rizzo cleaning up Philadelphia meant acting against these groups. In 1954, for example, police from Rizzo's precinct raided three clubs "in a drive against alleged obscene shows." At the Barton Sho-Bar, four "female impersonators," one "strip-tease dancer," and the owner were arrested. At a magistrate's hearing, police displayed a banner from the bar that read "Gay Boy Review—Direct from Hollywood." Against Rizzo's protests, the magistrate ruled that police failed to prove that the shows were more obscene than things shown on television and in magazines. In 1958, Rizzo's men raided a party at the home of painter-illustrator Emlen Etting. Rizzo reportedly told Etting, "Unless you and your goddamn pansy friends get back in the house, quiet down and shut up, I will put you all in the paddy wagon and throw you in with the drunks for the night." Also in 1958, Rizzo raided the Allegro, arresting patrons, bartenders, waitresses, and the owner. According to Joseph Yannone, who was Rizzo's driver,

> He hated all those fag joints. . . . On mischief night, especially, you know the night before Halloween, they'd all dress in drag and he would let them do that. But we got complaints about the clubs from the feds. The sailors when they pulled in the shipyard in South Philly would go to these bars, and when the "girl" would pull her dress down, then boom, he'd see it wasn't a girl. The sailors would want their money back, and they'd get the shit kicked out of them. So, we had to crack down. Rizzo was all for it. He really didn't like faggots.[10]

Rizzo had served in the navy and may have identified with the sailors' experiences of attraction and repulsion. In fact, police in this era were both subjects and objects of anti-gay crackdowns. At least one policeman was arrested on "morals charges" concerning "teen-aged boys" in the midst of the coffeehouse controversy.[11] Before long, Rizzo would have to confront public allegations that his son, Frank Jr., born in 1943, was gay.[12]

Breaking News

Although all four of these developments were linked with same-sex sexualities, it was not immediately apparent to readers of the city's newspapers that the story of the coffeehouse raids was about lesbians or gay men. The initial narratives positioned neighbors against patrons; an older generation against a younger one; police against beats, hipsters, intellectuals, and artists; and proponents of "law and order" against defenders of civil liberties. On 14 February, for example, two days after the first stories appeared, Philadelphia's *Bulletin* and *Inquirer* reported that police had raided the Humoresque again and that Rizzo had highlighted neighborhood complaints about "noise" and "profanity." In Philadelphia's *Daily News*, Rizzo referred to the concerns of "solid citizens who have lived in the neighborhood for 30 to 40 years." The *Inquirer* of 19 February also showed Rizzo raising neighborhood issues when he asked the city's Departments of Health and Licenses and Inspections and the state's Department of Labor and Industry to investigate four coffee shops: the Humoresque, Proscenium, Gilded Cage, and Artist's Hut. Heifetz responded by insisting that the music was played at low volume and was "classical, not rock 'n' roll." Granting that noise or rock music would be legitimate grounds for complaint, Heifetz fought back by representing himself as a good neighbor.[13]

The newspapers also portrayed the conflict as generational. According to the *Bulletin,* Rizzo stated that eight patrons found at the second raid were fifteen years old and that he had gone to the Humoresque "because the parents of some of the youngsters asked him to." Heifetz claimed that Rizzo told these four boys and four girls, "I'm going to take you into the police station and bring your parents there to let them know what kind of people you are associating with." These motifs also appeared in the *Bulletin*'s account of a third night of arrests, when Rizzo visited the Artist's Hut, Proscenium, and Gilded Cage. From the latter, "the policemen took a boy who admitted to being 16 and another who they said looked no older than that." Citing the city's 10:30 p.m. curfew for minors under sixteen years of age, the *Bulletin* noted that the boys were "collected" at the station by their parents.[14]

Coffeehouse defenders were not willing to yield the generational narrative. One response was to call attention to respectable adult patrons. According to Heifetz, while "four boys and four girls" were in the Humoresque when the second raid took place, there were thirty patrons in all, including "some married couples." Heifetz also enlisted the support of parents. While police were conducting their third set of raids, Heifetz, a group of patrons, and some of their parents were meeting with the Greater Philadelphia American Civil Liberties Union's (ACLU) Spencer Coxe. Meanwhile, the Philadelphia *Tribune* reported that the parents of an African-American man arrested at the Humoresque regarded the coffee shop as a "welcome substitute for 'juice joints' and houses of ill repute." Implicitly siding with coffeehouse defenders, the *Bulletin* mocked the police for targeting "kids who ought to be drinking milk." Similarly, a letter to the *Bulletin* praised Rizzo for attacking "highly suspect activities" that "smack of a subversive plot to lure the youth of the nation away from television watching or street corner lounging."[15]

Linked with the narratives of geographic and generational conflict was a narrative of cultural conflict between police and beats, hipsters, intellectuals, and artists. The first *Inquirer* story described the Humoresque as "a haven for 'beatniks' or followers of jazz music." Unlike the *Bulletin,* which reported that patrons under eighteen were released into parental custody and patrons over eighteen were arrested, the *Inquirer* distinguished between patrons dressed "in traditional garb of chinos and sweaters," who were released, and "beatniks," who were arrested. Two days later, the *Bulletin* reported that according to Heifetz, Rizzo had called him a "creep" and the Humoresque "a den of iniquity."[16]

Defenders of the coffeehouses responded in several ways. The *Daily News* editorialized that "maybe Capt. Rizzo doesn't understand why girls wearing leotards and men looking like beatniks want to sit around drinking espresso, listening to classical music on a hi-fi set, playing chess and talking about Art with a capital A. . . . Neither do we. . . . But we don't see why they should be arrested, finger-printed and mugged for doing it." A mocking letter to the *Bulletin* praised the police for their "unflinching heroism." These "fearless crusaders" had encountered "coffee-drinking, playing chess, reading, listening to music and, above all, talking," all of which were "menaces to our nation." Some observers denied that the coffeehouses were filled with beats. One letter asserted that "coffee houses in this city entertain fewer than one 'beatnik' for every 400 customers."[17]

Coffeehouse defenders also used the raids to criticize the police more generally. Several commentators focused on police inefficiency, inappropriate priorities, and a failure to address "real" delinquency. After the second raid, Heifetz stated that Rizzo spoke "very loudly and rudely," an indictment of the captain's cultural style. One letter writer claimed that he had "chuckled" in his "beard" at the *Bulletin*'s original story but that he was "pleased with the detectives' ability to recognize the music as 'classical.'"[18] In these class-marked accounts, coffeehouse proponents depicted a conflict between sophisticated coffee drinkers and ignorant police.

One coffeehouse defender positioned the patrons between and against both working-class police and well-to-do neighbors. Horace Proctor, Jr., wrote that he suspected that "wealthy people" who lived near the Humoresque had applied "political pressure" to bring about the raids. According to Proctor, these elites were "so narrow-minded and intolerant of people that are 'different,' that they might use their influence to deny these people their right to live as individuals." Proctor, however, was no celebrant of "difference" that he perceived to be declasse: "To discriminate against the type of people who prefer coffee, chess, and classical music over beer, gambling, and women is no better than discriminating against their race or religion." Proctor and his wife did not like "rock 'n' roll, baseball or inane television programs. . . . Should we for this be harassed?"[19]

The conflict between police and beats, hipsters, intellectuals, and artists was both cultural and political. While Rizzo and the police depicted the coffeehouses as threats to order, Heifetz and his patrons represented the police as threats to civil liberties. Rizzo, according to Heifetz, "behaved in the manner of one of Hitler's storm troopers." According to the *Daily News,* Manuel Rubin, owner of the Proscenium, was working with other owners to "end these Gestapo raids." Reporting on the involvement of the ACLU, which filed a complaint with the city's new Police Review Board, the papers framed the conflict as one that concerned basic civil liberties, in addition to geographic, generational, and cultural issues.[20]

News Updates

On 19 February, one week after the initial stories appeared, newspaper readers learned that Heifetz had made a bold next move. Using the federal Civil Rights Act enacted during Reconstruction, Heifetz had filed suit in U.S. District Court for $25,000, charging Rizzo and the city with damaging his business. Harvey Walters, who had been arrested in the first raid, also filed suit, asking $15,000 for damage to his reputation. Attorney Theodore Mann asked Judge Thomas Clary for a temporary injunction restraining Rizzo and his men from entering the Humoresque without a warrant, making arrests there "without reasonable basis," "interfering with Heifetz's right to conduct his business and with his right of privacy and with his and Walters' right to assemble peacefully," and "interfering with Walters' right to partake of refreshments" and "play chess." Helping to create an impression that the police were bullies, the *Bulletin* quoted Heifetz as saying that his business had been "permanently damaged" because customers were now afraid to come.[21]

Readers thus learned on 19 February that both Heifetz and Rizzo had escalated their conflict. Heifetz was taking Rizzo to court. Rizzo was asking for local and state investigations. But while the stories concerning Heifetz's action fit neatly into the existing narrative frameworks, other stories did not. The *Daily News,* for example, reported that police had raided the coffee shops "looking for 'known narcotics users or sellers.'" The *Inquirer* referred not only to complaints about noise, "foul language," and "'carrying on' between young girls and boys," but also "a report by an undercover policewoman disclosing how she arranged to purchase 'five sticks of marijuana in one of these shops.'"[22]

Letters to the *Bulletin* suggested other new angles. Walter S. Fraser of Willow Grove, Pennsylvania, wrote that he had been in the Humoresque when Rizzo raided it and, Fraser declared, "I haven't seen any alcoholics or homosexuals there." Referring to Humoresque patrons, Gertrude Fitzpatrick wrote, "I have been subjected to their loud conversation on perverted sex both from the alley behind my home and from the front of my home."[23] "Homosexuals" and "perverted sex" thus entered print media discourse on the raids in denials of the presence of the former and in opposition to the latter as a topic of conversation. Although Fitzpatrick complained about voices penetrating her domestic sphere from "behind" and "front," no one cited in the newspapers at this point had complained about the actual presence of lesbians, gay men, or same-sex sexual behaviors in or around the coffee shops.

What accounts for the week that elapsed between the initial coverage and the first mention of homosexuality? It is possible that the newspapers had known about complaints about homosexuality but had not reported on them. It is also possible that the police, neighbors, patrons, and owners had not shared these concerns with reporters, at least not on the record. Perhaps some of the language the newspapers used *had* signified homosexuality to some readers. Perhaps, after learning that Heifetz was taking the police to court, Rizzo, the police, and Fitzpatrick decided to use drugs and homosexuality to win their cases and rally public support. Whatever accounts for the change, residents were no longer said to be upset primarily about "'carrying on' between young girls and boys."

Drugs and same-sex sexualities were also highlighted when three hundred people, mostly members of the Center City Residents Association, met on 19 February to discuss the coffeehouses. Fitzpatrick handed Commissioner Gibbons a petition signed by thirty-three people demanding the closing of the Humoresque. Another neighbor, Eugene John Lewis, presented a petition with twenty-two signatures against the Gilded Cage. According to the *Inquirer,* Gibbons told the gathering that "statements that would shock adults were made by boys and girls, ranging in age from 14 to 17, after they were taken into custody." Gibbons claimed that one fourteen-year-old said "she had gone to the 'place for the sole purpose of becoming acquainted with sex deviates.'" The *Bulletin* reported that Gibbons said that this student "'admitted she had gone to the place [the Humoresque] to make acquaintances with Lesbians. That's my case,' he said. 'It's the case of all decent citizens in the city.'" Grafting the new narrative of sexual difference onto the earlier narrative of age conflict, Gibbons constructed homosexuality as deviant and youthful and he constructed deviance and youthfulness as homosexual.[24]

A similar process took place with the narrative of territorial conflict. According to the *Inquirer*'s account of the Center City meeting, "housewives living in the area" complained about patrons' "obscene language and immoral conduct." The *Bulletin* reported that Milo MacGoldrick charged that the Humoresque was "a gathering place for homosexuals" and that "it's a hangout for a lot of odd screwballs who live elsewhere." Eugene John Lewis claimed that he had been in the Gilded Cage several times and saw "homosexuals and Lesbians and young girls with old men." According to Lewis, "This place attracts groups of undesirables who, when they are not beating up each other, beat up people living in the neighborhood." Representing lesbians and gay men as violent and pedophilic, these accounts grafted new narrative conflicts between domesticated heterosexuals and disorderly homosexuals onto earlier narrative conflicts between neighbors and outsiders. Homosexuality was constructed as foreign to the neighborhood, and foreigners to the neighborhood were constructed as homosexual.[25]

The new attention to homosexuality and drugs also transformed the narrative conflict between police and beats. Displacing language describing the patrons as innocent, the newspapers now put forward more images of them as immoral and obscene. Meanwhile, opponents of the coffeehouses rushed forward to praise the police. According to the *Bulletin,* E. Walter Hudson, past president of the Center City Residents Association, called for "a tremendous vote of confidence for Rizzo." Reverend James Vallely of St. Patrick's Church noted, "We have to keep center-city respectable. . . . I'm on Captain Rizzo's side in that respect." The *Bulletin* reported, "Gibbons was also asked what interest the 'anti-egg head, anti-nonconformist, anti-intellectual feelings of the department played in the raids.' 'No interest at all,' Gibbons replied. 'We have quite a few intellects in the department ourselves.'"[26]

Homosexuality was also linked with drug use. Reporting on the Center City meeting, the *Inquirer* noted that six of the eighteen people arrested at the Humoresque had police records. The next sentence indicated that Bernard Lemisch, counsel for the Fraternal Order of Police, told residents that "more than 27 narcotics purchases had been made from patrons of the four coffee shops." The implication was that the prior arrests had been drug-related and that drug users were either consorting with "sex deviates" or were sexually deviant themselves.[27]

According to the media, defenders of the coffeehouses at the Center City meeting responded to these new attacks in several ways. The *Inquirer* presented no direct response to the accusations about homosexuality and drugs, focusing instead on civil liberties arguments. Several lawyers condemned the raids and suggested that residents should have obtained a court injunction, which one lawyer then immediately offered to do.[28] The *Bulletin* editorialized that "some patrons of some coffee houses are merely odd; but others are odd to a point offensive to public morality and perhaps dangerous to juvenile acquaintances." However, Rizzo's raids were "the wrong way to handle the complaints," not only because "dragnet technique[s]" were "offensive to normal civil rights," but also because they put "most citizens' sympathies where they may not really belong."[29] While criticizing the police, both the *Bulletin* and the lawyers who called for a court injunction implied that there were reasonable grounds for opposing the coffeehouses.

Another strategy was to promise cooperation with authorities. According to the *Inquirer* and the *Bulletin,* Jack Spiller, owner of the Artist's Hut, said he "always cooperated with the police." In the *Bulletin,* Edward Halpern, owner of the Gilded Cage, "disputed charges that homosexuals gathered at his shop." "'I'm not a doctor,' he said. 'I can't tell the differences.' He said certain undesirables might come to his shop but, he insisted, he always tries to get rid of them." Both Spiller and Halpern seemed to agree with opponents of the coffeehouses that their shops should not serve "undesirables."[30]

In the coverage of the Center City meeting, only one person explicitly supported the coffeehouses for their unique character. Near the end of its story, the *Bulletin* noted that according to one resident, "The coffeehouses gave center-city a touch of local color. 'It shows that we don't roll up our sidewalks at 7 o'clock at night,' he said. 'We need variety in center-city. These places give us a touch of Greenwich Village.'"[31]

More often than not, coffeehouse defenders stressed their respectability. In "A Visit to the Coffeehouses," *Bulletin* reporter James Smart took his readers on a tour, beginning with the Artist's Hut. Observing a sign "warning teenagers of the curfew" and another that read "No Parking, Temporary Police Regulation," Smart represented the coffee shop as law-abiding. After describing the physical environment and patrons, Smart traced the history of coffeehouses back to the Middle East in the sixteenth century, London and America in the eighteenth, and New York in the early twentieth. Countering the image of coffeehouses as recent creations of troubled youth, Smart's story stressed their long and illustrious history.[32]

Asking "Who goes to coffeehouses?" Smart answered by presenting the narrative conflict in clear terms: "The proprietors and habitues say they are college students, artists and art students, persons looking for a quiet place to spend an inexpensive evening in a nonalcoholic atmosphere. Neighbors of the places and policemen add to that list homosexuals, dope users and various types of odd characters." Conflict was also clear in Smart's answer to the question, "What do they do there?" "Proprietors and habitues" stressed eating, drinking, reading, playing chess and checkers, listening to music, and talking; "neighbors and policemen add that they make noise, park cars on the sidewalk and promulgate narcotics addiction and immorality."

While presenting both sides of the story, Smart offered more support for the patrons' version. Most of the customers described were in mixed-sex couples. Although members of these couples might mix and match gender codes (one man looked "Marlon Brandoish," a "girl" sported "khaki slacks," and another "girl" had on "black tights" under her "wool skirt"), most did not conform to common public images of lesbians and gay men. Although same-sex couples were mentioned ("two heavily made-up college girls in mannish blouses and wool skirts," a "well-dressed man in a derby" who stopped to "chat with a friend," and "two young men" sitting together), most were not clearly marked as lesbian or gay.

Quoting a variety of patrons, Smart lent support to their narratives of respectability. One art student noted, "We don't have a beatnik type in Philadelphia." His "companion" observed, "There are pseudos. . . . Kids who like to smoke a pipe and put on a European hat." But these were "phony." According to Smart, patrons "resent the branding of coffeehouses as hangouts for degenerates and dope users." One student said that while "odd characters" frequented the shops, "the same type, and worse," could be found elsewhere. He also said he had seen Rubin "order people out of the Proscenium because he didn't like the way they act." A "married" man explained that he and his wife did not drink alcohol and so did not go to bars. "If the police don't like some of the people here," he declared, "let them arrest those people. Why bother us?" As for the Humoresque, Smart reported that "the coffeehouse crowd" believed that Heifetz was "not responsible for any of the 'weirdos' who may have come to his place." One customer stated that "Mel's a naive sort of guy. . . . He wouldn't know an oddball if one walked in." Challenging the assault on the coffeehouses, defenders joined the campaign against oddballs.

Smart's biographical information on Heifetz highlighted his respectability. Readers learned that Heifetz had first encountered coffeehouses while in the army and stationed in Europe. On returning to Philadelphia, he began visiting the Humoresque, which opened in March 1958 and which he bought in May. Smart noted that on weeknights, the Humoresque served "neighbors, college students and regulars." On weekends, "Teenagers on dates fill the place from 9:30 to 11:30, clearing out before curfew [midnight]. The older set shows up a little later." Smart also revealed a few of Heifetz's "secrets," which included the awards he had received from the Boy Scouts and the Daughters of the American Revolution. One friend stated that Heifetz "doesn't see why he needs any character references." Representing Heifetz's patrons as neighbors, students, and teenagers on dates, Smart portrayed Heifetz as a patriot who was modest about his civic contributions.

While for the most part Smart's story presented the controversy within the narrative frameworks already established, toward the end of the article the reporter introduced a new one: "Underlying the complaints from some neighbors, coffeehouse regulars say, are questions of race. This produces diametrically opposed protests. One is that Negroes are welcome in several of the coffeehouses, and racially mixed couples have been seen. The other is that folk songs rendered by some customers date to the Civil War and are sprinkled with epithets objectionable to Negroes." While the latter claim was not repeated in the press, the former one was. The local ACLU's newsletter reported that "an illegal raid on an interracial gathering in a Mt. Airy residence was excused by the police on the grounds that the arrested persons were part of the 'crowd from those downtown coffee houses.'" Even when the *Tribune* quoted Rizzo as saying that the "contention that his squad staged the raids because colored and white—especially colored boys and white girls—mixed freely" was "a lie," the narrative link between coffeehouses and interracialism was strengthened.[33]

In a period in which the percentage of African Americans in Philadelphia was increasing but the percentage in Center City was decreasing, the presence of African Americans and interracial couples in Center City coffeehouses served as a reminder of the displacement of African Americans from the neighborhood and a symbol of new African-American and interracial transgressions. (In 1940, Center City was 21 percent African American, significantly above the city figure of 13 percent. In 1960, Center City was 20 percent African American, significantly below the city figure of 27 percent. In 1980, Center City was 6 percent African American, even more significantly below the city figure of 38 percent.) Although the media never discussed interracialism in same-sex sexual forms or same-sex sexuality in interracial forms during the coffeehouse controversy, homosexuality was linked by association with interracial sexuality, just as it was linked by association with drug use.[34]

Making Sex News

In some ways, these media discussions constructed same-sex sexualities as both male and female. For example, a column in the *Daily News* referred to "limp-wristed young men" and "girls in crew cuts" who frequented "Bohemian hangouts."[35] References to "homosexuals," "perverted sex," "obscene language," and "immoral conduct" could have signified male and female deviations. Given a larger cultural context in which same-sex sexualities were more often associated with the former, however, readers may have assumed that most or all of the stories concerned men and/or boys. In addition, as is suggested by the distinction Commissioner Gibbons made between "homosexuals" and "Lesbians," some theoretically sex-neutral words may have not been understood in sex-neutral ways. Moreover, even when patrons were depicted as gender transgressors, the dominant image was that of feminine men rather than masculine women. For example, the *Tribune* described one of the men arrested at the Humoresque as an aspiring "French teacher" and another as an honor society high school graduate who was working at Miss Adele Reed's "beauty school," teaching ballet, and planning to attend Fisk University.[36] Furthermore, to the extent that both female and male sexualities were discussed, they were discussed differently. Insofar as female adults were not arrested but male adults were, lesbianism was constructed more as a problem of minors. Teenage "girls" apparently were corrupting one another or were being corrupted by gay men. Male homosexuality, in contrast, was constructed as a problem of adult men, teenage boys, and intergenerational association.

After the court proceedings began, some stories again constructed homosexuality as neither specifically male nor female. For example, the *Bulletin* reported that thirteen neighbors of the Humoresque asked the Common Pleas Court to declare the shop a "nuisance" because it harbored "boisterous people who use vile and obscene language" and "openly flaunted their homosexuality in public." In other stories, homosexuality was portrayed as male. According to an *Inquirer* article that referred to the Humoresque as "a popular haunt of sex deviates," Sherry Goodman told Judge Clary in District Court that the "foul and obscene language is absolutely horrible." Implicitly suggesting that the objects of her complaints were male, Goodman explained that "the young people . . . see a woman approach on the street and are so insensible they won't stop that objectionable language." More explicitly, the *Bulletin* reported that an undercover policewoman testified that the Humoresque was "a gathering place for homosexuals" and that one "nightly visitor" was a man who "dressed as a woman." Similarly, the *Daily News* reported on testimony about "sex deviates and female impersonators." Although homosexuality was linked with effeminacy here, it was again presented as male.[37]

According to the *Bulletin,* Rizzo testified that he chased away "two men misbehaving outside the Humoresque." Rizzo also told the court that the second raid occurred after he witnessed "four girls enter the coffee shop," where he then saw "obvious homosexuals." His testimony made clear that while male homosexuality was the main problem, the protection of underage girls was his priority. Rizzo thus cast himself in the role of the male heterosexual defender of young female sexual virtue. Perversely and paradoxically, he was suggesting that these young girls were threatened by male "homosexuals."[38]

Along the same lines, the *Bulletin* reported that two undercover policemen claimed that "narcotics addicts and homosexuals" frequented the Humoresque and that one said he observed "adult young men keeping company with boys and girls." A woman testified that she saw "two persons in men's clothing kissing each other outside the coffee shop." While this phrasing raised some question as to whether these were in fact men, readers were more likely to conclude that they were male than to imagine that they were female cross-dressers. Describing the testimony of two neighbors who "heard girls crying outside the place," the *Bulletin* juxtaposed images of kissing men with those of crying girls. These stories simultaneously attacked intergenerational homo- and heterosexuality, constructed homosexuality as male, depicted homosexuality as offensive to women, and heterosexualized the "girls."[39]

How did coffeehouse defenders respond, and how did the media present these responses, after coverage shifted to the court proceedings? Heifetz highlighted the denial of civil liberties and challenged the disorderly image conveyed by the police. According to the *Inquirer,* Heifetz told the court, "I never permitted rock and roll. . . . We played practically all classical music since I wanted to attract a good class of customers." Supporting this respectable portrait, Walters testified that one day before the raid he had been discharged from the army and had gone to the Humoresque to see Heifetz, an "old friend" from the Boy Scouts. The *Bulletin* also noted that while Heifetz admitted that there had been complaints concerning "loud music or parking on the sidewalk," he also claimed that "he was never warned by police or neighbors that there were narcotics users or homosexuals frequenting his place." The implication was that had Heifetz been so warned, he might have excluded these two groups. Several days later, the *Bulletin* reported that six teenagers—three male and three female—testified that there was "neither obscenity nor 'running around'" in the Humoresque on the night of the first raid. One mother "backed up her daughter's account." Constance Matthews testified that "she had gone to the Humoresque three or four times herself 'because I always go to every place my daughter goes. I always investigate to make sure it's a proper place for her to go.'"[40]

Heifetz and his allies also attacked the police. While Philadelphians learned about developments in the federal case against Rizzo and the local case against Heifetz, they also read about the Common Pleas Court appeals filed by eight of the patrons convicted earlier. In March, the *Bulletin* reported that one witness testified that he, too, had been arrested at the Humoresque on 11 February, but that although "one officer threatened to kick him" at the police station, he was "slipped out the back door . . . after mentioning that his brother was a member of the Police Department."

Two days later, the *Bulletin* reported that Heifetz revealed that another patron seized at the Humoresque had been released when he mentioned that his brother was a policeman.[41]

In the end, however, Rizzo's arguments won more than they lost. In the Common Pleas Court appeals, Judge Ethan Allen Doty dismissed the charges against one appellant, set aside the convictions of three, and upheld the remaining four (including that of Walters). According to the *Bulletin,* two patrolmen testified that when they entered the Humoresque, "three boys were dancing ring-around-the-rosy around a table." The lawyer for the patrons argued that one of his clients (one of the two African-American men discussed by the *Tribune*) "had done nothing but sit at a table while two other boys were dancing." Although Doty dismissed the charges in this case, he "reprimanded" the appellant for "taking up the time of those who should be busy solving holdups and robberies." As for the others, when their lawyer argued that "there was not one scintilla of evidence that any of the defendants acted disorderly," the judge responded that if the lawyer "went across the street to the Girard Trust Corn Exchange Bank dancing, singing and shouting," he would "wind up at 12th and Pine Sts., too."[42]

In the three cases he set aside (including the other African-American case discussed by the *Tribune*), Doty ruled that "what the young men did, if anything, did not add up to disorderly conduct because it occurred within the shop, not on the public highway." In the cases he upheld, Doty accepted police claims that these four "were in a group of six young men they saw leaving the coffee shop, shouting and yelling, who bumped into two young girls and shouted obscenities at them."[43] The court thus dismissed the cases against the homosocially dancing men whose transgressions took place inside the Humoresque and upheld the cases against the heterosocially offensive men who "bumped" and "shouted" in "public."

Rizzo's victory was clearer in federal court, where Judge Clary declined to grant injunctions against the police because Rizzo had been transferred to Northeast Philly and would not likely raid the Humoresque again. Insofar as Rizzo had been made one of two new inspectors in command of the Northeast, his transfer amounted to a promotion. What's more, Rizzo's exile did not last long. Less than a year after his transfer, Gibbons moved Rizzo to West Philly. And in August 1960, less than eighteen months after leaving Center City as a captain, Rizzo was given command of the entire Central Division.[44]

Not long after Clary's ruling, Heifetz's isolation from the other coffeehouse owners became clear. In late March, the *Inquirer* reported that after meeting with Mayor Richardson Dilworth, city managing director Donald Wagner, Gibbons, and Rizzo, the owners of the Artist's Hut, Proscenium, and Gilded Cage promised "to police themselves and bar undesirable persons." According to Wagner, "These gentlemen said they wanted to cooperate with the police in every way possible" and would rely on the police to "point out the types of people who should be barred."

Around this time, Dilworth wrote to an ACLU leader who had been critical of the police raids: "Places where queers congregate do raise the devil with a neighborhood in very short order, and it is very difficult to break up such groups without some violation of civil rights. I will not say that some of my best friends are queers, or that I completely understand them, but I do know that while they are relatively harmless by themselves, when they get to running in packs they can be really vicious, and louse up a neighborhood in no time flat."[45]

Heifetz's neighbors won their case as well. On 26 September 1959, the Quarter Session Court jury found Heifetz guilty of running a disorderly house. According to the *Bulletin,* neighbors testified about "loud noises, disturbances on the steps and street, and the activities of homosexual patrons." Police testified that "six boys" pushed and exchanged obscenities with "two girls." The *Inquirer* reported that witnesses labeled the Humoresque "a hangout for 'beatniks,' sex deviates, dope addicts and pushers" and that police claimed they observed "a group of young men leave the coffee shop and shout obscenities at several young girls." One month later, Judge Leo Weinrott ordered Heifetz to shut down the Humoresque or go to jail. Heifetz chose the former. Meanwhile, in the aftermath of an incident in which Heifetz was accused of drawing a gun on a patron whom he claimed was stealing a coffeepot, the *Bulletin* reported that Heifetz was found guilty on new charges of "carrying a deadly weapon and playfully pointing a firearm." He received a suspended sentence for the first charge, a year's probation for the second, and an extra year's probation for the earlier disorderly house charge.[46]

The final federal court ruling on Heifetz's and Walters's suits also proved to be a victory for Rizzo. In December 1959, Judge Clary dismissed both. In his decision, Clary first referred to complaints about noise, the presence of minors, and "patronage from all parts of the City, rather than the immediate neighborhood." Declaring that he did not believe the statements of two neighbors who testified to the contrary, Clary also wrote that Rizzo had "received complaints from parents of persons of tender age." More prominent in the decision, however, were explanations that centered on homosexuality, drugs, and heterosocial offenses. According to Clary, the Humoresque had become "a gathering place of homosexuals and narcotic addicts." Clary gave credence to Rizzo's observation of "two men immediately after leaving the Humoresque hugging and kissing on the sidewalk," the testimony of a female neighbor who saw "similar occurrences," and evidence that "two of those arrested, boys, 18 and 19 years of age, were found hugging and squeezing each other."[47]

Clary also based his decision on police testimony that six men had left the Humoresque, "yelling, singing, and in a loud and raucous tone of voice using profanity." After these men ran back to the coffee shop, they were seen "brushing two young ladies who were leaving the place. When the young ladies protested they were answered profanely and the males then re-entered the establishment." Clary also highlighted male police heterosocial concern in relating that Rizzo had observed "four young girls, whom he judged from appearance to be of a rather tender age, enter the establishment," where they were joined by a seventeen-year-old "youth." According to Clary, Rizzo had also noted that "there were several people present, whom he knew to be homosexuals." Once again, the police appeared to be concerned about teenage girls associating with male homosexuals.

One story that had been critical in the earlier narratives was missing from Clary's decision and from all coverage of the court proceedings. Commissioner Gibbons had initially justified the raids by calling attention to the fourteen-year-old girl who had gone to the Humoresque to meet lesbians. Perhaps the most striking proof that the local media played an active role in linking same-sex sexualities more with men and boys than with women and girls is the fact that not once did the newspapers again mention the girl whose efforts to meet "sex deviates" had so moved Commissioner Gibbons. Why did her story and the stories of the other six girls arrested in the original raid fail to reappear? Had Gibbons fabricated the story and then dropped it? Did Clary hear testimony about these girls but not refer to it in his decision? Did the newspapers fail to report on this testimony? In the end, it seems likely that this story did not appear because the idea of a young woman seeking out lesbians failed to conform to the narratives offered by police. This was not a girl offended by straight or gay men and in need of Rizzo's protection. This was not a girl in danger of contamination or seduction at the coffeehouses; she herself was seeking out lesbians. This was not a girl whose "problem" could be blamed upon Heifetz, the Humoresque, or the coffeehouses. So her story disappeared.

Meanwhile, far from the local scene, gay activists offered a different story about Philadelphia's coffeehouses. Over the course of the coffeehouse controversy, the closest thing to a pro-gay local perspective came from the man who was quoted as supporting the coffeehouses for the "touch of local color" and "Greenwich Village" that they brought to Center City. Demonstrating the difference that organized lesbian and gay activism could make, the California-based homophile movement magazine *One* went much further. In April 1959, *One* published a campy report on Philadelphia's coffeehouses that linked the story of the raids with the politics of masculinity:

> Philly cop Captain Rizzo has an awful time trying to keep the center of the city clean and pervert-free. Extra terrible job with this Beat Generation. Imagine a 100%, patriotic, real he-man cop having to see things like grown men playing chess! And men (women too) sitting around arty little restaurants sipping coffee—and reading books yet—talking all that egg-head stuff! And that highbrow music! And those beards, and turtleneck sweaters, and tights and things! A he-man just doesn't have to stand for that sort of thing going on.[48]

One made three additional points. First, "Little evidence was presented that the coffeehouses are actually gay—and readers tell us that only a small percentage of the people in these places are gay." Second, "Homosexuals do have a right—and should exercise that right—to patronize any coffeehouse, bar, or other public establishment." And third, "Why not a few gay coffeehouses? Up to now, bars have been almost the only public places homosexuals could gather—and since many homosexuals don't drink—seems to me the coffeehouse would be a good addition."[49] In the absence of a local homophile movement in Philadelphia and at a safe distance from the local scene, *One* offered the most pro-gay interpretation of the raids. Significantly, *One*'s interpretation staged a conflict between "he-men" and perverts, with deviant women parenthetically set aside alongside their male counterparts.

Rewriting the News

More than thirty years later, the recollections of oral history narrators reaffirm some elements of the stories circulating in 1959, modify others, and introduce several new ones. For example, Heifetz remembers the objections of neighbors, but now believes that one of the neighborhood critics was gay himself. He also recalls the presence of interracial couples in the coffeehouses. "For a black boy to go out with a white girl," Heifetz explains, "there weren't many places that they would really feel comfortable. But the coffee shops, they were comfortable." According to Heifetz, "politically astute" people have told him that this was what triggered the raids: "The police, being very white and being very conservative, didn't like the idea of seeing black and white couples." While Heifetz remembers interracial mixing in the Humoresque, he thinks that the accusations about drugs were groundless.[50]

Heifetz's recollections also modify the narrative of police corruption. Not long after he bought the Humoresque, Heifetz remembers, a police sergeant suggested that he talk to Rizzo. Heifetz recalls Rizzo mentioning "complaints" and saying that "if I would cooperate with him, he was sure that it was no problem. . . . And I didn't know what he meant," Heifetz explains. "And as we talked, it was suggested that if I were supportive of the patrolmen on the beat, that were in cars, and if I were to make a gesture towards them, they would be very supportive of me." In a second conversation, Rizzo suggested that Christmas would be a "nice time" to show his "appreciation." Describing himself as "a little innocent," Heifetz remembers giving the police small bottles of alcohol. "Apparently that wasn't quite the gesture that he had in mind."

> What precipitated the whole thing was the fact that I didn't understand that there was a system of paying off the police in those days. And that if you had made an arrangement where you gave them 50 dollars a week, you would never be bothered for anything. And bars of the day all paid off. As I got older and as I became familiar with the bars and the people that owned them, I found out that there was an arrangement, that they used to go and pay off money every week, either to the police or to City Hall. I actually, years later, wound up walking with someone who

> owned a bar, and went into City Hall, and I knew what he was doing. He was paying them off. And he did that every week.[51]

Heifetz also describes backlash. The Humoresque "started to attract an undesirable clientele because the people that had been coming in were now scared away." At one point, "some young neighborhood kids" started to come and one night, after they walked out with his stainless steel pots, Heifetz began yelling. According to Heifetz, when they threatened him, he retrieved his unloaded gun and the troublemakers left. When Heifetz called to report the incident, the police charged him with gun violations, which he considers "payback." He also remembers incidents involving his lover, who was stopped by police a few times while driving Heifetz's car. After police saw Heifetz's name on the registration, his lover was harassed. In one incident, police took the car to Germantown (a neighborhood in northwest Philadelphia) and demanded that Heifetz claim it there. In another, two policemen took his lover to a South Philly park, where, according to Heifetz, "he had to submit to giving them oral sex . . . or they were going to beat him up."

One part of Heifetz's story that was never mentioned in the newspapers at the time but that he talks about today is that he is gay. In fact, Heifetz suggests that accusations about homosexuality in the coffeehouses contributed to his coming out. Born in 1935 and raised in Center City and South Philly, Heifetz recalls that he had his first same-sex sexual experiences in the Boy Scouts and the Market Street movie theaters. But he does not think that he was aware, when he was fifteen or sixteen, that there was a "gay society," "gay people," or a "gay lifestyle." After serving in the military and returning to Philly, Heifetz began his "first gay romance" with a man he met at the Humoresque. Discussing police accusations about the coffeehouses, Heifetz says, "That was probably the first time in my life that I was ever face to face with the word publicly: homosexual."

Heifetz now estimates that 25–40 percent of his patrons and 100 percent of his staff were gay. Asked why he thinks the Humoresque was singled out, Heifetz suggests that although "all of the coffee shops had some gay people," the Humoresque "probably had visibly more gay people." Moreover, when discussing the presence of gay men in the Humoresque, Heifetz sets the conflict into larger geographic terms. All four coffeehouses were in the vicinity of Rittenhouse Square, a park in the heart of a residential neighborhood that was very popular among lesbians and gay men. Symbols of the area's lesbian and gay presence, the coffeehouses in general and the Humoresque in particular offered those who opposed that presence a scapegoat. Defenders of the coffeehouses who did not publicly acknowledge that they were popular among lesbians or gay men may have been using the same type of strategic dissembling that often proved effective in everyday life. Denying that there were lesbian or gay patrons, that they knew about lesbian or gay patrons, or that they had been informed by police about lesbian or gay patrons may have been among the most promising strategies available for securing court victories, even though this strategy condoned attacks on lesbians and gay men.

Although Heifetz and several other gay narrators do not recall seeing lesbians in the coffeehouses, many lesbian narrators remember the coffeehouse scene as sexually and socially vital for them as well. Discussing the coffeehouses, Pat Hill says, "There was a very intense sort of network of attraction between several of us that centered around the Gilded Cage. . . . It was a straight slash lesbian scene." Becky Davidson remembers going to the Artist's Hut and Gilded Cage with lesbian and gay friends. Arleen Olshan says of the Gilded Cage, Humoresque, and Proscenium, "There were some lesbians there. There were some gay people there." Marcea Rosen remembers regularly meeting a woman with whom she was having an affair at Gilded Cage: "There were lesbians there, but it was my feeling that it wasn't overpoweringly a gay place. . . . Women weren't as visible," she argues. "We could blend in a little more. I was married, I had children, I had a family, I had a job. And wherever I went I was above reproach in a straight world. And I always enjoyed fooling them. I loved it. Just sort of humming to myself and saying, 'I may be married to a college professor and have three kids and a house in the suburbs, but I'm not what you think I am.'" One gay narrator does recall the lesbian presence. "Ray Daniels," who remembers the Artist's Hut, Gilded Cage, Humoresque, and Proscenium, says, "There was a mixture of lesbians, gay men, straight men, and straight women. There was a nice mixture there. In fact that was probably, when I come to think of it, the only place where there was that kind of mixture that took place openly."[52]

While lesbians and gay men may have converged in the coffeehouses, their narratives about Rizzo's raids diverge in significant ways. Pat Hill, for example, remembers Rizzo raiding the Gilded Cage and says that she "begged to go," but that Rizzo "brushed" her aside. "I wanted to be part of it," she recalls. "I *was* part of it. But I guess I just looked so innocent that he wouldn't take me. I wanted to get in the paddy wagon. Because they were taking everybody else off. And I felt very left behind." This image of Hill, part of the coffeehouse scene but "left behind" by the police, is emblematic of how lesbians and gay men often shared social and cultural space but experienced different forms of oppression and resistance.[53]

Conclusion

The roles played by lesbians and gay men in the coffeehouse narratives and in other public texts about same-sex sexualities in Philadelphia point to a number of conclusions about sex, gender, and sexuality in the postwar years. As Wini Breines has argued, "'Deviants' such as Beats, hipsters, juvenile delinquents, homosexuals, even communists, were almost always males . . . in the scholarly and public mind" in the 1950s.[54] This was in spite of the existence of dynamic "deviant" female cultures in the United States. The masculinization of lesbians and effeminization of gay men in public discourse failed to make lesbians any more visible, gay men any less visible, than would be expected given their sexes. And yet the stories of the fourteen-year-old girl looking for lesbians in the coffeehouses and Pat Hill trying to get arrested at the Gilded Cage suggest not only that lesbians were present in these cultural spaces, but that they were visible to one another.

In general, however, media narratives constructed gay men as visible, lesbians as invisible. Depending upon one's perspective, lesbians were either more successful or more unsuccessful than gay men were in avoiding public notice. When representations of lesbians did appear, they often were derived from, or conceived of in relation to, or overwhelmed in quantity and intensity by, their male counterparts. On the whole, the media constructed gay men as public, independent, and sexually active, and lesbians as private, dependent, and sexually passive. In turn, to the extent that public discourse shaped the views of lesbians and gay men, lesbians were more likely to define themselves in relation to gay men than the other way around.

The roles played by lesbians and gay men in the coffeehouse controversy and in other public debates in Philadelphia between 1945 and 1960 also point to a number of conclusions about relationships between the politics of everyday life and organized social movement politics.[55] First, both lesbians and gay men were part of an alternative late 1940s and 1950s culture that provided a vital public space for dissent from dominant norms. Second, these spaces were critical in the processes by which a variety of social groups moved from the politics of everyday culture in the late 1940s and 1950s to the politics of organized struggle in the 1960s. For example, a significant number of lesbians and gay men who became active in the Philadelphia homophile movement in the 1960s remember spending meaningful time in the coffeehouses in the 1950s. Although Heifetz's 1959 suit was an individual instance of gay resistance not sustained by a political group engaging in ongoing struggle, it helped create conditions that made it more possible to imagine the formation of a collective and organized Philadelphia homophile movement in 1960. Third, resistance to dominant culture in the late 1940s and 1950s involved a complex nexus of strategies that depended upon different types of visibility for different types of dissidents in different types of public places and populations. Finally, relationships between everyday resistance and organized political struggle across a range of U.S. social movements in the postwar era were sexed and gendered. In moving from the world of the everyday to the world of organized politics, lesbians and gay men encountered different problems and possibilities, even as their histories proved to be as intertwined as were the images of men in beards and girls in tights in the coffeehouse controversy.

Notes

1. "Police Raiders Break Up Chess Game, Seize Men in Beards, Girls in Tights," *Evening Bulletin* (*EB*), 12 February 1959, p. 3. The newspapers generally used "Haifetz," but Heifetz says he used and uses "Heifetz." Except in legal citations, I have standardized the spelling.

2. See Wini Breines, "The 'Other' Fifties: Beats and Bad Girls," in *Not June Cleaver: Women and Gender in Postwar America, 1945–1960,* ed. Joanne Meyerowitz (Philadelphia: Temple University Press, 1994), 399–400.

3. Sam Bass Warner, Jr., *The Private City: Philadelphia in Three Periods of Its Growth* (Philadelphia: University of Pennsylvania Press, 1968).

4. John D'Emilio and Estelle B. Freedman, *Intimate Matters: A History of Sexuality in America* (New York: Harper and Row, 1988), 275–76. See also Bruce Cook, *The Beat Generation* (New York: Scribner's, 1971), 24–27, 92–98; John D'Emilio, *Sexual Politics, Sexual Communities: The Making of a Homosexual Minority in the United States, 1940–1970* (Chicago: University of Chicago Press, 1983), 176–82; John D'Emilio, "Gay Politics, Gay Community: San Francisco's Experience," *Socialist Review,* 55 (January–February 1981): 461–62; Catherine R. Stimpson, "The Beat Generation and the Trials of Homosexual Liberation," *Salmagundi,* 58–59 (Fall 1982/Winter 1983): 373–92.

5. "City Teeners Account for 1/4 of Crime in 58," *Philadelphia Inquirer* (*Inq.*), 25 February 1959, p. 12. See also Allen J. Matusow, *The Unraveling of America: A History of Liberalism in the 1960s* (New York: Harper and Row, 1984), 107; James Gilbert, *A Cycle of Outrage: America's Reaction to the Juvenile Delinquent in the 1950s* (New York: Oxford University Press, 1986).

6. S. A. Paolantonio, *Frank Rizzo: The Last Big Man in Big City America* (Philadelphia: Camino, 1993), 110. See also Greg Walter, "Rizzo," *Philadelphia Magazine* (*PM*), (July 1967): 43, 71–89; Charles MacNamara, "The Tactics of Counterinsurgency," *PM* (March 1968): 50–53, 120–37; Charles MacNamara, "The Collected Love Letters of Frank Rizzo and Dick Nixon," *PM* (July 1972): 86–88; Fred Hamilton, *Rizzo* (New York: Viking, 1973); Nora Sayre, *Sixties Going on Seventies* (New York: Arbor House, 1973), 66–78, 112–32; Joseph R. Daughen and Peter Binzen, *The Cop Who Would Be King* (Boston: Little, Brown, 1977); Frank Donner, *Protectors of Privilege: Red Squads and Police Repression in Urban America* (Berkeley: University of California Press, 1990), 197–244.

7. Donner, *Protectors of Privilege,* 197, 200.

8. "Phila. Wins 3d Title of Cleanest U.S. City," *Inq.,* 13 March 1959, p. 29. See also Chester Rapkin and William G. Grigsby, *Residential Renewal in the Urban Core* (Philadelphia: University of Pennsylvania Press, 1960); Robert B. Mitchell, ed., "Planning and Development in Philadelphia," *Journal of the American Institute of Planners* 26(3) (August 1960); Edmund N. Bacon, "Downtown Philadelphia: A Lesson in Design for Urban Growth," *Architectural Record* 129(5) (May 1961): 131–46; Nathaniel Burt, *The Perennial Philadelphians: The Anatomy of an American Aristocracy* (Boston: Little, Brown, 1963), 539–40, 555–62; Sidney Hopkins, "Requiem for a Renaissance," *Greater Philadelphia Magazine* (*GPM*), (November 1964): 32–35, 54–59; *Time* (6 November 1964): 60–75; Nancy Love, "Paradise Lost," *PM* (July 1968): 72–75, 87–99; Edwin Wolf 2d, *Philadelphia: Portrait of an American City* (Harrisburg: Stackpole, 1975), 321–46; Peter O. Muller, Kenneth C. Meyer, and Roman A. Cybriwsky, *Metropolitan Philadelphia: A Study of Conflicts and Social Cleavages* (Cambridge: Ballinger,

1976), 3–5, 23–29; Paul R. Levy and Roman A. Cybriwsky, "The Hidden Dimensions of Culture and Class: Philadelphia," in *Back to the City: Issues in Neighborhood Renovation,* ed. Shirley Bradway Laska and Daphne Spain (New York: Pergamon, 1980), 138–55; Conrad Weiler, "The Neighborhood's Role in Optimizing Reinvestment: Philadelphia," in *Back to the City,* 220–35; Meredith Savery, "Instability and Uniformity: Residential Patterns in Two Philadelphia Neighborhoods, 1880–1970," in *The Divided Metropolis: Social and Spatial Dimensions of Philadelphia, 1800–1975,* ed. William W. Cutler, III, and Howard Gillette, Jr. (Westport, Conn.: Greenwood, 1980), 193–226; John F. Bauman, *Public Housing, Race, and Renewal: Urban Planning in Philadelphia, 1920–1974* (Philadelphia: Temple University Press, 1987), 90–208; Carolyn Adams et al., *Philadelphia: Neighborhoods, Divisions, and Conflict in a Postindustrial City* (Philadelphia: Temple University Press, 1991), 15–16, 66–123.

9. W. E. B. Dubois, *The Philadelphia Negro: A Social Study* (1899; repr. New York: Schocken, 1967), xix; Lincoln Steffens, "Philadelphia: Corrupt and Contented," *McClure's Magazine* (July 1903): 249–63; Estes Kefauver, *Crime in America* (Garden City, N.Y.: Doubleday, 1951), 218; Jonathan Rubinstein, *City Police* (New York: Farrar, Straus, and Giroux, 1973), 393–433; Pennsylvania Crime Commission, *Report on Police Corruption and the Quality of Law Enforcement in Philadelphia,* March 1974, pp. 1, 827. See also Senate Special Committee to Investigate Organized Crime in Interstate Commerce, 82d Cong., 1st sess., 1951, S. Rept. 307, 46–49; Senate Committee on Government Operations, Permanent Subcommittee on Investigations, 87th Cong., Hearings, 12 June 1962, 57–81; Joseph D. Crumlish, *A City Finds Itself: The Philadelphia Home Rule Charter Movement* (Detroit: Wayne State University Press, 1959), 5–22, 51–53; James Reichley, *The Art of Government: Reform and Organization Politics in Philadelphia* (New York: Fund for the Republic, 1959), 3–11, 57, 78–79, 89–92; Sayre, *Sixties Going on Seventies,* 123–25, 128–29; Blaze Starr and Huey Perry, *Blaze Starr: My Life as Told to Huey Perry* (New York: Praeger, 1974), 89–101; Joseph S. Clark, Jr., and Dennis J. Clark, "Rally and Relapse, 1946–1968," in *Philadelphia: A Three-Hundred-Year History,* ed. Russell F. Weigley (New York: Norton, 1982), 650–52; Paolantonio, *Frank Rizzo,* 43–44, 47–48, 59–63, 69–70, 175–178.

10. Joseph Yannone, cited in Paolantonio, *Frank Rizzo,* 61.

11. "10 Are Freed After Club Raids," *EB,* 28 April 1954, p. 3; "3 Dancers, 4 Men Held in Midcity Nightclub Raids," *Philadelphia Daily News* (*DN*), 28 April 1954, p. 3; Rizzo, cited in Walter, "Rizzo," 78; Joseph Yannone, cited in Paolantonio, *Frank Rizzo,* 61; "Policeman Fired in Morals Case," *Inq.,* 15 July 1959, p. 9. See also *Inq.,* 28 April 1954, p. 44; *EB,* 3 October 1958, p. 3; *Inq.,* 3 October 1958, p. 46; *DN,* 3 October 1958, p. 4.

12. See Mumia, "Occupation: Philadelphia, PA," *Black Panther,* 4 July 1970, 9; *DN,* 8 May 1973, p. 4.

13. "Rizzo's Raiders Strike Again at Midcity Coffee House," *EB,* 14 February 1959, pp. 1, 3; "'Beatnik' Place Raided by Police," *Inq.,* 14 February 1959, p. 9; Rizzo, cited in "Coffee House Steaming to Halt Rizzo's Raiders," *DN,* 17 February 1959, p. 4; Heifetz, cited in "Rizzo's Raiders Strike Again." See also "2 City Departments, State Agency Probe 4 Midtown Coffee Shops," *Inq.,* 19 February 1959, p. 13.

14. "Rizzo's Raiders Strike Again," *EB;* Heifetz, cited in ibid.; "Rizzo the Raider Tours Coffee Spots," *EB,* 18 February 1959, pp. 1, 19.

15. Heifetz, cited in "Rizzo's Raiders Strike Again," *EB;* Ruth Rolen, "Did Mixing of Races

Spur Coffee Shop Raids?" *Philadelphia Tribune* (*Trib.*), 21 February 1959, p. 11; "Rizzo the Raider Tours Coffee Spots," *EB;* C. A. S., Jr., letter to the editor, *EB,* 19 February 1959, p. 14.

16. "'Beatnik' Center Raided by Police," *Inq.,* 12 February 1959, p. 9; "Rizzo's Raiders Strike Again," *EB.*

17. "Cisco vs. Espresso," *DN,* 17 February 1959, p. 23; C. A. S., Jr., letter to the editor, *EB,* 19 February 1959, p. 14; Letter to the editor, *EB,* 19 February 1959, p. 14.

18. Heifetz, cited in "Rizzo's Raiders Strike Again," *EB;* Letter to the editor, *EB,* 19 February 1959, p. 14. See also letters to the editor, *Inq.,* 18 February 1959, p. 16; *DN,* 20 February 1959, p. 29.

19. Horace Proctor, Jr., letter to the editor, *EB,* 19 February 1959, p. 14.

20. Heifetz, cited in "Rizzo's Raiders Strike Again," *EB;* Rubin, cited in Stewart Klein, "Coffee Houses Hint Suit for 100Gs," *DN,* 19 February 1959, p. 5. See also "Rizzo the Raider Tours Coffee Spots," *EB;* "2 City Departments," *Inq.;* "Coffee House Steaming To Halt Rizzo's Raiders," *DN; Civil Liberties Record* (*CLR*), Mar. 1959, 1; *CLR,* May 1959, 2; *CLR,* Dec. 1969, 2; Coxe to Byrna Aronson, 14 May 1971, Harry Langhorne Papers, #7441, Box 1/f2, Human Sexuality Collection, Division of Rare and Manuscript Collections, Cornell University Library, Ithaca, New York.

21. "Coffee House Owner, Patron Sue Police over Raids," *EB,* 19 February 1959, p. 2. See also "Residents Protest Immoral Conduct at Coffee Houses," *Inq.,* 20 February 1959, p. 25; "'Shocking Talk' Laid to Coffee Shop Patrons," *DN,* 20 February 1959, p. 4.

22. Dave Racher and Jim O'Brien, "Fergy's Turn to Beard the Beatniks," *DN,* 18 February 1959, p. 3; "2 City Departments," *Inq.*

23. Letters to the editor, *EB,* 19 February 1959, p. 14. See also letter to the editor, *DN,* 19 February 1959, p. 17.

24. "Residents Protest Immoral Conduct," *Inq.,* 20 February 1959, p. 25; John H. Gordy, "Steamed-Up Residents Argue Coffee Shop Raids," *EB,* 20 February 1959, pp. 1, 3. See also *EB,* 19 February 1959, p. 2; "'Shocking Talk' Laid to Coffee Shop Patrons," *DN.*

25. "Residents Protest Immoral Conduct," *Inq.*

26. Ibid.

27. Ibid.

28. Ibid.

29. "Turning Down the Flame," *EB,* 21 February 1959, p. 6.

30. Gordy, "Steamed-Up Residents"; "Residents Protest Immoral Conduct," *Inq.*

31. Gordy, "Steamed-Up Residents."

32. James Smart, "A Visit to the Coffeehouses," *EB,* 22 February 1959, pp. 1, 16.

33. Ibid.; "Postscript on Coffee Houses," *CLR,* May 1959, 2; Rolen, "Did Mixing of Races Spur Coffee Shop Raids?"

34. See Philadelphia City Planning Commission, *Population Characteristics: 1960 and 1970 Philadelphia Census Tracts;* Philadelphia City Planning Commission, *Population and Housing Characteristics* (for 1970 and 1980 Philadelphia Census Tracts).

35. Jerry Gaghan, "Locust St. after Dark," *DN,* 19 March 1959, p. 39.

36. Rolen, "Did Mixing of Races Spur Coffee Shop Raids?"

37. "Thirteen Want Coffeehouse Ruled Nuisance by Court," *EB,* 25 February 1959, p. 21; "Coffee Shop Patrons Rowdy, Residents Say," *Inq.,* 28 February 1959, p. 13; "Coffeehouse

Witness Tells of Dope 'Buy,'" *EB,* 2 March 1959, p. 3; "Coffee House Brief Ordered," *DN,* 3 March 1959, p. 4. See also *Inq.,* 25 February 1959, p. 1; *DN,* 25 February 1959, p. 41.

38. "Rizzo Tells Federal Court of Coffeehouse Complaints," *EB,* 27 February 1959, p. 42.

39. "Narcotics Addicts Found in Coffeehouse, Police Say," *EB,* 28 February 1959, p. 3.

40. "Coffee Shop Asked to Cite Raid Ban Data," *Inq.,* 3 March 1959, p. 29; "Police Showed No Warrant, Coffeehouse Owner Says," *EB,* 27 February 1959, p. 3; "Teenage Witnesses Deny Disorders at Humoresque," *EB,* 3 March 1959, p. 11. See also *Inq.,* 27 February 1959, p. 23; *DN,* 27 February 1959, p. 3.

41. "Youth in Coffee Shop Raid Says Police Helped Him Flee," *EB,* 7 March 1959, p. 3; "3 Youths Freed of Charges in Coffee Raids," *EB,* 9 March 1959, p. 2. See also *Inq.,* 11 March 1959, p. 45.

42. "Youth in Coffee Shop Raid," *EB.*

43. "3 Youths Freed of Charges," *EB;* "Judge Upholds 4 Fines, Roasts Coffee Shop Set," *Inq.,* 10 March 1959, p. 29.

44. See *EB,* 20 March 1959, p. 13; *EB,* 26 March 1959, p. 42; Stewart Klein, "An Espresso of Sad Parting," *DN,* 27 March 1959, p. 4; *Haifetz v. Rizzo* 171 F. Supp. 654; Paolantonio, *Frank Rizzo,* 68–69; Hamilton, *Rizzo,* 59–60.

45. "3 Coffeehouses Vow to Police Themselves and Bar Undesirables," *Inq.,* 27 March 1959, p. 21; Richardson Dilworth to Henry W. Sawyer, III, 29 Mar. 1959, in the possession of Spencer Coxe, Philadelphia, Pa. See also Klein, "An Espresso of Sad Parting." I thank Fred Mogul for sharing Dilworth's letter with me.

46. "Coffee Shop Man Convicted," *EB,* 26 September 1959, p. 3; "Jury Convicts Owner of Raided Coffee Shop," *Inq.,* 26 September 1959, p. 11; "Close Place or Go to Jail, Coffee Shop Owner Is Told," *EB,* 28 October 1959, p. 32. See also *EB,* 23 May 1959, p. 1; *Inq.,* 24 May 1959, p. B2; *EB,* 27 May 1959, p. 58; *DN,* 23 May 1959, p. 3; *Inq.,* 28 October 1959, p. 43; *DN,* 29 October 1959, p. 10.

47. *Haifetz v. Rizzo,* 178 F. Supp. 828. See also *EB,* 9 December 1959, p. 52; *Inq.,* 10 December 1959, p. 41; *DN,* 10 December 1959, p. 19.

48. *One* (April 1959): 17–18.

49. Ibid., See also *One* (June 1959): 13.

50. Interview with Mel Heifetz. I interviewed forty-five oral history narrators from 1993 to 1997 in Pennsylvania, New York, California, and Massachusetts.

51. Interview with Mel Heifetz.

52. Interviews with Pat Hill, Becky Davidson, Arleen Olshan, Marcea Rosen, and "Ray Daniels" (pseudonym).

53. Interview with Pat Hill.

54. Breines, "The 'Other' Fifties," 383.

55. See D'Emilio, *Sexual Politics,* 4–5; James C. Scott, *Weapons of the Weak: Everyday Forms of Peasant Resistance* (New Haven: Yale University Press, 1985); James C. Scott, *Domination and the Arts of Resistance: Hidden Transcripts* (New Haven: Yale University Press, 1990); Elizabeth Lapovsky Kennedy and Madeline D. Davis, *Boots of Leather, Slippers of Gold: The History of a Lesbian Community* (New York: Routledge, 1993), 2, 150, 390; Esther Newton, *Cherry Grove, Fire Island: Sixty Years in America's First Gay and Lesbian Town* (Boston: Beacon, 1993), 236–39; Robin D. G. Kelley, "We Are Not What We Seem": Rethinking Black

Working-Class Opposition in the Jim Crow South," *Journal of American History* 80(1) (June 1993): 75–112; Robin D. G. Kelley, "The Black Poor and the Politics of Opposition in a New South City, 1929–1970," in *The "Underclass" Debate: Views from History,* ed. Michael B. Katz (Princeton: Princeton University Press, 1993), 293–333; George Chauncey, *Gay New York: Gender, Urban Culture, and the Making of the Gay Male World, 1890–1940* (New York: Basic, 1994), 5; Donna Penn, "The Present and Future of Recuperating the Past: A Review Essay," *GLQ* 2(3) (1995): 279–305.

12

Black Feminist Organizations and the Emergence of Interstitial Politics

KIMBERLY SPRINGER

THE sociopolitical conditions of the late 1960s prompted a resurgence of Black feminist awareness and the emergence of organizations dedicated to Black feminist ideals.[1] Black feminists defined their collective identity, those commonalities that bound Black women to one another, in reaction to the civil rights movement's masculinist definitions of rights for Blacks, the women's movement's limited definition of sisterhood among women, and the degradation of Black womanhood as matriarchal in social policy and popular culture. In essence, Black feminists conducted what one informant dubbed "politics in the cracks."[2] I call this moment the development of *interstitial politics*. Interstitial politics describes the development of Black feminist identity and the direction of Black feminist organizations' growth in two aspects. First, Black feminists squeezed their activism into their schedules whenever possible, serving as full-time unpaid staff for their organizations. Dedication to Black feminist activism was not just a matter of commitment, but of biographical availability—disposable time between familial, work, school, and other personal obligations—and constraints that dictated when and what kinds of resources members contributed to their organizations.[3]

Second, interstitial politics also applies to Black feminist organizations and their position relative to other twentieth-century U.S. social movements. Black feminist organizations took advantage of cracks in the social movement and political opportunity structures to garner for attention for Black women's race, class, and gender concerns. Black feminist organizations' naming of politics in the cracks sought to correct the gap left by masculinist Black politics and racist white feminist politics. In their emergence, Black feminist organizations did not forsake either movement and, instead, incorporated anti-racist *and* anti-sexist activism into the development of Black feminism. Additionally, Black feminist organizations introduced a critique of classist and heterosexist discrimination into the Left social movement community. This development was critical to the evolution of attention to the intersecting nature of socially constructed identities used in the humanities and the social sciences.

Interstitial politics, as a social movement dynamic, function not only outside social movement organizations, but also within them. To assume that because a group of people belong to the same social movement they hold the same ideas about collective identity or ideology is to leave the movement open to potentially crippling disruptions. Thus, interstitial politics can effectively address these fissures by bringing tensions out into the open as a tool for organizational strengthening. Rather than surprise and dismay, organizational leaders can anticipate the issues heterogeneity within the group will raise and turn those differences into positive aspects of the organization's identity or objectives.

In the case of the Black feminist movement, Black lesbian feminists enacted interstitial politics in their claims against racism, sexism, and heterosexism. As this essay shows, the significant Black lesbian, feminist, socialist membership of the Combahee River Collective simultaneously named oppression based on gender and race, as well as oppression based on sexual orientation. By doing so, Combahee broadened the range of issues considered relevant to Black liberation, women's liberation, and gay liberation in the 1970s.

Overview of Black Feminist Organizations

Within a protest cycle, there are "early risers," or those individuals and organizations whose confrontations with elites significantly reduce the costs of collective action.[4] For example, the civil rights movement was an early riser in the articulation of the equal rights framework of social justice. Black, Asian, Puerto Rican, Chicana, and Native American nationalist movements, feminists of all races, and gay/lesbian/transgender movements of the early 1970s all benefited morally and organizationally from the challenges issued by the civil rights movement.[5] These movements adopted known strategies (e.g., sit-ins, civil disobedience) and structural forms. In the late 1960s and 1970s, Black feminist organizations relied on social networks forged in the civil rights and women's movements to mobilize Black women, as well as challenge established social movements and political structures. However, Black feminist organizations also expanded upon strategies of protest, in theory and practice, through their explanation of how race, class, and gender intersected in their lives.

From the mid- to late 1960s, Black women active in civil rights and women's organizations discovered that these movements did not include the simultaneous eradication of sexism and racism, respectively. Additionally, Black women encountered structural obstacles as promoted in racist and sexist theorizing, such as Daniel Patrick Moynihan's 1965 report that proposed the theory of the "Black Matriarchy."[6] Lastly, Black women faced discrimination in popular culture that included stereotypes of the "Mammy" or the hypersexual Black woman of Blaxploitation films, such as Shaft. These stereotypes were not new, but they gained new currency as producers of mass culture attempted to capitalize on the new Black Pride aesthetic.

All of these occurrences created sociopolitical conditions that incited Black women's racial consciousness and rising gender awareness.

Despite these negative media images, some Black women did hold leadership positions in the civil rights and Black Nationalist movements that challenged traditional gender and race norms.[7] These leadership opportunities provided Black women with a wealth of strategies and ideologies that they later employed in feminist organizations, such as a critique of hierarchy and commitment to democratic decision-making. Yet, the inability of the civil rights movement to extend its objectives to include anti-sexist struggle alienated some Black women. Similarly, Black women active in the women's movement found that the movement's definition of women did not take into account discrimination based on race and class. Overall, Black feminists' gains from these two movements were mixed: they experienced discrimination rooted in racism and sexism but gained the tools to overcome and form their own organizations.

Case Study: Combahee River Collective

There were at least five Black feminist organizations known to be active from 1968 to 1980: the Third World Women's Alliance (New York and San Francisco-Oakland); the National Black Feminist Organization (New York); the National Alliance of Black Feminists (Chicago); the Combahee River Collective (Boston); and Black Women Organized for Action (San Francisco-Oakland). There are striking similarities between these groups and their members, including activist histories in the civil rights movement, adherence to democratic decision-making (at least, in theory), difficulties in the mobilization of resources, and collective identities centered around being Black, female, and often working-class or poor.

However, there were also differences between Black feminist organizations as their members struggled to define Black feminism, Black womanhood, and strategies for liberation from Black women's common oppression. In particular, Black women discovered that all Black women did not share the same life circumstances around sexual orientation and class. This heterogeneity proved to be a challenge to Black feminists as they attempted to construct Black feminist identity. The Combahee River Collective serves as a case study of the complexity of Black feminist organizational emergence and forging Black feminist identity. The case of Combahee demonstrates that while Black feminists did unite around a common racialized and gendered identity, there were concrete differences between Black women, and those differences became apparent in building Black feminist organizations.

Emergence

Started as the Boston chapter of the National Black Feminist Organization (NBFO) in January 1974, the Combahee River Collective split from the NBFO by the summer of 1975.[8] Despite its decline after 1980, Combahee is most remembered for its pivotal statement of Black feminist politics originally titled "A Black Feminist Statement." Solicited for inclusion in Zillah Eisenstein's *Capitalist Patriarchy and the Case for Socialist Feminism,* the statement was reprinted and cited in numerous texts as representative of Black feminist ideology, theory, and practice.[9] Yet, there is more to the story of Combahee than this statement, specifically the evolution of the organization and its experiment with nonhierarchical, collectivist organizing.

The radicalization of Combahee's principal organizers occurred not unlike that of other founders of Black feminist organizations. As Barbara Smith explained in an interview with me, she and her sister Beverly came to political consciousness during the civil rights movement in Cleveland, Ohio.[10] As high school students, Barbara and Beverly participated in the school desegregation struggle through a school boycott sponsored by the Congress on Racial Equality (CORE) in 1964. Following graduation from high school, the Smith sisters volunteered with CORE as telephone operators and canvassers in Cleveland's housing projects. Cleveland CORE's female executive director helped cultivate Barbara's activist abilities, and she credits the director with giving her an opportunity for active politicization that might not have happened under the supervision of a male leader.[11]

Barbara Smith attended Mount Holyoke College as an undergraduate, and it was there that she began to see the interlocking nature of oppression. Involved in the anti–Vietnam War movement through an organization called "Civil Action," which focused on both anti-war and civil rights support work, Smith witnessed the vagaries of racism and imperialism as the U.S. government drafted young Black men to fight for democracy, while discriminating against them domestically.[12]

About the same time Smith graduated from Mount Holyoke and went on to graduate studies, the civil rights movement took a turn toward Black Nationalist politics. The articulation of a masculinist view of revolution and liberation motivated Smith's gravitation toward the women's movement. She explained:

> I went to a major anti-war mobilization in Washington, D.C., in the fall of 1969 [the National Moratorium]. . . . I thought it was the last demonstration I'd ever go to; one of the reasons being Black people back at Pitt [University of Pittsburgh] had so many nasty things to say about the fact that I was involved in what they say was a "white" entity, namely, the anti-war movement. There were not that many Black people involved at that time . . . but it was a very hard time to be a politically active Black woman, who did not want to be a pawn. . . . I actually imagined that I would never be politically active again because nationalism and patriarchal attitudes within Black organizing was *so* strong—we're talking early '70s now—was so strong I just thought there would be no place ever for me to be politically active the way I had been in my prior life. But, then, I got involved in the women's movement through Black feminism, the National Black Feminist Organization in 1973, and then I've been able to be active ever since.[13]

Smith's comments echo those of Margaret Sloan of the NBFO and Brenda Eichelberger of the National Alliance of Black Feminists (NABF), who, in more than one instance, were challenged on their commitment to Black struggle and their adherence to feminist principles. Rather than seeing the connections between racism, imperialism, and sexism, Smith's detractors believed that opposition to the Vietnam War was not a "black issue" and that she betrayed her race by participating in coalition work.[14] Nevertheless, Smith's negative experience with patriarchal attitudes was a positive move toward Black feminist organizing.

In addition to these radicalizing political experiences, Barbara's sister Beverly played a central role in the emergence of Combahee. While on staff at *Ms.* magazine when it was still a fledgling publication, Beverly met Margaret Sloan, a founder of the NBFO. Part of a preexisting network of Black feminists through which Barbara received information, Beverly was in a central position to relay information about the NBFO's upcoming Eastern Regional Conference to be held in December 1973.[15]

The Eastern Regional Conference was significant for Barbara, and many other Black women who attended, because its consciousness-raising sessions highlighted the connections between Black women and feminist issues. The conference showed Barbara that though she encountered only white women in Boston consciousness-raising groups, feminism was not their exclusive property:

> So, it was really pivotal for me because, see, I could never see myself joining a white women's organization. I just couldn't even imagine that. The first time I heard about feminism I thought those women were *crazy.* I thought they were *perfectly crazy.* I could not even understand it. And my sister says the same thing because, see, my sister, being at the University of Chicago, she was at the place where some of the strongest feminists—early feminists in the country—was growing up. Heather Booth, you know, and all the rest of them. . . . We both talked about how we thought these people were just crazy because we couldn't understand what white women had to complain about. . . . It [the Eastern Regional Conference] was a very positive experience for me, but there were days when it was like, "Oh, my goodness, I'm the only black woman/woman of color in this room." But I had never gone to a NOW [National Organization for Women] meeting. I never did that. So having something called the National Black Feminist Organization made it possible for me to be a Black feminist because I just couldn't imagine being involved in a white women's group.[16]

The Smith sisters voiced the sentiments of many Black women during that period who thought that feminism was a crazy invention of privileged, white women. Yet, unlike many of the women who rejected feminism as a "white thing," the women who attended the Eastern Regional Conference sought to move beyond media stereotypes of feminism and explore feminism's liberatory potential for Black women. Smith confirms, "And then, of course, we found ourselves identifying with feminist issues." The conference was called for the eastern region, but women came from all over the United States to network and connect with other Black feminists. Smith, who by this time lived in Boston, recalled caucusing with women from the Boston area in a stairwell because there were so many other women present from different cities searching for meeting space in the church.[17]

In January 1974, the first meeting of women interested in forming a Boston chapter of the NBFO met in Roxbury, a predominately Black neighborhood.[18] About a dozen women attended the meeting, including a woman who attended the Eastern Regional Conference and was opposed to Black feminism. Smith credited this woman with scaring off a number of potential members, particularly those women who had not attended the meeting in New York:

> And, see, what was so horrible about it is that for those of us who had been at the NBFO conference, we had something that we could build from as far as having a model and experience in our head of, "Yeah, you can do this. Yeah, 400 people can be with you. Yeah, Shirley Chisholm can be there and Eleanor Holmes Norton and it can be like that." For those who had not been at the conference in New York, I think that what Brenda Verner did was much more frightening and, as I said, some of those women never ever came back. They never came back.[19]

Just as lesbian-baiting was used to discourage women of all races from joining the women's liberation movement, some Black nationalists declared feminism antithetical to Black liberation. Lacking the empowering experience of the Eastern Regional Conference, potential members, who may have come to the meeting ambivalent about Black feminist politics, did not perceive the building momentum of a Black feminist movement. Also, since the Black feminist movement's vision was still in formation, it was susceptible to misinterpretation or distortion by anti-feminist opponents. Yet, regardless of anti-feminist sentiments, interest in forming the Boston chapter remained high.

Smith's personal interest in NBFO grew during a brief stay in Washington, D.C., from May to November 1974. During that period Smith met members of the Washington NBFO chapter, who kept her informed about the development of Black feminism in the area. Also, while she was in Washington, Smith still received letters from Black women expressing interest in joining the Boston NBFO chapter, including one from Demita Frazier. In her letter Frazier wrote to say that she was relocating to Boston from Chicago and detailed her interest in Boston NBFO. Frazier's description of her Black feminist activism and her enthusiasm for starting an NBFO chapter prompted Smith to contact Frazier and let her know that she would be returning to Boston. They later met and began the process of reconstituting the local chapter.

In the early months of 1975, Frazier and the Smith sisters convened the first Boston NBFO meeting at the Cambridge Women's Center. It was open to all Black women who wanted to attend. Their meetings focused on consciousness-raising and, as they recall in the Combahee River Collective Statement, members experienced "the overwhelming feeling that . . . after years and years we had finally found each other."[20]

Radical Black Feminist Identity and Organizational Objectives

As a result of their initial meetings, the women who attended the Boston gatherings critiqued the incipient politics of NBFO and determined that the organization was headed in a reformist direction. Several leftist, socialist, or Marxist members had a significant impact on Combahee's critical stance toward capitalism. One woman, Sharon Bourke, was what Smith called an "educated Marxist" with a wide breadth of political knowledge as well as life experience that was useful to the group. Bourke

> had been very involved in the Black Liberation Movement. She actually lived . . . in Atlanta. She was involved with the Institute for the Black World. I don't know if you know about that, but that was an important cultural and political formation during those years. She also was a trained Marxist and she was one of the most brilliant people I ever met. . . . So, it wasn't like somebody who was in their 40s—like Sharon was when I was in my late 20s—it wasn't like she was lording it all over us and saying, "You all don't know what you're doing." She was very self-effacing and she just knew how to work politically with all different people. So it was really an incredibly positive experience.[21]

Bourke also brought to the table a class-based analysis of Black women's issues. She and other Combahee members influenced the Boston chapter's move away from NBFO and toward socialist politics.

The Boston chapter also experienced many of the same frustrations as the Chicago, Atlanta, and Washington, D.C., chapters around the National NBFO Office's lack of communication and structure. But, greater than the lack of communication, the Boston women discovered that their politics were more radical than those being espoused by NBFO. In fact, they believed that NBFO was "parroting NOW and taking a 'NOW-approach' to feminist issues."[22]

The Boston women participated in consciousness-raising on a highly sophisticated political level that, much like the Third World Women's Alliance, combined consciousness-raising *with* political theorizing. Reflecting on the outcomes of the civil rights and women's movements, Boston NBFO members determined that

> you do need reform simultaneous with radical or revolutionary kinds of demands and initiatives. But the difference, of course . . . between a radical and a reformist is that reformists think that those reforms are enough. And they have much more faith in a system that has proven itself to be motionless and exploitative than people like the ones who eventually made up Boston Combahee.[23]

This observation echoed social movement theorists and historians of the women's movement who attest to radical and reformist demands as complementary.[24]

The Boston women did not advocate the dissolution of the NBFO, but they decided to split from the national body because of its reformist politics. Smith summarized:

> I don't think we were happy with NBFO. I remember being incredibly disappointed with them and being very skeptical and very—we tried to maintain good relationships because—I can't remember exactly how the communications continued after we decided we were Combahee. . . . I remember a huge amount of talk about, "Are we 'Combahee'? Are we the National Black Feminist Organization calling ourselves Combahee or are we something entirely different? Are we completely independent?" I think, of course, we opted to be completely independent, but those were complicated questions because we certainly did not want to alienate or cut off contact with other Black feminists.[25]

Black feminists could not afford to alienate one another, so the Boston women formed Combahee as a branch of the burgeoning Black feminist movement and worked locally for a socialist, Black feminist agenda.

A unique aspect to Combahee is that its members remained connected to the broader movement through their individual political work in lesbian feminist politics, reproductive rights, and other common areas of feminist activism. The inclusion of a plurality of forms of feminist activism and lesbian feminist theorizing in Combahee was the result of the networks through which members came to the organization. As previously mentioned, Beverly Smith's link to the women's movement through *Ms.* magazine was critical to the formation of the Boston chapter of the NBFO and Combahee. Similarly, preexisting ties to other Black lesbians in the Boston area served as a recruitment tool for Combahee. Mercedes Tompkins, for example, lived in the same cooperatively-owned house as Combahee member Margo Okazawa-Rey and was therefore privy to information about the formation and meetings of Combahee.[26] An organization of mostly Black lesbian feminists did not exist in Boston before Combahee, so in regard to recruitment, Combahee was attractive to Black lesbians who wanted to explore their potential involvement in the women's movement with an organization that welcomed women regardless of sexual orientation.

Much to the organization's credit, however, Combahee members did not assume that because most of its members were Black lesbians, they held the same political views or objectives. To delve deeper into the broader ramifications of Black feminism, the Boston-based members of Combahee initiated a series of seven retreats from 1977 to 1980. Invited to these retreats were friends and acquaintances of Boston members who lived mostly on the East Coast. Audre Lorde, Sharon Page Ritchie, and Cheryl Clarke were among the writers, artists, academics, and social workers who attended Combahee's Black Feminist Network Retreats. These informal members of Combahee made valuable contributions to Black feminist theory and served as members-at-large when they returned to their local communities by reinvigorating their activities with Black feminist praxis.

Connecting Black Lesbian Feminism to Black Communities

In crafting a statement on Black feminist politics, Combahee was the only Black feminist organization in this sample to mention "heterosexual oppression" in its mission statement; however, the statement did not thoroughly explain this form of oppression and its impact on Black women's identities. The term "heterosexism"—the normativity of heterosexuality—was not yet in use among activists.[27] However, most readers of Combahee's statement may have deduced the implicit meaning of heterosexual oppression as heterosexism or homophobia. For other readers, the Combahee statement was possibly the first time they were forced to recognize *publicly* that lesbians and gay men faced oppression or that considerable sexual diversity existed within Black communities.

Combahee was on the front lines of Black lesbian feminist struggle in the 1970s, yet the statement neglected to specify the ways that Black communities were complicit in perpetuating heterosexism. Barbara Smith explains this omission as the result of an intersection of the personal and political:

> I think for the record, it's important to know that I was coming out in '74, '75. What's important about that is that I declared myself—considered myself to be a Black feminist before I came out. So for those who—who telescope . . . Black feminism and Black lesbianism, I think it's important to know that one can be a Black feminist. Some would say the reason we were Black feminist is 'cause you were gonna be a lesbian and just didn't know it [laughter].[28]

The Combahee statement omitted an explicit challenge to heterosexism due to the timing of organization members' individual coming-out processes and the desire to explain feminism on its own merit. Smith and other Combahee members strategically claimed a Black and feminist identity *before* they claimed a lesbian one, though they claimed all of these as integral to Black feminist identity. The separate emergence of individuals' feminist and lesbian consciousness undermined stereotypes of all feminists as lesbians and all lesbians as feminists. Feminist and lesbian were conflated identities in the popular mind, but the coming-out process and rise in feminist consciousness, as illustrated here, disrupt that conflation.

Combahee included anti-heterosexism as part of its organizational objectives, surely a daring move then and now; however, its statement places lesbianism in the background of Black feminism's connection to Black communities: "*Although we are feminists and Lesbians. . . .*" Such a statement acts as a disclaimer that despite lesbian and feminist identity, Combahee was still dedicated to Black liberation. The position of Black feminism was clearly articulated, but Black *lesbian* feminism was, in 1977, an allusion in the text. An explication of Black heterosexism was underarticulated in the interest of establishing the foundational basis of solidarity between Combahee's Black feminism and Boston's Black communities. Still, lesbian visibility was a courageous and revolutionary move for Combahee to make, particularly in a social movement environment often divided by homophobia and hostility toward lesbian, bisexual, transgender, and gay activists.

Black Lesbian Socialist Feminist Identity as a Resource

Combahee, as a local organization, incurred few expenses. Their coalitions with other Boston area political groups lessened the financial burden of preparation for rallies, such as in the rental of audio equipment and copying informational flyers. For their Black Feminist Network retreats, women would contribute as little as ten dollars for food and lodging. Combahee's organizers never rented space for the retreats because they relied on in-kind donations from white feminists and other allies.

In essence, Combahee used its members' collective identity as currency in Boston's social justice community. As the only Black lesbian, socialist, feminist organization in the Boston area, Combahee was at the vanguard of articulating the parameters of Black feminism and the complex functioning of socially constructed identities. In market economy terms, its brand of theorizing was in demand in the marketplace of leftist ideas. Mercedes Tompkins, a Boston member of Combahee, explained how Combahee's political analysis and collective identity garnered influence in Boston's feminist, leftist, and socialist communities:

> Within Boston people looked to Combahee for anchoring around things—around the whole issue of race and culture. So that if you touch base with us or we were involved in giving support to a certain position, it almost gave them a rubber stamp. . . . "Combahee was involved in this."[29]

Combahee did not sell its name or position as Black feminists, but signed on to events in line with its political agenda and ideology of an anti-racist, anti-sexist, anti-heterosexist, and socialist revolution. In effect, Combahee bartered for a position on the political agenda of like-minded organizations. In addition, as with other Black feminist organizations, Combahee's organizers remained vigilant of tokenization or being used to give a seal of approval to other organizations that did not offer principled coalitions of social justice. Instead of dues, donations, or foundation grants, Combahee negotiated its unique political position as a valuable local resource.

The Challenges of Collectivity

The Combahee River Collective did not have an articulated definition of collectivity, but decision-making was informal within the group. However, similar to Honor Ford-Smith's experience in Sistren, a Jamaican women's collective, discrepancies in how members defined collectivity masked power differentials between Black feminists within Combahee.[30] Jo Freeman points out that though groups claiming structurelessness believe all members have equal power, "structurelessness becomes a way of masking power, and within the women's movement it is usually most strongly advocated by those who are the most powerful (whether they are conscious of their power or not)."[31] In an unpublished essay on Black feminism, Smith wrote that

> major elements of our [Black feminist] movement seem bent upon parodying the hierarchy and power-mongering of "mainstream" organizations. The only way Black feminism can survive is as a radical movement whose goal is the overturning of patriarchy, the complete questioning of things as they are. In our internal structure we should strive for collectivity and reject the tokenism and careerism that has undermined other movements.[32]

In advocating collectivity, Smith aspired for Combahee to observe lessons from other civil rights and women's movement organizations and make an effort to organize nonhierarchically. Members of Combahee did work together on a broad range of issues, but interpersonal dynamics, biographical availability, and the needs of the movement were key considerations when attempting collectivity and an informal organizational structure.

Smith was aware that her position as a leader in Combahee gave her a different perspective on the organization's collectivity than others who felt they were outside of leadership positions. Smith's understanding of the leadership of the organization was based on a distinction between collective decision-making and the role of the leader. She defines leadership as "really based upon someone who did the work and who had the capacity in their lives to fit in doing the work. . . . It wasn't a male model of leadership."[33] No one was officially in charge of the organization, but biographical availability and personality played a large part in who assumed leadership roles.

Barbara Smith, Demita Frazier, and Beverly Smith emerged as the central leaders in Combahee, jointly authoring the statement of the organization's principles. These women were not solely responsible for the organization, but their biographical availability allowed them to invest more time in the organization. Members of Combahee were undergraduates or pursuing advanced degrees, working full-time jobs, and/or engaged in other political causes in addition to their involvement with Combahee. Without establishing a subjective hierarchy of who was the most committed, it is difficult to measure availability to the organization. How individual members prioritized their obligations to Combahee, to family, and to their political ideals played a significant role in the development of an elite within Combahee.

As a result, two other members, Okazawa-Rey and Tompkins, disagreed with the view of Combahee as collectively run. Tompkins and Okazawa-Rey learned of Combahee through word of mouth and joined in the winter of 1975. Okazawa-Rey, a social worker, participated in consciousness-raising with a branch of the lesbian group Daughters of Bilitis, but later joined Combahee to meet with other Black lesbian feminists. Tompkins, at twenty-one, was not politically active with any particular group when she joined Combahee because she was only beginning to define her lesbian feminist identity.

In contrast to Smith's view of Combahee's collectivity, Tompkins and Okazawa-Rey contested the use of the term collective when applied to Combahee. Tompkins noted that Combahee's members discussed issues as a group, but she also acknowledged being outside of an "underground network" within the group. In her words, "Before things came to the group, things got filtered. So most of the requests for information or participation, or anything that was sort of on the docket for Combahee, went through Barbara Smith."[34] Tompkins believed she was outside of the elite leadership core because she "pushed the envelope around the whole issue of class and educational elitism."[35] I also maintain that, again, submerged friendship networks, while good for recruitment, had adverse effects on democratic decision-making in collective women's movement organizations. Friendship loyalties often made egalitarian decision-making difficult in Black feminist organizations.

Okazawa-Rey concurred with Tompkins's perspective on the collectivity of the organization, believing Smith held disproportionate power within Combahee:

> I think "Collective" was probably a misnomer. I think the ideal was to have it a collective, but because it was really loose—first of all, for a collective to be a collective there needs to be . . . clear ideas about decision-making that are consensus and all that. . . . So, in a way, it was kind of hierarchical in the sense that Barbara was kind of—and this gets really tricky to even talk about this—but Barbara was kind of in the center and she was certainly a driving force and it was hard to know to what extent we kind of acquiesced to her influence and to what extent she really was domineering. You know what I mean? It was tricky. It was a tension there.[36]

Smith's talents as a writer put her in a privileged position in a movement that valued connecting the personal to the political through the written word and verbal acuity. Additionally, by the late 1970s, the women's movement began to make inroads into academia as women's studies, creating another space for Smith's work as a feminist theorist and literary critic. As Smith accurately assessed, in social movements "people who write get far more visibility than those who don't."[37]

Though the collective structure was an effort to avoid hierarchy, Combahee encountered internal and external difficulties in devising a leaderless leadership strategy that was truly egalitarian. Like all organizations, Combahee was susceptible to a leader who gained predominance through her prolific writings and connections to Boston's feminist, socialist, and Black communities. Additionally, other organizations and local media chose Combahee's leader for them by contacting Smith as the group's representative.

As Okazawa-Rey pinpointed, it is difficult to ascertain where a leader's asserted dominance ends and members' acquiescence begins. In the case of Combahee, founders and rank-and-file members raised valid issues about the dangers of organizational leadership and the tyranny of structurelessness in masking power where there was thought to be none. Determining when a person crosses the boundary from dedicated leader to exerting inordinate power is a dilemma organizations must remain vigilant for from their inceptions.[38]

Biographical availability issues also played a role in complicating the leadership conflicts of Black feminist organizations. It is possible that for Smith, one of Combahee's founders, Black feminist organizing held a higher priority at that particular point in time than it did for other members. In light of this founder/organization connection, regardless of hierarchical or collective structure, it is possible that new members initially accepted the existing leadership structure, but by the time new members gained organizing skills and wanted a chance to use them, the founders were firmly installed in their leadership positions. For an organization based on preexisting friendship networks, these leadership conflicts were even more damaging to the continuance of the organization because the political and personal were so thoroughly intertwined.

It is worth noting that, for Combahee, these preexisting networks included friendships and romantic relationships, adding an additional layer to leadership conflicts. Barbara Smith's archived notes from the third retreat refer to a conflict that involved the impact of her personal, intimate relationship on the Combahee River Collective:

> I would like to do criticism/self-criticism about the political discussion we had on Saturday morning about what it means to be out. The reason we decided to have that particular discussion had to do with a personal situation-conflict between me and another person in the group, which only the women from Boston were aware of. They have pointed out how uncomfortable they felt knowing this dimension of what was going on and it not being out on the table for everyone. I think it did put a strain on the discussion for which I apologize. Perhaps we can discuss this in New York on May 20 or in the summer.[39]

Because of Smith's powerful position in Combahee, an individual personal conflict meant disruption for the entire collective. As an organization consisting of activists who were also friends, political discussions on lesbianism and the politics of being out overlapped with the joys and perils of intimate relationships. Intimate involvement is not uncommon in social movement organizations, but there is little research on the consequences of this involvement for organizational functioning. How do the emotional aspects of political engagement interact with the political practice of leadership?[40] For Combahee, it meant that the person in conflict with Smith was asked to leave the organization or felt uncomfortable remaining, like her friend who felt implicated in the conflict by association. More than gossip, this example provides an illustration of the difficulty of organizing Black women, lesbian and heterosexual, who might assume unity around their mutual identities.

The Combahee River Collective's organizers held their last Black feminist network retreat in February 1980, but organizational records do not indicate when the Boston-based collective ceased meeting. For an organization such as Combahee, it is difficult to determine a precise date of decline because many of its members came to the group through preexisting friendship and activist networks. Though Combahee may have stopped meeting as an organized body, members still encountered one another in the Boston women's community and in the Black feminist movement nationally. Yet, of all the possible reasons for Combahee's decline, leadership and interpersonal disputes stand out as decisive factors. Combahee members' developing collective identity as Black socialist lesbian feminists collided with their individual ideas about organizational collectivity and interpersonal relationships.

Summary

As demonstrated here, there was much more to the story of Combahee than "A Black Feminist Statement." The emergence of the organization from the National Black Feminist Organization—critiqued for its lack of in-depth class and sexual orientation analysis—compelled Combahee to include anti-heterosexist and anti-classist goals in its organizational Black feminist objectives. Additionally, the failings of the NBFO and experience with other civil rights organizations showed Combahee's members that a bureaucratic structure was not an organizational structure they wanted to pursue. Yet, Combahee's struggle with collectivity shows the potentially divisive effects of power, regardless of a nonhierarchical structure.

On a broader level, I propose that just as white feminists were challenged to expand the category *woman* to include women of color, lesbians, disabled women, and working poor women, Black feminists must also challenge themselves and their organizations to fully interrogate the plurality of Black feminist identities and visions that exist within the Black feminist movement. Perhaps one reason that the Combahee River Collective is the most well-known Black feminist organization, aside from the relative obscurity of other Black feminist organizations, is that its statement incorporates the ideal aspirations of the Black feminist movement at a particular point in history: a world free of race, gender, sexual orientation, and class discrimination. The new challenge for Black feminists and organizations is to increase engagement around issues of sexism and heterosexism, building on the legacy of Combahee and other Black feminist organizations through radical intervention within and outside of Black communities on multiple fronts.[41]

Notes

1. I say there was a "resurgence" of Black feminist organizational activism because Black feminist organizations of the 1970s were part of a legacy of feminist activism by Black feminism. This activism included resistance of enslaved women to forced reproduction, free Black abolitionist women, nineteenth-century clubwomen, Black women labor activists, and civil rights proponents.

2. Linda Burnham, interview with author by phone, 12 February 1998.

3. For more on biographical availability, see Doug McAdam, "The Biographical Consequences of Activism," *American Sociological Review* 54 (October 1989): 744–60. See also "Gender as a Mediator of the Activist Experience: The Case of Freedom Summer," *American Journal of Sociology* 97(5) (1992): 1211–40.

4. Sidney Tarrow, *Power in Movement: Social Movements, Collective Action, and Politics* (1994; repr. Cambridge: Cambridge University Press, 1998), 154.

5. See, for example, Vicki Crawford, Jacqueline Anne Rouse, and Barbara Woods, *Women in the Civil Rights Movement: Trailblazers and Torchbearers, 1941–1965* (Brooklyn: Carlson Publishing, 1990); Alice Echols, *Daring To Be Bad: Radical Feminism in America, 1967–1975* (Minneapolis: University of Minnesota Press, 1989); Sara Evans, *Personal Politics: The Roots of Women's Liberation in the Civil Rights Movement* (New York: Vintage Books, 1979).

6. Moynihan argued that due to slavery's economic crippling of the Black family, Black women assumed a dominant role in the family. This Black "matriarchy," as Moynihan labeled it, resulted in the emasculation of Black men and pathological Black families. Moynihan proposed that the cure for this pathology was for Black men to reassume a dominant position in Black families.

7. Texts that analyze the leadership of Black women in the civil rights movement include: Cynthia Griggs Fleming, *Soon We Will Not Cry: The Liberation of Ruby Doris Smith Robinson* (Lanham, Md.: Rowman and Littlefield, 1998); Charles Payne, "Men Led, But Women Organized," and Anne Standley, "The Role of Black Women in the Civil Rights Movement," in *Trailblazers and Torchbearers: Women in the Civil Rights Movement, 1941–1965,* ed. Vicki Crawford, Jacqueline Rouse, and Barbara Woods (Brooklyn: Carlson Publishing, 1990), 183–201; Belinda Robnett, *How Long? How Long?: African-American Women in the Struggle for Civil Rights* (New York: Oxford University Press, 1997); Regina Werum, "Women in the Civil Rights Movement," in *Women and Work: A Reader,* ed. Paula J. Dubeck and Kathryn Borman (New Brunswick, N.J.: Rutgers University Press, 1996), 58–59.

8. The name Combahee comes from "the guerrilla action conceptualized and led by Harriet Tubman on June 2, 1863, in the Port Royal region of South Carolina. This action freed more than 750 slaves and is the only military campaign in American history planned and led by a woman." Combahee River Collective, "The Combahee River Collective Statement: Black Feminist Organizing in the Seventies and Eighties." Foreword by Barbara Smith (1977; repr. New York: Kitchen Table Women of Color Press, 1986), 9.

9. Other texts that reprint or include analysis of Combahee's statement include: Gloria Anzaldúa and Cherríe Moraga, *This Bridge Called My Back: Writings by Radical Women of Color* (New York: Kitchen Table Women of Color Press, 1981); Patricia Bell-Scott, Beverly

Smith, and Barbara Smith, *All the Women Are White, All the Blacks Are Men, but Some of Us Are Brave: Black Women's Studies* (New York: The Feminist Press, 1982); Patricia Hill Collins, *Black Feminist Thought* (Boston: Unwin Hyman, 1990); Beverly Guy-Sheftall, *Words of Fire: An Anthology of African-American Feminist Thought* (New York: The New Press, 1995); bell hooks, *Ain't I a Woman: Black Women and Feminism* (Boston: South End Press, 1981); Stanlie James and P. A. Busia, *Theorizing Black Feminisms: The Visionary Pragmatism of Black Women* (London: Routledge, 1993); Gloria Joseph and Jill Lewis, *Common Differences: Conflicts in Black and White Feminist Perspectives* (1981; repr. Boston: South End Press, 1986); Miriam Schneir, *Feminism in Our Time: The Essential Writings from WWII to the Present* (New York: Vintage Books, 1994); Barbara Smith, *Homegirls: A Black Feminist Anthology* (New York: Kitchen Table Women of Color Press, 1983).

10. Barbara Smith, interview with author, 15 July 1998.

11. Ibid.

12. Ibid.

13. Ibid.

14. One wonders if these same detractors would have said the same about Black male leaders such as Dr. Martin Luther King, Jr., Muhammad Ali, or Huey P. Newton, who all opposed the Vietnam War.

15. Smith, interview with author, 15 July 1998.

16. Ibid.

17. Ibid.

18. Margaret Sloan, "Black Feminism: A New Mandate," *Ms.* (May 1974): 97–100; Smith, interview with author, 15 July 1998.

19. Smith, interview with author, 15 July 1998. Brenda Verner, the woman Smith spoke of, wrote a highly critical cover story about NBFO's Eastern Regional Conference for *Encore* magazine (April 1974).

20. Combahee River Collective [1977] 1986, 16.

21. Smith, interview with author, 15 July 1998.

22. Ibid.

23. Ibid.

24. Social movement theorists who address this positive aspect of movement bifurcation include: Steven M. Buechler, *Women's Movements in the United States* (New Brunswick, N.J.: Rutgers University Press, 1990); Herbert H. Haines, "Black Radicalization and the Funding of Civil Rights: 1957–1970," *Social Problems* 32 (October 1984): 31–43; Barbara Ryan, *Feminism and the Women's Movement: Dynamics of Change in Social Movement, Ideology and Activism* (New York: Routledge, 1992).

25. Smith, interview with author, 15 July 1998.

26. Mercedes Tompkins, interview with author by phone, 6 May 1998.

27. The *Oxford English Dictionary* (*OED*) (http://www.chaucer.library.emory.edu) dates 1979 as the first printed use of the word "heterosexism" in J. Penelope's *Articulation of Bias*. The *OED* also cites an article in the January 1979 issue of *Ms.* magazine as the first use of the word "heterosexist."

28. Smith, interview with author, 15 July 1998.

29. Tompkins, interview with author by phone, 6 May 1998.

30. Honor Ford-Smith, "Ring Ding in a Tight Corner: Sistren, Collective, Democracy, and the Organizing of Cultural Production," in *Feminist Genealogies, Colonial Legacies, Democratic Futures,* ed. M. Jacqui Alexander and Chandra Talpade Mohanty (New York: Routledge, 1997), 213–58.

31. Jo Freeman, *The Politics of Women's Liberation: A Case Study of an Emerging Social Movement and Its Relation to the Policy Process* (New York: David McKay, 1977), 203.

32. Barbara Smith, unpublished essay, Barbara Smith Papers (1975), Lesbian Herstory Archives, Brooklyn, New York.

33. Smith, interview with author, 15 July 1998.

34. Tompkins, interview with author by phone, 6 May 1998.

35. Ibid.

36. Margo Okazawa-Rey, interview with author by phone, 20 October 1997.

37. Smith, interview with author, 15 July 1998. This is particularly true when we consider the civil rights movement where women performing in the private sphere were not recognized as leaders, unlike men who represented the movement publicly. In the same way, until more scholars reconstruct narratives of the Black feminist movement, and until more Black feminist movement participants record their memoirs, well-known personalities of the movement will continue to predominate in the historical record.

38. Ford-Smith, "Ring Ding in a Tight Corner"; Starhawk, *Truth or Dare: Encounters with Power, Authority, and Mystery* (San Francisco: Harper & Row Publishers, 1987).

39. Barbara Smith, Memorandum to retreat participants. Folder 12. "Black Feminist Retreats, Fourth Retreat." Barbara Smith Papers (1978), Lesbian Herstory Archives, Brooklyn, New York.

40. For an insightful look into the interaction of intimate relationships and leadership roles, see: Elaine Brown, *A Taste of Power: A Black Woman's Story* (New York: Pantheon Books, 1992); and Margo Perkins, "'Inside Our Dangerous Ranks': The Autobiography of Elaine Brown and the Black Panther Party," in *Still Lifting, Still Climbing: Contemporary African American Women's Activism,* ed. Kimberly Springer (New York: New York University Press, 1999), 91–106.

41. For more research detailing Black women's contemporary activism around gender, sexuality, race, and class, see Kimberly Springer, ed., *Still Lifting, Still Climbing: Contemporary African American Women's Activism* (New York: New York University Press, 1999).

13

Protest and Protestantism

Early Lesbian and Gay Institution Building in Mississippi

JOHN HOWARD

AS Christmas 1982 approached, readers of *This Month in Mississippi*, published by the Mississippi Gay Alliance (MGA), took notice of an exceptionally vitriolic article in the December issue. Entitled "Christianity's Intolerance of Gays," the piece opened in a deliberate, rational tone:

> Today, there seems to be an attempt on the part of many Gay people to accommodate Christianity into their lifestyles. This seems . . . like . . . fitting round pegs into square holes. Unfortunately, many Gay people find it difficult to take an honest look at the history of Christianity. They have been so thoroughly indoctrinated since childhood that to question these dogmas can be compared to renouncing one's parentage or even truth itself.[1]

A historical enumeration of church abuses followed. By the conclusion, gay Christians were dubbed (oxy)morons, as inconceivable as Jewish Nazis or black Klansmen. "Some Gays may consider themselves Christians," the author surmised, "but when I think of what Christianity has done to Gay people, I can only regret the lack of lions in the Roman Empire."[2]

Written by Don Sanders, vice-president of the Gay Atheists League of America, Houston, Texas, the article likely drew few sympathizers. While Christianity, especially Protestant evangelicalism, increasingly fueled much of the bigotry directed at them, many queer Mississippians were reluctant to fully relinquish ties to their religious past. Brought up in the heart of the Bible Belt, often in communities so small that the church served as the primary sociocultural institution, they sometimes drifted away, especially when acknowledgment of their sexuality left them feeling alienated, but they rarely severed all connections.

In fact, the institutional merging of Christian faith and homosexual orientation was about to attain a watershed in the state. Just after the new year, 1983, in the capital of Jackson, organizers announced plans to form a local congregation of the Metropolitan Community Church (MCC), a Protestant denomination ministering mainly to lesbian and gay parishioners. Founded by a Southerner in Los Angeles almost fifteen years earlier, MCC boasted a national and international following. Affiliated churches flourished in urban centers across the country, such as Nashville and New Orleans. Yet their spread had only lately reached many smaller cities in the South. Political and popular resistance in Mississippi would be fierce, just as allegiance from spiritually inclined lesbians, gays, bisexuals, and transgender persons would be intense. By December 1983, *This Month in Mississippi* reported that after a "long, rough row . . . things [we]re definitely looking up for the Metropolitan Community Church of Jackson."[3] In its wake, public discourse on homosexuality had mushroomed in Mississippi. The state's fledgling gay movement—scarcely twenty-five years old and only ten years active—was radically altered in its direction. And for a couple dozen members of MCC and many more across the state who followed the events, personal religious reconciliation had begun.

Protestant Christianity became the center around which lesbian and gay life and politics turned. Whereas since the 1960s persecution had been directed from religious sectors and patterned on scriptural references, perhaps a majority of queer Mississippians clung to other aspects of church doctrine and ritual. These queer Christians, black and white, rarely responded to a narrow gay movement driven by identity politics. Instead, they joined only when a more expansive definition of gayness was fashioned. Leadership came to recognize this phenomenon and eventually encouraged MCC's entry into the local arena. The backlash from religious right fundamentalists and mainline churches meant an increased level of hostility in the short run, but the discourse it fostered and the attention it focused on lesbians, gays, bisexuals, and transgender persons forged greater levels of community solidarity and political power over the long run. With the successful establishment of the Metropolitan Community Church in Jackson, a new era dawned on lesbian and gay organizing and institution-building in Mississippi.

Homophile Rights, Civil Rights, Gay Rights

Queer organizing in Mississippi began as early as 1959, with the establishment in Texas of a local branch of an Austin-based organization. Wrapped in the language of science and education, Wicker Research Studies was the brainchild of college student Randy Wicker. Wicker had met Mississippian Eddie Sandifer in the summer of 1958 at a New York meeting of the secretive Mattachine Society,[4] and by early 1959 Sandifer was an officer of the tri-state Wicker Research Studies, convening meetings in Jackson. In this sense, Wicker Research Studies was a Southern manifestation of a national "homophile movement," of which Mattachine was but a part. Wicker Research Studies took its credo verbatim from the San Francisco-based lesbian organization, Daughters of Bilitis (DOB), as printed in DOB's monthly publication, *The Ladder.*[5]

No less than Mattachine and DOB, Wicker Research Studies relied on secrecy—false names and clandestine operations. Such measures well suited the quiet accommodationism characteristic of queer life in 1950s Mississippi. As Eddie Sandifer remembers,

> The founder, the one that started it—Randy Wicker, who uses that name still, Charles G. Hayden, Jr.—he was in Texas at the University at the time. There was Randy one, two, and three. Randy was number one, a [college student in] Louisiana was number two, and I was number three, Randy Wicker three. We had a local meeting here at my house, and the mail came down on McDowell Road here to Meadowlane Station, a little store. That was the mailing address. We had a pamphlet [and] only one paper we put out.[6]

Wicker Research Studies quickly passed. The State of Mississippi denied its request for incorporation. Worse still, "it was hard to get blacks *or* whites to come to meetings," Sandifer remembers.[7] Upon graduation, Wicker left Texas for New York. Sandifer toughed it out in Mississippi.

As civil rights activism took Mississippi by storm in the 1960s, police targeted homosexuals in and outside the movement. Queer organizing all but ceased. On occasion, a coalition of leftists—not specifically gay-identified—protested anti-homosexual initiatives, utilizing broader calls for free speech and freedom of expression. Queer writing found outlets in late-sixties, left-wing, counterculture publications such as the underground newspaper *Kudzu,* printed in Jackson and distributed on high school and college campuses throughout the state. But Sandifer remembers it as a time of retrenchment, a time of great repression as compared to the forties and fifties.

In 1968, when the Jackson Federation of Women's Clubs forced the city council to ban local screening of *The Fox,* pickets formed outside City Hall. Women and men carried signs reading, "The Truth Shall Set You Free." But official Mississippi dug in its heels. *Jackson Daily News* editor Jimmy Ward acknowledged that he had "not seen the film." Nonetheless, he understood its hazards: "All the reviews by responsible critics I have read describe the movie as a sack of trash featuring the love affair between two women. . . . Few mature persons would want to view sordidness of that nature unless afforded the facilities to take a shower before, during and immediately after the show."[8] *Kudzu* editors made fun of Ward's puritanism: "Mr. Ward, if you need a shower after thinking about a movie on homosexuals, if you get *that* sexually excited, we suggest that you see a psychiatrist, or can the crap and go enjoy the movie!"[9]

In late-sixties Mississippi, counterculture advocates of free (heterosexual) love and a particular kind of gender nonconformity rarely espoused homosexuality and gender-nonconformity, at least in public. More commonly, male long-hairs resented the fact that their parents and other authority figures called them "fruits." Many white left-wingers—supporters of sex, drugs, rock 'n' roll, and radical politics—disavowed queer tendencies.[10]

Like lesbian and gay movements in other American sections, concerted and highly visible gay political activity in the South emerged in the early 1970s. Partially informed by New York's Stonewall riots of June 1969 and descended from the Civil Rights, women's, and student movements, early organizations such as the Gay Liberation Front (GLF) championed a holistic, radical politics encompassing a wide array of leftist causes.[11] The South harbored high-minded revolutionary sentiment, as a core group of Atlanta organizers started a vibrant but short-lived local cell of the GLF in 1971. Weekly meetings, one former member recalls, borrowed from feminist consciousness-raising techniques. Participants discussed "the evils of sexism, racism, capitalism" and learned "a smattering of Marxism." However, they mostly "focused on the plague of sexual objectification, sexist language, and oppressive looksist standards running rampant among gay men."[12]

Lesbian and gay political dissent in Mississippi was no less radical in its tenets. In 1973, the Mississippi Gay Alliance appeared on the scene with its founding chapter in Starkville, led by lesbian faculty and students at Mississippi State University. Soon headquartered in Jackson and spearheaded by the daringly outspoken Eddie Sandifer, the group's stance on many issues inevitably reflected his own political worldview. A self-described Trotskyist, Sandifer was born in Cotton Valley, in rural Webster Parish, Louisiana, in 1929, the son of a Baptist preacher. He moved to McComb, Mississippi, in 1945. Involved from that time in the American Communist Party, he attracted considerable attention. "It was out and about town," he says, "that I was a Commie, a queer, and a nigger lover."[13]

Sandifer, like Randy Wicker, was involved in civil rights protests in the South and, like so many early homophile activists, participated in a range of leftist causes, including equal treatment initiatives for senior citizens and the disabled. Sandifer's experience, perhaps more than any others', demonstrates how queer rights were linked to and thwarted in the wake of the black struggle for equality, a struggle consistently red-baited as well. Though he was well-known since the 1940s as a communist, homosexual, and civil rights activist, Sandifer never suffered harassment based on his sexual orientation until the 1960s, when he hosted freedom riders in his Jackson home. As historian Donna Smith concludes, "His account of the ways in which his sexuality was used as a weapon in local battles to maintain white dominance parallels similar reports surfacing in research on lesbian/gay experience throughout the South during the 1960s. [It] reveals how ideologies of race and sex have been inextricably intertwined in the South."[14]

Though he was "a strong believer in armed revolution," Sandifer also possessed enough political savvy to moderate his statements during the MGA's early years.[15]

In 1975, he told a reporter that MGA's official position was that "homosexuals have the same rights as heterosexuals. This includes the right to sexual acts between consenting adults . . . [and] the right to show affection in public—kissing and holding hands."[16] In a state with a strict sodomy code, Sandifer alluded to the specter of civil disobedience by supporting sexual intercourse between women and between men, but he tempered his words with references to public displays of affection—acts that, while no doubt repulsive and confrontational to many Mississippians, at least were not illegal. Moreover, Sandifer characterized the MGA's primary purpose as alleviating prejudice through education, a common programmatic method in traditional, liberal interest-group politics. The MGA supported "educational programs on campuses and [on] radio and television, counseling for members, and activities including gay pride week"[17]—again, a local manifestation of a broader gay cultural phenomenon.

The same reporter questioned an unofficial and unnamed spokesperson for the Gay Activist League of Mississippi (GALM), a Jackson organization that didn't enjoy the longevity of the MGA. In a rare mainstream press engagement with issues of religion and homosexuality, the GALM member responded directly and caustically. Persecution of lesbians and gays amounted to a violation of the First Amendment protection of freedom of religion because, he said, "anti-homosexual statutes [we]re based on Judeo-Christian moral codes" and as such they represented "an imposition of religion on the majority of us." While not defining its parameters, he referred to a monolithic "Judeo-Christian culture . . . that is unequivocally anti-sexual."[18] He pointed out several European and Latin American countries that, though no less devout, had decriminalized homosexual practices, and he suggested that the United States, collectively and individually, follow suit.

The MGA attacked religious fundamentalism in the person of Anita Bryant. After her successful campaign in Florida to overturn Dade County's anti-discrimination ordinance, the pop singer and orange juice spokesperson took her anti-homosexual "Save Our Children" message on the road to Southern Baptist conferences and various other public engagements in 1977. "Once you allow special privileges for a radical group like that," she chimed, "then you have to do it for the prostitutes, you have to do it for the one who has a sexual preference with [*sic*] a German shepherd."[19]

While hundreds, sometimes thousands protested her appearances in major American cities, the MGA was able to mobilize twelve for a rally when Bryant came to town for the Mississippi State Fair. In his speech to those assembled on October 12, Eddie Sandifer, state president of the MGA, said, "I feel the same way towards Anita Bryant that I do toward any fascist right-winger that is oppressing other people."[20] A few months earlier, a group of MGA members had driven three hours south, where they took part in what *Workers' World* called "the largest lesbian and gay demonstration ever in New Orleans," in reaction to Bryant's appearance there.[21] The MGA was said to be one of the largest contingents among the estimated three thousand marchers.

More typical of MGA activities during the 1970s was the monitoring and reporting of police harassment of queer Mississippians, especially in the Smith Park area. Covering one city block directly behind the governor's mansion, between it and the new capitol building, Smith Park had long been an after-dark meeting place. It sometimes attracted Jackson's gay bar-goers. Known for drag shows and dancing, the predominantly white Mae's Cabaret (later renamed Jack's) and the predominantly black Bill's Club were located just three blocks down Amite Street, across the street from one another. But more commonly, the park was frequented by persons who couldn't or wouldn't support the bars. Some refused to patronize Mae's, calling it "a social club run for friends of the owner."[22] "Smith Park People"—mostly white but also black males—cultivated varied styles of identification and visibility. At one end of the spectrum, they included married, middle-class, middle-age men who circled the park in their cars, hoping to discreetly meet a partner for the most anonymous of sexual encounters or for ongoing relations of many kinds. For many such men, being seen in a gay bar was unthinkable. At the other end were out-of-the-closet gay men, cross-dressers, and male sex workers. Estranged from the self-acknowledged but circumspect bar crowd, they were often young, from lower income groups, willing to hustle for a living. Still, this spectrum simplifies. Smith Park harbored a queer miscellany of individuals, marked by diverse configurations of age, race, class, gender, identity, desire—and place. As many oral history narrators attest, rural and small-town motorists regularly "checked out" such notorious queer haunts whenever driving through the area—just as city dwellers frequented the park's rural equivalent, the roadside rest area.

The Jackson Police Department (JPD) targeted the men at Smith Park. According to one gay member of the JPD, superiors instructed officers to "give hell" to "those queers at the park."[23] Implicit in these orders, in the view of many gay men, was a proviso to lay off the bars, which they said made payoffs to the police.[24] Thus, Jackson law enforcement lent legitimacy to the quasi-private, sequestered spaces of gay commercial establishments while attempting to cordon off public spaces from use by so-called undesirables.

Eddie Sandifer personally was the victim of police harassment in Smith Park on the night of September 25, 1976. Three uniformed policemen confronted Sandifer, William McLemore, and Steve Pond around midnight and threatened to arrest them for disturbing the peace and interfering with an officer in the line of duty. As described in his formal complaint against the department, Sandifer and his two friends were patrolling the park as part of a safety and visibility campaign by the MGA and its supporters—"ministers, lawyers, reporters, young and old, from babes in arms to 75 years old, male and female, black and white, gay and straight."[25] Volunteers cleaned the park, monitored police activity, and advised persons against sleeping there or making disparaging remarks to officers. Sandifer had informed the department of the MGA patrols, adding that volunteers could be readily identified by the pink triangles they wore. Despite (or perhaps due to) the triangles, Sandifer and his two friends, one in a wheelchair, were forcibly removed from the park that September evening.

A U.S. Civil Rights Commission advisor labeled the incident one of "a series of police department maneuvers to harass members of Jackson's gay community."[26] In assessing these reports, along with an unrelated case of police brutality resulting in wrongful death, the official concluded in 1977 that the department's complaint process was shrouded in secrecy, completely closed to outside review, and that internal investigation procedures remained undefined. Not only queer citizens, but a significant portion of the city's residents—especially African-Americans—had come to distrust the police force. Disputes raged in the local newspapers between Jackson mayor Russell Davis and police chief Lavell Tullos, on the one hand, and Civil Rights Commission regional director Bobby Doctor, on the other.

Thus another explicit linkage between gay rights and civil rights was manifested. That a U.S. Civil Rights Commission official addressed gay issues and that its regional body consciously focused on bias against queer Mississippians were particularly significant, given that the principal, enabling federal legislation—the Civil Rights Act of 1964—did not cover discrimination based on sexual orientation. Still, racial bigotry and queer-baiting had long been entangled. Indeed, Eddie Sandifer became a target of queer bias in Mississippi not for his communist sympathies, but for his involvement in the African-American struggle for equality. It was Sandifer and the MGA that subsequently pressed the Civil Rights Commission to intervene in Mississippi on behalf of lesbians and gays.

In September of 1979, Sandifer again appeared before the commission charging Jackson police officers with soliciting and entrapping gay men in illegal sex acts in Smith Park. Specifically, he singled out officer David Pinson, the subject of numerous complaints. Captain Joe Alford, head of the vice and narcotics division, defended Pinson. "You can't entrap somebody who starts playing with your legs," he said. "We don't have to approach anybody up there [in Smith Park]. You can't stay there for five minutes any night without one of them trying to play with you."[27] Alford thereby confirmed the considerable police presence in the small Jackson park. And chief of detectives J. L. Black acknowledged "furnish[ing] the bait" by utilizing undercover officers. Black was intransigent in the face of criticism: "The officers are already performing an unpleasant task and don't deserve this kind of abuse. We are going to enforce the law against homosexual acts, and we will not be intimidated."[28]

Mississippi Gay Alliance activities also included occasional legal actions, educational forums, and hate group monitoring through its Jackson headquarters and through a handful of local chapters elsewhere in the state. In 1976 at the U.S. Circuit Court of Appeals in New Orleans, MGA unsuccessfully challenged the refusal of Mississippi State University's student newspaper to print an MGA advertisement.[29] (As recently as 1990, the newspaper, *The Reflector,* rejected an ad from the newly organized campus group, Gays, Lesbians and Friends.) MGA found a reliable ally in the American Civil Liberties Union of Mississippi, which sponsored a forum on sexual privacy in 1975, but this and other events garnered relatively little support from lesbian and gay Mississippians.[30] Though he did amass a protest group of thirty in 1976—fewer still in 1979—in response to police harassment allegations, Eddie Sandifer was the sole MGA observer at an anti-gay Ku Klux Klan rally held on October 10, 1981, in Smith Park. The lead speaker, Grand Dragon Gale Gordon, advocated the caging of homosexuals, and he encouraged listeners to take back "Queer Park." Robed member Jessie Sanford snapped photographs of Sandifer.[31]

Though constantly under siege, the Mississippi Gay Alliance proved a vital lifeline for queers in Jackson and across the state. Its mere existence gave heart to those who, due to a sheer lack of numbers, felt alienated in the countryside. Its high profile meant greater ease in connecting previously disparate and sometimes incohesive networks of men like that. Even official Mississippi had to own up to MGA's determination and resilience. Jimmy Ward's *Jackson Daily News* received queries of its advice columnist as early as 1974 from readers who wanted to contact the MGA. "I can't reveal my name," one letter writer confided, "because of the small town in which I live." The columnist supplied the invaluable data to the writer, who signed his letter, "One of them."[32]

But Sandifer candidly recalls the frustrations of mounting a gay political movement in Mississippi, a movement he continues to lead as director of the renamed Mississippi Gay and Lesbian Alliance: "You have a few people that'll do all the work, and you have a lot of people willing to pay dues if you ask for dues, but they're not willing to get politicized."[33] In the 1970s, MGA membership never totaled more than a few dozen, with white membership always vastly outnumbering black. Influenced as it was by identity politics, most notably an increasingly national lesbian and gay movement, gay organizing clashed with local sensibilities, queer and non-queer. For decades, sexual deviants and gender-nonconformists in Mississippi had functioned quietly but effectively within rural and small-town contexts, outmaneuvering hostile forces. Queer Mississippians even in remote parts of the state were nonetheless visible and available *to one another.* Gay politics required a *different* sort of visibility. Most disturbingly, it required clear-cut identity statements, individuals' open and *public* avowal of homosexuality, a speech act that some belligerent lawmakers and law enforcers interpreted as a felony in and of itself (attempted sodomy). And many queer Mississippians found Sandifer unkempt, his methods brusque and shrill.[34]

Further, the category gay didn't well-encompass the range and inventiveness of sexual and gender non-normativity in Mississippi. And it made few allowances for those whose sexual and gender non-normativity served as a relatively insignificant component of identity. For African Americans, for example, to participate in gay organizing meant to participate in yet another white-controlled, white-dominated institution. Though homosexuality and gender insubordination clearly weren't just a white thing, gay political organizing for the most part was.

As the seventies gave way to the eighties, and as the effects of the Reagan revolution began to be felt, the Mississippi Gay Alliance languished. Administration policies crippled the U.S. Civil Rights Commission. Hopes for lesbian and gay political struggle in Mississippi reached their nadir. Despite Eddie Sandifer's diligence and what must have seemed at times his singlehanded effort, MGA failed to attract a wide following. The mainstream press mostly ignored its activities; state attorney general Bill Allain, citing the sodomy statute, denied its bid for incorporation and a potentially lucrative, nonprofit status.[35] And as attitudinal surveys showed that Southerners' feelings toward lesbians and gays were akin to those toward radical student activists and marijuana users, queer Mississippians appeared destined to languish on the political margins.[36] For the most part, this liminality would remain intact until interrupted by stirrings of religious activism initiated by Southerner Troy Perry.

Gay Churches

Troy Perry was born in 1940 to a Pentecostal family in north Florida.[37] After running away from home in his early teens, he lived with relatives in south Georgia before becoming an itinerant evangelist in Alabama. In his late teens he married a preacher's daughter just graduated from high school. Perry passed a high school equivalency exam, and despite his denomination's distrust of seminary training, he attended a nonaccredited Bible college. At the same time, he pastored a Church of God congregation in Joliet, Illinois.

Church officials excommunicated Perry after they learned of his adolescent affair with another boy, but he was able to secure preaching engagements at the rival Church of God of Prophecy when he, his wife, and their two young sons moved to southern California. After his refusal to disavow homosexuality, clerics again forced Perry out. This time, his wife left him, taking the children with her. In 1965, the U.S. Army drafted Perry, by now a seasoned pastor at the ripe old age of twenty-five. (The military, according to Perry, was less concerned with his sexual orientation than was the church.) Still attending Pentecostal worship services, he came under the influence of a fellow gay enlistee, an Episcopalian who posed a prophetic question: "Why don't you think about starting your own church?"[38]

The Metropolitan Community Church (MCC) was founded on October 6, 1968, when Perry and his partner Willie Smith hosted twelve persons at an afternoon service in their Los Angeles home. Vowing to preach a three-pronged gospel of salvation, community, and Christian social action, Perry saw his following expand rapidly. Initially conceptualized as "not a homosexual church, but a special church that [would] reach out to the lesbian and gay community," only 5 to 15 percent of the membership was heterosexual. The church's appeal, according to Perry, was its doctrine of acceptance, its belief in a God of unconditional love: "We were the first Christian bulwark against a determinedly ignorant society whose homophobic cruelty masked a callous indifference to humanity."[39]

MCC became the Universal Fellowship of Metropolitan Community Churches in 1969, with Troy Perry as general moderator. In the wake of a splashy, impromptu service/demonstration in the dignified National Cathedral in Washington, D.C., congregations continued to spring up throughout the United States. Thirty-five were represented at the Third General Conference, held in 1972 at the "Mother Church" in Los Angeles. Such ecclesiastical gatherings, in stark relief to in-your-face activism, could generate the support of some liberal politicians. California assembly member Willie Brown delivered a well-received speech at the MCC conference, though a small faction, dismayed over the so-called politicization of the church, walked out.

Congregations attempted to incorporate elements from various Protestant traditions into their worship services, but usually the format and tone mirrored those of the more middle-class, mainstream, "mainline" Protestant faiths. Troy Perry attempted to distance himself from inherited Pentecostal customs—speaking in tongues, shouting, and a healing ritual known as the "laying on of hands"—though they sometimes were practiced at MCC meetings. Heeding the advice of gay Congregational minister Revel Quigley, Perry wore liturgical robes at his first service and was commonly seen thereafter in clerical collar. Furthermore, as Perry later stated, Revel helped raise his "parochial Pentecostal view of religion to a more sophisticated level where individuals worshipped God with a devotion similar to mine, but without the great public display of emotion I had previously assumed was the only way to be a good Christian."[40] Like that first gathering, a typical MCC service, held on Sunday, opened with singing; included communion, along with prayers for various concerns, personal and public, local and national; and featured a sermon by the congregation's pastor. Services were conducted in private homes, in gay bars, in public spaces, or in facilities owned by other religious or secular organizations. Over time, MCCs in many cities came to occupy their own houses of worship.

MCC's growth was not without its setbacks. Nor was it immune to criticism from within and without lesbian and gay circles. Its overwhelmingly male laity and leadership left it open to charges of sexism. Not until its fourth year did MCC license a female minister, Freda Smith, then assistant pastor at MCC-Sacramento. Yet it was hardly surprising that even a gay church would mirror the patriarchal structure of mainstream social, cultural, and political institutions, given the inherently patriarchal biases of Christian teaching. Intense hostility from outside forces surfaced in 1973, when three worship sites burned. Presumably the results of arson, fires consumed meeting places first in Los Angeles and then Nashville, without personal injuries. But a fire that summer in New Orleans claimed thirty-two lives. Perhaps not directly aimed at MCC, the deliberately set fire engulfed the Upstairs Bar, at the corner of Chartres and Iberville in the French Quarter, where the congregation often met. The bar was filled with revelers, as it was the last day of Gay Pride weekend, held in June on the anniversary of Stonewall. Many of the dead were MCC members. Perry says seventeen such blazes have been set over the years, including a fall 1982 firebombing in Atlanta.

In terms of doctrine, the Metropolitan Community Church suffered from a perplexing identity crisis. MCC bylaws lacked any reference to homosexuality, and as of 1974, the church had made no official statement on lesbian and gay sexuality.[41] "We are *not* a gay church," said MCC-Boston pastor Larry Bernier. "We worship God like anybody else worships God, and the fact that we're gay has very little to do with it."[42] Sociologists Ronald Enroth and Gerald Jamison refuted such claims in their disparaging but informative 1974 study, *The Gay Church,* for which Troy Perry declined to be interviewed. While acknowledging the church's importance in the lives of its parishioners, the two self-described heterosexuals condescendingly chided MCC as "merely an extension of the gay life-style clothed in religiosity."[43]

Enroth and Jamison nonetheless were astute in their observation that

> the straight church is, in part at least, responsible for the emergence of the gay church. Gay churchmen [*sic*] are correct in the charge that conventional churches fail to minister to homosexuals. The attitude of many Christians toward gay people is one of repugnance and even contempt.[44]

Indeed, beginning in the late 1960s, primarily as a result of rumblings made by evermore politicized lesbian and gay members, the Catholic Church and major Protestant denominations issued increasingly condemnatory proclamations and doctrines. Despite the concomitant growth of lesbian and gay affiliate groups, such as Episcopal Integrity and Methodist Affirmation, mainline church policy proved decidedly antagonistic.

Mainline Churches

The nation's largest religious body, the Southern Baptists, published relatively temperate articles on homosexuality during the late 1960s and early 1970s. While hardly accepting of homosexuality, Baptist writers advanced a policy of benevolent care-taking. Seen as either psychologically maladjusted or especially prone to sin, lesbians and gays could be accommodated within the church given humble attitudes and repentant hearts. By the late 1970s, however, as gay activism spread inside and outside the church, ecclesial statements became more caustic, focusing on biblical injunctions against homosexuality. The 1976 meeting of the Southern Baptist Convention pronounced its "commitment to the biblical truth regarding the practice of homosexuality and sin" and discouraged congregations from hiring homosexual preachers or church employees.[45] The 1977 convention members lauded fellow Baptist Anita Bryant for her "courageous stand against the evils inherent in homosexuality."[46] State conventions joined in. Thirteen issued condemnations of homosexuality in 1977, and of those, Mississippi and six others further expressed their support for Bryant's campaign to stop gay rights legislation in Dade County.[47] Bryant delivered the opening address to the Southern Baptist Pastors' Conference in Atlanta in 1978, but she lost her bid for first vice-president at the denomination-wide convention that followed. By this time, Baptist ministers and church members were leading the backlash against numerous local initiatives designed to recognize or protect lesbian and gay citizens. Baptist sentiments continued to harden through the 1980s.

Ordinarily more liberal-minded and less reliant on concepts of scriptural inerrancy, United Methodists, America's second largest Protestant denomination, were scarcely less hostile to lesbians and gays. The 1972 General Conference declared "the practice of homosexuality . . . incompatible with Christian teaching," in what one Mississippi minister described as the "famous paragraph 71F" of the denomination's *Book of Discipline*.[48] He and others would rely on it through the years to guide their interpretations of homosexuality. The 1972 conference also recommended against marriage between two persons of the same sex. The next quadrennial conference, held in 1976, exposed a developing rift between national officers of the United Methodist Church and local church clergy and laity. The former attempted to add a conciliatory clause to the otherwise condemnatory "Social Principles" doctrine. But the statement "we welcome all persons regardless of sexual orientation" was soundly defeated by the evangelical "Good News" wing, as was a proposed study of human sexuality. The grassroots elements further forbade the ordination of lesbian and gay clergy and forced through a resolution that would cut funding from any church agency using money to support homosexual organizations or to "promote the acceptance of homosexuality."[49] In 1979, the Mississippi Conference of the United Methodist Church voiced strong support for these positions, which the national body reaffirmed in 1984.[50]

Among smaller religious denominations, responses covered a broad range. As summarized by Robert Nugent and Jeannine Gramick,

> Other churches, such as the Moravian, the Friends, and the Unitarian Universalist Association, not only have voiced official and strong support for lesbian and gay people in the area of civil rights, but also have endorsed same-sex genital expression as fully compatible with Christian morality and human sexuality. Not surprisingly, many Evangelical, Pentecostal, and smaller, independent Bible churches remain adamantly and vociferously opposed both to homogenital behavior and to any support for societal or ecclesial recognition of what they see as a moral or psychological evil and a serious threat to family values.[51]

The latter churches greatly outnumbered the former in the South, a section that, according to sociologist David Greenberg, was less tolerant of homosexuality and more opposed to gay rights than any other in America, at least as publicly articulated.[52] Moreover, Baptists and Methodists, which predominated in Mississippi, described homosexual relations as "always wrong," in survey proportions of 88 percent and 77 percent respectively.[53]

In his otherwise perceptive study of American churches and homosexuality, Thomas Hewitt mistakenly asserts that "there was no struggle within any Christian denomination over the issue of accepting or rejecting homosexuals until after 1969," the year of Stonewall.[54] Methodist quadrennial conference attendees debated homosexuality at least as early as 1968, though it was not taken up by the entire assembly until 1972.[55] More impressive still, Southern Baptists' "Brotherhood Commission" grappled with church responses to homosexuality as early as 1908.[56] As in all histories of sexuality, a dearth of readily accessible sources should not be construed as an absence of concern.

Over the course of the twentieth century, Protestant denominational engagement with homosexuality likely waxed and waned in the South. My research shows a hushed church in Mississippi during the 1940s and 1950s. As Methodist minister Ted Herrington recalls, homosexuality then "wasn't viewed in any sense [as] a great threat, a bugaboo."[57] He and his colleagues rarely if ever preached against it or counseled members about it. Even as late as the early 1960s, Loyd Star native Vince Jones heard not a single condemnation of homosexuality from clergy at his rural Baptist church, nor at the Baptist college he attended in Clinton.[58] Still, most assumed that this quiet reflected certain unspoken understandings: The "love that dare not speak its name" was clearly forbidden by church proscriptions against extramarital sex.

By the 1970s and 1980s, a significant change had taken place. Even a parishioner ill-attuned to church doctrine as adopted by the national body could not fail to learn the prevailing attitudes toward homosexuality from within the local church. A survey of Southern Baptist, independent Baptist, and Assemblies of God pastors—half of whom were attached to congregations in the South—found that of all "public issues addressed . . . in sermons," homosexuality was among the most frequently mentioned. It was matched only by pornography and surpassed only by the more generic category, "Christian attitude toward civic responsibility." It superseded prayer in schools, abortion, equal rights for women, and the state of Israel, among others.[59]

Now some of the most influential and persuasive discourse flowed from preachers' sermons, which in many Mississippi Protestant congregations tended toward the "hellfire-and-brimstone" variety.[60] In rural north Mississippi in the 1980s, one eighteen-year-old churchgoer, Bud Thomas, felt the wrath of a fanatical pastor after he confided his homosexuality to the pastor's son. When the friend in turn told his father, the preacher confronted Thomas during the Sunday morning worship service, in front of the entire congregation. Thomas was kicked out of his church and told never to return.[61] Papal hostility made it difficult for others. As one gay Mississippian, a self-described "ex-Catholic," put it, "An awful lot of the Catholic church will fuck you up."[62]

Religiously inclined lesbians and gays in Mississippi were at an impasse with the state's major churches, at the same time that the Universal Fellowship of Metropolitan Community Churches had come to a standstill in relations with national denominational bodies. In 1983, the National Council of Churches, to which most major Christian faiths belonged, again denied membership to MCC and moved to postpone indefinitely any future vote on its eligibility.[63] Yet MCC was undaunted. With 150 U.S. congregations—including new Southern groups in Little Rock, Shreveport, Memphis, Montgomery, and Birmingham—and 30 more in seven foreign countries, they were determined to continue their expansion, with or without ecumenical support.[64] They found fertile soil in Mississippi.

Mississippi Churches

Palm Sunday services of the Metropolitan Community Church of Jackson, on March 27, 1983, resembled those held at other Protestant sanctuaries across the state that morning. The service began with hymn singing: "Amazing Grace" and "Jesus Loves Me." The Reverend Gilbert Lincoln of Nashville, coordinator of MCC's South Atlantic District, delivered a brief sermon to nine women and men. The group celebrated holy communion, eating crackers and drinking grape juice—a common substitute for wine among teetotaling congregations in the South. And Lincoln offered a prayer for "Mr. Wells and all of the Moral Majority, . . . for everybody who fears . . . and mistrusts us."[65]

Since Lincoln had first come to Jackson over a month prior to initiate meetings and plan for this, MCC's first worship service, the Reverend Mike Wells, pastor of Mountainview Baptist Church in nearby Raymond, had emerged as the church's most adamant opponent. President of the state chapter of the national Moral Majority, founded by Baptist minister Jerry Falwell of Lynchburg, Virginia, Wells had been stirring controversy, trying to raise money to combat homosexuality in Mississippi. Indeed, homosexuals were popular scapegoats for what Kathy Rudy calls "the 'new' Christian Right." Highly influential in "setting the agenda for national Christian politics," this movement sprang up prior to the 1980 election with the advent of four conservative organizations—the Christian Voice, the National Christian Action Coalition, the Religious Roundtable, and the Moral Majority. These and other conservative Christian organizations "did not limit their political organizing tactics to television," Rudy demonstrates. "Radio, mass mailings, rallies, book and sound recordings sales, telephone, leafleting, and personal contacts . . . helped."[66] Mike Wells and the Mississippi Moral Majority utilized most of these methods.

Wells's initial salvo in the battle against Mississippi's first MCC congregation was a letter dated 7 March 1983, sent to ten thousand people throughout the state. In their mailboxes, recipients found an envelope with a red computer-generated, "handwritten" message on the outside. In all capital letters, it read, "please, open at once. homosexuals invade jackson, mississippi."[67]

In the letter, Wells told readers he "just couldn't believe" the recent news that "a sodomite church" was forming in Jackson. Raising the looming specter of homosexual teachers and public officials, he denounced lesbian and gay attempts at "disguising this perverted life style in a normal light by building a homosexual church." Compelled to "alert God-fearing Mississippians statewide," Wells insisted that he needed support to prevent Jackson from becoming "another San Francisco or Houston." "With a massive budget," he warned, "the homosexual pressure groups are gripping our city now. *Perhaps your home town is next.*"[68] Opposition had to be rallied, and he was the person to lead:

> I have prayed to God, "Lord, someone needs to go on local radio and television across Mississippi and call forth the God fearing people to do all, then stand." Then God called me to do just that. But He calls you to stand with me. Take a stand now, *before it's to [sic] late.*[69]

Wells asked for three things. First, he needed suggestions. On which radio and TV stations should he buy air time? Second, he needed prayers. Would God make audio and film equipment available to him in order to produce radio and television programming? Third, he needed money. Would the recipient "help in paying for these specials to expose the truth to the people of Mississippi"? In a "handwritten" postscript, he made an offer: "If you will send a gift of $29.00, I will send by return mail a casett [*sic*] tape of a message preached in my church and broadcasted on Radio." In yet another postscript, he said he would accept "whatever you can send" as a show of support, for he knew that "most Mississippians view the practice of homosexual sodomy among the worst imaginable form [*sic*] of perversion."[70]

Clearly, sodomy was a problem of the imagination. For something so alien, so unimaginable, homophobes in Mississippi seemed to think a great deal and in detailed, projective fashion about homosexual acts. Beyond hypocrisy, this contradiction was fueled by an epistemic dilemma. Preachers and police needed to know about homosexuality in order to combat it. Yet, too great a knowledge compromised the moralists' integrity and masculinity (for, with the exception of Bryant, there were few female leaders among the opposition). Such knowledge might implicate them, especially when so corporeally involved. Jackson police captain Joe Alford described the sexual interactions between "Smith Park People" and his officers—presumed heterosexual—in infantile language reminiscent of queer youth. They *played.* That is, Smith Park people allegedly played with officers' legs. Wells, on the other hand, deployed a rhetoric of deception. A gay church could only be a disguise—worship in drag, masking what any right-minded person *knew* to be inherently sexual activity.

Wells's letter was effective. A media bonanza ensued. Never before had Mississippi's lesbian and gay communities received such attention. Both Jackson newspapers, the morning *Clarion-Ledger* and the evening *Jackson Daily News*, carried stories, as did the Memphis *Commercial Appeal*. On March 23, the *Jackson Daily News* published an editorial cartoon by Jimmy Johnson, who attempted to frame the principal combatants in the debate. In the foreground, Johnson depicted an elderly minister clad in Puritan hat, small round spectacles, and lengthy black frock labeled "Moral Majority." Wielding a smoldering hot branding iron with the letter "Q," the zealot chased a stereotypically gay figure—a limp-wristed, frailly slender young man wearing flip-flops, tight pants, and a tank-top reading "Mississippi Gay Alliance." Pinky finger outstretched, he attempted to fend off his pursuer by swinging his handbag. In the background was a middle-aged couple, presumably married and representative of average Mississippians. While she stared in fright, hand to her chest, he began walking away. With the classic will to ignorance, he declared: "I'm not sure I want to know what's going on here."[71]

Johnson seriously misread and oversimplified the discourse. Opposition to the MCC was hardly limited to a radical right fringe. Leaders of various well-established local and regional church bodies weighed in with derogatory remarks. Reverend F. L. Langley, superintendent of the Assemblies of God Mississippi district, stated, "We are dynamically [*sic*] opposed" to a gay church. Bishop Joseph Brunini of the Catholic Diocese of Jackson said homosexuality was "condemned by all Christian people as a way of life." He acknowledged lesbians' and gays' right to form a church—"It's a free country" after all—but he felt they needed to be "ministered to." He emphasized the importance of salvation.[72] The Reverend Michael Schneider of St. Paul Presbyterian Church in Jackson said that "biblically speaking, a church for those who engage in homosexual acts is the equivalent of a church for practicing adulterers, prostitutes, murderers, drunkards or thieves."[73] An editorial in the *Baptist Record* made a backhanded swipe at MCC, ironically proposing that a church for lesbians and gays, "a group that has openly embraced a sinful lifestyle," might not be such a bad idea: "After all, where would the gospel find a more needy audience than this?"[74]

Cartoonist Johnson correctly surmised that the Mississippi Gay Alliance was at the forefront of support for the Metropolitan Community Church. The leadership of the two organizations was intimately intertwined, as MCC's first worship coordinator, Kathy Switzer, recalls: "Many of us who were on the board of the Church were also on the board of the Alliance."[75] Notable among those was Eddie Sandifer who, along with Switzer, Johnny Estes, Bryan Homeyer, and Denita Claypool, had first solicited MCC expansion into Mississippi. Regularly contacted by reporters, Sandifer attempted to discredit Mike Wells's letter, saying it was "just something to raise funds."[76] As the rhetoric heated up through April 1983, MGA issued a press release that compared Wells's mail-outs and flyers to fascist pamphlets and Hitlerian edicts from Nazi Germany.[77]

Johnson inaccurately gauged the level of feeling among ordinary Mississippians. Many reacted with anything but indifference to the issue. Mid-century Mississippi's trademark pretense of ignorance and quiet accommodation suggested by the cartoon's middle-aged male passerby was now eclipsed by the fascination and shock of his wife, the willful onlooker. The *Clarion-Ledger/Jackson Daily News* reported that "a heavy stream of letters—pro and con—poured in" after their own liberal columnist Raad Cawthon urged the Moral Majority to lay off MCC.[78] Cawthon had scoffed at assertions of a homosexual invasion, saying that such language implied "the homosexuals are from somewhere else. Perhaps Wells thinks citizens of Mississippi are immune to homosexuality." While carefully pointing out his own heterosexuality, Cawthon clearly sided with MCC, echoing the MGA argument that "the Moral Majority is just using this issue as a straw man to be set up, screamed at, and knocked down for monetary gain."[79]

Even the *Jackson Daily News* ombudsman/advice columnist "Jack Sunn" fielded letters from concerned Mississippians. Normally prone to folksy conservatism, his response was surprisingly sympathetic to MCC, reflecting a libertarian strain in his thinking. When Mary wrote in, declaring homosexuality a "deformity," Jack Sunn good-naturedly demurred. "Now that's a new one on us," he wrote. "We think folks have the right to believe just about anything they want to, and to worship just about any way they want to, as long as it doesn't interfere with anybody else."[80]

In his crusade to "go on . . . television across Mississippi and call forth the God fearing people," Mike Wells was beaten to the punch by adversaries, the People for the American Way. The New York-based advocacy group, founded in 1980 by TV producer Norman Lear, had created a half-hour documentary about the national Moral Majority's attacks on First Amendment rights, previously aired in thirty-six American cities. Donors in Mississippi paid to have the show broadcast on the biracially-owned NBC-affiliate, WLBT, Channel 3, at 6:30 p.m. on Saturday, 19 March 1983. Because the local telecast purportedly was funded only by individuals, neither the Mississippi Gay Alliance nor the national Urban League was allowed to contribute.[81] Yet its timing, during the midst of the MCC controversy, was a clear indication of both national and local support for queer Mississippians and their quest for a church.

Many Protestant pastors denounced the People for the American Way documentary. The Reverend Don Patterson castigated WLBT the next day during Sunday worship services at First Presbyterian Church, a large downtown congregation filled with white middle- and upper-class families. He said the telecast "maligned" the Moral Majority, "a Christian organization seeking to alert the American people to the trends in our country." He insisted that Mississippians must "take seriously the teachings of scripture," especially proscriptions against homosexuality.[82]

The Mississippi Moral Majority's rebuttal was less than swift. While president Mike Wells reported "a tremendous response" to his direct-mail campaign,[83] months passed before he completed his video project. When he did, its reach apparently was limited. Perhaps for lack of funds, the documentary seems mostly to have been aired in bits and pieces. Portions were shown in Jackson on at least one local evening news program, but it may never have been broadcast in its entirety. More likely, copies of the tape were distributed to church groups and other organizations. Evidence of any radio broadcasts by Mississippi Moral Majority remains inconclusive.[84]

Most importantly for advocates of lesbian and gay rights in Mississippi, the debate over the Metropolitan Community Church fostered a print media discourse that ultimately aided organizing efforts and promoted community development. According to Eddie Sandifer, the Mississippi Moral Majority campaign and the subsequent press coverage did "more to solidify gays in Jackson and throughout the state" than "even Anita Bryant."[85] Moreover, in the wake of the controversy, the *Jackson Daily News* ran a crucial series of stories on Mississippi lesbian and gay cultures. Published in early June, these features addressed lesbian and gay spirituality, bar culture, committed partnerships, employment discrimination, Smith Park cruising and socializing, hate crimes against lesbians and gays, and—two years after the initial report in the *New York Times*—the spread of AIDS cases, at that point numbering only two in Mississippi.[86]

The liberatory potential of such news accounts should not be underestimated. Though hardly celebratory, often serving to further marginalize lesbians and gays in the consciousness of many Mississippians, the coverage often empowered its subjects. As I have demonstrated elsewhere, queer Mississippians had long employed against-the-grain readings of even the most phobic representations in print and song, on film and stage. As John D'Emilio writes about an earlier period in American life,

> Systematized oppression . . . exerted contradictory influences on gays. In repeatedly condemning the phenomenon, antigay polemicists broke the silence that surrounded the topic of homosexuality. Thus the resources available to lesbians and homosexuals for attaching a meaning to otherwise dimly understood feelings expanded noticeably. The attacks on gay men and women hastened the articulation of a homosexual identity and spread the knowledge that they existed in large numbers. Ironically, the effort to root out the homosexuals in American society made it easier for them to find one another.[87]

This certainly was the case in Mississippi, where never before had issues surrounding homosexuality been afforded such a public forum. Suddenly, valuable information abounded in the daily press. Queer Mississippians contemplating their first forays into lesbian and gay cultures learned the locations of gay bars. They read the names of community leaders and activists, organizations and working groups. They found out about Smith Park. They were informed that committed relationships were a common complement or (normalizing) alternative to the relative abandon of the bars and parks.

But such information did not *clarify* "dimly understood feelings"—for as oral history narrators attest, their feelings and those of non-gay-identified queers were regularly acknowledged and acted upon. Rather, this discourse *channeled* queer feelings into particular modes of gay being and homosexual identity. Undeniably, this discourse promoted or expanded gay community, enlisting new individuals into the ranks and shoring up the allegiances of old guard activists such as Sandifer. But even more so, it shaped that community, setting boundaries, parameters, standards of conduct. While the enumeration and articulation of gay institutions appeared an invitation to many, it seemed a barrier to others, a signal that an identity-based community, by its very nature, excluded some as it smoothed out differences among the elect.

Now more than ever before, however, those with deeply-held religious faith—a vast majority in Mississippi—were welcomed into a gay community. Queer Mississippians learned that a new congregation existed to address their spiritual concerns. They learned that their spirituality and sexuality were not antithetical.

The importance of spirituality for many gay Mississippians might best be summed up by Darryl Jeffries, a working-class Warren County native who describes his first encounter with the Metropolitan Community Church in this way:

> I had met one gay person through my cousin's wife. A waiter at Tuminello's [in Vicksburg]. He wasn't really a sexual partner. More like a gay confidante. Somebody that I could talk to, that could give me information on something that I knew nothing about, but I knew I was a part of. He really enlightened me a whole lot.
>
> But what *really* gave me the message that it was okay to be gay was when I was nineteen. I looked in the *Clarion-Ledger.* And it was really strange, because I *never* looked at the *Clarion-Ledger.* I had no interest in it. It didn't mean anything to me. Jackson was a place that I had been maybe two or three times in my life; I had no reason to even look in it. But I looked in it this one Sunday. There was a write-up. There was the Baptist church, I think, opposing the Metropolitan Community Church on the same page. I called the gay minister out in California and started talking to him on the phone.[88] I called him; I got information from him on my sexuality. He wanted me to move out to California. I was too afraid to, of course.
>
> So at that point I got the message that it was okay to be gay. That God loved me regardless. It was not a sin to be homosexual. So I started developing a whole new belief about myself. That's when I started coming out to other people. It was like, I'm not bad, you know. All this shit that I've believed all my life is bullshit. It's just bullshit. It's a bunch of lies that people have concocted out of their own fears and their own ignorance. That's when I really started coming to life, really. I used to be a very shy person. And after that, it was just like boom. The energy was in me then to live, actually. My depression started lifting. I had a reason to live then.
>
> I felt like an alien up to that point. Then I found out there were people like me. This was a very big turning point in my life. It was so strange that I happened to pick up that paper at that point. It was like a God thing, you know. It was meant to happen.[89]

Jackson's Metropolitan Community Church appealed to queer Mississippians who personally had felt the sting of church-sponsored oppression, yet had retained the commitment to Christian spirituality. Ever larger groups of men like *that*—a category given to occasional dissembling and disidentification—began to band together with, as Daryl Jeffries put it, people like *me*—a distinctive form of identification and association. Where gay identity politics flagged, a gay social gospel flourished.

MCC reached Harold, a conflicted fifty-five-year-old who, having been kicked out of his church and told he would be barred from heaven, still considered homosexuality a sin. Kathie likewise was told she was destined for hell. However, after "going from church to church, counselor to counselor," she concluded that "it's not me that's screwed, it's them." Young Johnny Estes so thoroughly absorbed fundamentalist teachings into his psyche that "I prayed to God that he would allow me to be straight." Estes later overcame his guilt, even after a painful divorce. He became one of the five founding members of MCC-Jackson in 1983.[90]

After the success of their Palm Sunday gathering, MCC began regular Sunday services two weeks later on April 10. The first lesbian and gay organization to be incorporated by the State of Mississippi, the Metropolitan Community Church met thereafter at two o'clock every Sunday afternoon, just two doors up North State Street from First Baptist Church downtown. The Human Coalitions Building, which housed various nonprofit organizations including the Mississippi Gay Alliance, remained the MCC's home throughout the early period. Membership expanded from the initial five to twenty-two within five months. Thereafter, it grew exponentially.

The early numbers were deceptively small. Truly, they promised MCC's continued presence in Mississippi for years to come. Many who worshiped at MCC never transferred their letter of membership from their home church, ordinarily their parents' church. Many people visited and took part in services and activities without ever becoming members. Of these, many went on to help strengthen local gay affiliates of mainline Protestant churches, such as the Methodist group Affirmation, and the even stronger Episcopal Integrity, local founding of which predated MCC of Jackson.

Some visitors to MCC felt particularly unwelcome. As Kathy Switzer recalls, the congregation was entirely white. Though African Americans visited, "they would always go back to their home churches because they felt more comfortable there." One black worshiper explicitly stated the dilemma to the group: "It's hard enough to be black. You want me to be gay too?" "Yes," came the response. "You play with the boys, honey. Don't you think it's time to identify yourself?"[91]

Indeed, identity was the issue. Just as gay organizing privileged a particular form of outness as a primary and sometimes prerequisite political act, gay worship mandated and affirmed a gay identity that in theory was stable and thus in practice was often inflexible. Further, as we have seen, particular styles of worship were valorized. If MCC in Mississippi minimized emotive and charismatic elements of the liturgy, as even Pentecostal Troy Perry did, then the resultant complexion of the membership should not surprise. Gay worship, we can assume, not only excluded African Americans; it also alienated those whose desires and self-conceptions did not comport to these gay standards.

Of those who did join MCC, most shied away from leadership roles, given the degree of disclosure entailed—for example, signing official papers of incorporation. Under Kathy Switzer, Johnny Estes became assistant worship coordinator, and Denita Claypool served as secretary. The founders tapped as treasurer longtime gay activist, MGA president, outspoken revolutionary, and committed communist, Eddie Sandifer.[92]

Sandifer's involvement was less a reflection of his own religious values and upbringing—as son of a Baptist minister—than an indication of the nature of lesbian and gay politics in Mississippi. Sandifer, who first invited MCC officials to come to Jackson, realized that after ten years of MGA activity, political organizing would falter if it did not address the spiritual concerns of a vast number of queer Mississippians. For these individuals, Protestant Christianity, while the source of much oppressive activity in the state, nonetheless informed their identity as much as, if not more than, sexuality. According to Switzer, the Metropolitan Community Church offered them "a place where they could actually be themselves, where their faith was validated and their lives were affirmed."[93] Just as parishioners came to MCC from throughout Mississippi, gay people of faith in Jackson and across the state formed their own informal groups, prayer circles, and gatherings.

So pervasive was Christianity in Mississippi—the state with the third largest percentage of self-declared Christians[94]—that one's existence was fairly predicated on one's adherence to a Christian worldview. *To be,* in many ways, meant *to be Christian,* as Darryl Jeffries's narrative suggests. Jeffries said that he "had a reason *to live*" once he discovered "that it was okay to be gay," "that God loved [him] regardless." His very sense of having or being a self was informed by a particular religious culture of meaning. Before, he had "felt like an alien"—in a sense, a nonbeing. The struggle over a gay church was consequently a struggle over gay existence, over *being* as defined by a broader culture. Queer Mississippians' spiritual need was a conflicted need for assimilation, no less or more so than the needs of other Mississippians, including members of the religious right.

The strident backlash against MCC suggested the nonetheless subversive potential of queer religious organizing. Right-wingers like Mike Wells no longer enjoyed the comfortable distance constructed between us and them, the devout and the sinful, the saved and the damned. Early MGA activity had never occasioned this level of reactionary diatribe. Wells and other religious and political figures felt more threatened by MCC because it muddled lines of distinction. Gay people now seemed startlingly similar to average Mississippians in their desire for safe communities, work environments, and houses of worship—in short, in their desire for normalcy. Once a danger from without—Wells presumed the "invasion" originated elsewhere, say San Francisco or Houston—homosexuality proved a hidden threat from within. When Sandifer asserted that "we are everywhere including [Wells's] Mountainview Baptist Church," the reply of the Mississippi Moral Majority president rang conspicuously hollow. While Wells professed having counseled and "reformed" lesbians and gays in Christian congregations, he paradoxically denied the possibility of homosexuals at Mountainview as "the most ridiculous thing I ever heard."[95]

Finally, the MCC controversy demonstrated that the discourse of lesbian and gay rights could no longer ignore religious right arguments, but would have to refute them on moral grounds. Organizers could not presuppose that the taking on of a lesbian or gay identity was accompanied by the shedding of a spiritual identity. Queer Mississippians, as a group, were not atheistic, as Don Sanders of Houston's Gay Atheists League assumed logical. Instead of discarding their religious upbringings, many were learning to accommodate them to new ways of living—and also to accommodate their new ways of living to their religious upbringings.

As Meredith Raimondo writes of Atlanta during the 1980s,

> While [Christian] religion clearly fueled homophobia . . . it also energized AIDS [and gay] activism. Actions often took the form of memorial services, prayer services, and protests in which ministers spoke. . . . Religion served as a basis for political organization as well as personal strength.[96]

Likewise in Mississippi, this historical moment signaled the necessity for a complex change in tactics for political movement and institutional development. Though the shift was not a wholesale departure from radical left systemic critique—as in Sandifer's early communist alliances and Atlanta's Gay Liberation Front—it clearly was a turn toward an articulation of aims and objectives within Christian discourses. Given the life histories of members like Sandifer and the recent regional history of a church-based African-American civil rights struggle, the time and place were opportune. Queer Christian community building was not a mere rhetorical reaction to religious persecution. It was instead an enunciation of the rich, complex spiritual convictions of many Mississippians.

The most effective affirmation of queer life in Mississippi could no longer preclude Christian faith. Instead, it would increasingly comport itself to a different model. That model was elaborated in a 5 June 1983 op-ed piece for the *Clarion-Ledger* by the Reverend Ken Martin—a Mississippi native, pastor of MCC-North Hollywood, California, and long-distance telephone mentor to nineteen-year-old Vicksburg resident, Darryl Jeffries. To the paper's point-counterpoint query—"Is it possible to be homosexual and still be a Christian?"—Martin responded with a series of supportive biblical interpretations and answered the question with a vigorous, reassuring "YES."[97]

Notes

1. Don Sanders, "Christianity's Intolerance of Gays," *This Month in Mississippi* 9 (December 1982): 20–21.

2. Ibid.

3. "Metropolitan Community Church of Jackson," *This Month in Mississippi* 10 (October/November 1983): 17.

4. On Mattachine and on Randy Wicker's involvement, see John D'Emilio, *Sexual Politics, Sexual Communities: The Making of a Homosexual Minority in the United States, 1940–1970* (Chicago: University of Chicago Press, 1983), 125, 158–61.

5. "New Homophile Organization," *The Ladder* 8 (May 1959): 7.

6. Eddie Sandifer, interview with author, Jackson, Mississippi, 29 July 1998.

7. Ibid.

8. "Expose Short-Haired Anti-Intellectual Queers," *Kudzu* 1 (12 November 1968).

9. Ibid.

10. "Heavy Hog," *Kudzu* 1 (17 December 1968). On the official backlash against *Kudzu* and its staff, see *Clarion-Ledger* (*CL*), 10, 11 October; 19, 20 December 1968; 31 May 1970.

11. Martin Duberman, *Stonewall* (New York: Dutton, 1993), 190–221. On the GLF in New York, see Terence Kissack, "Freaking Fag Revolutionaries: New York's Gay Liberation Front, 1969–1971," *Radical History Review* 62 (Spring 1995): 104–34.

12. David Hayward, "Where Were You in '72? Atlanta Was Proud and Gay," *The Gazette* (n.p., n.d.; 1981).

13. Darrell Yates Rist, *Heartlands: A Gay Man's Odyssey Across America* (New York: Plume, 1993), 267–69. For more, see "History of the MGA," *This Month in Mississippi* 9 (September 1982): 20.

14. Donna Jo Smith, "Queering the South: Constructions of Southern/Queer Identity," in *Carryin' On in the Lesbian and Gay South*, ed. John Howard (New York: New York University Press, 1997), 382.

15. Rist, *Heartlands*, 267.

16. Joe Nix, "Jackson Gay Community Speaks Its Mind," *Reporter* 20 (30 January 1975): 1.

17. *ACLU/Memos* (Newsletter of the American Civil Liberties Union of Mississippi), January–February 1975.

18. Nix, "Jackson Gay Community Speaks Its Mind," 1.

19. (Jackson, Miss.) *Steppin' Out*, 4 November 1977.

20. *Workers' World*, 21 October 1977. See also Anita Bryant, *The Anita Bryant Story: The Survival of Our Nation's Families and the Threat of Militant Homosexuality* (Old Tappan, N.J.: Revell, 1977).

21. *Workers' World*, 18 June 1977.

22. Nix, "Jackson Gay Community Speaks Its Mind," 10.

23. Ibid.

24. Ibid. The white owner of Mae's regularly put off all my attempts at an interview. Though accounts differ, many narrators assume that he and/or his family likewise owned the black bar, Bill's.

25. "Jackson Police Department Personnel Complaint," 28 September 1976, Files of the

Mississippi Gay Alliance (hereafter MGA), Mississippi Department of Archives and History (MDAH), Jackson, Mississippi. See also the *CL*, 30 September 1976.

26. Mary Ramberg, letter to John Buggs, Washington, D.C., 18 March 1977, Files of MGA, MDAH.

27. *Jackson Daily News* (*JDN*), 14 September 1979. See also Laus Humphreys, *Tearoom Trade: Impersonal Sex in Public Places*, rev. enl. ed. (New York: Aldine de Gruyter, 1975), 46, 64. In this groundbreaking study, sociologist Laud Humphreys shows that men interested in homosexual encounters in public places only make overtures to those who indicate, through various in-group signals, a willingness to participate.

28. *JDN*, 14 September 1979.

29. *Mississippi Gay Alliance v. Goudelock* (1976) 536 F 2d 1073. See also Defendants' Brief, *Mississippi Gay Alliance and Anne Debary v. Bill Goudelock, Mississippi State University, et al.*, In the United States Court of Appeals for the Fifth Circuit, No. 74–4035, Files of MGA, MDAH.

30. Nix, "Jackson Gay Community Speaks Its Mind," 1.

31. "Mississippi Gay News," *This Month in Mississippi* 8 (December 1981).

32. *JDN*, 23 August 1974.

33. Sandifer, interview with author, 29 July 1998.

34. For example, Joe Holmes (pseudonym), interview with author, Brandon, Mississippi, 6 July 1996.

35. *Worker's World*, 29 December 1983.

36. Earl Black and Merle Black, *Politics and Society in the South* (Cambridge: Harvard University Press, 1987), 62, 69.

37. The following discussion of Perry's life and early MCC history is informed by his two memoirs: Troy D. Perry with Charles L. Lucas, *The Lord Is My Shepherd and He Knows I'm Gay* (Los Angeles: Nash Publishing, 1972), and Troy D. Perry with Thomas L. P. Swicegood, *Don't Be Afraid Anymore: The Story of Reverend Troy Perry and the Metropolitan Community Churches* (New York: St. Martin's Press, 1990). See also *Mobile Register*, 8 June 1997.

38. Perry and Swicegood, *Don't Be Afraid Anymore*, 28.

39. Ibid., 35, 42.

40. Ibid., 36.

41. Ronald M. Enroth and Gerald E. Jamison, *The Gay Church* (Grand Rapids, Mich.: William B. Eerdmans Publishing, 1974), 41.

42. Ibid., 140.

43. Ibid., 106.

44. Ibid., 137.

45. Thomas Furman Hewitt, "The American Church's Reaction to the Homophile Movement, 1948–1978" (Ph.D. diss., Duke University, 1983), 289.

46. Ibid., 291.

47. Ibid., 292–93. Interestingly, Hewitt cites Rev. Dr. John R. Claypool of Jackson—no relation to Denita, later mentioned—as one of the more "compassionate, non-judgmental" members of the Baptist leadership, 307.

48. Ibid., 263–64. Ward Tillman (pseudonym), interview with author, Jackson, Mississippi, 13 January 1996. The full General Conference statement reflected conflict among the church's clergy and lay delegates. Among the more conciliatory yet patronizing statements:

"Homosexual persons no less than heterosexual persons are individuals of sacred worth. All persons need the ministry and guidance of the Church in their struggles for human fulfillment, as well as the spiritual and emotional care of a fellowship which enables reconciling relationships with God, with others, and with self. Further we insist that all persons are entitled to have their human and civil rights ensured." For an account of the floor debate, see Bruce Hilton, *Can Homophobia Be Cured? Wrestling with Questions That Challenge the Church* (Nashville: Abingdon Press, 1992), 84–86.

49. Hewitt, "The American Church's Reaction to the Homophile Movement," 268.

50. *JDN,* 15 June 1979. *CL,* 17 November 1984.

51. Robert Nugent and Jeannine Gramick, "Homosexuality: Protestant, Catholic, and Jewish Issues; A Fishbone Tale," in *Homosexuality and Religion,* ed. Richard Hasbany (Binghamton, N.Y.: Haworth Press, 1989), 26.

52. David Greenberg, *The Construction of Homosexuality* (Chicago: University of Chicago Press, 1988), 468.

53. Hewitt, "The American Church's Reaction to the Homophile Movement," 63.

54. Ibid., 260.

55. Tillman, interview with author, 13 January 1996.

56. Ellen Rosenberg, *The Southern Baptists: A Subculture in Transition* (Knoxville: University of Tennessee Press, 1989), 89.

57. Ted Herrington (pseudonym), interview with author, Hattiesburg, Mississippi, 13 January 1996.

58. Vince Jones (pseudonym), interview with author, New Orleans, Louisiana, 21 July 1998.

59. J. Kathleen Bills Harder, "The Role of the Local Pastor in the Political Mobilization of Evangelical Protestants" (Ph.D. diss., University of Maryland, 1988), 62.

60. Thomas Hal Phillips, interview with author, Corinth, Mississippi, 27 December 1995.

61. Janet Watson and Tommy Ross, "Afterword," in *Rural Gays and Lesbians: Building on the Strengths of Communities,* ed. James Donald Smith and Ronald J. Mancoske (Binghamton, N.Y.: Harrington Park Press, 1997), 114–15.

62. Frederick Ulner (pseudonym), interview with Mississippi Oral History Program, Hattiesburg, Mississippi, 22 July 1993.

63. Perry and Swicegood, *Don't Be Afraid Anymore,* 267.

64. *CL,* 6 February 1983.

65. *CL,* 28 March 1983.

66. Kathy Rudy, *Sex and the Church: Gender, Homosexuality, and the Transformation of Christian Ethics* (Boston: Beacon Press, 1997), 6–8.

67. Mike Wells to "Family Member," 7 March 1982 [*sic;* 1983], Files of MGA, MDAH. *CL,* 12 March 1983. (Memphis) *Commercial Appeal,* 12 March 1983.

68. Mike Wells to "Family Member," 7 March 1982 [*sic;* 1983], Files of MGA, MDAH. *CL,* 12 March 1983.

69. Ibid.

70. Ibid.

71. *JDN,* 23 March 1983.

72. *CL,* 28 March 1983.

73. *CL/JDN,* 5 June 1983.

74. Don McGregor, "The Homosexual Church," *Baptist Record* (April 1983).

75. Kathy Switzer, interview with author, Jackson, Mississippi, 28 March 1994.

76. (Memphis) *Commercial Appeal,* 12 March 1983.

77. "Mississippi Gay Alliance: The Moral Majority is Neither," 27 April 1983, Files of MGA, MDAH.

78. *CL/JDN,* 5 June 1983.

79. *CL,* 13 March 1983.

80. *JDN,* 22 March 1983.

81. Ibid.

82. Ibid.

83. Ibid.

84. *CL/JDN,* 5 June 1983, shows the video as still yet to be produced. No further references to television or radio spots appear in the Files of MGA, MDAH. Kathy Switzer remembers seeing the clips on a Jackson evening news telecast. Mike Wells declined my request for an interview.

85. *JDN,* 22 March 1983.

86. *CL/JDN,* 5 June 1983. *JDN,* 6, 7, 8 June 1983.

87. D'Emilio, *Sexual Politics, Sexual Communities,* 52.

88. This is not a reference to Troy Perry, but rather Mississippian Ken Martin, mentioned below.

89. Darryl Jeffries (pseudonym), interview with author, Brandon, Mississippi, 6 July 1996. It is important to note that this memory was unprompted. It arose within the context of the narrator's broader life history. At this point in the interview, I had not mentioned religion or spirituality.

90. *CL/JDN,* 5 June 1983.

91. Switzer, interview with author, 28 March 1994.

92. "Metropolitan Community Church of Jackson," 17.

93. Switzer, interview with author, 28 March 1994.

94. James L. Cox, ed., *Mississippi Almanac: The Ultimate Reference on the State of Mississippi* (Yazoo City, Miss.: Computer Search and Research, 1995), 53.

95. *JDN,* 28 April 1983.

96. Meredith Raimondo, "Dateline *Atlanta:* Place and the Social Construction of AIDS," in *Carryin' On in the Lesbian and Gay South,* ed. John Howard (New York: New York University Press, 1997), 355.

97. *CL/JDN,* 5 June 1983.

Part Five

Public Debates and Public Policy

14

Health Care, the AIDS Crisis, and the Politics of Community

The North Carolina Lesbian and Gay Health Project, 1982–1996

Ian K. Lekus

> When I was 18, I told my dermatologist, whom I expected to be sympathetic, that I feared I was lesbian. He practically raped me.
>
> When treated recently for a viral infection, the health care provider based his diagnostic work-up on the fact that I was gay. I was unnecessarily tested for STDs [sexually transmitted diseases] because he assumed all gays are promiscuous—despite the fact that I told him I'd been monogamous for two years.
>
> One psychiatrist led me into trying to convert from gay to straight for 13 years while I stayed closeted, anxious, and depressed.
>
> I saw a male resident at a North Carolina hospital three years ago. Said I was a lesbian. He couldn't deal with it. Got very embarrassed. Obviously wasn't ready to deal with it.
>
> David H. Jolly, *The North Carolina Lesbian and Gay Health Survey: Final Report*, June 1985, pp. 32–34

IN the fall of 1982, Carl Wittman, an environmental activist in Durham, North Carolina, gathered a few friends to discuss reports of homophobic health care providers mistreating their lesbian and gay male patients. These stories of neglect, ridicule, and harassment convinced Wittman and the others to organize to address the quality of health care available to lesbians and gay men in the area. Wittman proposed the creation of a grassroots self-help organization modeled after feminist health clinics founded in the 1970s. In contrast, David Jolly, one of Wittman's friends and a graduate student in public health in Chapel Hill, wanted to make existing health care institutions more responsive to the specific needs of lesbians and gay men. These two competing notions coalesced into the founding vision for the organization—the North Carolina Lesbian and Gay Health Project (LGHP)—established by Jolly, Wittman, Timmer McBride, and Aida Wakil.[1]

Reports of a new illness striking down gay men raised Wittman's eyebrows. He collected newspaper clippings documenting the medical and grassroots responses to this poorly understood cluster of diseases. The epicenters of the illness were in the largest gay male communities in the United States, but cases quickly appeared in smaller cities and towns across the country. About the same time that Wittman and his friends gathered to discuss lesbian and gay health concerns, the lead story of *The Front Page,* a Raleigh-based gay newspaper covering the Carolinas, warned "UNC-CH Researchers Study Baffling Illness." The September 1982 article mentioned that the five hundred cases of this illness reported to date nationally included a handful of local gay men. While at least one of the patients treated at North Carolina Memorial Hospital had moved to the state after developing symptoms of what was then called Gay-Related Immune Deficiency (GRID) in New York, the hospital staff cautioned against assuming a causal relationship between illness and residence in major metropolitan gay communities. Dr. Myron Cohen explained that "the problem is not limited to New York City or San Francisco. We have encountered patients in this area, some of whom have had no exposure or travel to endemic areas."[2]

The LGHP's founders did not anticipate that this illness, renamed Acquired Immunodeficiency Syndrome, or AIDS, would soon dominate the daily business of the organization. The history of the LGHP is rare among lesbian and gay health organizations of its time, in that it was neither launched specifically in response to AIDS nor dedicated solely to the needs of gay men or lesbians. Its defining mission to serve the general health concerns of both men and women and its original grassroots self-help philosophy distinguished the LGHP from later AIDS service organizations (ASOs) founded upon traditional public health and social work models—even when the LGHP itself professionalized to meet the demands created by the AIDS crisis. Yet the most distinct legacy of the LGHP remains the instrumental role it played in developing a sense of community among both lesbians and gay men in Durham and the broader Triangle area.[3]

In this essay, I will explore how successful the LGHP was in fulfilling its goal of developing "a model of lesbians and gay men working together for the good of the community."[4] Its founders took for granted that such a community existed between the two populations, when in fact their work proved critical to forging the necessary emotional and institutional bonds across gender lines in the first place. While the organization committed itself to addressing the needs of both sexes, the social, economic, and cultural pressures brought to bear upon the LGHP and the local population by the AIDS crisis exposed limits in popular notions of who belongs to a community (in this case, a community defined primarily by sexual identity), who the community excludes, how a community operates, and how those processes are intrinsically connected. AIDS forced the LGHP to struggle regularly with two specific dilemmas created by the gap between its commitment to fostering community and the differences of power within that community. First, trying to balance the needs of men and women and maintain egalitarian gender relations in the face of an epidemic afflicting far more gay men than lesbians proved very challenging. Second, the LGHP found it extremely difficult to provide AIDS prevention education and support services to those individuals who did not claim the sexual identity at the core of the lesbian and gay community. This population included many African-American men who engaged in homosexual sex but continued to identify as straight.

A brief discussion of the frequently invoked, inadequately understood term "community" is in order. Communities do not exist as static entities—they are public, dynamic systems created, fostered, and sustained by their members, who often assume and invoke the existence of a community. Community can be said to be performed in that it simultaneously takes place in and derives from the actions of its members and of the institutions those members create. Rituals—that is, practices routinized by a specific group whose members attach a commonly understood meaning to participation in such events—are one benchmark frequently used to measure community. Shared territory and culture are intrinsic to the composition of and membership in a community, including accepted notions of what individuals and groups, and which places and actions, *do not* belong to the given community. Yet notions of a shared sense of belonging to a single united community obscure internal conflicts—conflicts rooted in the uneven power among members and members' allegiances to other communities and social networks. The history of the LGHP, from its 1982 birth through its collapse in early 1996, demonstrates how this theory of belonging and community is played out in everyday life.[5]

BEFORE the early 1980s, no institutional bonds held white lesbians and gay men together in the Durham area, though both groups did form their own communities. Gay liberation groups at Duke University and the University of North Carolina at Chapel Hill in the early 1970s purported to serve the needs of both lesbians and gay men. However, these groups, especially the original Duke Gay Alliance, were dominated by men who did not sponsor programs or events of interest to lesbians. Lesbian feminists, frustrated by gay male sexism and by the homophobia of local heterosexual feminists, organized their own groups, publications, and women-only events in the name of a shared (predominantly white) sisterhood. These women explicitly declared their lack of interest in working with gay men. The Triangle Area Lesbian Feminists (TALF) and the Durham-based journal *Feminary* were particularly explicit about their woman-centered politics. At the same time, many white gay men were comparably invested in their own community institutions such as bars and social clubs—spaces often notorious for excluding nonwhite men and all women. Plenty of white gay men and lesbians enjoyed personal friendships with each other, but no groups or events and few public spaces catered to the needs and interests of both populations. The limited evidence available suggests that African-American lesbians and gay men established "leisure clubs" and socialized together at regularly scheduled parties, but these networks remained too underground to be considered public communities.[6]

Several events of the early 1980s brought Triangle-area lesbians and gay men together in political coalition. The April 1981 Little River murder of Ron Antonevich by two men looking "to beat up some faggots" gave rise to a memorial rally (co-organized by Carl Wittman) and two months later to the state's first gay and lesbian pride march in Durham. Lesbians and gay men also worked together to attempt to repeal the state's sodomy laws and to challenge Senator Jesse Helms's 1984 reelection campaign. Confronting deeply entrenched homophobic institutions, attitudes, and actions, they recognized the urgency of organizing across gender lines and of educating and recruiting heterosexual allies.[7]

The LGHP also understood the necessity of such tactics. Carl Wittman brought two decades of experience using these strategies in the draft resistance, gay liberation, and environmental movements. In his 1968 tract, "A Gay Manifesto," he demanded that gay men challenge their own sexism and urged them to form alliances with the women's liberation movement. For some lesbian feminists in Durham, Wittman and his lover Allan Troxler were the first gay men with whom they worked politically. When Wittman and his friends discussed the horror stories lesbians and gay men told of homophobic mistreatment received from health care professionals, they took for granted that they would address the needs of both sexes.[8]

The LGHP founders recognized that they needed to survey the specific health concerns of North Carolina lesbians and gay men. They designed and distributed a questionnaire asking respondents about their physical and mental health history, sexual practices, and demographic background. Respondents were asked to describe the quality of the medical and mental health care they had received and whether their health care providers were prepared to address issues with specific ramifications for lesbians and gay men. The 459 returned surveys testified to the need to confront homophobia in the health care system. The LGHP received dramatic accounts of homophobic harassment, abuse, and mistreatment. Numerous respondents recounted that when their health care provider learned of their sexual orientation, the quality of the services provided was directly and adversely affected. The hardships endured included neglect, needlessly rough treatment, and breaches of confidentiality. Some doctors told gay men that they deserved the sexually transmitted diseases they had contracted. One psychologist told a client questioning her sexual identity that "lesbians were immature and unfulfilled." Lesbian and gay male health care providers expressed frustration with their colleagues' hostile attitudes and fear for their own careers if their sexual orientation become known.[9]

The survey solicited suggestions for remedying these problems. The information collected provided the LGHP its first template for programming and services, including a referral system for gay-sensitive health care professionals and education about lesbian and gay health issues for both health care providers and the lesbian and gay community. The results were affected, no doubt, by the fact that the questionnaires, distributed in the spring of 1983 as inserts to *The Front Page* and

The Newsletter (a local lesbian-feminist publication) and at gay academic conferences, reached visible, self-identified adult gay men and lesbians. Not surprisingly, the services the LGHP then developed best served the needs of women and men who could afford health care, who were willing to make use of health services explicitly identified as lesbian or gay, and who were comfortable discussing their homosexuality with their doctors and therapists.

David Jolly acknowledged that "the very groups we missed are likely to have the most health problems and the least access to adequate care: the elderly, minorities, and less educated persons." He also speculated that the pool of respondents did not include persons who engaged in homosexual sex but identified themselves as heterosexual, since "it is unlikely that they read gay and lesbian publications or participate in community activities." The inability to reach these persons as well as lesbian and gay youth, elders, African Americans, and working-class people raises questions about these populations' status as full members of the lesbian and gay community. Notwithstanding individual exceptions, these groups are often subject to the power of white, middle- and upper-class, self-identified adult lesbians and gay men to define the qualities of their community. From the beginning, LGHP volunteers were aware of the populations they failed to reach, yet unable to recognize how their own circumstances as middle-class white men and women encouraged them to overlook the presence and needs of less privileged members of the lesbian and gay male community. Thus the LGHP, even while bridging the power differentials between lesbians and gay men, reinforced the marginalization of other community members along the lines of race, class, age, and even sexual identity.[10]

Despite the LGHP's shortcomings, its Healthline referral network proved remarkably effective in putting those women and men willing to call an explicitly lesbian and gay service in contact with community resources far beyond the realm of health care. Launched in March 1985, Healthline was the only listing in the Durham telephone book for years under either "gay" or "lesbian," so many lesbians, gay men, and bisexuals new to the area, and those people just beginning to identify as such, called Healthline to meet other people and find supportive social and political organizations, churches, and bars. Some volunteers began working with Healthline after calling the service themselves. They provided emergency counseling over the telephone to crisis-stricken callers, who were often anguishing over their sexual orientation or reeling from being diagnosed with AIDS and turning to the only visible resource for support. The service not only provided accessible information about health issues, it also helped build community by connecting people and organizations, laying the groundwork for subsequent social and political action.[11]

The telephone referral network comprised one leg of the LGHP's efforts to build channels of communication with health care providers. Healthline volunteers collected and maintained a list of providers through recommendations from volunteers and friends and through mass mailings of questionnaires to area general and nurse practitioners, psychologists, dentists, gynecologists, chiropractors, acupuncturists, nutritionists, and other specialists. Some health care providers asked to be listed after participating in LGHP educational presentations. David Jolly and other LGHP volunteers, including Nancy Thompson and Tony Adinolfi, frequently presented a "Homo 101" program to Duke and University of North Carolina (UNC) medical students, at nursing and physical therapy schools, human sexuality classes, and churches and synagogues. This program, the second component of the organization's outreach to the local health care system, provided its heterosexual audiences an introduction to lesbian and gay health issues and made local professionals aware of the LGHP's services. "Homo 101" presenters sought to challenge notions that homosexuality was inferior to heterosexuality and that it was either a medical pathology or a moral weakness, thus undermining the basis for much anti-gay discrimination and hostility.[12]

The public health backgrounds of LGHP presenters helped build relations with local providers. Jolly found audiences receptive to what he described as their "responsible, credible presentation[s]." He explained that the presenters made sure not to appear "militant." The volunteers spoke to professionals through their common language of the scientific study of lesbian and gay male health concerns, complete with overheads of statistics and graphs. Nancy Thompson believed that the professionals responded well to LGHP presentations and services in part because their mission was to reform and supplement—rather than replace—the health care system. Long after Jolly, Thompson, and Adinolfi left the organization, the LGHP Speakers' Bureau continued to offer revised educational programs to local health care professionals.[13]

Healthline, "Homo 101," and the increasing number of doctors, nurses, and therapists who volunteered with the LGHP provided the internal catalyst driving the group's evolution into a service-providing organization. Carl Wittman, whom David Jolly remembered as "much more interested in grassroots political activism, in challenging the system and working politically to change things" than in supplementing the existing system, gradually withdrew from the LGHP. After battling AIDS for a year, Wittman followed his philosophy of self-reliance to its ultimate conclusion, taking his life on January 22, 1986, in the company of friends and family, rather than spend his last days suffering in a hospital room. Virtually no other people with AIDS (PWAs) shared Wittman's ideological opposition to receiving professional medical treatment. Instead, the severity of the AIDS crisis made Wittman's goal of organizing lesbians and gay men to reject corporate and public health institutions appear to be a utopian luxury. It was in fact the needs of PWAs in and out of hospitals and of the people who provided them clinical, legal, and emotional support that drove the LGHP to professionalize its structure and services.[14]

As the LGHP surveyed and publicized the needs of the lesbian and gay community during its first three years, the urgency of the AIDS crisis became dramatically apparent. The association of AIDS with homosexuality and the unrelenting silence from public officials regarding the epidemic made the LGHP the most visible source of AIDS information in the Triangle. The organization received a deluge of letters and phone calls from people desperately searching for information and support in confronting the crisis. The LGHP received such requests from gay men in North Carolina prisons, from students preparing research reports, and from groups organizing to provide their own AIDS education programs and support groups throughout North Carolina, the Southeast, and even as far away as Winnipeg and Mexico City. A Birmingham lesbian wrote for "advice, encouragement," and training materials for a support group started after two men committed suicide following their diagnosis with AIDS. One mother wrote searching for an AIDS support group for her "very depressed and lonely" son in Charlotte. A South Carolina man whose lover recently had sex with two other men asked for information and advice, as did a Durham man trying to decide whether to take the new HIV antibody test and whether or not to abstain from sex altogether. Responding to these requests and providing support services consumed the majority of the LGHP's human and financial resources for the remainder of its existence.[15]

The LGHP's buddy program, originally an informal response to the immediate needs of one gay man with AIDS, grew into the organization's hallmark service. Mike W., originally from a western North Carolina farming family, had moved to San Francisco years before. He became involved with the Shanti Project's residential program for people with AIDS in San Francisco, but returned to North Carolina in 1983 to be closer to his family. The LGHP learned about Mike through Tony Adinolfi, his nurse at the Durham VA Hospital. Mike W., Adinolfi, McBride, Troxler, and two new volunteers, Doug Ruhren and Dante Noto, used Mike's training with the Shanti Project and materials from Gay Men's Health Crisis in New York to organize a buddy program for PWAs in and out of the hospital. Adinolfi explained that "buddies did those things for us that our families would do for us if we were dying of cancer for instance. And you don't have your family around, so someone's gotta do it."[16] LGHP buddies helped Mike with simple chores after he left the hospital, such as shopping for groceries or taking him to doctors' appointments. Other tasks required greater coordination and financial commitment. Mike lived in a hotel after leaving the hospital until the hotel staff discovered he had AIDS and evicted him. Troxler and Ruhren found him an apartment, helped pay for bus tickets for his impoverished family to visit him, and drove them around Durham while they visited Mike. Though Mike died in 1984, the forms of support provided him were institutionalized into the buddy program.[17]

By the mid-1980s, AIDS dominated the daily business of the LGHP. Dante Noto and other volunteers handled a wide range of AIDS-related issues, duties later supervised by paid staff members. These services included investigating social services available to people with AIDS and arranging and running support groups for them and bereavement groups for their surviving partners. The LGHP advertised for buddies in local newspapers; other buddies volunteered, having heard of the program through word of mouth. Buddies moved PWAs into new apartments, took care of their pets, cut their hair, and offered emotional support. The LGHP also arranged legal counseling and hospice care and sponsored emergency loans. In serving as an information resource and in offering the psychological, logistical, and financial assistance biological families could not or would not supply, the LGHP offered the institutional and emotional support communities are expected to provide to their members. Furthermore, the commitment of lesbian volunteers to running the LGHP and providing direct support to gay men with AIDS demonstrated vividly the personal bonds of community developed between lesbians and gay men.[18]

Nonetheless, the demands of the AIDS epidemic meant that other lesbian and gay male health issues were all but ignored, leading to conflict and anger. Timmer McBride noted that "we got some flak from the women in the community about our full and undivided attention being devoted towards men."[19] Tony Adinolfi, acknowledging this resentment, explained the lack of attention paid to lesbian health: "there was no reaction, no one thought about it, [our work] was more crisis-oriented."[20] Plans to provide programs on alcoholism, depression, eating disorders, and other concerns identified by lesbians in the survey remained on the shelf for the most part during the 1980s.

Riki Friedman, who had worked with feminist self-help clinics in Berkeley before moving to Durham, organized a lesbian health committee in 1986. The committee trained Healthline volunteers and male LGHP organizers in the details of lesbian health, sponsored body image discussions at TALF meetings, and developed brochures outlining how HIV can and cannot be transmitted by lesbians. Friedman dissolved the committee a year later, frustrated by the LGHP steering committee's failure to write grants or provide volunteer support for lesbian health programming. Based on the limited grant money available for such programs a decade later, it appears unlikely that such applications would have been funded, but the steering committee's passivity reveals the limits of its vision and the drain on its resources. Friedman acknowledged that defining lesbian health needs was often difficult in the 1980s and noted the pall cast by the AIDS epidemic in the lesbian and gay community. She recalled arguing at the time that "it's very hard to talk about quality of life issues when you're looking at people dying."[21]

Not surprisingly, this remarkable energy generated its own variety of problems. As the LGHP expanded its services and programming, funding became its paramount concern. Lack of funding limited the services it could offer and directed its structural development. At the same time, most grants from government, foundation, or corporate sources specifically addressed AIDS issues, not general lesbian and gay male health concerns. From 1985 to 1990, the LGHP thus evolved from an activist organization that provided services to the local lesbian and gay male population to a professional service agency rooted in the community but focused largely on a single, critical disease.

Community fund-raising events and grants became the two most reliable sources of income for the LGHP. Margie Sved hosted the first LGHP yard sale in 1986 in front of her Trinity Park home, the same year that the LGHP sponsored a dance party (at the Chapel Hill American Legion Hall) the night before the first statewide lesbian and gay pride march in Durham. The LGHP continued to sponsor yard sales and Pride Dances on and off through the next ten years. Annual bike-a-thons, beginning in 1987, supported LGHP AIDS support services, while another yearly event, the Triangle Gourmet Gala dinner, subsidized other expenses. These fund-raisers became important rituals for the local lesbian and gay community.[22]

Notwithstanding the financial importance of these events, the LGHP recognized the necessity of larger, more stable sources of income. Grants from nonprofit foundations, the state government, and Research Triangle Park-based pharmaceutical giants Glaxo and Burroughs-Wellcome provided the bulk of the LGHP's funding starting in the mid-1980s. These institutions required grant recipients to account for the use and supervision of their money. Corporate sponsors preferred to fund organizations that could demonstrate stability and efficacy, favoring those headed by a board of directors including health care professionals with whom final responsibility rested. Tony Adinolfi recalled how the LGHP recruited "more people with initials after their name, so it legitimized us [to these institutions], having the MDs especially." The LGHP could not survive without grants for AIDS-specific programs from such institutions—it almost ceased operations several times during the late 1980s—and reorganized itself in order to bring in more funding.[23]

Hiring staff members was the first major change for the previously all-volunteer organization; creating a board of directors was the second major step towards professionalization. Previously, the steering committee (composed of equal numbers of women and men) made all decisions by consensus at monthly meetings, usually potluck dinners. As more people with AIDS asked for buddies, more people called with questions about AIDS, and more requests for educational programming came in, the steering committee could no longer manage these demands through monthly meetings and casual division of responsibility. In 1986, the LGHP hired Jill Duvall to coordinate volunteers and Scott Hustead to develop and direct HIV/AIDS educational programming. With Duvall and Hustead in the office every day, the LGHP was able to respond far more swiftly to events and requests.[24]

Determining lines of responsibility and authority proved a delicate task and generated various conflicts during this transition era. Dedication to consensus decision-making grew more challenging as the demands upon the LGHP multiplied. Spending monthly meetings arguing details in search of unanimity took time away from providing urgently needed services. The decentralization of responsibility among steering committee members gave way as paid workers made more and more of the daily decisions. Duvall and Hustead at least served on the steering committee; once a board of directors was created, staff members reported directly to the board. In 1987, Duvall, a graduate of the UNC social work program, was hired as a full-time project coordinator; the BOARD subsequently promoted her to executive director, giving her final responsibility for day-to-day operations.[25]

Duvall's tenure as executive director proved tumultuous. Volunteers accustomed to running the LGHP now had to cede the authority and media attention to the executive director. Tony Adinolfi, now a board member, questioned how many people with AIDS the LGHP was actually serving, claiming that only one PWA at the Duke University AIDS Clinic had a buddy from the LGHP; Duvall denied his charges.[26] In addition, the director won enemies in certain segments of the local gay male community through her outspokenness. In an interview with *The Front Page,* Duvall expressed anger that in North Carolina, "men are asked to give speeches on AIDS ethics and policy, and women are brought in to discuss nurturing and care-providing."[27] She recalled how frequently gay men commented on her dress or appearance, doubting that her male peers received similar comments. The only woman leading an AIDS organization in the state, she found herself excluded from the "good old gay male boys network . . . [of] all upper-class" men who were the state's most powerful AIDS activists. Comments were attributed to Duvall about gay men not changing their sexual practices to avoid HIV transmission. Former board member David Jones, recently a vice president at Abbott Laboratories, rebuked such claims, noting that conservatives made the same charges in government hearings to justify not funding HIV/AIDS education programs.[28]

Understandably, the financial stress on the organization, which more than once forced the board of directors to consider eliminating Duvall's position or even closing the LGHP's doors, heightened tensions, as did the workload and the emotional stresses involved in dealing with AIDS on a full-time basis. In the spring of 1989, Jones called for Duvall's resignation, due to "the long history of her political views restraining the organization. . . . Her politics interfered with the delivery of services" provided by the LGHP, he argued.[29] She wavered over whether to stay until she decided that she lacked the board's support and resigned that May. After the board of directors clarified staff job descriptions and the responsibilities of board and staff members, she returned in the fall of 1989 to the same job for another year.[30]

The flurry of letters and articles in *The Front Page* and the intensity with which interviewees recalled this turmoil illustrate how an organizational crisis was simultaneously a community event. Such moments reveal the contradictions between how members conceive of community and how the community operates. Duvall declared that

> I said something bad about our community, and that our community was not, and probably is not still, sophisticated enough to deal with internal conflict. We don't like it, we want to pretend that everything's peachy, and we don't like dissent, at all, and we'll get real mad real fast if you do.[31]

Duvall's analysis is supported by the extent to which interviewees emphasized the apologies made and the disagreements settled since 1989, including the reconciliation between Duvall and Jones. The need to smooth over past strife not only reflects the desire to lay personal anguish to rest, but also demonstrates the importance among community members of muting differences in power and the conflicts caused by those differences. These battles and the collective healing that often follows are as central to performing community as are the institutions and events by which communities are usually measured.

The daily work of training volunteers and coordinating buddies, and of writing grants and sponsoring fund-raisers, went on during the turmoil over professionalization. The LGHP organized its HIV/AIDS programming and services under the umbrella of The AIDS Services Project (TASP) in 1987, in order to circumvent homophobic roadblocks to its work. This decision institutionalized the question over the LGHP's mission: was it first and foremost interested in general lesbian and gay health, or was it primarily an AIDS service organization? This debate exposed what appear as contradictions to presumed unity of community, especially along the fault lines of class, race, and gender.[32]

The LGHP consistently encountered hostility from foundations, government agencies, and individuals unwilling to fund an organization with the words "lesbian" and "gay" in its name. TASP, lacking that burden, proved more successful at winning grants from groups willing to support organizations specifically devoted to AIDS issues. Resistance to the so-called "L" and "G" words in the LGHP's name also came from some gay men and lesbians. Stan Holt, Duvall's successor as executive director, reported offers to serve on the board or make donations on the condition that the LGHP remove the words "lesbian" and "gay" from its name, claiming that the LGHP "would never become mainstream as long as it had a name reminiscent of the radical '60s."[33]

Other potential donors or board members backed away from getting involved with the LGHP, skeptical that it served its clientele efficiently or unwilling to support an organization whose representatives reportedly criticized local wealthy white gay men and corporate and patriarchal institutions at large. Despite the LGHP's efforts to professionalize, it remained committed to a broader vision of organizing lesbians and gay men to manage their own health care. This explicit refusal to redefine itself as solely an AIDS service organization suggested to some of its affluent gay male critics that the LGHP remained "too radical" to be effective. Many of these critics preferred to donate to the more recently founded Triangle-area ASOs, organizations committed from the start to a case management approach to assisting people with AIDS regardless of sexual identity.[34]

Despite these concerns, North Carolina-based pharmaceutical research corporations, notably Burroughs-Wellcome and Glaxo, sponsored fund-raisers and provided grants to the LGHP and other ASOs in the region. Through their philanthropy, these businesses reemphasized popular notions that health care, even related to AIDS, was a humanitarian concern and not a political issue. Such ideas made it possible for closeted individuals just beginning to get involved with the lesbian and gay community to justify volunteering with TASP as a matter of compassion without making any political statement or bringing suspicion onto themselves. The LGHP acknowledged the financial and cultural power of the local health care culture, taking pains not to criticize Burroughs-Wellcome (upon whom it depended for grants) for the high price and toxicity of azidothimidine (AZT). This reticence distinguishes the LGHP from other AIDS activists around the country in the late 1980s, though Riki Friedman did acknowledge one protest "not by the Health Project, but [by] some people [who] had been connected with the Health Project" against the cost of AZT. The need to secure funding from corporations, foundations, and local community members pushed the LGHP to present itself as respectable and apolitical.[35]

It is no accident that this "respectability" question resurfaced regularly for the LGHP. Debates over what is acceptable at any moment are a matter of both what society at large sanctions and what the marginalized community in question allows. The conflicts within local communities cannot be separated from broader social divisions. External strategies and internal processes are inextricably linked.[36] The loudest battles over the LGHP's ideology and political tactics came from those community members with the greatest power to define what the LGHP *should have* been doing—from individuals employed by or connected to hospitals and pharmaceutical corporations who may have resented the organization's refusal to completely conform to their models of professionalized AIDS client case management. However, the LGHP's inability to fully incorporate the needs of those community members lacking this power may have been its undoing.

Stan Holt's arrival as executive director in September 1990 marked a fundamental shift in how the LGHP approached issues of power and community. Holt, a graduate of the UNC School of Public Health, committed the organization to seriously addressing the health issues of lesbians and bisexual women and of African-American lesbians, gay men, and bisexuals for the first time. To do this, the LGHP needed income not saddled with restrictions on how money could be spent. Many of the groups funding LGHP and TASP, especially government agencies, clearly dictated how their monies could be used in order to prevent charges that they were promoting or encouraging homosexual sex. Holt directed major donor campaigns that brought in unrestricted donations. Additionally, the public identification of breast cancer as a specific threat to lesbians led some foundations to sponsor unprecedented grants for lesbian health programming.[37]

While the LGHP included gender parity in structure and programming in its original plans, it made no such provisions to address the needs of African Americans. David Jolly acknowledged the LGHP's awareness that it remained and was perceived "as a project of white gay men."[38] In discussing this issue, he echoed Tony Adinolfi's aforementioned comment that the demands of the AIDS crisis consumed the LGHP's energies, explaining that "as the Health Project became fairly well established, I think it could begin to address other very important issues like crossing lines of race and class." Local activist Mandy Carter challenged this logic, arguing that though the white founders of the AIDS movement (including the LGHP) correctly took the initiative to confront the epidemic without waiting for government action, they shortsightedly overlooked that AIDS was hitting black gay men, not just white gay men, from the beginning. She questioned whether the LGHP was able to develop community across racial lines, pointing out that the LGHP maintained offices in a series of white middle-class Durham neighborhoods and doubting whether African Americans felt comfortable "coming onto Ninth Street, knowing what Ninth Street is."[39]

Longtime Healthline volunteer Jake Lehrer expressed the frustration of many LGHP white activists who accepted the importance of addressing the needs of African Americans but maintained that "it's real hard for . . . white folks to reach out and really make a meaningful connection to the African-American community as far as gay and lesbian health-related issues are concerned." Echoing these activists, Lehrer explained that blacks "feel that they've already got a lot of social constrictions anyway" because of racism and therefore "to be gay or lesbian is even more of a handicap."[40]

Scott Hustead, in his one year as the LGHP's AIDS educator, rejected white assumptions of widespread black homophobia. He refused to accept that he could not do programming for African Americans merely because he was white. Building upon his friendships with Mandy Carter and Gary Lipscomb (two cofounders of the Triangle Coalition of Black Lesbians and Gays) and his local work with Black and White Men Together, he made himself a presence in the Triangle-area African-American lesbian and gay community. He discovered many places to do AIDS education overlooked by the LGHP. He made presentations to private black social groups such as The Stable and hung out with African Americans at the Power Company, a predominantly gay dance club in downtown Durham, giving out condoms and talking about AIDS to anyone who happened to be there. Godfrey Herndon, Mandy Carter, and Gary Lipscomb all testified that his persistence, creativity, and access, and his "easy to listen to, nonthreatening" presentation style made Hustead the LGHP's first effective link to African Americans in Durham.[41]

Yet Gary Lipscomb also agreed with Jake Lehrer that many African Americans felt that "I'm already oppressed for being black. Why add my sexual orientation to that oppression?" The LGHP hired Lipscomb, formerly a Healthline volunteer, in 1993 to direct Black Men United, a program designed to educate African Americans about the dangers of AIDS and how to avoid HIV infection. Black Men United, first under Lipscomb and Don Jackson, then later under Rodney Hunter and Jerry Harris, issued newsletters, distributed condoms, and talked about these concerns in bars and other places African-American men met to have sex with men, and sponsored regular discussions among African-American men regarding HIV/AIDS and sexuality issues. Lipscomb and other African Americans working with the LGHP reported large numbers of blacks who either regularly engaged in homosexual sex but did not identify as gay or lesbian, or did identify as such but remained closeted around heterosexual friends and family members. They explained this reluctance to claim a lesbian or gay identity by referring to the burdens mentioned above and to the continued centrality in African-American communities of churches that regularly featured sermons denouncing homosexuality and AIDS.[42]

The LGHP found it difficult to incorporate the ambiguities of same-sex behaviors among African Americans, and more broadly among all individuals who engaged in homosexual sex but did not identify as lesbian or gay. Do such individuals belong to the lesbian and gay community? Did they fall under the scope of the LGHP's mission to organize lesbians and gay men? Stan Holt recalled the hostile reception the LGHP received as a white-led, openly lesbian and gay organization from African Americans on a committee formed to address the AIDS crisis in the Durham black community. He explained that the grudging willingness of these public figures to work with TASP to confront the devastation wrought by AIDS in this community offered the most convincing rationale for keeping TASP a separate entity.[43]

The LGHP proved most successful working with African-American lesbians and gay men whose experiences and identities closely resembled those of their white counterparts. The organization thus turned to the most visible, self-identified black lesbians and gay men to get access to those harder to find. Godfrey Herndon, who served on the board of directors for almost a decade, described himself and other prominent African-American lesbians and gay men: "We tend to be fairly well-educated professionals . . . people who have been around a little bit, people who are comfortable dealing with white people and people of other races, and people who are comfortable enough with their sexuality" to be publicly identified as lesbian or gay. Herndon distinguished these visible individuals from the majority of black lesbians and gay men "who are not willing to be out, who are not willing to work for organizations with people of other races . . . and whom you will never reach with efforts aimed at black lesbians or black gay men. They simply won't take the time to self-identify with those messages."[44] Gary Lipscomb explained that

> a lot of these men assume that if you're gay, you're a flaming queen. That's their definition of gay. It's not the sexual act, it's not identifying with a certain community. It's "this behavior is gay," which means usually being very effeminate, playing the passive role in sexual acts, . . . dressing as women, or quasi-dressing as women, and if you don't do that, then you're not gay.[45]

LGHP educational materials and services targeting these men could not simply substitute black gay male images and cultural references in place of white ones;

they needed to address sexual behavior, not sexual identity. The increasing numbers of AIDS cases among African Americans spurred the LGHP to develop programs such as Black Men United, to provide information regarding HIV transmission and safer sex recommendations to men regardless of their sexual identity. Through its outreach programming targeting these men—indeed, through the very language of "outreach"—the LGHP simultaneously reiterated and tried to contravene the definitions of lesbian and gay community requiring a public sexual identity.[46]

The new programming directives targeting African-American men and lesbian and bisexual women of all races included the commitment of the LGHP staff to allow these community members to define their health needs and tell the LGHP how those needs should be addressed. Stan Holt described his role as a gay man planning a lesbian health conference:

> All I did was answer phones and answer questions and get the money . . . this was not a conference for me. . . . It's real important that . . . lesbians define what it is they need and what it is that needs to go into a conference. So who cares what they spend their money on, as long as it's what they need and want.[47]

Lucy Harris discussed designing a proposed lesbian health clinic to meet the needs of black lesbians and bisexual women from its inception, including her offer to "trash the health clinic and start from scratch if I find that a large section of the women of color population say that what we're looking at is not going in the right direction." Board member Bernadette Carr explained that African-American lesbians and gay men "have to tell us what [their] issues are—we shouldn't be telling them." The LGHP revised its original mission to foster community across lines of class and race, trying to shed its image as the "White Gay Male Health Project" in the process. By doing this, the organization demonstrated how when white gay men in lesbian and gay male communities surrender administrative, financial, or symbolic power to women or to people of color, they tacitly acknowledge that white men generally have the power to cede in a community, and that their interests represent the standard from which these other groups' issues deviate.[48]

Lucy Harris, hired to coordinate Healthline volunteers and the buddy program, kept these concerns in mind as she directed most lesbian health programs during her tenure with the LGHP. With grants from the Ms. and ASTRAEA foundations, Harris organized a lesbian health conference in November 1992 in Chapel Hill. This retreat brought 130 women together to talk about breast cancer, lesbian parenting, HIV transmission among lesbians, substance abuse, sexual and homophobic violence, eating disorders, and other issues, and reinvigorated lesbian health organizing in the area. The LGHP sponsored health nights at the lesbian community center, Our Own Place, and inserted articles on breast cancer into local newspapers. Harris, Liza Rankow, and Bernadette Carr took 15 lesbians to a breast cancer summit in Winston-Salem in April 1994. The group, described by Carr as "black, white, and Latino, poor and not, older and younger," was selected to hold the conference organizers accountable for rendering lesbians invisible among the groups—women of color, older women, poor women, rural women—they had identified as facing particular risks for breast cancer. These were the women least likely to have satisfactory access to health care and to fit stereotypes of lesbians as young, white, middle-class, and urban.[49]

Harris brought to the LGHP the credibility she had built in the local lesbian-feminist community through her work as director of Our Own Place and as a promoter of women's music concerts. Mandy Carter explained that as Harris "started organizing some lesbian-specific things, then people said, 'hey this ain't bad'." Though her job was volunteer coordinator, she was determined to "figur[e] out a way to equally service the lesbian community and the gay men's community." For the previous decade, those lesbians devoted to building community with gay men donated their time and energy as buddies, AIDS educators, Healthline volunteers, and steering committee and board members. The AIDS crisis transformed the personal networks of lesbians and gay men into a community of both groups, complete with institutions and events, explosive conflicts and commitment to overcoming the divisions between the two populations. The lesbian health programming that Harris and her volunteers organized, particularly efforts to establish a lesbian health clinic and programs addressing breast cancer, mobilized the women involved with local lesbian-feminist organizations and institutions to a degree that AIDS—still considered a gay men's disease within the white lesbian and gay community—never could.[50]

Under the leadership of Holt and Harris, the LGHP expanded its efforts to encourage the growth of other lesbian and gay community institutions. Before their arrival, the steering committee assisted groups organizing to provide AIDS services around the state. Locally, Lester Lee secured a grant in 1987 from North Carolina Hands Across America to cover startup costs for a residence house for people with AIDS, a program that soon evolved into the independent AIDS Community Residence Association (ACRA). In the 1990s, the LGHP sponsored several organizations, sharing office space and equipment, staff and volunteers, and 501(c)(3) tax-exempt status. These groups included OutRight! (a support group for lesbian, gay, bisexual, and transgender youth), the North Carolina Coalition for Gay and Lesbian Equality (an anti-violence project), and the Piedmont HIV Health Care Consortium (the regional AIDS services program funded by the Ryan White Comprehensive AIDS Resources Emergency Act of 1990). The LGHP also provided meeting space to ACT-UP/Triangle, which lobbied to keep anonymous HIV testing available in North Carolina. By the mid-1990s, the LGHP served as the hub of an emerging community center, composed of these organizations and Our Own Place. Groups struggling to reduce their expenses and attempting to improve communications within the lesbian and gay community recognized the benefits of sharing human, financial, and physical resources and other tools crucial to community organizing.[51]

In July 1994, Stan Holt left the LGHP to explore other career opportunities. The LGHP went through a series of interim executive directors while trying to replace Holt; during the year following his departure, the major donor campaign faltered, many grants remained unwritten, and traditional community fund-raisers fell by the wayside. Jeff Prince, hired as executive director in the summer of 1995, resigned after just three months on the job. The financial crisis forced the LGHP to lay off all staff members in December 1995 and close its doors permanently three months later.[52]

While this financial crisis sent the LGHP into its fatal tailspin, two community crises destroyed interest in saving the organization. At the same time that Jeff Prince was hired, the co-chairs of the board of directors, David Doss and Anne Dornberg, fired Lucy Harris for alleged misuse of funds. Reed Williams attacked the LGHP in a *Front Page* column, claiming Harris "was given no notice nor was she given the opportunity to answer any of the allegations levied against her. . . . She was asked to leave the premises immediately, and the organization changed the locks on the door, implying criminal behavior on her part." Some LGHP board and staff members, infuriated and baffled by this unexpected move, expressed their deep skepticism of the co-chairs' claims. They suggested that this incident was an excuse to silence the politically outspoken Harris, despite the perception that she was the key to keeping the organization afloat during this crisis.[53]

Meanwhile, Jerry Harris, coordinator of TASP and Black Men United, tried to pull those projects out of the LGHP, criticizing the organization for deciding that its mission "did not include HIV/AIDS programming outside of gay society." The LGHP's African-American critics questioned whether an organization whose mission relied upon sexual identity could ever serve the needs of the local black population beyond the very small numbers of self-declared lesbians, gay men, and bisexuals comfortable dealing with white-led organizations. As a result, Jerry Harris, with the assistance of Lucy Harris and other LGHP supporters, set up a short-lived TASP office of their own in downtown Durham closer to the working-class African-American neighborhoods they sought to serve. The LGHP, already under fire for the recent dismissal of Don Jackson, lost further credibility in the African-American community. These two major controversies, muddied by public charges and countercharges, ruined the goodwill the organization had built over the previous five years trying to reconceptualize the local lesbian and gay community to account for the unequal power of community members across lines of race, class, and gender.[54]

THE decision to establish the Kerr/Lee Community Center from the ashes of the LGHP, rather than from an AIDS service organization, is perhaps the final testimony to the LGHP's legacy as a dynamic community-building force. Even the LGHP's critics at *Out in Black*, a newsletter for African-American gay men, lesbians, and bisexuals that grew in part out of Black Men United, expressed optimism that the new group taking over "the helm of this lost flagship of the community" would address its readers' needs. The new center's organizers (still mobilizing as of this writing) have begun their work where the LGHP left off before collapsing into financial and administrative crisis. This includes recognizing that members of the lesbian, gay, bisexual, and transgender (LGBT) communities are simultaneously members of other communities and social networks. One allegiance, whether of sexual orientation, gender, race, class, or age, may take precedence at any given moment, but the others do not disappear.[55]

LGBT communities are composed of members who contribute the interests, experiences, and assumptions built through their other allegiances and in their everyday participation in "work, politics, worship, voluntary associations, and civic affairs" where sexual identity may not be a central concern.[56] Women and people of color have been blamed for claiming additional identities that undermine the presumed sameness of LGBT people and the supremacy of issues related to sexual orientation, but all community members—from the most powerful to the least—have these conflicting allegiances. In another context, historian Elsa Barkeley Brown writes that "it is important to recognize that middle-class women live the lives they do precisely because working-class women live the lives they do. White women and women of color not only live different lives, but white women live the lives they do in large part because women of color live the lives they do."[57] The fundamentally *relational* nature of identity cited here by Barkeley Brown offers explanations of how differences in power produce the ideological divisions that split activists initially drawn together by their common dedication to improving the quality of health for lesbians and gay men and to serving the needs of people with AIDS.

For most of the LGHP's existence, it proved capable of fostering community among mostly white, middle-class, politically active lesbians and gay men. Some staff and volunteers cut their political teeth on community organizing; others came from careers in public health policy and administration, direct primary care, or pharmaceutical research. Many of these activists bridged the divides between these worlds. For example, Jill Duvall and Stan Holt applied their training in social work and public health, respectively, to grassroots community organizing. Riki Friedman moved from organizing feminist health clinics to becoming a physician's assistant, while David Jones retired from Abbott Laboratories to devote himself to full-time HIV/AIDS lobbying and organizing. These fluid boundaries between belonging to the mainstream health care culture and battling the system from the outside, between shifting places in and outside the lesbian and gay community, both framed by common overarching political aims, made the conflicts over how to achieve those goals all the more agonizing for those involved with the LGHP. The LGHP structured itself, through organizational gender parity and dedication to remaining a lesbian and gay health project, to take into account that gay men, as men, live the lives they do because lesbians, as women, live the lives they do. The demands of the AIDS crisis prevented the LGHP from developing services addressing the needs of lesbians until money became available to do so and until other organizations began to share the burden of providing AIDS educational and support services. Yet the LGHP did succeed in fostering community among lesbians and gay men in Durham, even as attempts to bridge divides of race and class remained far from complete when the organization collapsed. Nonetheless, should a LGBT community yet emerge in Durham that acknowledges and addresses its intrinsic dynamic, relational nature, it will do so expanding upon the legacy of the North Carolina Lesbian and Gay Health Project.[58]

Notes

Acknowledgment: The author wishes to express his appreciation to the many people who have contributed to this project in a myriad of ways. Special thanks must go to David Cecelski, William Chafe, Derek Chang, John D'Emilio, Lawrence Goodwyn, Lisa Hazirjian, Nancy Hewitt, Wesley Hogan, Erik Ludwig, Greg Millett, Philippe Rosenberg, Michael Tino, Kathy Wallerstein, and Mary Wingerd, and to those women and men of the LGHP and the Durham lesbian, gay, bisexual, and transgender communities who graciously lent me their time, memories, and papers to make it possible to preserve this history.

1. Interview with David Jolly, February 3, 1994. Interview with Timmer McBride, December 9, 1993. Interview with Allan Troxler, December 7, 1993. Three of the four LGHP founders were white; the fourth, Aida Wakil, was originally from the Middle East and left the project not long after its inception. Wakil and Wittman worked as community organizers for the Public Interest Research Group (PIRG), while McBride was a nurse.

2. Interview with Allan Troxler, December 7, 1993. Papers of Carl Wittman, in possession of the author. Mike McLaughlin, "UNC-CH Researchers Study Baffling Illness," *The Front Page*, September 28, 1982, p. 1. The most detailed account of the early years of AIDS remains Randy Shilts, *And the Band Played On: Politics, People, and the AIDS Epidemic* (New York: St. Martin's Press, 1987). Readers should also consult the critiques of Shilts's account, in particular Douglas Crimp, ed., *AIDS: Cultural Analysis, Cultural Activism* (Cambridge: MIT Press, 1988); and Cindy Patton, *Inventing AIDS* (New York: Routledge, 1990). For histories of AIDS in the South, see Meredith Raimondo, "Dateline *Atlanta:* Place and the Social Construction of AIDS," in *Carryin' On in the Lesbian and Gay South,* ed. John Howard (New York: New York University Press, 1997), 331–69; and Abraham Verghese, *My Own Country: A Doctor's Story* (New York: Vintage Books, 1994).

3. Throughout this essay, I refer to lesbian and gay male communities. Given the current preference to discuss lesbian, gay, bisexual, and transgender communities, it is worth pointing out that while the LGHP began to address the health concerns of self-identified bisexuals (as opposed to those individuals identifying as heterosexual while having sex with both men and women) during the 1990s, that process was still beginning when the organization collapsed in 1995 and 1996. While the staff and board of directors' intentions moved in this direction, one cannot say that the LGHP systematically fostered a lesbian, gay, and bisexual community. The issues of transgendered people were just beginning to be raised by staff at the time of the LGHP's demise. More broadly, I believe the evidence does not yet support

the conclusion that the local lesbian and gay communities have refashioned themselves into lesbian, gay, bisexual, and transgender communities, despite the intentions and sympathies of some individuals and organizations.

The Triangle area of central North Carolina encompasses Raleigh, Durham, Chapel Hill, and several smaller towns in Durham, Orange, and Wake Counties. The lesbian, gay, bisexual, and transgender communities of the Triangle are best understood as overlapping communities, both divided and united along the lines of regional and personal identities. The LGHP's record of developing community is most visible in Durham but extended through the entire Triangle area.

4. Lesbian and Gay Health Project of North Carolina, Inc., *Annual Report,* 1986, p. 3.

5. My analysis of the performance of community, and more generally of a theory of practice and structure, draws primarily on two works of anthropology: Sherry B. Ortner, *High Religion: A Cultural and Political History of Sherpa Buddhism* (Princeton, N.J.: Princeton University Press, 1989), and Marshall Sahlins, *Islands of History* (Chicago: University of Chicago Press, 1985). My discussion of the limits of community is formulated in response to Robert N. Bellah et al., *Habits of the Heart: Individualism and Commitment in American Life* (Berkeley: University of California Press, 1985), and to Stephen O. Murray, "Components of Gay Community in San Francisco," in *Gay Culture in America: Essays from the Field,* ed. Gilbert Herdt (Boston: Beacon Press, 1992), 107–46. In their conceptualizations of community, Bellah et al. emphasize similarity and inclusion, while Murray pays close attention to the importance of boundaries and difference. My position is that it is impossible to consider these issues separately, because they are not two distinct processes but one integral process. Including someone in a group based upon some shared quality requires distinction from those who do not belong and/or who are excluded, whether explicitly or implicitly.

My analysis of community also takes into consideration the work of Cindy Patton. In *Inventing AIDS,* Patton argues that "the term 'community' has political valency in the United States, but fails as an analytic concept; for it cannot illuminate the shifting personal or network allegiances lived by individuals in face-to-face relations" (7). My research suggests that this may not be a useful distinction. As long as individuals and groups—both those presumed to belong to a community and those on the outside—assume the existence of a community and base their actions accordingly, their allegiances cannot be isolated from that assumption. Communities are not stable, monolithic entities, but Patton's cautions regarding the limits of community should not be taken to mean that communities do not occur. Patton needs to offer more systematic evidence to support her insights; lacking such evidence, her provocative insights are organically speculative.

6. Jennifer L. Gilbert, *"Feminary" of Durham-Chapel Hill: Building Community through a Feminist Press,* master's thesis, Duke University, 1993. Deirdre M. Lutz, *Lavender Triangle: Evolution of the Gay and Lesbian Rights Movement in a North Carolina Community, 1969–1990,* master's thesis, University of North Carolina at Greensboro, 1991. The evidence collected to date on African-American lesbian and gay history in North Carolina is extremely limited, though it does outpace the total dearth of research into white working-class lesbian and gay histories.

The literature on lesbian and gay desire, identity, communities, and politics is both rich and expanding rapidly. The seminal works in the field include George Chauncey, *Gay New*

York: Gender, Urban Culture, and the Making of the Gay Male World, 1890–1940 (New York: Basic Books, 1994); John D'Emilio, *Sexual Politics, Sexual Communities: The Making of a Homosexual Minority in the United States, 1940–1970* (Chicago: University of Chicago Press, 1983); and Elizabeth Lapovsky Kennedy and Madeline D. Davis, *Boots of Leather, Slippers of Gold: The History of a Lesbian Community* (New York: Routledge, 1993). In addition to these works, my research is informed by extensive discussions with John Howard, especially in regard to the distinction between communities and networks. For further details, see John Howard, *Men Like That: A Southern Queer History* (Chicago: University of Chicago Press, 1999.)

For a national perspective on the divisions between lesbians and gay men in the 1970s, see John D'Emilio, "After Stonewall," in D'Emilio, ed., *Making Trouble: Essays on Gay History, Politics, and the University* (New York: Routledge, 1992), 234–74.

7. Lutz, *Lavender Triangle*. Paul Falduto and Janelle Lavelle, "Fighting CAN," *The Front Page*, November 12, 1993, Special Supplement: *Creating Change* in North Carolina, pp. 4–5.

8. Interview with Mab Segrest, August 12, 1994. Carl Wittman, "A Gay Manifesto," in Karla Jay and Allen Young, eds., *Out of the Closets: Voices of Gay Liberation* (New York: New York University Press, 1992, Twentieth Anniversary edition), 330–42. Carl Wittman, "Waves of Resistance," *Liberation* (November 1968): 29–33. Papers of Carl Wittman, in possession of the author. For further details regarding Wittman's experiences in draft resistance and gay liberation organizing, see Ian Lekus, *Queer and Present Dangers: Homosexuality and American Anti-War Organizing, 1960–1985*, Duke University, Ph.D. diss., forthcoming.

9. Interview with David Jolly, February 3, 1994. Interview with Timmer McBride, December 9, 1993. Interview with Allan Troxler, December 7, 1993. David H. Jolly, *The North Carolina Lesbian and Gay Health Survey: Final Report*, June 1985, pp. 30–35. "Largest Survey Ever on Lesbian/Gay Health," *The Front Page*, October 8, 1985, sec. 1, pp. 7–11. Papers of Carl Wittman, in possession of the author.

10. Interview with David Jolly, February 3, 1994. Interview with Timmer McBride, December 9, 1993. Jolly, *The North Carolina Lesbian and Gay Health Survey*, pp. 7–14. It is necessary to point out that for these particular populations to have the power to determine membership in a lesbian and gay community is hardly unique to Durham. Such dynamics reappear throughout modern lesbian and gay history, particularly in the quest for "respectability," from the first homophile organizations to debates of the mid-1990s over the military ban on gay service members, the campaigns for same-sex marriage rights, and the policing of public sex. Nonetheless, I will resist the temptation to place this local history in a broader perspective, because, to quote David Sabean, "the *local* is interesting precisely because it offers a *locus* for observing relations." The social relations of the local may be obscured or even disappear against the backdrop of broad comparative perspectives. David Warren Sabean, *Property, Production, and Family in Neckarhausen, 1700–1870* (New York: Cambridge University Press, 1990), 10.

11. Interview with Tony Adinolfi, February 3, 1994. Interview with Mandy Carter, February 22, 1994. Interview with Jake Lehrer, February 22, 1994. Interview with Doug Ruhren, February 13, 1994.

12. Interview with Tony Adinolfi, February 3, 1994. Interview with David Jolly, February 3, 1994. Interview with Nancy Thompson, January 28, 1994. Duke University Special Collections Library, North Carolina Lesbian and Gay Health Project Papers (hereafter LGHP

Papers), Programming and Services Series, Healthline Subseries. "Health Referrals," *The Front Page,* October 23, 1984. "The Health Project Helps and Needs Help," *The Front Page,* November 20, 1984. "Healthline Opens," *The Front Page,* April 9, 1985. Lesbian and Gay Health Project, *Newsletter,* February—March 1986, p. 3.

13. Interview with David Jolly, February 3, 1994. Interview with Nancy Thompson, January 28, 1994.

14. Interview with Riki Friedman, February 12, 1994. Interview with David Jolly, February 3, 1994. Interview with Mab Segrest, August 12, 1994. Interview with Allan Troxler, December 7, 1993. Mab Segrest, *Memoirs of a Race Traitor* (Boston: South End Press, 1994), 52–64. Carl Wittman, Obituaries, *Durham Morning Herald,* January 24, 1986, p. 14A.

15. LGHP Papers, Correspondence Series, 1983–1985. The LGHP assisted other North Carolina groups responding to the AIDS crisis, including Metrolina AIDS Project (MAP) in Charlotte, the Triad Health Project (THP) in Greensboro, and other groups in Asheville, Winston-Salem, and Wilmington. Though it appeared at first that the LGHP might act as an umbrella organization for the state, and though Healthline's referral network listed health care providers from across the state, it quickly became clear that the LGHP did not have the financial or human resources to do so, that the new organizations would function independently, and that most LGHP programming would target the Triangle area. The LGHP offered advice and assistance to these new AIDS service organizations (ASOs), such as inclusion under the LGHP's tax-exempt 501(c)(3) nonprofit status while the ASOs applied for their own tax exemption. The "North Carolina" in the LGHP's full name reflects original intentions to address the health care concerns of lesbians and gay men across the state. Interview with Timmer McBride, December 9, 1993. Interview with Dante Noto, February 11, 1994. Interview with Doug Ruhren, February 13, 1994. LGHP Papers, Community Connections Series.

This prominence included profiles and contact information in newspaper articles appearing throughout North Carolina, including a 1985 Independent Citizen Award from *The North Carolina Independent.* Grace Nordhoff, "The Lesbian and Gay Health Project: Filling the Void of Silence," *The Independent,* December 20, 1985, pp. 12–13.

16. Interview with Tony Adinolfi, February 3, 1994.

17. Ibid. Interview with Timmer McBride, December 9, 1993. Interview with Dante Noto, February 11, 1994.

18. *The Lesbian and Gay Health Project of North Carolina: 1984—A Report to the Community,* pp. 4–5. Interview with Dante Noto, February 11, 1994. Interview with Doug Ruhren, February 13, 1994.

19. Interview with Timmer McBride, December 9, 1993.

20. Interview with Tony Adinolfi, February 3, 1994.

21. Interview with Riki Friedman, February 12, 1994. Interview with Nancy Thompson, January 28, 1994.

22. LGHP, *Newsletter,* June 1986, p. 2. LGHP, *Newsletter,* June 1987, p. 4. Papers of Lester Lee, in possession of the author. Interview with Tony Adinolfi, February 3, 1994. Interview with Bernadette Carr, May 26, 1994. Interview with Godfrey Herndon, June 2, 1994. Interview with Jake Lehrer, February 22, 1994. Interview with Margie Sved, February 24, 1994.

23. "Health Project Awarded Two Grants," *The Front Page*, March 27, 1984, p. 9. Letter from Jack Beckford, Program Officer, Fund for Southern Communities, to the author, November 17, 1994. Letter from Janis DiGiovanna, Associate Director, Chicago Resource Center, to the author, April 24, 1995. *The Lesbian and Gay Health Project of North Carolina: 1984*, p. 2. Interview with Tony Adinolfi, February 3, 1994. Interview with Lester Lee, June 1, 1994. Interview with Dante Noto, February 11, 1994. Interview with Margie Sved, February 24, 1994. Interview with Nancy Thompson, January 28, 1994. LGHP Papers, Financial Papers Series, Grants Subseries.

24. Interview with Jill Duvall, March 2, 1994. Interview with Julie Johnston, May 31, 1994. Papers of Nancy Thompson, in possession of the author. Papers of Riki Friedman, in possession of the author.

25. Interview with Tony Adinolfi, February 3, 1994. Interview with Jill Duvall, March 2, 1994. Interview with Riki Friedman, February 12, 1994. Interview with Dante Noto, February 11, 1994. Interview with Nancy Thompson, January 28, 1994.

26. Interview with Jill Duvall, March 2, 1994. Letter from Tony Adinolfi to Fellow Board Members, July 19, 1989, LGHP Papers, Correspondence Series.

27. "Women in the AIDS Movement Face Criticism from Within and Without," *The Front Page*, March 7, 1989, p. 3.

28. Interview with Jill Duvall, March 2, 1994. Interview with David Jones, February 23, 1994.

While Duvall confirmed her comments challenging sexism, racism, classism, and homophobia within the gay male community, she neither remembered nor denied the comments regarding gay men's sexual practices. The article on women in AIDS activism cited above juxtaposes her criticism of unchallenged privilege and prejudice among white middle-class gay men with comments about those men's fears and ethics, *implying* that she claimed that sexual practices remained unchanged. Perhaps the only common element of this crisis agreed to by those interviewees involved was the degree to which irresponsible journalism greatly exacerbated these tensions.

29. "Internal Conflicts Challenge LGHP," *The Front Page*, June 6, 1989, p. 1.

30. Interview with Tony Adinolfi, February 3, 1994. Interview with Jill Duvall, March 2, 1994. Interview with Julie Johnston, May 31, 1994. Interview with David Jones, February 23, 1994. Interview with Lester Lee, June 1, 1994. Interview with Dante Noto, February 11, 1994. Interview with Nancy Thompson, January 28, 1994. LGHP Papers, Administrative Files, Board Minutes, March 27, 1989. "Letters" and "In Response to Your Letter . . . ," *The Front Page*, June 20, 1989, pp. 12–19. "Letters," *The Front Page*, July 18, 1989, pp. 4–5.

In between Duvall's resignation and return to the LGHP, Julie Johnston served a term as interim executive director. These clashes over structure, power, and ideology have torn apart AIDS service organizations across the industrialized world. For a comparative perspective, see Dennis Altman, *Power and Community: Organizational and Cultural Responses to AIDS* (London: Taylor & Francis, 1994).

31. Interview with Jill Duvall, March 2, 1994.

32. Ibid. Interviews with Stan Holt, March 15 and May 13, 1994. Interview with Julie Johnston, May 31, 1994. Interview with Dante Noto, February 11, 1994.

33. Interview with Jill Duvall, March 2, 1994. Interview with Julie Johnston, May 31,

1994. Interview with Lester Lee, June 1, 1994. Interview with Dante Noto, February 11, 1994. Interview with Margie Sved, February 24, 1994. Stan Holt, "God Don't Make Mistakes," *Southern Exposure* (Spring 1996): 18.

34. Interviews with Stan Holt, March 15 and May 13, 1994. Interview with David Jolly, February 3, 1994. Interview with David Jones, February 23, 1994. Interview with Dante Noto, February 11, 1994.

35. Interview with Jill Duvall, March 2, 1994. Interview with Riki Friedman, February 12, 1994. Interview with Stan Holt, May 13, 1994. Interview with Mab Segrest, August 12, 1994. For different perspectives on the connection between AIDS activism and pharmaceutical corporate philanthropy, see The ACT-UP/NY Women and AIDS Book Group, *Women, AIDS, and Activism* (Boston: South End Press, 1990), and Philip M. Kayal, *Bearing Witness: Gay Men's Health Crisis and the Politics of AIDS* (Boulder: Westview Press, 1993).

36. Marc Stein recently observed the same dynamic, arguing that ultimately "the conditions of life for lesbians and gay men in Philadelphia would be set not only in ongoing negotiations with straight society, and not only in ongoing negotiations between lesbians and gay men within their own communities, but in the ways that these two processes were intricately linked." Marc Stein, "Sex Politics in the City of Sisterly and Brotherly Loves," *Radical History Review* 59 (Spring 1994): 66.

37. Interviews with Stan Holt, March 15 and May 13, 1994. Interview with Don Jackson, July 18, 1994. Interview with Liza Rankow, July 7, 1994. For example, state and Centers for Disease Control restrictions are exemplified by regulations of the content of LGHP- and TASP-produced pamphlets for the state-funded "Reducing Our Risks" program. The program was designed to prevent HIV infections among gay and bisexual men and other men engaging in homosexual sex, through programs at bars, adult bookstores, and other places where men met to have sex with each other. The restrictions limited the ways the pamphlets could describe safer sex, including how penises were drawn, requiring the use of dictionary English rather than slang when referring to body parts or sex acts, and so on. Such regulations interfered with the ability of programs to communicate with their intended audiences through the language and images most familiar to them.

38. Interview with David Jolly, February 3, 1994. His assessment was echoed by many other interviewees.

39. Interview with Mandy Carter, February 22, 1994.

40. Interview with Jake Lehrer, February 22, 1994.

41. Interview with Mandy Carter, February 22, 1994. Interview with Godfrey Herndon, June 2, 1994. Interview with Lester Lee, June 1, 1994. Interview with Gary Lipscomb, May 23, 1994. Lutz, *Lavender Triangle,* 43–46. Hustead left the LGHP in 1987 for a position with the state government's AIDS Control Program. Since his June 13, 1988, death due to AIDS, he remains remembered by many local activists for his enthusiasm and passion for AIDS education. Wake County AIDS Service Agency named its residence house for PWAs Hustead House in his memory.

42. Interview with Godfrey Herndon, June 2, 1994. Interview with Don Jackson, July 18, 1994. Interview with Gary Lipscomb, May 23, 1994.

43. Interview with Stan Holt, March 15, 1994. See Altman, *Power and Community,* for a comparison of how gay-defined or gay-dominated ASOs have wrestled with the question

"who owns AIDS?" It must be noted that plenty of whites engage in homosexual behavior without identifying as lesbian, gay, or bisexual, and that their membership in a queer community is as contested as that of their African-American (and Latino, Asian-American, and Native-American) counterparts. In all the interviews conducted for this project, no one mentioned specific efforts to reach white men who do not identify as gay or bisexual except in general references to outreach work in adult bookstores and other spaces where men look for male sex partners.

44. Interview with Godfrey Herndon, June 2, 1994.

45. Interview with Gary Lipscomb, May 23, 1994.

46. These experiences offer evidence to support Cindy Patton's assertion that "the notion of 'community' required adherence to identity categories; yet AIDS activists were increasingly concerned to delink practices and identity, so that for example men-having-sex-with-men could recognize the risks involved without having to reorganize their identity and claim to be gay." Patton, *Inventing AIDS,* 8.

47. Interview with Stan Holt, May 13, 1994.

48. Interview with Bernadette Carr, May 26, 1994.

49. Interview with Lucy Harris, March 4, 1994. Interview with Bernadette Carr, May 26, 1994. Interview with Liza Rankow, July 7, 1994.

50. Interview with Mandy Carter, February 22, 1994. Interview with Lucy Harris, March 4, 1994. Suzy Angle, "Lesbian Health Center Plans Move Forward," *The Front Page,* June 9, 1995. As the higher rates of breast cancer among lesbians became public knowledge, some lesbians came to resent the failure of gay men to mobilize in comparable numbers on their behalf, given all the work of lesbians responding to the AIDS epidemic. Most male interviewees for this project considered the issue of breast cancer among lesbians to be very important, but the political sympathies of these men, all directly involved in the politics of health care, cannot be assumed to extend to the local gay male community as a whole.

51. Interview with Lucy Harris, March 4, 1994. Interview with Julie Johnston, May 31, 1994. Interview with Andy Knapp, March 2, 1994. Interview with Lester Lee, June 1, 1994. LGHP Papers, Community Connections Series. LGHP Papers, Financial Papers Series, Grant Subseries, AIDS Community Residence Association.

52. Beth Harrison, "LGHP Ends Search for Director," *The Front Page,* August 11, 1995, sec. 1, p. 7. "Prince Leaves LGHP Post," *The Front Page,* October 27, 1995, sec. 1, p. 20.

53. Harrison, "LGHP Ends Search for Director." Reed Williams, "Open Letter to All Lesbians," *The Front Page,* September 15, 1995, pp. 4–5. Conversations with anonymous board members.

54. Jim Duley, "LGHP Faces Financial Crisis," *The Front Page,* January 19, 1996, sec. 1, p. 17. Conversations with anonymous board members. For the record, Lucy Harris, a white lesbian, and Jerry Harris, an African-American gay man, are not related.

55. Tim Vercellotti, "Struggling Gay Group Decides to Keep Going," *Raleigh News and Observer,* March 31, 1996, p. 5B. "Is Lesbian & Gay Health Project Dead or Alive?", *Out in Black,* July / August 1996, p. 7.

56. John D'Emilio, "Homophobia and the Trajectory of Postwar American Radicalism: The Career of Bayard Rustin," in this volume's chap. 7.

57. Elsa Barkeley Brown, "'What Has Happened Here': The Politics of Difference in Women's History and Feminist Politics," *Feminist Studies* 18(2) (Summer 1992): 298.

58. Interview with Jill Duvall, March 2, 1994. Interview with Riki Friedman, February 12, 1994. Interviews with Stan Holt, March 15 and May 13, 1994. Interview with David Jones, February 23, 1994.

15

The Immigrant Infection

Images of Race, Nation, and Contagion in the Public Debates on AIDS and Immigration

JENNIFER BRIER

ON June 1, 1987, President Ronald Reagan gave his first speech exclusively devoted to Acquired Immune Deficiency Syndrome (AIDS) at the American Foundation for AIDS Research (AMFAR) Awards Dinner. The speech began with a dramatic introduction that trumpeted the ability of scientists to find a cure for the disease. Reagan then explained that AIDS was not a "casually contagious disease. . . . Experts tell us you don't get it from telephones or swimming pools or drinking fountains,"[1] a line that received widespread applause from the audience. But within minutes, boos and hisses drowned out his words in the large banquet hall when Reagan concluded his speech with a call for widespread testing of several groups of people, including couples applying for marriage licenses, inmates incarcerated in federal prisons, and foreigners seeking legal immigration status in the United States. He claimed that "AIDS is surreptitiously spreading throughout our population, and yet we have no accurate measure of its scope. It is time we knew exactly what we were facing. And that is why I support routine testing."[2] In language reminiscent of the Cold War he fought with the Soviet Union, Reagan wanted to stop the supposed invasion by finding all the people who tested positive for Human Immunodeficiency Virus (HIV). Clearly many audience members disagreed with the proposal, including Elizabeth Taylor, the founder of AMFAR, who thought testing was a flawed strategy for dealing with AIDS. But this limited display of dissent did not stop the Reagan administration's efforts to screen certain people's blood for the presence of the HIV antibody and then use the results to dictate where they could live.

Even before Reagan's call to action, a public debate about the risks and benefits of testing for HIV had been brewing for several years. While scientists and public health officials initially believed that AIDS could be spread through the sharing of blood products (semen and blood in particular), their ideas were not "scientifically" confirmed until French and American scientists identified HIV late in 1983. It took another two years for the development of a test to detect the presence of the virus. Soon after, word of the ELISA test, the fastest way to detect the existence of the HIV antibody in blood, began to appear in the news media and scientific press. Beginning with the blood-products industry's decision to test donations to blood banks in the first months of 1985, AIDS organizations and public health officials discussed the value and accuracy of the HIV test. They questioned the relationship between a positive result and the onset of AIDS, as well as the real possibility of false readings.[3] Most gay groups also opposed the test on the grounds of potential privacy violations. Would positive antibody status be used to discriminate against gay men? Would lists of infected individuals' names be kept and subsequently shared with health insurance providers? As a result of these concerns, gay organizations told people to refuse testing. People involved with helping IV drug users, a less politicized and less powerful group than gay men, took their lead from gay organizers in opposing HIV testing.[4]

Ignoring these issues and assuming that testing was an efficacious strategy to deal with the spread of AIDS, Reagan's AMFAR speech was only one manifestation of the growing desire to mark people infected with HIV. Just months before, Congress passed an amendment to the Immigration and Nationality Act (INA) that prohibited people with AIDS/HIV from seeking legal resident status. The amendment required that Immigration and Naturalization Service (INS) test all people applying for residency before they crossed the U.S. border. The congressional debates not only illuminate the production and maintenance of a naturalized connection between AIDS and outsiders, but also how foreign policy considerations influenced public health legislation. This immigration legislation existed at the nexus of domestic and foreign policy decision-making. Here the state was able to regulate relations with other nations by using arguments that focused *only* on the needs of the American people. The assumptions behind the approach inferred that U.S. citizens deserved protection from the illness brought in from the outside world. But not all U.S. citizens would find equal protection under the legislation. The legislators seemed most concerned with protecting the "general public," a group set in opposition to homosexuals, Haitians, and heroin intravenous drug users, people considered high risk by the Centers for Disease Control (CDC). Ultimately, the state would shield these citizens by externalizing the threat of AIDS and preventing it from crossing the border. In addition, by excluding infected foreigners, attention was deflected away from potential public health solutions. Policymakers tried to isolate and contain AIDS outside the country, in much the same way they did nations and ideas perceived as harmful to "democracy."

This essay looks at the rhetoric deployed in the government's decision to add HIV to the list of excludable diseases in 1987—a critical year in the first decade of the AIDS epidemic. It not only marked the passage of immigration legislation, it also witnessed a dramatic increase in public awareness of the disease. By examining the decision to contain the spread of AIDS by testing immigrants and stopping those infected with HIV in tandem with growing knowledge of the disease, it is possible to see part of the process by which AIDS was racialized and externalized in the late 1980s. While policymakers rarely spoke of race directly, images of people of color as sources of contagion suffused the public language spoken in Washington. The discourse reified notions about the causal connection between AIDS and nations other than the United States, particularly African countries. Examining this externalization process highlights the complex relationship between race and sexuality, and exposes how particular groups of people and geographic locations became dangerous in the first decade of the AIDS epidemic. The essay concludes with a description of the critiques of this policy made by several different groups. These responses focused on the xenophobic tenor of the language and legislation barring HIV-positive immigrants, who played a critical role in international, national, and local AIDS activism that culminated in civil disobedience at the 1990 International AIDS Conference in San Francisco.

Initial discussions of AIDS described Haiti as a place of origin, but by the late 1980s African nations, especially Kenya and Zaire, increasingly appeared as the epidemiological starting point for AIDS.[5] In early 1985, the *New York Times* ran a series of articles documenting the possibilities of infection among heterosexual populations in central Africa. In the first article, Lawrence Altman, the *Times*'s lead medical reporter, explained that "suspicion is growing stronger that the disease may now pose a threat to the heterosexual community, though [some medical experts] hasten to add that this suspicion is based on preliminary interpretations of figures collected mainly from Africa and Haiti and on only scant data from the United States. Other health authorities still contend, however, that the risk to heterosexuals in the United States is so small that no new public health recommendations are warranted."[6] Later in the article Altman quoted Dr. Thomas Quinn of the National Institute of Allergy and Infectious Disease: "AIDS 'is starting to break out in heterosexuals in the United States but it is primarily hitting those who are very promiscuous, and that is exactly what we see in Africa and what initially was the most common risk factor in the homosexual group in the United States.'"[7] Quinn asserted that heterosexual sex in Zaire and Rwanda was quite different from most heterosexual sex in America. Whether it was because of particular sexual practices African couples enacted or the sheer quantity of sexual activity they had with multiple partners, Americans who had heterosexual sex had little cause to worry. This categorization made the spread of AIDS to the "general" population in America unlikely because "heterosexuals" were considered completely isolated and shielded from others at risk of infection. At the same time, the unquestionable connection between AIDS and the world outside the United States was taking root. Few journalists, if any, questioned the idea that AIDS was a threat that originated outside the United States, and almost all believed that that place was Africa. According to theorist Paula Treichler, AIDS journalism in the mid 1980s "sustain[ed] our sense of what [was] true."[8]

As the popular media increasingly represented AIDS as an externalized disease, public awareness of the disease grew sharply. This can be seen in two developments occurring in 1987. First, the sheer amount of news coverage exceeded that of all the previous years combined: the *New York Times* ran just over 370 articles on AIDS in 1985, while in 1987 almost 900 pieces appeared in its pages. While quantity of coverage does not necessarily mean that the quality of public knowledge grew, it does indicate that people became more aware of AIDS as a medical disease and social problem. Knowledge about the disease also expanded with the unprecedented mailing of C. Everett Koop's *Surgeon General's Report on Acquired Immune Deficiency Syndrome* to millions of American households beginning in 1987.[9] The thirty-six page booklet gave the public information about the growing epidemic, including risk behaviors, methods of protection (both condom use and abstinence), and actions that posed no risk (children with AIDS in schools and donating blood). But these images presented contradictory ideas for most American citizens. Popular representations of AIDS portrayed the disease as one that overwhelmingly affected heterosexuals of color outside the United States and white homosexual men within America, not everyone equally.

The Public Health Service (PHS) proposal to add AIDS to the list of dangerous and contagious diseases, and the congressional debate about how that would affect immigration law, must be understood within this larger context of increasing pubic discussion of AIDS, an awareness that was shaped by ideas about sexuality, race, and citizenship. In April 1986, the PHS—the government agency charged with crafting policy to protect the public from health threats—recommended mandatory testing for all applicants seeking permanent residence in the United States, but the proposal was not finalized until May 1987.[10] The PHS first asked to bar aliens with AIDS using section 212(a)(7) of the INA, which states that "physical defects, disease or disability" can prevent the immigration process. The final proposal, and the one that was ultimately included in the legislation, maintained that immigrants with AIDS/HIV should be excluded from the United States under section 212(a)(6), which states that a "dangerous contagious disease" can bar entry. This was not a trivial distinction to make. The PHS originally justified exclusion solely on economic grounds. Immigrants who could not provide for themselves medically would become dependents of the state. By excluding only those who could not afford care, the discriminatory implications made few, if any, scientific claims. The fear was not that AIDS would spread quickly if HIV-positive immigrants entered the country, rather that too many poor people would come seeking medical care. By changing the final ruling to argue that AIDS was a "dangerous contagious disease," the government characterized infected individuals in a much more threatening way. Under 212(a)(6), the PHS implied that AIDS was an easily transmittable disease, one that could only be controlled by excluding those who carried it. This clause enabled complete interdiction, sealing the border for HIV-positive immigrants.

One week after the PHS's final recommendation, the U.S. Senate began a debate about an amendment to the INA proposed by North Carolina Republican Jesse

Helms. In this amendment, Helms called for the testing of both potential immigrants to the United States and U.S. couples seeking marriage licenses. He went on to argue that the precedent existed to exclude people if they had, and here he quoted from the statute, "'a dangerous contagious disease'."[11] Over the course of two months, the Senate twice debated the merits of the Helms amendment. The first time the amendment appeared, it called for testing soon-to-be married couples in addition to potential immigrants; the second time, only immigrants were considered. The discussions in both its content and structure relied on and expanded a longstanding association between foreigners and disease. The debates also presented immigration control policy objectives in the form of public health actions, revealing the Reagan administration's AIDS policy in general and the congressional decision in particular as substitutes for action that could actually stop the spread of the disease.

The Helms amendment was certainly not the first time Congress attempted to change the INA or limit the number and origin of immigrants entering the country. Over the course of the twentieth century, legislation had been used on many occasions to keep selected groups of "undesirable" people out of the United States. In 1882 and again in 1924, the state limited and prevented Asian immigration, basing the exclusion on racist conceptions of the Chinese. In 1952, over President Truman's veto, the Senate passed the McCarran-Walter Act that prevented the immigration of "sexual deviates" (read "homosexuals") and members of the Communist Party. Legislation in 1961 gave the PHS flexibility to change the specific grounds for exclusion based on "medical progress," under the assumption that public health officials could best determine what diseases threatened U.S. citizens.[12]

The 1987 proposal to add AIDS to the list of diseases by which an immigrant could be excluded from the United States touched on issues addressed in earlier immigration legislation but, in its oversimplification of health and economic problems, went beyond previous government actions. Neither Helms nor any of the amendment's supporters offered for the record stories of specific infected immigrants trying to enter the United States. Rather, they relied on descriptions of the African continent's ability to export the disease beyond its border to paint a picture of an imagined invasion threat for the nation. Helms stated that "the disease is no longer confined to Africa. We have all heard the statistics on Americans who have it. . . . But, the epidemic extends beyond our borders. In December 1982, the World Health Organization reported 711 cases of AIDS from 16 countries. By January 1987, 5 years later, 85 countries reported 37,872 cases of AIDS."[13] Even though Helms mentioned other countries in his remarks, only African nations ultimately appeared as dangerous. "It is not clear how many individuals infected with the virus have been allowed to enter the United States. We do know that between January 1, 1981, through and including December 1985, more than 2.8 million people have come to the United States from foreign countries. There are 43,312 persons who have emigrated here from various countries in Africa, and we know statistically that Haiti and central Africa are very high-risk areas."[14] While the text of the legislation named no specific countries, its effect was to reify a racialized image of AIDS. Helms's rhetorical strategy defied logic. He simply attached two ideas to one another, without proving a causal relationship. Helms's amendment assumed that immigrant's infected blood would find its way into America through some unnamed route of transmission.

No other senator offered scientific data for the record. Instead, Senator Steve Symms, a first-term Republican from Idaho, asked to include an article he had recently read in the June edition of *Reader's Digest* entitled "AIDS: The Plague That Knows No Bounds." John Pekkanen, the article's author, reported that the "African Crisis" was on the scale of the Black Death. Throughout the article Pekkanen compared events in central Africa, such as widespread prostitution in Zaire, to the situation in the United States, especially New York City.[15] Ultimately, the images presented on the floor of the Senate not only assumed, but also actively shaped, the identification of AIDS with Africa. The implication was that immigrants from the continent posed the greatest risk to American citizens. These would-be immigrants came from central African nations where heterosexual transmission of AIDS was "rampant." But instead of forcing the general population to see the risk inherent in unsafe sexual contact, hetero or homo, the images mollified fears growing among many heterosexuals in America that they were at risk for contracting AIDS. They could now see their own practices as fundamentally different from those of Africans, and at the same time believe they would be protected by the policy of physical exclusion.

While the Helms amendment only mentioned legal immigrants, its impact on illegal aliens soon became apparent. The Immigration Reform and Control Act of 1986 made it possible for illegal aliens to apply for amnesty, and, with the passage of the Helms amendment, those individuals would need to be tested for HIV. Arguing that "we are going to bring 2 to 6 million people into the United States that we have no idea from whence they came or how they got here," Senator Alan K. Simpson of Wyoming claimed that testing illegal immigrants was as necessary as testing legal ones.[16] The new policy could then serve as an implicit check on amnesty applications. If aliens tested positive in their physicals, whether they were infected in the United States or in their country of origin, immigration officials could force them to return home. Here the potential immigrant appeared not as an African, but rather as a Mexican attempting to cross the border in the Southwest. In support of the PHS policy of exclusion, others in the government wrote that nations would literally invade the United States by sending HIV-infected individuals to our shores. Ultimately, "the exclusion of those with HIV infection is entirely justified in the national interest on public health grounds, based on both medical and economic considerations."[17]

Senate debate on the first version of the Helms proposal did not question the testing of immigrants. Senators seemed most concerned with the section that encouraged testing soon-to-be married couples for AIDS/HIV. While the idea that heterosexuals were at risk for AIDS was still a relatively new concept, this piece of legislation assumed that testing heterosexuals couples could slow the spread within the "general" population. Most of the senators who opposed the Helms amendment pointed out that screening citizens was untenable, expensive, and even unconstitutional. Senator Daniel Patrick Moynihan, the senior Democratic senator from New York, argued that such actions would be perceived as harassment, while Senator David Durenberger, a Republican from Minnesota, claimed that the limited testing of marriage applicants would ultimately lead to universal mandatory testing.[18] Instead they wanted the government to offer voluntary HIV testing for heterosexual couples supplemented with counseling before marriage. This policy made sense, senators argued, not only because few heterosexuals had actually been exposed to the virus, but also because it would prevent falling down the "slippery slope" to forced testing of American citizens. Not one legislator hypothesized that screening the blood of immigrants would lead to universal mandatory testing. The senators, even those who opposed the Helms amendment, defined which specific group of individuals were worthy of government protection.

Those who opposed the Helms amendment because of the marriage clause implicitly accepted and contributed to the idea that Africans posed the most serious risk to Americans, and in so doing imbued that risk with racial characteristics. Senator Edward Kennedy argued for site-specific testing. Instead of testing all immigrants, the INA should require screening of people only from areas where the incidence of AIDS was high. While Kennedy never specified where those places might be, he suggested targeting businessmen, because they were the only people who had the ability to transmit the disease here. Unlike the poor immigrants who might come to the United States seeking government-sponsored medical care described by Senator Simpson, the businessmen Kennedy imagined posed a threat of AIDS transmission precisely because of their class position. They had the resources and mobility to travel from place to place, prostitute to prostitute, infecting someone new each time.[19] Kennedy's claim presented a representation of immigrant threat consistent with the original Helms amendment. Foreign businessmen were so careless in their sexual practices that they could infect the American population.

In the first round of decision-making, the opponents of the Helms amendment got their way. They defeated by a vote of 63 to 32 the amendment that called for testing immigrants and couples seeking marriage licenses.[20] Several weeks later, Helms proposed the amendment again. This time he removed the testing requirement for a marriage license, leaving only the demand that immigrants be tested. In a considerably shorter debate, the new amendment passed with 96 senators voting yes, no dissenters, and four abstentions. Clearly, most senators only opposed tests on heterosexual citizens.[21] HIV was added to a list of excludable diseases that cited five other venereal diseases, as well as infectious leprosy and active tuberculosis.[22]

At the same time, a similar debate took place in the House of Representatives. Representative Bill McCollum, a Florida Republican, introduced a bill that claimed to "curb the spread of AIDS to our citizens by denying entry by immigrants into the United States who are carrying this dreadful disease." McCollum expressed his concern by noting that "it is becoming more evident with each passing day that AIDS is just as easily spread through heterosexual contact as it is through homosexual contact. We have a major health risk for the entire society looming ahead of us. America faces a disease that is fatal and spreading. We must take steps now to do what we can to stop people who have AIDS from seeking permanent-resident status in our country and spreading the disease to Americans."[23] In McCollum's analysis, immigrants presented the largest threat to heterosexual Americans. Testing them was therefore palatable because it purported to contain AIDS outside the boundaries of the United States. With the disease isolated, Americans were safe. This model of prevention failed to describe the route of transmission. How would those "seeking permanent-residence status" spread "the disease to Americans"? Would they have heterosexual sex with citizens? Would they donate blood? Would they do these things intentionally? The epidemiological answers never materialized. But apparently the questions, alone, were enough to create a recognizable threat.

With congressional approval, Attorney General Edwin Meese announced President Reagan's policy to test both immigrants and federal prisoners.[24] Ultimately, potentially infected immigrants were the perfect people to test because the government had no duty to protect them. Better suited than the original plan to test immigrants and would-be married couples, both immigrants and federal prisoners could be imagined as dangerous to the larger American public if not isolated properly, while neither had the constitutional rights to disagree with the decision. Even Surgeon General C. Everett Koop, who opposed testing generally, accepted the need for mandatory tests of all immigrants and federal prisoners. A *New York Times* editorial appearing on the heals of Reagan's AMFAR speech rejected forced testing for everyone except these two groups.[25]

The general public also seemed convinced by the debate, even though it remained skeptical of the public health benefits. A July 1987 Gallup Poll found that 90 percent of the 1,005 people questioned felt that prospective immigrants should be tested for AIDS, and 66 percent wanted testing of all foreign visitors. Slightly fewer, 52 percent, thought all American citizens should be screened. Strangely, however, only 6 percent believed testing was the best way to prevent AIDS.[26] Even though testing would not retard the spread of AIDS, it made people feel like they were doing something. It allowed them to imagine themselves quarantined from the dangerous world around them.

With passage of the Helms amendment, the federal government now had to redefine a series of regulations to address what would happen to potential immigrants. Within months, the INS distributed screening manuals to "examining physicians worldwide," providing a detailed order of events for considering the immigration applicant for the first time. Unlike tuberculosis, where "the likelihood of transmission rather than the presence of disease determines whether an applicant is excludable," the presence of HIV alone was enough to exclude a hopeful immigrant.[27] The instructions provided a suggested script that could be enacted by the screening physician. The doctor should tell the applicant:

> A blood test for antibody to the human immunodeficiency virus (HIV) is required as a part of your medical examination. . . . Infection with HIV causes a defect in a person's natural immunity against disease. This defect leaves infected people vulnerable to serious illnesses that would not usually be a threat to anyone whose immune system was intact. This test is not to diagnose AIDS but to detect antibodies to the virus. The results of your test will be provided to a consular officer. Also, it may be necessary to report results to the health authorities in this country. A positive test result will mean that you may not be eligible to receive a visa. A positive test result could also have other local consequences on your day-to-day activities in this country.[28]

What the script did not describe was how this "defect" threatened others. There was no mention of contagion, only illness. Immigrants could contaminate America by merely entering the United States. However, if immigrants stayed in their country of origin, would the effects of the illness remain controlled and contained? While the people who argued against testing U.S. citizens cited the harmful effects of government intervention into the lives of heterosexuals, they never applied that logic to foreigners. Neither the U.S. government, nor apparently their own country's government, had a responsibility to respect their privacy rights.

Even people who sought permission to stay in the United States temporarily had to reveal their HIV status. The application for a visa questioned whether or not the applicant had HIV. If the person said he had tested positive, he could request a waiver to be granted entry into the country. But first the attorney general's office needed to grant the request, a process that required the applicant's health information to be communicated without regard to confidentiality. With the waiver approved, officials stamped the visitor's passport at the bottom with a "6," referring to the list of dangerous and infectious diseases. While this marking could have applied to any of the excludable diseases, it almost always indicated the person was HIV-positive, as officials often told people to treat other conditions and then reapply for visas.[29] With a "6" printed on his passport, the applicant could then enter the United States.

Neither legislators nor public health policymakers could provide an adequate theory of how transmission of the disease would occur if HIV-positive immigrants were allowed into the country. Entry was falsely equated with transmission of the disease. On the one hand, they assumed that the disease was easily passed from one person to another, a claim that had little, if any, scientific support. On the other, they imagined that immigrants would intentionally spread the virus because they were incapable of controlling their own actions. Even the Health and Human Services (HHS) Final Rule recognized this lacuna. HHS wrote that the decision to exclude HIV-positive immigrants was "made specifically in the context of the requirement of the Immigration and Nationality Act. This designation has not been made on the basis of any new scientific knowledge about the transmission or natural history of AIDS, nor should any such interpretation be drawn."[30] In this case, immigration control and other domestic policy agendas took precedent over scientific understanding and public health policy. Just as the lack of scientific information was not problematic in Congress, it would not cause paralysis for the INS.

By amending the INA, politicians not only substituted threat for public health action, but also created health policy guided by foreign policy objectives. That is, if the political objectives of the Cold War containment policy of the Soviet Union and its satellite states were jeopardized by the HIV rule, the foreign policy needs took precedence. The policymakers at PHS made the government's intentions clear in the Final Rule: "The potential effect of testing refugees in camps in first-asylum countries and the difficulties posed by some admissions programs, such as those for Soviet Jews, Vietnamese, and Cuban political prisoners, are of particular concern. The Department will work closely with the Department of State to ensure that the testing program is implemented with respect to refugees in a way that will protect both the affected refugees and U.S. foreign and humanitarian policy interests served by the refugee admissions program."[31] Unlike the policy that sent potential Haitian immigrants fleeing a dictatorial regime to detention camps at the military base in Guantanamo Bay, Cuba, the imperative to isolate Soviet allies politically and physically would not be disrupted by the need to test and restrain infectious immigrants. Whenever possible, the U.S. would accept refugees from the Soviet bloc regardless of HIV status.

The containment ideology promulgated by Cold War foreign policy affected more than relations with the Soviet Union; it also shaped domestic policy decisions. The Reagan administration's attempt to shrink social services, under the guise of helping the poor, has been well documented by a wide range of people, including academics, public intellectuals, and people who experienced the breakdown of the welfare state firsthand.[32] At one level, the debate over adding AIDS to the list of excludable diseases could be read as just that. Testing allowed for the appearance of action but ultimately did little to control the spread of HIV within the United States. However, unlike what historians of the Reagan administration have described as complete inaction on AIDS, clearly the administration's policies amounted to much more than inactivity. The decisions reflected what political scientist Michael Rogin sees as Reagan's unique ability to "split the good within the country from the bad without. Evil, he reassures us, is out there in visible spots that can be identified and removed."[33] The isolation model enacted to contain AIDS within the nations where the disease supposedly originated worked well in combination with an ideology that marked homosexuals outside the moral order of American life. With the groups most likely to infect the American public identified, and even visibly marked in the case of immigrants, the disease's surreptitious spread ceased.

While the federal government mobilized a potent trope of foreigners infected with AIDS, it was not the only image created in the public sphere. In opposition to the government policy of exclusion, a diverse group of associations formulated action plans to address the problems of HIV infection in America. From legal associations to international health organizations to grassroots activists, these varied positions had mixed results. Ultimately, the responses using direct action techniques of boycott and protest, spearheaded by activists, presented a powerful alternative vision of the AIDS crisis at the local, national, and international levels.

Days after the Helms amendment passed, the American Civil Liberties Union's (ACLU) Nan Hunter, in a *New York Times* op-ed piece, called the policy "too little, too late and tragically beside the point."[34] In the ACLU Annual Report, the organization went even further, claiming that the United States was "much more an 'exporter' than an 'importer' of AIDS."[35] In so doing, the ACLU presented an argument that turned the idea that AIDS originated in Africa on its head. The United States could be viewed as an original source for AIDS. Monica Hernandez, a member of the Coalition for Immigrant and Refugee Rights and Services HIV/Immigration Task Force, formed in December 1987, argued that most of the people who would be tested under the 1986 amnesty had lived in the United States for at least eight years.[36] The unmistakable implication was that these people had been infected within American borders, not in their native lands.

Outside the United States, the World Health Organization (WHO) also opposed the policy of testing immigrants. The international health group, with connections to the United Nations, contended: "The social and political consequences following imposition of an HIV screening programme for international travellers could include a marked deterioration of bilateral or regional relations and the heightened stigmatization of certain groups or nationalities. These effects would likely be aggravated if the screening programme were to be applied according to geographical or geopolitical criteria."[37] Interestingly, this argument pointed out that health objectives could actually work against geopolitical goals. WHO predicted that other nations would be angered by the association with AIDS to such an extent that relations could be strained. This attacked the premise behind the U.S. HIV-containment policy. Despite such conclusions, no national or international organization was able to change the course of the legislation in 1987.

On a more local level, the course of events was quite different. Looking at the development of protest in San Francisco, California, provides an opportunity to understand the complicated nature of AIDS activism in America in the late 1980s. San Francisco was unique in two important ways. First, as one of the hardest hit cities in the AIDS epidemic, San Francisco had a large number of AIDS agencies. In addition to organizational strength, the city had an active history of AIDS protest. This was driven, in part, by a vocal gay voting bloc, well tied to the Democratic Party machine. Second, the 1990 International AIDS Conference was scheduled to meet in the city. This event had profound implications for those who objected to the immigration policy of HIV exclusion.

Long before the government's immigration decision, the Third World AIDS Advisory Task Force (TWAATF) was formed out of a series of community meetings that included participants from the Human Rights Commission and the San Francisco AIDS Foundation (SFAF), the oldest AIDS organization in the city. In Fall 1983, TWAATF, an association composed exclusively of people of color, began to serve the needs of people in underrepresented communities.[38] By the end of 1985, TWAATF wrote a public health brochure entitled "Information for People of Color." The SFAF then produced the pamphlet in one of its first attempts to reach out to groups other than the largely white, gay male community. Less than a year later, TWAATF planned and coordinated the first Western Regional Conference on AIDS and Ethnic Minorities, held at University of California-San Francisco (UCSF).[39] By 1987, with years of activism behind it, TWAATF criticized the new legislation that sought to control immigration. At the monthly meeting that coincided with its passage, members discussed the implications of the law for "Third World people," arguing that they would be disproportionately affected. Here, the membership reasoned that immigrants and people of color in the United States were viewed similarly by those in power. TWAATF presented an alternative construction of the "slippery slope" alluded to in the congressional debate. In this case, TWAATF reasoned that once mandatory testing happened for immigrants, people of color in America would not be far behind. Both groups were represented as dangerous people whose actions needed to be monitored, either in the form of residence exclusion or limitations to welfare.[40]

TWAATF, and other San Francisco AIDS associations, laid the groundwork for the most visible and, one might argue, lasting public disagreement with the Helms amendment: the international boycott of, and mass protest at, the VI International AIDS Conference held in San Francisco in 1990. In the five years before the 1990 conference, scientists, public health professionals, and some activists from across the globe attended the annual conference without much incidence.[41] But the San Francisco meeting proceeded much differently precisely because of the immigration restrictions that kept even HIV-positive visitors out of the country. For the first time, conference attendees were prevented from participating in the event.

The City of San Francisco tried to combat the legislation. Mayor Art Agnos made San Francisco a "City of Refuge" on October 24, 1989. He ordered that "no department, agency, commission, officer or employee of the City shall use any funds of resources to assist in the enforcement of federal immigration law or to gather or disseminate information regarding the immigration status of individuals in the City unless required by state or federal law."[42] In creating this legislation, Agnos defied the ban enacted by the immigration amendment. But even this action could do little to allow people access at the border.

More than eighty-five AIDS organizations and thousands of activists did not participate in the meeting. From the League of Red Cross and Red Crescent Societies to Britain's largest AIDS organization, the Terrence Higgins Trust, groups explicitly protested the U.S. government's policy of excluding HIV-positive foreigners by refusing to even register at the 1990 conference. Some groups even went further: TWAATF cosponsored the AIDS Activists Conference held concurrently at the Women's Building in the Mission District.[43]

With the international boycott limiting the number of participants at the 1990 conference, members of the AIDS Coalition to Unleash Power (ACT UP) changed the tenor of protests by orchestrating a demonstration for each day of the week-long conference. The grassroots group used direct action techniques of marching and civil disobedience to insert a dissenting voice into the discussions at the meeting. Members demanded better health care, faster drug approval, and an end to discrimination against people with AIDS.[44] For the most part, each protest was a tightly choreographed event, a process that prevented all but limited confrontations with the police.[45]

Direct action against the U.S. government's immigration restrictions took the form of three separate protests and were the only demonstrations in which the police used force. On the evening before the 1990 conference began, several hundred members of ACT UP paraded past the local offices of the INS. The Federal Protective Service, with the help of the San Francisco Police Department (SFPD), barricaded the building. Some of the activists attempted to break through the blockade and were arrested.[46] Several days later a similar protest took place in downtown San Francisco. On June 23, conference planners and participants joined ACT UP members in a march through the city. Generally peaceful, the march turned violent when police contained people near the INS building. The *New York Times* reported that "then, as mandated by the department's new crowd control manual, the commanding officer warned that batons would be used if demonstrators did not desist. When banging of the barricades continued, officers struck the protesters' hands, bruising and bloodying knuckles."[47] The protests ended at the closing session of the conference, an event that featured a speech by Dr. Louis Sullivan, Secretary of the Department of Health and Human Services. Protesters drowned out Sullivan's speech with whistles and air horns. Among other things, the demonstrators criticized the government's immigration restrictions.[48]

The ACT UP protesters at the conference called attention to the limits placed on public health policy by the Helms amendment to the Immigration and Nationality Act. They would stop any and all discussions of AIDS treatment and prevention that excluded HIV-positive foreigners. In so doing, they rearticulated a critique that had its roots in older AIDS organizations. The argument was quite simple: the disease was not contagious, was not spread through casual contact, and therefore did not require public health measures that treated AIDS the way leprosy had been approached earlier in the century. Discrimination against people with AIDS was a substitute for neither treatment nor prevention.

In the aftermath of the events in San Francisco, Congress proposed legislation that would have allowed the Department of Health and Human Services to remove AIDS from the list of excludable diseases, but the measure did not pass.[49] Throughout the course of the 1987 congressional debates, foreign policy agendas took priority over those that would protect the public's health. The strategies were anything but inaction. In the case of Helms's proposal, the Senate unanimously favored a policy of containment instead of ones that promoted treatment and prevention. Looking at the language and rhetoric of those debates has opened a window into the constructions and implications of governmental policy actions.

Analyzing the government's actions in this brief yet critical period of 1987–1990 also pushes us toward a historical account of AIDS, particularly by exposing the changing images of the disease. Once HIV infection could be used as grounds for excluding residence seekers, blame for AIDS was effectively displaced outside the United States, in terms of origin and spread, etiology and epidemiology. Initially linked exclusively with Haiti and Africa, it now threatened Americans precisely because it could come from anywhere in the world. According to those in favor of testing immigrants, AIDS could be stopped at the physical border of the nation. That illusion of containment obfuscated the need for more internal solutions. While AIDS was becoming a global crisis by the late 1980s, the domestic course of the epidemic required strategies that emphasized education and prevention, not identification and control.

Notes

Acknowledgment: I would like to thank the members of the 1998–1999 Black Atlantic Seminar at the Rutgers Center for Historical Analysis for their comments on this essay. Karen Balcom and Steve Brier each read an even earlier draft and offered sound criticisms and suggestions. Roxanne Panchasi provided an invaluable reading of the final draft.

1. Ronald Reagan, "Remarks to the American Foundation For AIDS Research Awards Dinner," May 31, 1987, Ronald Reagan Library, Robert Sweet Files, Box OA 16629, folder HPWG: AIDS #2 [2 of 6], 2.

2. Ibid., 4. See also Philip Boffey, "Reagan Urges Wide AIDS Testing but Does Not Call for Compulsion," *New York Times* (*NYT*), June 1, 1987, p. A1.

3. Cindy Patton, *Inventing AIDS* (New York: Routledge, 1990) 32–34. She provides a useful description of the differences between the ELISA and Western Blot tests.

4. Ronald Bayer, *Private Acts, Social Consequences* (New Brunswick: Rutgers University Press, 1991), chaps. 4 and 5. See also Patton, *Inventing Aids,* 36–40.

5. The connections between AIDS and Haiti are almost as old as the association between AIDS and gay men. Haitians faced discrimination almost immediately. They were stigmatized and marked as an AIDS threat, even though little, if any, scientific evidence could connect Haiti or Haitians with AIDS. For work on Haiti see Paul Farmer, *AIDS and Accusation: Haiti and the Geography of Blame* (Berkeley: University of California Press, 1992); Paula Treichler, "AIDS and HIV Infection in the Third World: A First World Chronicle," in *AIDS: The Making of a Chronic Disease,* ed. Elizabeth Fee and Daniel Fox (Berkeley: UC Press, 1992), 377–412. Treichler's recent monograph puts together her work on AIDS over the last decade; see Paula Treichler, *How to Have Theory in an Epidemic: Cultural Chronicles of AIDS* (Durham: Duke, 1999). Two theorists in particular have talked about how the process of differentiation between Americans and Africans works in the popular media. See Cindy Patton, "From Nation to Family: Containing African AIDS," in *The Lesbian and Gay Studies Reader,* ed. Henry Abelove et al. (New York: Routledge, 1993), 127–40; and Simon Watney, "Missionary Positions: AIDS, 'Africa,' and Race," *Differences* 1 (1989). I hope to show here how similar ideas were circulating in other arenas.

6. Lawrence Altman, "Heterosexuals and AIDS: New Data Examined," *NYT,* January 22, 1985, p. C1.

7. Ibid., p. C11.

8. Treichler, "First World," 383.

9. C. Everett Koop, *Surgeon General's Report on Acquired Immune Deficiency Syndrome* (U.S. Department of Health and Human Services, 1986). For reports of dissemination see C. Everett Koop, M.D., *Koop: The Memoirs of American's Family Doctor* (New York: Random House, 1991), 234–37; Gerry Studds, "Distribute the Surgeon General's Report on AIDS," *Congressional Record—House* (*CR-H*), Extension of Remarks, May 21, 1987, p. 13673. Discussion about AIDS and immigration began in the Senate on May 21, 1987.

10. See House Committee on the Judiciary, *Grounds for Exclusion of Aliens under the Immigration and Nationality Act,* 100th Cong., 2d sess., September 1988, pp. 73 and 85. See also Bernard Weinraub, "Health Officials Seek AIDS Test for Immigrants," *NYT,* May 16, 1987, p. A1.

11. Jesse Helms, *Congressional Record—Senate* (*CR-S*), May 21, 1987, pp. 13451–2.

12. House Committee on the Judiciary, *Grounds for Exclusion of Aliens under the Immigration and Nationality Act,* 100th Cong., 2d sess., September 1988, pp. 74–76. The McCarran-Walter Act was not fully rescinded until October 1990. See "Two Reasons to Rejoice on Immigration," *NYT,* October 29, 1990, p. A20. For a historical overview of the specific connections between immigration control and disease see Alan Kraut, *Silent Travelers: Germs, Genes, and the "Immigrant Menace"* (New York: Basic Books, 1994); David Reimers, *Unwelcome Strangers: American Identity and the Turn against Immigration* (New York: Columbia University, 1998).

13. Helms, *CR-S,* June 2, 1987, p. 14285.

14. Ibid., p. 14285.

15. Steve Symms, *CR-S,* May 21, 1987, pp. 13460–3. The connection between central Africa and New York City was regularly made in the late 1980s and early 1990s. The assumed similarities between places were most likely the result of high rate of HIV infection among people of color in New York City in the mid-1980s, as contrasted to San Francisco where the population most affected was white gay men.

16. Alan Simpson, *CR-S,* May 21, 1987, p. 13464. For a good discussion of the 1986 Reform Act see Michael C. LeMay, *Anatomy of a Public Policy: The Reform of Contemporary American Immigration Law* (Westport: Praeger, 1994).

17. The quote was included in the Final Rule published in Department of Health and Human Services, 42 CFR Part 34, *Federal Register,* August 28, 1987, p. 32543.

18. Daniel Patrick Moynihan, *CR-S,* May 21, 1987, p. 13466, and David Durenberger, *CR-S,* May 21, 1987, pp. 1468–71.

19. Edward Kennedy, *CR-S,* May 21, 1987, p. 13454. This sentiment about businessmen was echoed in the popular press only a few months earlier. See "A One Man AIDS Epidemic," *U.S. News and World Report* (January 12, 1987): 65.

20. Jonathan Fuerbringer, "Senate Votes to Require Tests of Aliens for AIDS Virus," *NYT,* June 3, 1987, p. B8.

21. Roll Call Vote No. 142 Leg., *CR-S,* June 2, 1987, p. 14290. One of the four senators who did not vote was Bob Dole. He believed that false positives meant that marriage applicants should not be tested because the risk of incorrect results were likely and quite painful. He did not, however, apply this argument to immigrants.

22. House Committee on the Judiciary, *Grounds for Exclusion of Aliens under the Immigration and Nationality Act,* 100th Cong., 2d sess., September 1988, p. 84.

23. Bill McCollum, "Aliens with AIDS," *CR-H,* June 3, 1987, p. 14602.

24. Department of Justice, "For Immediate Release," Press Release, June 7, 1987, Ronald Reagan Library, Robert Sweet Files, Box OA 16629, folder "HPWG: AIDS #2 [4 of 6]," 1. See also Robert Pear, "AIDS Test Ordered for U.S. Prisoners and Immigration," *NYT,* June 9, 1987, p. A1. I have not discussed in this essay the process by which federal prisoners were added to the list of testable people. For the most part, no debate on this piece of the proposal happened; more historical work needs to be done on AIDS policy created for the prison population.

25. For Koop see *NYT,* June 1, 1987, p. B5; Editorial, "Forced AIDS Tests. Then What?", *NYT,* June 7, 1987, sec. 9, p. 28.

26. CRS Report for Congress, *American Public Opinion on AIDS,* February 1989, p. 20.

27. Department of Health and Human Services, 42 CFR Part 34, Federal Register, August 28, 1987, p. 32541.

28. Centers for Disease Control, *Technical Instructions for Medical Examination of Aliens,* 1991, pp. III-1, III-5 (http://www.cdc.gov/ncidod/dq/pdf/ti-alien.pdf). While this is the not the manual first created after the Helms amendment, it is the only one available.

29. Barbara Wallace to Dr. June Osborne, November 29, 1989, in House Committee on Energy and Commerce, *HHS Authority Over Immigration and Public Health,* 101st Cong., 2d sess., June 27, 1990, p. 58.

30. Department of Health and Human Services, 42 CFR Part 34, *Federal Register,* June 8, 1987, p. 21532.

31. Department of Health and Human Services, *Federal Register,* August 28, 1987, p. 32542.

32. The academic work on AIDS over the last ten to fifteen years has documented the critical lack of attention the Reagan administration paid to the growing problem of AIDS in the 1980s. For works on Reagan's presidency see Paul Boyer, ed., *Reagan as President:*

Contemporary Views of the Man, His Politics, and His Policies (Chicago: Ivan R. Dee, 1990); Lou Cannon, *President Reagan: The Role of a Lifetime* (New York: Simon and Schuster, 1991); Haynes Johnson, *Sleepwalking through History: America in the Reagan Years* (New York: Norton, 1991); and Michael Paul Rogin, *Ronald Reagan, The Movie* (Berkeley: University of California, 1987). Cheryl Cole, "Containing AIDS: Magic Johnson and Post[Reagan] America," in *Queer Theory/Sociology,* ed. Steven Seidman (Cambridge: Blackwell, 1996), looks at Reagan's ideological connection to AIDS and the politics of race in the 1980s. Even Koop's autobiography describes the president's failure to address AIDS fully.

33. Rogin, *Ronald Reagan,* xvii.

34. Nan D. Hunter, "Reagan's 'Weak, Coercive' AIDS Plan," *NYT,* June 12, 1987, p. A31.

35. ACLU, "Annual Report," Report, 1987–88, Princeton Library, ACLU Records, Box 390, folder 3, p. 10.

36. Monica Hernandez, "The Immigrant's Dilemma: HIV Testing and Amnesty," *Multicultural Inquiry and Research on AIDS Quarterly Newsletter* (*MIRA*), 4(2) (Spring 1990): 1. (Housed in AIDS Office Collection at the San Francisco Public Library.)

37. Special Programme on AIDS World Health Organization, "Report of the Consultation on International Travel and HIV Infection," Pamphlet, March 2–3, 1987, New York Public Library (NYPL), Lawrence Mass Collection, Box 14, folder "Printed Material about AIDS," p. 6.

38. For work that investigates the failure of both the government and AIDS activists to address the needs of people of color within the United States see Cathy Cohen, *The Boundaries of Blackness: AIDS and the Breakdown of Black Politics* (Chicago: University of Chicago, 1999); Cathy Cohen, "Contested Membership: Black Gay Identities and the Politics of AIDS," in *Queer Theory/Sociology,* ed. Steven Seidman (Cambridge, Mass.: Blackwell, 1996); Evelynn Hammonds, "Race, Sex, AIDS: The Construction of 'Other'," *Radical America* 20 (1987): 328–40; Evelynn Hammonds, "Seeing AIDS: Race, Gender, and Representation," in *The Gender Politics of HIV/AIDS in Women: Perspectives on the Pandemic in the United States,* ed. Nancy Goldstein (New York: New York University, 1997), 113–26.

39. TWAATF, "Organizational Chart," Report, August 12, 1986, UCSF Special Collections, TWAATF Records, Box 1, folder "History, Organization, and Policy Statements (1987–1991)."

40. "Minutes of meeting held on June 10, 1987," TWAATF Records, Box 1, folder "Meeting Minutes (9/86–10/90)." This sentiment was echoed by the National Minority AIDS Council. "But as citizens of color who are considered by many lawmakers as among that population directly responsible for overburdening the health and welfare systems, we must consider their action as one in a series that will play itself out against all of us fighting against both the spread of HIV and the discrimination against those infected with HIV. We must not miss this opportunity to stop what is intended by many to become the basis for a federal government ruling on mandatory testing and discrimination in all of the communities impacted by HIV." National Minority AIDS Council, "HIV: A National Public Health Threat," 1990, San Francisco Public Library, AO Records, Carton 6, folder "Immigration Law and HIV," p. 1.

41. The conference in Montreal the year before also witnessed protests by ACT UP, but the direct actions did not address travel restrictions. For good descriptions of the protests

in 1989 see Media Committee ACT UP, "ACT UP Takes Over Montreal, Media Report," Report, June 4–9, 1989, NYPL, ACT UP/NY Records, Box 1, folder 4. Ronald Rowell, "Special Issue: Transition for NMAC," 1989, TWAATF Records, Box 1, folder "General POC Events, Issues and Clippings."

42. David Werdegar (San Francisco's Director of Health), Memo sent to all employees, April 20, 1990, TWAATF Records, Box 1, folder "Immigration."

43. "Resolution," April 11, 1990, TWAATF Records, folder "History, Organization, and Policy Statements (1987–1991)."

44. For works on the formation of ACT UP, as well as the kinds of political strategies the group used, see Peter Cohen, "'All They Needed': AIDS, Consumption, and the Politics of Class," *Journal of the History of Sexuality* 8 (1997): 86–115; Gilbert Elbaz, "The Sociology of AIDS Activism: The Case of ACT UP/New York, 1987–1992" (Ph.D. diss., CUNY, 1992); Maxine Wolfe, "The AIDS Coalition to Unleash Power (ACT UP): A Direct Model of Community Research for AIDS Prevention," in *AIDS Prevention and Services: Community Based Research*, ed. Johannes P. Van Vugt (Westport: Bergin and Garvey, 1994), 217–48.

45. Jane Gross, "City Hears Harmony, with a Few Jarring Notes," *NYT*, June 24, 1990, p. A23. The police also attempted to limit their own reactions. Recognizing the problems the city would face if the world witnessed protesters beaten by police, the SFPD trained officers to disperse demonstrators. See Jane Gross, "Warily, San Francisco Braces for AIDS Forum," *NYT*, June 18, 1990, p. A14.

46. Jane Gross, "Immigration Laws Protested on Eve of AIDS Conference," *NYT*, June 20, 1990, p. A15.

47. Gross, "City Hears Harmony," p. A23.

48. Philip J. Hilts, "Jeers at AIDS Gathering Drown Out Health Chief," *NYT*, June 25, 1990, p. A12.

49. Amy Fairchild, "Policies of Containment: Immigration in an Era of AIDS," *American Journal of Public Health* 12(84) (1994): 2011–22.

16

The Myth of Lesbian (In)Visibility

World War II and the Current "Gays in the Military" Debate

LEISA D. MEYER

THIS essay emerged from my initial confusion and eventual irritation over the ways in which the debate about "homosexual" military service has been framed these last several years. The crux of my disorientation was the product of two contradictory issues: first, the "gays in the military" public debate and academic response seemed to only briefly and infrequently address lesbians; second, I knew that most evidence suggests that lesbians in the military have been from four to ten times more likely to be targeted and discharged for homosexuality than gay men.[1] This essay, then, is a product of my attempt to reconcile this seeming paradox.

Initially, I thought that the invisibility of lesbian military personnel within the "gays in the military" debate might be due to the chronic invisibility of women in the military generally. This invisibility can certainly in part be explained by the smaller numbers of women relative to men in the military. And ironically, this invisibility can also in part be explained through the incidents of "visibility" that gain public attention. I am speaking here of the most recent occasions during which public attention has been directed (by military leaders and the press) to the consequences of a female military presence: the media and military portrayal of women as "victims" in either sexual scandals or of misguided military "affirmative action" policies that bring allegedly "untrained" women into "nontraditional" (read "male") positions of power and authority with tragic results. These "incidents" of "visibility" highlight women's status as at best "nonmilitary" and at worst as a danger to the American military's mission.

The lack of attention to lesbians in the current debate might also be a factor of the intensive public focus on the ramifications for openly including gay men in the military and the many questions about the crisis of "masculinity" that such acceptance raises. Would men be "cruising" other men, "looking" at other men in the same ways that some men "cruised" and "looked" at women? In other words, would some men be the "objects" of other men's desires or "gazes"? I was equally confused, however, by the frequent invocation of the "close quarters" of a submarine and male "showers" as the sites of a great deal of this hysteria. These anxieties seemed to coexist with the as-frequent manifestation of the stereotype of the effeminate gay man or "limp-wristed fairy" as antithetical to the "hypermasculine" ethos of, say, the Marine Corps. Neither image, however, easily lends itself to the implicit (and often explicit) reference to "predators" that the anti-gay "shower" discourse seemed to evoke. In fact, the "predatory" inflection of the anti-gay rhetoric that was and is rife in this debate more aptly suggests long-held cultural stereotypes of lesbians as "masculinized" women "preying" on their more "feminine" counterparts. So, why were lesbians so absent from this controversy?

The lack of popular attention to the question of a lesbian presence within the military, or the "invisibility" of lesbians in current debates about "gays in the military," is also mirrored by scholars' interpretations of the lack of formal military policies addressing lesbians or "female homosexuals" historically as a decisive indicator that overall lesbians were ignored, tolerated, or a less significant threat than gay men within the military institution. I would like to suggest that this tale of toleration does not tell the whole story. Focusing on the formal regulation of sexual acts based on a male military model regulating the sexuality of gay men misses the extent to which the issue of female masculinity or "mannishness" became one of the major informal means through which issues of lesbianism were addressed and lesbian soldiers themselves were "regulated."[2]

Through a brief comparison of the situations of lesbians in the WWII army and in today's military I argue that the particular position of lesbians within the military, both historically and currently, can only be understood by situating lesbians not only as "homosexuals" within a largely heterosexual and homophobic military but also as women within a predominantly male and misogynistic institution. In other words, frameworks that highlight *both* gender (as it specifically applies to women) and sexual hierarchies in the military are required to illuminate the experience of lesbian soldiers. In saying this I am suggesting that one of the unexamined implications of lesbian absence from both contemporary debates as well as historical regulatory frameworks is the broad-based and "commonsense" assumption of a lesbian presence (or suspected lesbian presence) within the "ultimate" masculine institution of the military.

Part of this assumption is supported by the oppositional division between the concepts "woman" and "soldier," an opposition based on constructions of military service as a critical measure of cultural "masculinity." It is also one that begs the question, if the military turns "boys into men" what does it turn women into? What is a "female soldier"?

Historically and currently this question has defined the parameters of the double bind facing military women—to be a "good soldier" is to be *ipso facto* masculine. Military women during WWII and today, then, could be *too* good at soldiering and therefore vulnerable to accusations of masculine appearance and behavior. Or, if they performed poorly, they might be deemed incompetent because of their "femininity." This framework under which female soldiers operated required a defensive posture from women; in effect they had to walk a tightrope trying to appear not to challenge male power in the military while proving their ability to do all that men can do.

Cultural associations between "masculine" women and female homosexuality formed the basis for public suspicions during WWII that at least some female soldiers would be lesbian. While gay men were perceived as a threat to the military because they were homosexual, their presence did not necessarily endanger *men's* position within the military generally. In contrast, accusations of lesbianism within the Women's Army Corps (WAC)[3] and other women's services were the embodiment of cultural anxieties over the disruption of gender and sexual norms seen as potentially following from women's entrance into the military. The entirety of women's military experience was organized against the cultural assumption that military women were masculine and masculine women were lesbians. In response, the female administration of the WAC designed enlistment and discharge criteria that were distinct from the male military and that were organized around defining "respectable" behavior and appearance in ways that excluded "masculine" women on the grounds of gender deviance, not sexual transgression.

Within the WAC regulatory framework a woman's expressed desire to join the military could in itself be cause for suspicion, because "real women" would not want to be "soldiers" at all. In fact, popularly articulated fears of the kind of woman who might flourish in a martial environment were rife with allusions to lesbianism. Jack Kofoed, a reporter for the *Miami Florida News,* for instance, could imagine no "female soldiers" other than "the naked amazons . . . and the queer damozels of the isle of lesbos."[4] One female reporter, pleasantly surprised at the appointment of the "feminine" Oveta Culp Hobby to head the women's corps, wrote that "left to guess, most of us would have said that if ever a woman's army got under way in this country a man or an unmarried woman with worlds of experience and a *Gertrude Stein haircut* would direct it."[5] Although explicit references to female homosexuality in the women's corps were seldom made in the mainstream press, army reports addressing public opinion about the WAC demonstrated that public concern with female homosexuality was pervasive.[6]

Fears that the WAC would either attract or produce lesbians were in part generated by what historian Esther Newton has called the "fusion of masculinity, feminist aspirations, and lesbianism."[7] Women's entrance into the military and their assumed usurpation of men's duties, for instance, became a symbol of women claiming traditionally male power. In contrast, joining the military reinforced men's claim to a "masculine" identity that was presumed to be a heterosexual one as well. WAC director Colonel Oveta Culp Hobby articulated this connection between mannishness, female power, and lesbianism in a postwar interview in which she drew an analogy between women's claim to suffrage and women's entrance into the military, stating that "just as a startled public was once sure that woman's suffrage would make women unwomanly, so the thought of 'woman soldiers' caused some people to assume that WAC units would be hotbeds of perversion."[8] As the official WAC historian Mattie Treadwell recalled, during WWII there was a "public impression that a women's corps would be the ideal breeding ground" for homosexuality because of the "mistaken" popular belief that "any woman who was masculine in appearance or dress" was a homosexual.[9]

It was within this context that the female leaders of the WAC created a regulatory framework that focused not only on specific sexual "acts," but more importantly on the "appearance" of impropriety as a means of eliminating women they deemed dangerous to the corps' reputation and legitimacy. Most WAC policies that affected lesbians, for instance, were not specifically addressed toward female homosexuals but fell within this larger WAC regulatory system addressing female sexuality in general. The predominant concern of this design, based in WAC policies regulating women's "conduct," was to portray women within the corps as sexually respectable and to eliminate those whose *behavior* or *appearance* undermined this goal. In contrast to their male counterparts, then, Wacs could be discharged not only for actions that were deemed inappropriate by WAC leaders, but for "seeming" (through dress or circumstance) to act in inappropriate ways.

Within this regulatory paradigm, sexual agency in general was defined as a threat to the legitimacy of the women's corps, no matter *who* was the object choice of the female sexual actor. Wacs who acted on their sexual desires were violating both gender and sexual norms, as the potentially "masculinizing" effect of the military on women was not only defined as women's taking on male characteristics, appearance, and power, but also as women adopting an aggressive, independent, and "masculine" sexuality.[10] Within this framework, "masculine" appearance and behavior, not only sexual acts between women, were the key criteria for defining the "lesbian threat" within the corps. Consequently, throughout the war, the WAC administration's efforts to address the "problem" of female masculinity were aimed at women whose dress, demeanor, and/or behavior linked them with the popular cultural stereotype of the "mannish lesbian" who was by definition a sexual agent.[11]

The procedures developed by WAC officials for evaluating applicants to the corps did not specifically address lesbians until the war was near an end. Because the WAC was a volunteer organization whose requirements for enlistment were much higher than those used by the army to rate men, military leaders and psychiatrists affiliated with the women's corps believed that the process of self-selection would be sufficient for screening out "undesirables."[12] Yet, while no formal system for identifying lesbians existed, the WAC *did* develop and use screening procedures that were partially aimed at detecting and rejecting lesbian applicants to the corps. This informal setup focused on class background, education, personality, and behavior and worked to eliminate women who demonstrated characteristics culturally associated with female homosexuality. WAC policies for selecting women for the first "Officer Candidate" class and for subsequent officer training, for instance, included criteria for the exclusion of women whose manner was "rough or coarse," whose build was "stocky or shapeless," and whose demeanor, including dress and "voice type," was "masculine." While these policies did not name *lesbians* as persons to be refused admission to the corps, WAC leaders' efforts to eliminate "masculine" women from the corps most likely resulted in some female homosexuals being denied entrance.[13]

Within the WAC regulatory paradigm, however, not all lesbians were considered equally threatening; class and cultural divisions made some same-sex female relationships more acceptable than others. Certainly butch/femme couples (consisting of a "masculine" and "feminine" partner) were the most recognizable lesbians during the 1940s, but their culture defined only one tier of a class system of relationships between women that existed in the twentieth century. While butch/femme culture and butch/femme dyads were a largely working-class phenomenon, for instance, these cultural creations were paralleled by the continuation of traditions of "romantic friendships" between white middle-class and upper-class women.[14] The middle- and upper-class predominantly white women who were involved in these "romantic friendships" structured their associations in relation to contemporary standards of white, middle-class sexual morality, including their de-emphasis of explicitly sexual components in their ties to other women. The differential treatment and perception of butch/femme women vis-à-vis those women involved in "romantic friendships" paralleled popular assumptions and psychiatric understandings of the class-based nature of heterosexual behaviors. Contemporary Euro-American middle- and upper-class cultural attitudes toward working-class people ascribed to them a more vulgar and obvious sexuality and assumed their greater sexual immorality. Both the greater visibility and assumptions about sexual aggressiveness contributed to the general hostility toward butch women.[15]

The formal and informal procedures for dealing with "suspected" lesbians within the women's corps were consistent with this larger framework and supported WAC leaders' overall emphasis on the recruitment of white middle-class women into the corps. "Romantic friendships" were often "tolerated," although not encouraged; so long as they remained invisible to the public, they were not considered a threat to the larger aims of the WAC sexual regulatory system, which defined threats to the public legitimacy of the corps as the primary criterion for punishing sexual misbehavior. Rooting out lesbians who maintained their "femininity," and did not call attention to themselves, would have made the "lesbian problem" more visible to the public than the WAC leadership desired.

Thus, Wacs' appearance played a crucial role in public accusations of lesbianism and informed the responses of the WAC administration to allegations that the military "masculinized" women. As the focus of constant public criticism during WWII, the WAC uniform became one area in which the "problem" of "masculinity" within the women's corps was addressed. Gallup polls addressing the corps made it clear that many civilians felt that army women's uniforms were the most "unfeminine" and "unattractive" of all the services.[16] The masculine appearance of the WAC uniforms was due in large part to the fact that the Philadelphia Quartermaster's Depot for most of the war based its patterns and sizes for women's attire on male models.[17] In response to the "masculine" appearance of women's uniforms, the WAC administration tried throughout the war to "feminize" women's uniforms by adding brightly colored accessories, including scarves and gloves, designing off-duty dresses, and encouraging the "feminine" WAC pompadour courtesy of the Elizabeth Arden salons (conveniently located at most WAC posts).[18]

Servicewomen's position within these debates can be viewed through the metaphor of the "cross-dresser," a "woman" assuming a "masculine" identity by embracing the role of "soldier" and the male garb that went with it. But unlike the cross-dresser, who might "pass" without being discovered, GI Jane's secret was "out" and Wacs, whether heterosexual or homosexual, were forced to negotiate within cultural and medical frameworks that viewed their desires to enter the army and their role within the WAC as possible evidence of lesbianism.

A 1944 segment of the popular military camp comic strip "Male Call" quite literally equated military service with cross-dressing. The strip's creator, Milton Caniff, explored the interaction between his femme fatale protagonist, "Miss Lace," and a WAC private. The segment's title, "Know Which Army You're In," aptly described this cartoon's content as "Miss Lace" awakens from an evening's sexual encounter and is startled by the sound of a female voice in bed beside her. Somewhat shocked, she stares at the uniform hanging on the chair next to the bed as the WAC private in bed with her asks her what's wrong. "Lace" replies, "They should have more distinctive insignia on those WAC uniforms!"[19]

Although this segment was censored by the army and therefore not distributed to military camp newspapers, it suggests in a humorous fashion the correlations between masculine appearance and female homosexuality, in particular the explicit connections between women in uniform and lesbianism. The predicament of "Miss Lace" arises from a case of mistaken identity—her assumption that army uniforms are worn only by men. Caniff's cartoon suggests that Wacs wearing army uniforms were "passing" in a very concrete sense if they can be mistaken for men by "Miss Lace," a perennial heterosexual male GI favorite.

Analyzing female soldiers as cross-dressers within the male military allows for the illumination of the links between gender and sexuality in the construction of lesbianism in the women's corps and the broader culture. Despite some historians' arguments that "female masculinity, unlike male effeminacy," was perceived by military officials as a positive attribute, it was clear during WWII that WAC officials saw "mannish" Wacs as a danger to the legitimacy of the corps and to women's position in general within the military.[20] The WAC administration especially feared any public linkage between the masculine aspects of military service in general and some Wacs in particular to the presence of lesbians. The efforts of Colonel Hobby and her staff to "femininize" the appearance of female soldiers, including the prohibition of "mannish" hairstyles and pants, highlighted the importance of a symbolic conformity to gender norms as a means of claiming sexual respectability and also framed one set of parameters for identifying and eliminating lesbians from the women's corps.

This focus on "masculinity," as well as overall more stringent guidelines for regulating female soldiers' behavior, provided the possibility for the WAC in particular to eliminate "suspected" lesbians without calling specific attention to their homosexuality, and thus avoiding the threat to the legitimacy of a women's corps and female soldiers that such publicity might entail.[21]

Thus, the construction of the "lesbian threat" in the WWII Women's Army Corps requires that we look beyond formal regulations addressing female homosexuality and analyze the many ways in which lesbianism was informally addressed within the women's corps. These more informal and often contradictory procedures were shaped by an intense focus on female masculinity as *the* marker of "deviant" behavior. While some formal policies, such as prohibitions on "witch hunting," seemed to suggest tolerance, characterizing WAC policies as generally "tolerant" of lesbians misses the extent to which the WAC administration targeted "masculine" women and tried to eliminate "suspected" lesbians with the least publicity possible. Corps' leaders screened for "masculine" women at enlistment and discharged women whose "homosexuality" was "suspected" but could not be "proven." They accomplished both by invoking the more stringent regulations governing Wacs' social behavior. WAC leaders were thereby able to address what they defined as the "lesbian threat" to the corps with a minimum of publicity about the issue. Consequently, understanding the position of lesbians within the WWII Women's Army Corps demands that we situate them not only like their gay male counterparts, as "homosexuals" in the military, but also unlike their gay male counterparts, within their precarious site as women within a male military.

This "cross-dressing" paradigm is useful for understanding current debates over "gays" in the military and the seeming invisibility of lesbians within these discussions. Indeed, this framework as a means of analyzing the contemporary predicaments of many military women is still relevant for several reasons: first, military service continues to be equated with a masculine rite of passage; second, being a "good soldier" continues to be equated with masculinity; and third, "lesbian" continues to be popularly associated with "masculinity" or "mannishness" in women, including both appearance and job performance. Therefore, simple entrance into the military in general raises the possibility of lesbianism among heterosexual and lesbian servicewomen alike. Such assumptions are reinforced if military women are in "male-defined" job categories, perform their jobs exceptionally well, or do not have sex with men.

The dilemma this creates for many military women is demonstrated by several recent studies and issues raised by women currently serving. In 1987, 1989, and again in 1991, the Defense Advisory Committee on Women in the Services (DACOWITS), for example, was asked to consider adding "dyke-baiting" to the list of prohibited behaviors under military sexual harassment guidelines because of its widespread use to harass and intimidate servicewomen.[22] In fact, many contemporary servicewomen and female officers report being accused of lesbianism or subject to rumors of same if they refuse dates with male counterparts, or are perceived in any other way as "too masculine."

Moreover, sociologist Melissa Herbert designed a study to specifically examine how women in the military negotiate an environment that has been both structured and defined as masculine. In her 1995 investigation of six hundred women who served in the military from 1976–1990, Herbert found that 85 percent believed that perceptions of "masculinity" could lead to accusations of lesbianism and more than 40 percent, both self-identified lesbians and heterosexual women, actively strategized for ways to appear and seem "less masculine" to avoid the difficulties arising from such rumors and accusations, including possible investigation and dismissal. Thus, Herbert discovered that it was and is violations of broader social understandings about gender that serve as markers for women's sexual orientation in the military.[23]

The consequences of Herbert's results in light of current policies on "gays" in the military are fairly obvious. If "masculine" tags are enough to "inform" peers and coworkers within the military of a woman's sexuality, or allow them to assume her sexuality, this has broad implications in the context of the new "don't ask, don't tell, don't pursue" policy. A woman might be "telling" simply by refusing a date with a male colleague or cutting her hair "too short."

Why, given our absence from current debates over "gays" in the military, in the last ten years have lesbians been far more likely to be pursued and discharged than gay men? Part of the answer is that the absence of lesbians from contemporary public discourse on "gays" in the military is not an indication of our invisibility, but rather a marker of a lesbian presence so "normalized" that it is assumed. Thus, there is a need for developing new frameworks within which to understand lesbian experience and constructions of lesbian identity historically and currently. Analyses focusing on questions of formal regulations of male homosexuality and gay male visibility within the military, or other social institutions, by eliding the particular gendered position of women miss much that is unique about lesbians' positions as *women* within preeminently masculine institutions. We must analyze both gender and sexuality together and place constructions of lesbianism and female homosexuality within a broader context of female sexuality more generally to begin to fully understand the constructions of lesbian identity historically.

Notes

1. See, for example, Tamar Lewin, "Gay Groups Suggest Marines Selectively Prosecute Women," *New York Times,* December 4, 1988, p. 14. As Lewin points out, since 1983 Defense Department statistics show that lesbians had been discharged for homosexual conduct at a rate of almost ten times that of gay men in the military. This trend seems to be continuing in the current "don't ask, don't tell, don't pursue" era.

2. Allan Berube, *Coming Out Under Fire: Gay GIs During World War II* (New York: Free Press, 1991), 28. Lillian Faderman in her synthetic work on the history of lesbians in the United States picks up Berube's point and simply reiterates it: that lesbian military personnel during WWII were generally tolerated, infrequently discharged, and certainly not viewed as threatening to the military mission as gay men. See Lillian Faderman, *Odd Girls and Twilight Lovers: A History of Lesbian Life in Twentieth-Century America* (New York: Columbia University Press, 1991).

3. The Women's Army Auxiliary Corps (WAAC) existed from May 1942 to September 1943 when it was replaced by the Women's Army Corps (WAC). Throughout this article I use the acronym WAC to refer to the organization and Wac (lower case) to refer to individuals within the corps. In addition, to avoid repetition I use the terms "corps" and "women's corps" interchangeably with WAC. To avoid confusing terminology I use the acronym WAC in most discussions of the women's corps throughout World War II. When I discuss material that is specific to the early auxiliary years of the Corps I specifically note this by referring to the corps as "the auxiliary" or the WAAC. See Leisa D. Meyer, *Creating G.I. Jane: Sexuality and Power in the Women's Army Corps during World War II* (New York: Columbia University Press, 1996).

4. Jack Kofoed, *Miami Florida News,* May 20, 1942, in Center for Military History Manuscript Files, Mattie Treadwell's Background Files, Box 9, RG 319, National Archives (NA).

5. July 13, 1942, Mrs. Walter Ferguson on the appointment of Oveta Culp Hobby as Director, WAAC, File "Newspaper Clippings," WAAC 21–40, Box 8, Oveta Culp Hobby Papers, Library of Congress (LC). My emphasis.

6. See, for example, Reports on Rumors: Headquarters Minneapolis Recruiting District, Minneapolis, Minnesota, July 3, 1943, Harrisburg Armed Forces Recruiting and Induction District, 1st Officer Lovella M. Jones, Assistant WAAC Recruiting Officer, File "Rumors," Box 192, S55, RG 165. See also Reports on Rumors, 5th Service Command, Fort Hayes, Columbus, Ohio, July 10, 1943, 1st Officer Helen Y. Hedekin to Col. Oveta Culp Hobby, Box 92, S54, RG 165, NA.

7. Esther Newton, "The Mythic Mannish Lesbian: Radclyffe Hall and the New Woman," in *Signs: The Lesbian Issue,* ed. Estelle B. Freedman et al. (Chicago: University of Chicago Press, 1982), 16.

8. Interview of Colonel Oveta Culp Hobby by Joan Younger of the *Ladies Home Journal,* File "*Ladies Home Journal,*" Article on WAC, 1952, Box 9, Hobby Papers, LC.

9. Mattie Treadwell, *The U.S. Army in World War II: Special Studies, The Women's Army Corps* (Washington, D.C.: Office of the Chief of Military History, 1954), 625.

10. John D'Emilio and Estelle B. Freedman, *Intimate Matters: A History of Sexuality in*

America (New York: Harper and Row, 1988), 260, 288–89. Elaine Tyler May, *Homeward Bound: American Families in the Cold War* (New York: Basic Books, 1988), 69.

11. Army policies addressing male homosexuals and WAC procedures for dealing with lesbianism differed during WWII. Historian Allan Berube has meticulously documented the influence of modern psychiatry on the development of the army's anti-homosexual apparatus. The most significant change in army policies toward male homosexuality was a movement away from longstanding regulations criminalizing sodomy, and thus punishing identifiable homosexual acts, toward policies that defined the homosexual soldier as mentally ill and therefore in need of psychiatric treatment and rehabilitation, not imprisonment. Berube contends that this change allowed the military to cast a substantially wider net in screening for homosexuals and thus affected a much larger number of gay men than had the original sodomy restrictions. Berube, *Coming Out Under Fire,* 8–33. It should also be noted that Berube makes clear in his study that this change was not smooth or complete during the war and that some gay men continued to be imprisoned under the older sodomy regulations.

12. Major Albert Preston, *History of Psychiatry in the Women's Army Corps,* Spring 1946, pp. 8–10, File 700, Box 143, Series 54, RG 165, NA.

13. "Waac News," *WAAC Newsletter,* 1(33) (June 5–12, 1943): 3, Fort Des Moines, Iowa, Box 212, Series 55, RG 165, NA.

14. For an explanation of this "two-tiered" system of lesbian relationships in the twentieth century and public attitudes toward each see Leila Rupp, "Imagine My Surprise: Women's Relationships in the 20th Century," in *Hidden from History: Reclaiming the Gay and Lesbian Past,* ed. Martin Duberman, Martha Vicinus, and George Chauncey, Jr. (New York: Penguin Books, 1989), 398. Much of the discussion of lesbians generated within the field of women's history has focused on these "romantic friendships" and women's homosocial networks. See Lillian Faderman, *Surpassing the Love of Men: Romantic Friendship between Women from the Renaissance to the Present* (New York: William Morrow, 1981); Blanche Wiesen Cook, "Historical Denial of Lesbianism," *Radical History Review* 20 (1979): 60–65; Cook, "Women Alone Stir My Imagination," *Signs* 4 (1979): 718–39; and Adrienne Rich, "Compulsory Heterosexuality and Lesbian Existence," in *Powers of Desire,* ed. A. Snitow et al. (New York: Monthly Review, 1983), 177–205. For a case study of one working-class butch/femme community, see Elizabeth Lapovsky Kennedy and Madeline D. Davis, *Boots of Leather, Slippers of Gold: The History of a Lesbian Community* (New York: Routledge, 1993).

15. As historian George Chauncey contends, degeneration theory in particular embodied white middle-class assumptions concerning the class nature of sexual morality. George Chauncey, "From Sexual Inversion to Homosexuality," in *Passion and Power,* ed. Kathy Peiss and Christina Simmons (Philadelphia: Temple University Press, 1987), 100. Thus, although female "romantic friendships" came under stricter scrutiny throughout the twentieth century, many white middle- and upper-class women forming same-sex relationships were perceived as sexually respectable. See, for example, Leila Rupp, "Imagine My Surprise," 407.

16. Letter Commanding General Fourth Air Forces to Commanding General Western Flying Training Command, February 8, 1944, RE: Results of January 1944, Gallup Poll, pp. 249–50, Section V, 4th Air Force Historical Study, #V-4, Box 450.01–13, 1941–45, Vol. 1, Air Force Center for Historical Research, Maxwell Air Force Base, Montgomery, Alabama. See also Maxson F. Judell to Colonel Hobby, April 24, 1944, RE: Uniforms, and James E.

Dunlap to Colonel Hobby, February 21, 1944, RE: Uniforms, Box 21, Series 54; Memo for the Record, November 8, 1948, From: H. M. Boutell, Major, GSC, Chairman, Subject: Plans and Policy Committee Meeting, October 27, 1948, Item #3, "Discussion: Uniform Consideration," File "WAC Committee Chairman's Book," Box 222, Series 55. All in RG 165, NA, "Reform for a Uniform," *Colliers* 113(2) (June 3, 1944): 82. And also see Treadwell, *The U.S. Army in World War II,* 158–66.

17. Treadwell, *The U.S. Army in World War II,* 156–58.

18. Berube, *Coming Out Under Fire,* 59–61. See also Correspondence: May 19–October 15, 1943, Elizabeth Arden Corporation on WAAC Hairstyles, File 062.001, 1942–43, Box 9, Series 54, RG 165, NA; Historian, WAC Section, Headquarters, Fourth Air Force, 1 January 1944–40, [4?] September 1945, p. 46, Historical Section Files, pp. 249–50, Section V, 4th Air Force Historical Study, #V-4, Box 450.01–13, 1941–45, Vol. 1, p. 73, Part Two: "Plans and Policies," Chapter 2, "Supply," File: Study of the WAC in the ETO, V.I, Box 502.101-3 thru -11 (43–45) ETO, Air Force Center for Historical Research, Maxwell Air Force Base, Montgomery, Alabama.

19. Milton Caniff, "Know Which Army You're In," from "Male Call," 1944, in *Male Call Rejects, Featuring Miss Lace,* ed. Peter Poplaski (Princeton, Wis.: Kitchen Sink Press). "Male Call" was distributed by the Camp Newspaper Service and appeared in over three thousand military newspapers in the United States and overseas. I am indebted to Allan Berube for bringing this material to my attention.

20. Berube, *Coming Out Under Fire,* 29. See also Faderman, *Odd Girls,* 123. Berube bases his argument on the assertion that such a policy reflected "the military's need for women who could perform traditionally male work." During WWII, however, the army did not anticipate utilizing women in "male" jobs and the vast majority of Wacs were placed in jobs defined as traditionally "feminine."

21. Exemplifying this attitude, a WAC officer reporting on her visit with the New Zealand women's corps observed:

> The wisdom of the director's emphasis on maintaining femininity was certainly stressed. Apparently nothing has been done along that line and the masculine characteristics of some of their leaders, added to the natural tendency of regimentation, probably have influenced the women to adopt mannish haircuts, long strides, etc. It . . . has been responsible, I think, for many of the depreciating [*sic*] comments I heard made by some of the civilians I met.

See Captain Ethel F. Hoffman, Headquarters USAFISPA to Lt. Colonel Jessie Pearl Rice, Deputy Director, WAC, Washington, D.C., May 28, 1944, File 314.81, Box 57, Series 54, RG 165, NA.

22. "Military Witchhunt Victims Charge Sexual Harassment," *National NOW Times* (April 1989): 5.

23. Melissa Herbert, *A Fine Line: The Management of Gender and Sexuality among Women in the Military,* Ph.D. diss., University of Arizona, 1995, chaps. 3, 4, and 6.

Conclusion

17

Where Are We Now, Where Are We Going, and Who Gets to Say?

VICKI L. EAKLOR

OCCASIONALLY I am asked if I think lesbians and gay men (or homosexuality) will be "accepted" in my lifetime.[1] The question has been posed in a variety of circumstances—at the end of a talk or panel presentation, an informal conversation, a classroom discussion—but with one common denominator: I am being asked for my opinion as both activist and historian, as participant in "the movement" on some level and as professional observer of the past. In attempting to construct an answer to this question (probably a simple "yes" or "no" would suffice, but what academic has ever stopped there?), I have found at least three elements of the process intriguing and ultimately revealing of some of the tensions that beset the study of this or any social/political movement.

First, I am struck by the assumption that my study of history qualifies me as a prophet. Not that it is surprising in any way, but rather it reminds me how thoroughly we historians have sold ourselves and our profession on the basis of teaching others (to paraphrase Santayana) to remember the past so as not to repeat it.[2] Second, I am torn repeatedly between two immediate and equal responses to the question: "yes, it will," and "no, I don't think so." When I examine why this is (and exclude schizophrenia as an answer), I find that these contrary impulses reflect the recent divisions both within queer scholarship and between "academic" and "activist" queers that it is part of my project here to explain. Finally, other questions arise in the wake of "will acceptance come . . . ?" questions whose answers demand a historical perspective. Among them might be: How accepted are queers now? How does our present status compare with various points in the past? What conditions have fostered greater and less acceptance, and are they possible in the future? As important as these questions are, though, the one that seems most salient is *how will we know?* That is, what exactly constitutes acceptance, to whom, and what are its signifiers?

My purpose is to explore the implications of these questions and to delineate some recent queer history and theoretical issues in the process. In light of this, I depart from what might be expected from a concluding article: a summary of the previous chapters, a summary of events of the last two decades, an explanation of recent and current issues and controversies, and most especially an assessment of "where" we are now in terms of successes, failures, and the future of queer history, politics, and life in the United States.[3] While I provide some narrative, I take a more postmodernist stance toward the issues of relative success and failure on the one hand and predictions for the future on the other. Rather than merely list any gains or losses (from a pro-queer perspective) for the reader to accept passively, I ask for participation in the thought processes involved and ask questions about the motives and politics behind such assessments. Rather than providing a too facile "we've come a long way, but have a long way to go" conclusion that actually concludes nothing, I challenge the reader to decide for yourself what has been gained and lost—or even whether that is a useful question. Finally, I ask what different interests have at stake in their varying pronouncements about the past, present, or future.

Beginning at the End: *Ellen* and the Future

On April 30, 1997, the ABC television network aired the "coming-out" episode of the sitcom *Ellen,* in which the star, Ellen Morgan, declares—realizes? decides? even this language reflects contested theories—that she is a lesbian.[4] Previous to the airing, Ellen DeGeneres, the actress playing the role, also came out in the mainstream media and herself became as hot a topic as the impending episode.[5] The same day the episode aired, DeGeneres appeared on *The Oprah Winfrey Show* with girlfriend Anne Heche, and the latter created yet another stir by saying, "I was not gay before I met her [DeGeneres]."[6] After the April 30 episode, two more episodes aired focusing on the ongoing process of coming out—to her parents and boss and the reactions of her friends and family—and the show returned for one more season, amid further controversy over whether selected episodes would be preceded by a "parental advisory" and, ultimately, the reasons for its cancellation.[7]

Several topics of interest here intersect: the media's role in alternately helping or hurting any cause; coming out as a strategy for acceptance and issues surrounding its definition and process; and questions regarding sexuality itself, such as whether it is fixed or fluid, whether shaped more by biology or experience, and why any of this matters. Not the least of these topics is to what degree the episode and the (very postmodern) life-imitating-art-imitating-life character of the events before and since represent "progress" toward the day when sexuality will be a nonissue and coming out rendered pointless, even anachronistic.

On the one hand it is difficult *not* to see a sitcom starring an out lesbian as an out lesbian as a giant leap for queerkind; of all media genres, none is more indigenously American than the TV sitcom, and none (except possibly the soap opera) has been as important a form for the introduction of "controversial" topics. The numbers viewing the episode and the series' subsequent success also appear to support the notion that the visibility of the two Ellens is both cause and effect of greater acceptance. (A similar sentiment attended the 1997 release of the film *In and Out,* in which Tom Selleck and Kevin Kline kiss: the *New York Times* went to the Mall of America to gauge responses and found the film the most popular show at the mall, with viewers in America's heartland decidedly *not* scandalized by the kiss.[8])

On the other hand, two caveats might be voiced, both relative to power and paradox. One is simply recognizing that the star who comes out does so in a different context than that of the average queer, and so the results, especially if positive, may not be those upon which a more general level of acceptance can be measured. A "star" by definition is both known and liked, both familiar and distant. However close one feels to the star, though, it remains an impersonal relationship on the part of the audience. To embrace that star as gay or lesbian may or may not mean a decrease in homophobia closer to home. This dynamic is related to the second warning: not to mistake the ability of entertainers—often marginal figures—to entertain the mainstream for full entrance into the mainstream. An analogy would be to assume that the popularity of African-American jazz musicians and their art among Euro-Americans early in this century signaled a decrease in racism in general and the "acceptance"—social, political, and economic—of African Americans as equal partners in U.S. society. The paradox of entertainment media, then, lies in its central role in offering widespread visibility to people and issues, offering a type of power to entertainers, but within a system in which the real power ultimately resides in the structure that *allows* them to perform. "We [the mainstream] will let you [African Americans, Jews, women, gay men and lesbians] entertain us," might be their call, "but it does not mean we want you as equals in our neighborhoods, businesses, and families."[9] What all this suggests is that there are two parallel and sometimes intersecting realms at issue, political and cultural, but that a "gain" or "loss" in one cannot necessarily be equated with the other.[10] This raises again the question of reality: Which realm is real if they offer contradictory examples?

The dynamics revealed in attempting to assess *Ellen*'s historical importance to the movement are precisely those that affect my own reactions to the request to predict the future and reflect the more general trends in reactions to events associated with the queer movements. Any lack of general agreement on the issue of *Ellen* is predictable in the sense that for every perceived "advance" in the last two decades or so, there is a real or imagined negative result, and vice versa.

Gains as Losses, Losses as Gains

> Since the Stonewall Riots, the gay and lesbian movement has achieved a level of success that would astound its early leaders. . . . At the same time, the recent years have been times of struggle for gays as well.
>
> Kevin Jennings, *Becoming Visible*

The phenomenon of gains as losses might be summarized as that of a backlash, a reaction hardly unique to queer politics but rather following the same timing and patterns of those of other movements.[11] To say that America has been for two decades or so engaged in "Culture Wars"—wars whose battlegrounds are school and college curricula and arts and entertainment media as well as the floors of various legislatures—is now a cliché, as is the accusation that the changes of the 1960s are to blame. If the first three decades after World War II saw the rise of a social consciousness as expressed in minority movements and occasionally codified, as in 1964, 1965, and 1973 (the Civil Rights Act, the Voting Rights Act, and *Roe v. Wade*, respectively), the period since the late 1970s has been characterized by reaction to those events: the rise of the Moral Majority and the New Right, the elections of Ronald Reagan and George Bush, and during their tenures the undermining of governmental commitment to social programs, affirmative action, immigrants, and a woman's control over her body.

By the late 1970s, of course, lesbian and gay communities were clearly part of this pattern and helped to define it: they expanded, divided, and generally became more visible, and following the historic removal of homosexuality from the American Psychiatric Association's list of mental disorders in 1973–74, sexual orientation was added as a nondiscrimination category by several professional organizations and localities, while homosexuality was decriminalized in a few states. It was also at this time, however, that efforts to repeal nondiscrimination ordinances began, most notably in Florida in Dade County's successful "Save Our Children" campaign of 1977, while similar child-molester imagery was utilized the next year in California with the failed attempt (Proposition 6, or the Briggs Amendment) to keep homosexuals and mention of homosexuality out of the public schools. Tensions culminated in that fall of 1978 with the murder of San Francisco Mayor George Moscone and city supervisor Harvey Milk in November, the manslaughter verdict given the convicted assassin Dan White the following May, and the riot that rocked the city—"sparked," but not "caused," by the verdict alone.[12]

To add insult to injury, the dynamic of "blame the victim" often accompanies a backlash: if only activists had not been so, well, *active*, queers would not be facing such hostility. Such a mentality is hardly unique to the lesbian/gay movement—everyone from the unemployed and homeless to victims/survivors of rape and harassment routinely have been blamed for their condition (an act that has the paradoxical effect of keeping power away from the powerless while attributing to them a great deal of it)—but it is particularly notable when we consider the 1980s and the overshadowing presence of AIDS.

As if the general political mood of voters wasn't enough, the deadly condition known as AIDS was reported in the summer of 1981 and from the beginning associated with gay men.[13] In a now well-known history, it rapidly unfolded as a "lose-lose" situation for gay men and lesbians. If it was an exclusively gay issue—indeed a gay male issue—sympathy, and funding for a cure, in a homophobic society would be difficult to come by, while news of the equal vulnerability of nongays merely accentuated the homophobic wrath now directed at gays as "typhoid Marys." The gay and lesbian communities divided along lines not only of gender, but also of support or rejection of anonymous sex and its institutions, notably the bathhouses.[14]

AIDS surely has been a disaster in many ways, especially in the lives lost to it as well as the justification it seemed to offer homophobes to escalate anti-gay attacks, whether verbal, legal, or physical. At the same time, it is the prime example of the ability to find the positive in the most negative of circumstances, as the onset of AIDS is also seen as a turning point in queer unity, visibility, and activism: the leadership of gay male and lesbian communities in organizing effectively both medically and politically (and showing the connection) is recognized, while, pertinently, the deaths of previously closeted entertainment figures such as Rock Hudson became key events. Film historian Vito Russo, who himself succumbed to AIDS-related complications in 1990, told Eric Marcus of being a founder of ACT UP (AIDS Coalition to Unleash Power):

> This is a new kind of activism. It's a coalition that we were never able to achieve in the 1970s. Back then the ideal and the dream were that gay people would come together with other oppressed groups like blacks and Asians and women to form a coalition. That didn't happen because we had too many differences. . . . Now AIDS has brought us together in ways that we could not have foreseen. . . . So AIDS has been a catalyst for people to become more involved. This has made others more aware of gay life and of gay people than they ever were before. So maybe something good is going to come out of this.[15]

Subsequently media coverage not only increased, but sympathetic portrayals of even gay patients increased in both the news and entertainment genres, and questions of the limits of civil rights—to whom they apply and under what conditions—were reminiscent of those of the eras of anti-communism, African-American freedom marches, and anti-Vietnam protest. Perhaps as a result, AIDS became a national rather than a gay crisis, with civil rights now clearly intertwined with issues of health, medicine, and sex in general. John D'Emilio's summary thus became typical of a general tone of assessment within queer activism: "Although AIDS was an unparalleled tragedy for the gay community around the nation, it also fostered a heightened level of political organizing. . . . By the mid-1980s, AIDS was pushing gay issues toward the center of public debate."[16]

In similar fashion, almost any setback might be mined for some kind of positive outcome, and not without merit. Whether we consider the 1986 *Bowers v. Hardwick* Supreme Court decision that declared laws against sodomy constitutional, or the more recent 1993 "don't ask, don't tell" compromise in the anti-homosexual policy of the U.S. military, we can always fall back on visibility.[17] No matter the disaster, as seen from this perspective, if it makes news it may have the effect of raising consciousness about continuing discrimination and stimulate yet more opposition from yet more people, queer and nonqueer. At the least, these events helped foster two of the three large marches on Washington for lesbian/gay/bisexual/transgender rights in 1979, 1987, and 1993, with the latter two following *Hardwick* and the military debates, respectively, and the mainstream media blackout of the 1987 march leading to the 1988 establishment of National Coming Out Day on its anniversary of October 11.

The debate over losses and gains continued through the 1990s, and the confusing mixture that fueled it continues. Nothing is more symbolic of the situation than the votes taken in the U.S. Senate on September 10, 1996, on the Defense of Marriage Act (DOMA) and the Employment Non-Discrimination Act (ENDA). While the first, with the intent of outlawing same-sex marriage in the United States, was approved overwhelmingly by a vote of 85–14, the latter, which would have protected workers from discrimination due to sexual orientation, nearly passed (49 yeas, 50 nays). More recently, a July 14, 1997, GLAADlines includes the headline "Studies Show State, Local Advances and Challenges to Gay Civil Rights" and cites parallel increases in civil protections of and hostility toward lesbians and gay men. How to perceive this situation, it seems, is up to the perceiver, and ultimately begs the question of reality itself.

Why the Differences?

The fact that there is no consensus on what constitutes progress, or even if there is such a thing, is rooted in several factors related to progressive history as well as divisions within and among groups inside and outside the academy. Not the least of these is the inherent tension between the psychological need of the activist to believe in ultimate victory (I am reminded of the Susan B. Anthony button, quoting "Failure Is Impossible") and an equal mandate not to take it for granted. Indeed this may be any activist's most fundamental dilemma: to work for change one must believe that it is possible to accomplish it (or why bother?), but one cannot slip into the assumption that some historical force of destiny is at work that will accomplish it "in time" regardless of human agency. In short, one must believe that change is possible but not inevitable.

On the surface achieving the balance necessary to maintain this kind of cautious optimism does not seem so difficult. However, the way U.S. history is usually presented exacerbates the potential for complacency, while reaction against that presentation can degenerate into a cynicism equally unsupportive of activity. Elsewhere I have examined the possible relationships among the progressive "grand narrative" of the U.S., lesbian/gay history, and lesbian/gay politics.[18] The now well-known "great America" story, I argue, fostered a secondary reform grand narrative that, while it appears to be subversive of the dominant view, actually reinforces it. The reform narrative, a product of the New Social History and paralleling the upheavals of the 1960s and after, focuses on the oppression of self-defined minorities (including women) and has been praised (by liberals, at least) as a necessary antidote to the cloying and incomplete story of great Euro-American men building an infallible nation based on liberty and equality. A pattern is established, however, wherein victories for these groups are emphasized as much as or more than their struggles, justice triumphs in the end, and the United States and its history remain progressive because of, rather than in spite of, the minorities' experiences. Although more subtle than the more traditional American narrative, in the end this version supports the notion of progress and its inevitability. At the same time, reactions against all versions of progressive history, particularly when coupled with the realization that some positive changes may have been due to political or economic expediency rather than justice, can lead to a cynical rejection of *any* progress whatsoever. At the extremes, then, the pervasiveness of the progressive view produces the same end result: removal of human agency from history in favor of forces, good or evil. This historical determinism in turn can either discourage the potential activist and/or lead to a narrow interpretation of one's actions because they are placed within a storyline already written; victory is always just around the corner or, at the other extreme, will never really come because it is all an illusion.

If various grand narratives have contributed to varying interpretations of our past and future success, we can locate their sources also in recent developments in queer history, politics, and theory. The growth of the field of lesbian/gay history has itself produced paradoxical results; in effect, that the success and acceptance of any scholarly area sows the seeds of its own de(con)struction. Central to the definition of acceptance is a type of "trickle-down" effect wherein the information leaves the realm of the specialist and enters the textbook, the media, and hence the mainstream. To accomplish this, a clear, linear narrative is usually the most effective, the outlines of which often emphasize progression or regression along a linear model, as outlined above. Add to this a focus on attainment of civil rights on an identity politics model, and lesbian/gay history since World War II can be reduced fairly neatly to perhaps three periods (periodization being another inevitability of canonization), characterized by the degree of advancement toward that end. The first two eras share a general if uneven sense of progress, and might be (and are) termed simply pre- and post-Stonewall, to designate not only an event but a perceived change toward even more nonaccommodationist theory and action. The third era, actually a subheading under "post-Stonewall," begins around 1980 with, as previously mentioned, a growing backlash against gains made in the 1970s (lesbian/gay rights victories, the growth of lesbian/gay culture and communities, greater visibility in general, for example), the election of Ronald Reagan as a signal of America's general "turn to the Right" and, of course, the discovery of AIDS.[19]

On the one hand, such a narrative and its periodization signify the "arrival" of lesbian/gay history: We now have a coherent narrative that can be transmitted fairly easily—it is teachable—and thus can contribute to the increasing visibility of queer people while enriching the study of history. On the other hand, it is this very narrative that is already subject to critique, not only for its general message of overall progress (again) but because of broader intellectual trends of which queer theory and history is both partial cause and effect.

Interestingly the decade of the backlash, the 1980s, also saw the advent and development of queer theory in conjunction with both AIDS activism and several intellectual strains, the latter of which might be grouped under the rubric "postmodern."[20] A term used in the arts and humanities, postmodern only incidentally designates an era ("following modern") and might be better understood as an attitude that rejects much of that associated with the "modern" world, especially the presence of an objective Truth, whether in the sciences, humanities, or arts (often posing here as Beauty), which is discovered by the disinterested observer. Further, a modern view (according to postmodernists) would include the assumption that humans have gradually "progressed" toward gaining this Truth, with particular advances having been more steadily made since the scientific revolution in Europe.

Conversely, a postmodern stance denies the existence of this Truth and seeks to define the implications of that act. Associated variously with deconstruction in literature and poststructuralism in the social sciences, and the growing areas of critical theory and cultural studies, postmodernism posits objectivity as a myth and therefore the existence of the disinterested observer as well. These areas all have in common, then, a resistance to any one "right" reading of a cultural product, whether it be textual (literature or history), visual (fine arts, film, TV) or material. This resistance is enhanced by emphasizing the role of the reader/viewer/observer/consumer at one end and continually asking the question of power relations at the other: What various interpretations might one ascribe to this text/piece/product? What/whose interpretations prevail in a given case? *And* can we explain *why* certain interpretations prevail by analyzing whose interest they serve? The question of power is further complicated, finally, by the assertion that it is possible for the less powerful to appropriate texts, images, etc., for their own purposes, and a debate ensues as to whether this is truly subversive of power or merely a defensive act. Through it all, however, the previously "objective" observer is now expected to be aware of her/his role in the process of observing, and convey that self-consciousness in some fashion (at times this is done through the deconstruction of language, which also is seen as a product of power relations, spawning those annoying parentheses, dashes, and slashes that have themselves become part of a newer language of power—one of the many conundra of postmodern theory!).[21]

At any rate, these strains have generated the critique of two already entrenched modes of presenting the queer past and present: the linear presentation of a history of homosexuals/homosexuality/homophobia, and the "identity politics" generated from the minority group status that such a history can either create or reinforce (depending upon one's view). In the first instance, the general deconstruction of grand narratives not only has raised doubts about the type of "gay history canon" outlined above due to its progressive tilt, but in the case of sexuality the linear form itself has seemed less appropriate as more scholars have argued for a "social constructionist" over an "essentialist" position.

Briefly, social constructionists have challenged an "essentialist" view of sexuality that assumes the universality across time and place not only of specific types of human behavior and desire, but of identity based on those elements as well; what the two camps agree on, it should be noted, is that the question of whether sexuality is fixed by biology or environment is still open, and basically irrelevant to the social/historical issue (that is, we might distinguish between biological and historical essentialism).[22] Social constructionists have been especially critical of the dichotomizing of human sexuality into two basic categories—heterosexual and homosexual—with a third, bisexual, existing in an uneasy space between them but no less defined by them. They assert, rather, that even if similar desires and actions can be discovered in various times and cultures, the *meaning* of those desires and actions will be particular to the time and culture in which they are found.[23]

Second, this sensitivity to the specificity of identities that change over time undermines a simple, linear narrative of homosexuals who have "always" identified as such and whose group or political identity has been shaped as much by a history of oppression as by a shared sexuality. Called the "myth of the 'eternal homosexual'" by John D'Emilio, this essentialist history in question becomes to the postmodernist the grand narrative on which modern or identity politics necessarily rests: homosexuals, like other minorities, gradually achieve a group identity as a minority, and their progress is charted according to the degree to which they approach parity, especially in civil rights, with the majority.[24] When social constructionists assert the fluidity of sexual categories, then, they cast doubt simultaneously upon both identity politics and the goal of that politics, civil rights; even if they are acquired, they may not be a sign of progress to a postmodernist, hence the kinds of divisions at issue here.[25]

Social constructionist theory does support a history, then, but it is more the history of change than progress, and an assessment of both losses and gains resulting from change is not unusual. It is becoming more common, for example, to note a perennial dialectic between such "gains" as the formation of homosexual identity, communities, and movements on the one hand, and the stigmatization and oppression possibly stimulating that formation on the other, all the while charting the options (romantic friendship, multiple categories of sexuality, etc.) that may have been lost in the process.[26] To a postmodernist, conditions are usually different than previously, but designations of times "better" or "worse" lose their meaning. In this way, historical theory is no less related to queer politics than was the traditional marriage of linear history and identity politics. A nonlinear or postmodern history of sexuality based on its social construction does not merely deny that progress has occurred; it denies that progress is a viable concept. Once irrelevant, progress can no longer be assessed in the past, present, or future.

The advent of postmodern thought has exacerbated, if not caused, a rift perceived to exist between activists, who generally remain wedded to a minority model and hence a linear history of progress towards lesbian/gay rights, and the academics who, by questioning the notions of fixed identity, linear history, and progress, are seen as undermining the very project some perhaps studied history to aid. That this rift is relatively new is all the more disturbing: Those who advocated the social history and minority histories in the 1960s and 1970s often perceived themselves as either activists or at least contributing to rights agendas by telling previously unknown histories of oppression, heroism, and/or the contributions of women and minorities that supplemented arguments of a need for redressing wrongs. As gay/lesbian history entered its infancy in this climate, its practitioners assumed a natural alliance between the academy and the street.

The academic/activist division, then, may be partly generational, but still is not so simple. Certainly, as with all movements, agreement has never existed within lesbian/gay activism as to ideology or methodology. Among the various splits have been those between men and women, whites and nonwhites, "accommodationists" and "protesters," rights advocates ("moderates") and liberationists ("radicals"), and so on; continuing divisions are manifest in the ongoing analysis of queer politics, theory, and history.[27] On the academic side, further divisions have been noted between those who "do" history (who may represent various combinations of social constructionism and essentialism) and those who engage primarily in theory and are most associated with the postmodern/social constructionist stance.[28]

Given these divisions, one can see that any event is going to be interpreted in a variety of ways, not the least of which will be assertions of progression, regression, a denial of "movement" altogether in favor of change, or even the denial that anything really changes. This situation is not unique to queer politics and history but certainly has developed in a symbiotic relation to the greater visibility of queers through politics and history, and so is especially relevant both to this inquiry and any broader consideration of life in twenty-first-century America.

Who Gets to Say?

A December 1, 1997, GLAADAlert begins, "A November 22 *Washington Post* story entitled 'Gay Chic' raises many interesting questions about the 'normalization of gay and lesbian life in America,' but ultimately rests on some major false assumptions."[29] It goes on to quote writer Richard Harwood as listing some notable gains for lesbians and gays in politics, education, and the media, and then begins a point-by-point critique:

> The story paints a curious and false picture of the political and cultural landscapes faced by lesbian and gay Americans today. Phenomenal progress has been made by gay Americans towards full inclusion in society. But there is a long, hard road ahead, and Harwood dismisses just how far we have to go.[30]

What is illustrated here is not only the very dynamics that are my subject—the cautious acknowledging of gains immediately followed by the "we're not that far" argument—but the larger postmodern question of power as well. Typically, this power operates as the power of domination (in Starhawk's words, "power-over" as opposed to "power-from-within"[31]), and is manifested between so-called straight and gay societies, or dominant and marginal, respectively, as well as *within* the latter.

That the *Washington Post* runs a story at all, for example, can be seen as a sign of progress, but that it can is indicative of the very power of the mainstream media to determine what is and is not "real," including progress towards lesbian/gay equality. Similarly, as already noted, queers are no more equal among ourselves—hence the divisions—than we are to the dominant culture, so that the statement of GLAAD (Gay and Lesbian Alliance Against Defamation) represents the ability of some queers *to* respond while others are marginalized through lack of access to the institutions and devices of power.

As a postmodernist, at this point I must note my own power: I have written something you are reading and possibly was assigned to you by others holding a similar (if marginally respected) societal power. Given this, I choose to use it to speculate on signs of acceptance after all. How will we know, for example, when queer history and theory are genuinely embraced? Not, perhaps, by their becoming obsolete because so thoroughly adopted into "larger" topics (as we once hoped for most minority studies), but instead when that adoption has changed the questions, methods, and approaches sufficiently to alter the very conception of the field. Just as reclaiming women's and African-American histories has led from documenting the contributions of individual women and African Americans to assessing the social histories of their groups to deconstructing gender and race themselves, so it might be with sexuality: when the necessity of studying it as a category in human history is no longer questioned, much less ridiculed and reviled, we may say it has "arrived" (as is already happening to some degree).

In the larger culture, however, I wonder whether a sort of obsolescence will indeed be the sign. Beneath all the paradoxes of this society there may lie one most profound one: that full integration of queers into American society will be charted by the degree to which we once again approach silence about sexual orientation. This will be a silence born not of fear of exposure, however, but of its lack of relevance to such public discourses as employment, law, politics, housing, and medicine. "Progress" toward this end might be signified when the tabloid press and TV no longer find it a sensational topic because queerness will be only as titillating as heterosexual cohabitation is now. In other words, nonheterosexuality will cease to be exploitable by those in power, and thus also cease to be a political issue. As a result, sexuality—perhaps for the first time in history—will be a genuinely *private*, as distinct from a *hidden* or *unmentionable*, concern.

A truly postmodern approach would posit that you, the reader, also gets to say what is and is not progress, or whether it exists, and would suggest that you, like everyone else, has an investment in seeing things the way you do. Asking what this investment might be is one way to place a supposed observer *inside* history as part of the object of study rather than as some alienated being without a stake in the outcome. History can be a parade one watches from the sidelines but is at its most challenging when we decide to get in the street, figuratively if not literally, and try to keep up with the march.

Notes

1. Although these are common phrases, I am indebted to John Cage's "Where Are We Going? And What Are We Doing?", in *Silence* (Middletown, Conn., 1983), 194–259, for my inspiration. That Cage was gay, and that his title denotes four lectures intended to be delivered simultaneously to better approximate a "real" experience of information reception, only make the source all the more appropriate here, as I see his ideas as forerunners, or perhaps early examples, of postmodern thinking.

2. George Santayana, "Reason in Common Sense," in *The Life of Reason*, one-volume ed. (1905; repr. New York: Charles Scribner's Sons, 1953). The actual quote (p. 82) is: "Those who cannot remember the past are condemned to repeat it."

3. I have chosen "queer," though still a contested term, to include any one or combination of the following: lesbian, gay, transgendered, and transsexual, and political movements associated with these categories. This issue is but one, and symbolic of, the very divisions in "the movement" that I will discuss.

4. The bulk of this essay was written in the fall of 1997, at the beginning of what turned out to be *Ellen*'s last season. The main points of this discussion remain relevant, however.

5. Bruce Handy, "Roll Over, Ward Cleaver," *Time*, April 14, 1997 (cover story), and related features, "He Called Me Ellen Degenerate?", "Is Coming Out Going Too Far?", and "Not Always Ready For Prime Time," in the same issue. (www.pathfinder.com/time/magazine/1997/dom/970414)

6. *The Oprah Winfrey Show*, April 30, 1997. See Ted Gideonse, "The Sexual Blur," *Advocate* (June 24, 1997): 28–43; Heche is quoted on p. 28.

7. The "parental warning" is usually used for "explicit violence, sex or language"; DeGeneres protested its use on her show as representing a double standard regarding sexual orientation, since many more explicit heterosexual situations air without it.

8. Neal Karlen, "Ho-hum. The Kiss That Didn't Rock the World," *New York Times*, October 5, 1997, sec. 1, pp. 45, 48. While Karlen writes (p. 45), "Indeed, the kiss is, as they say in the Midwest, *different*, yet the fact that it has caused nary a peep marks it in some way as a gay liberation milestone," he also points out that films more focused on the topic of gay sex (*Jeffrey* and *Love! Valour! Compassion!*) did not do well at the box office.

9. A good treatment of this relationship between minorities and entertainment is Lewis A. Erenberg, *Steppin' Out: New York Nightlife and the Transformation of American Culture, 1890–1930* (Westport, Conn.: Greenwood Press, 1981). Interestingly, readers of the national lesbian/gay magazine the *Advocate* were asked in the April 29, 1997, issue, "Whose coming-out do you think has the most impact on your daily life?" The results, published May 27, 1997, were typically mixed and inconclusive on the question of figures like Ellen: sports celebrity, 7 percent; high ranking politician, 12 percent; *show business personality, 12 percent;* well-known leader in the business world, 16 percent; they would all have equal impact, 53 percent (p. 13, my emphasis).

10. Urvashi Vaid, *Virtual Equality: The Mainstreaming of Gay and Lesbian Liberation* (New York: Anchor Books, 1995), also notes these two realms throughout, as in the section, "The Cultural is Political" (195–202).

11. An excellent overview of the fate of women, for example, is Susan Faludi, *Backlash: The Undeclared War Against American Women* (New York: Crown, 1991).

12. Quoted from John D'Emilio, "Gay Politics and Community in San Francisco Since World War II," in *Hidden From History: Reclaiming the Gay and Lesbian Past,* ed. Martin Duberman, Martha Vicinus, and George Chauncey, Jr. (New York: NAL Books, 1989), 471. Also see Barry D. Adam, *The Rise of a Gay and Lesbian Movement,* rev. ed. (New York: Twayne Publishers, 1995), esp. 104–24, for an overview of these years; David Jernigan, "Why Gay Leaders Don't Last: The First Ten Years after Stonewall," *Out/Look* (Summer 1988): 33–49, provides a context for a brief celebration of Milk's leadership style.

13. Lawrence K. Altman, "Rare Cancer Seen in 41 Homosexuals," *New York Times,* July 3, 1981, p. A20.

14. The most comprehensive account of the crisis in the early 1980s remains Randy Shilts, *And the Band Played On: Politics, People, and the AIDS Epidemic* (New York: St. Martin's Press, 1987).

15. Eric Marcus, *Making History: The Struggle for Gay and Lesbian Equal Rights, 1945–1990, An Oral History* (New York: HarperCollins, 1992), 415–17.

16. D'Emilio, "Gay Politics," 472.

17. Good discussions of *Bowers v. Hardwick* include those in Kevin Jennings, ed., *Becoming Visible: A Reader in Gay & Lesbian History for High School & College Students* (Boston: Alyson Publications, 1994), 227–39, and Nan D. Hunter, "Banned in the U.S.A.: What the *Hardwick* Ruling Will Mean" and "Life After *Hardwick,*" in *Sex Wars: Sexual Dissent and Political Culture,* ed. Lisa Duggan and Nan D. Hunter (New York: Routledge, 1995), 80–100; a critical summary of the military policy is J. Jennings Moss, "Losing the War," *Advocate* (April 15, 1997): 22–25, 29–30.

18. Vicki L. Eaklor, "Learning from History: A Queer Problem," *Journal of Gay, Lesbian, and Bisexual Identity,* July, 1998. For the concept of the grand narrative see, for example, Jean-Francois Lyotard, *The Postmodern Condition: A Report on Knowledge* (Minneapolis: University of Minnesota, 1984).

19. Quotation from the title of Chapter 33 of Mary Beth Norton et al., *A People and a Nation,* 4th ed., vol. 2 (Boston: Houghton Mifflin, 1994), 1023, an American history survey text. Other common titles for chapters on the 1980s include the "Reagan Revolution" (or "Counter-Revolution"), the "Triumph of Conservatism," and the "Resurgence of

Conservatism." Norton's fifth edition (1998, p. 955), in fact, changes this section from the title cited to "The End of the Postwar Boom: Stagflation, Immigration, and the Resurgence of Conservatism, 1974–1989."

20. For AIDS see, e.g., Lee Edelman, "The Plague of Discourse: Politics, Literary Theory, and AIDS," *South Atlantic Quarterly* (Winter 1989): 301–317; Daniel Harris, "AIDS and Theory," *Lingua Franca*, June 1991, pp. 1, 16–19; and Thomas Yingling, "AIDS in America: Postmodern Governance, Identity, and Experience," in *Inside/Out: Lesbian Theories, Gay Theories*, ed. Diana Fuss (New York: Routledge, 1991), 291–310.

21. Among the major figures who have shaped postmodern theory are Jacques Derrida, Michel Foucault, Fredric Jameson, and Jean-Francois Lyotard. A relatively concise statement of principles can be found in *After Truth: A Post-Modern Manifesto*, of the Second of January Group, (n.p., 1986); its preface (p. 3) begins, "This manifesto presents no programme or principles. It does not seek converts or adherents. It supports no 'position' or party. It is not a 'theoretical' document. The time of theory has now passed. We must learn to live after truth." I am indebted also to my colleagues in philosophy at Alfred University, William Dibrell, Beth Ann Dobie, and John Gilmour, who have shared their knowledge and advice on this topic in conversation with me.

22. A lack of agreement on this point also, in fact, is evidenced in the results of an *Advocate* poll, "Sexuality: Fixed or changing?" Of the respondents, 46 percent said that "sexual orientation is fixed," 41 percent agreed that "sexual orientation can change," and 13 percent voted that "we are all bisexual" (July 22, 1997, p. 6; see also the letters on that page).

23. It should be noted that, like all polarizations, the poles actually represent few "purist" adherents, with many theorists, while favoring social constructionism, representing various combinations of views. For the social constructionist position and its implications, see, e.g., Michel Foucault, *The History of Sexuality, Vol. 1: An Introduction* (New York: Vintage Books, 1980); Jonathan Ned Katz, *The Invention of Heterosexuality* (New York: Dutton, 1995); and Edward Stein, ed., *Forms of Desire: Sexual Orientation and the Social Constructionist Controversy* (New York: Garland Publishing, 1990).

24. John D'Emilio, "Capitalism and Gay Identity," in *Powers of Desire: The Politics of Sexuality*, ed. Ann Snitow, Christine Stansell, and Sharon Thompson, (New York: Monthly Review Press, 1983), 101; reprinted in John D'Emilio, *Making Trouble: Essays on Gay History, Politics, and the University* (New York: Routledge, 1992), 3–16 (quote p. 5).

25. For identity politics generally see, e.g., *Socialist Review* 20 (January–March, 1990). Among works on lesbian/gay identity, politics, and their application or relation to postmodernism, literary and historical, see especially Scott Bravmann, "Telling (Hi)stories: Rethinking the Lesbian and Gay Historical Imagination," *Out/Look* (Spring 1990): 68–74; Ed Cohen, "Who Are 'We'? Gay 'Identity' as Political (E)motion (A Theoretical Rumination)," in Fuss, ed., *Inside/Out*, 71–92; John D'Emilio, "Making and Unmaking Minorities: The Tensions between Gay History and Politics," in D'Emilio, *Making Trouble*, 181–90; Steven Epstein, "Gay Politics, Ethnic Identity: The Limits of Social Constructionism," *Socialist Review* (May–August 1987): 9–54; Jeffrey Escoffier, "Sexual Revolution and the Politics of Gay Identity," *Socialist Review* (July–October 1985): 119–153.

26. For the dialectic between oppression and identity, see John D'Emilio, *Sexual Politics, Sexual Communities: The Making of a Homosexual Minority in the United States, 1940–1970*

(Chicago: University of Chicago Press, 1983). Among those who have suggested a more complicated history of sexuality in America that includes changing or narrowing of options are George Chauncey, *Gay New York: Gender, Urban Culture, and the Making of the Gay Male World, 1890–1940* (New York: Basic Books, 1994); and Elizabeth Lapovsky Kennedy and Madeline D. Davis, *Boots of Leather, Slippers of Gold: The History of a Lesbian Community* (New York: Routledge, 1993).

27. Vaid, *Virtual Equality,* is an impressively thorough critique. Other recent works include Charles Kaiser, *The Gay Metropolis: 1940–1996* (Boston: Houghton Mifflin, 1997); and Rictor Norton, *The Myth of the Modern Homosexual: Queer History and the Search for Cultural Unity* (London: Cassell, 1997).

28. For various aspects of these divisions see especially Duggan and Hunter, eds., *Sex Wars,* 144–206. See also Caleb Crain, "Pleasure Principles: Queer Theorists and Gay Journalists Wrestle Over the Politics of Sex," *Lingua Franca,* October 1997 (www.linguafranca.com/9710/crain.html); and Epstein, "Gay Politics."

29. GLAADAlert of November 26, 1997, posted on the internet December 1, 1997, quoting Richard Harwood, "Gay Chic," *The Washington Post,* p. A19.

30. Ibid.

31. Starhawk, *Dreaming the Dark: Magic, Sex and Politics,* new edition (Boston: Beacon Press, 1988), esp. 1–14.

About the Contributors

HOLLY A. BAGGETT teaches American and Women's History at Southwest Missouri State University. She is the editor of *Dear Tiny Heart: The Letters of Jane Heap and Florence Reynolds.*

BRETT BEEMYN has edited or coedited a number of texts in *LGBT Studies: Bisexuality in the Lives of Men: Facts and Fictions*; *Bisexual Men in Culture and Society*; *Creating a Place for Ourselves: Lesbian, Gay, and Bisexual Community Histories*; and *Queer Studies: A Lesbian, Gay, Bisexual, and Transgender Anthology*. He is currently writing a history of LGBT life in Washington, D.C., during the twentieth century.

ALLIDA M. BLACK is Research Professor of History and International Affairs at The George Washington University, where she is also Project Director and Editor of The Eleanor Roosevelt Papers. She is the author of *Casting Her Own Shadow: Eleanor Roosevelt and the Shaping of Postwar Liberalism* and the editor of *Courage in a Dangerous World: The Political Writings of Eleanor Roosevelt* and *"What I Hope to Leave Behind": The Essential Essays of Eleanor Roosevelt.*

JENNIFER BRIER is a Ph.D. candidate in American and Gender History at Rutgers University, New Brunswick. Her dissertation focuses on "infectious ideas"—exposing the cultural transmissions of AIDS in the 1980s.

JOHN D'EMILIO is Professor of Gender and Women's Studies and History at the University of Illinois at Chicago. He is the author of *Sexual Politics, Sexual Communities: The Making of a Homosexual Minority in the United States, 1940–1970* and coeditor of *Creating Change: Sexuality, Public Policy, and Civil Rights*. He is writing a biography of Bayard Rustin.

VICKI L. EAKLOR is Professor of History and Chairperson of the Division of Human Studies at Alfred University. She currently holds the Margaret and Barbara Hagar Chair in the Humanities, and she teaches and publishes in the areas of American culture and lesbian/gay history and theory. She is researching the history of the Human Rights Campaign and its founder, Steve Endean.

ESTELLE B. FREEDMAN, Professor of History at Stanford University, is the author of *Their Sisters' Keepers: Women's Prison Reform in America, 1830–1930* and *Maternal*

Justice: Miriam Van Waters and the Female Reform Tradition and coauthor of *Intimate Matters: A History of Sexuality in America* (rev. ed., 1997). She coedited *The Lesbian Issue: Essays From Signs* and *Victorian Women: A Documentary Account.*

CHRIS FREEMAN holds a Ph.D. in English from Vanderbilt University. He teaches in English, film, and popular culture / gay and lesbian studies at St. John's University in Minnesota. He is writing a biography of Paul Monette and is a regular contributor to the *Gay and Lesbian Review.*

MARGARET ROSE GLADNEY is Associate Professor of American Studies at the University of Alabama. She is the editor of *How Am I to Be Heard? Letters of Lillian Smith* and the author of "Personalizing the Political, Politicizing the Personal: Reflections on Editing the Letters of Lillian Smith," in *Carryin' On in the Lesbian and Gay South.*

JULIA GRANT is Associate Professor of History at James Madison College, Michigan State University. She is the author of *Raising Baby by the Book: The Education of American Mothers* and is currently working on a new book, *Sugar and Spice: Girls and Boys in American History.*

JOHN HOWARD is Lecturer in American History at the University of York, U.K. He is the author of *Men Like That: A Southern Queer History* and the editor of *Carryin' On in the Lesbian and Gay South.*

IAN LEKUS is a Ph.D. candidate in the Department of History at Duke University. He is completing his dissertation on homosexuality and American antiwar activism, 1964–1973, and is Project Coordinator of the Rainbow Triangle Oral History Project at the Duke University Center for Lesbian, Gay, Bisexual, & Transgender Life.

LEISA D. MEYER is Associate Professor of History and the Director of Women's Studies at the College of William and Mary. She is the author of *Creating G.I. Jane: Sexuality and Power in the Women's Army Corps During WWII.*

LEILA J. RUPP is Professor and Chair of the Department of History at Ohio State University. She is the author of *Mobilizing Women for War: German and American Propaganda, 1939–1945; Survival in the Doldrums: The American Women's Rights Movement, 1945 to the 1960s* (with Verta Taylor); *Worlds of Women: The Making of an International Women's Movement;* and *A Desired Past: A Short History of Same-Sex Love in America.* She also edits the *Journal of Women's History.*

KIMBERLY SPRINGER is the Mellon Fellow in Women's and Gender Studies at Williams College and is also in residence at WAMC Northeast Public Radio in

Albany, New York. She is editor of *Still Lifting, Still Climbing: African American Women's Contemporary Activism*. Her research, teaching, and radio work focus on Black feminist activism and social movement organizations.

MARC STEIN is Assistant Professor of History at York University, Ontario, Canada. He is the author of *City of Sisterly and Brotherly Loves: Lesbian and Gay Philadelphia, 1945–1972*, the former coordinating editor of *Gay Community News* (Boston), and the current Chair of the Committee on Lesbian and Gay History, an affiliate society of the American Historical Association.